Gods, Goddesses, and Mighty Ones

Faces of the God

The God of the Witches is often viewed as the Horned God, Sun King, and Lord of the Greenwood. Within Wicca, he is seen as the consort or child of the Goddess, while Traditional Witchcraft views him as the Magister, the Dark and Wild God who brings initiation, liberation, and enlightenment. Like the Great Goddess, the God is often approached under the guise of one of his many archetypes, as evidenced by his many aspects throughout the world.

The Sun & Fire God
Apollo, Horus-Ra, Belanus, Helios, Sol, Kane, Freyr, Heimdall, Bielobog, Lucifer, Lugh

The Lord of the Greenwood
Cernunnos, Herne, Robin Goodfellow, Puck, Dionysos, Pan, the Greenman, Silvanus, Gran Bois, Krishna, Buccos, Basajaun

The Heroic Son
Herakles, Arthur, Cuchulain, Achilles, Hektor, Perseus, Jason, Theseus, Fionn MacCumhaill, Amergin, Gilgamesh

The King & Father God
Arthur, Zeus, Jehovah, Allah, Vishnu, Dagda, El, Damballah

The Warrior God
Ares, Thor, Ogun, Bran, Tyr, Nuada

The Craftsman God
Hephaestus, Ptah, Wayland the Smith, Tubal Cain, Goibhnu, Simbi, Lugh

The God of the Oceans
Poseidon, Manannan MacLyr, Agwe, Njord

The Sacrified God
Tammuz, Mithras, Adonis, Jesus Christ, Osiris, Baal, Lyr, Baldur, Attis, John Barleycorn

The Death Lord
Hades, Anubis, Ghene, Baron Samedi, Saturn, Gwyn ap Nudd, Holt

The Wisdom God/Sage
Oghma, Thoth, Legba, Odin, Hermes, Merlin, Shiva, Taliesin, Apollo, Math ap Mathonwy, Solomon, Baphomet

The Trickster/Anti-God
Loki, Seth, Raven, Coyote, Iblis, Lucifer, Prometheus, Chernobog, Melek Taws, Azazel

Copyright Asteria Books 2017

Faces of the Goddess

The Great Goddess of the Witches is a universal Goddess figure honored in such foundational Craft literature as "The Charge of the Goddess" and Robert Graves' *The White Goddess*. She is equal to the God, and in some aspects is considered more powerful.. This great, all-encompassing Goddess is frequently identified by a number of archetypes, which we see in the faces of specific Goddesses from various cultures.

The Maiden/Virgin
Kore, Flora, Hebe, Mary, Artemis, Idun

The Moon Goddess
Diana, Selene, Ixchel, Mawu, Chang-O

The Bright Lady/Sun, Fire & Light
Brighid, Arianrhod, Aine, Amaterasu, Uzume, Sarasvati, Holle, St. Lucia, the Muses

The Wisdom Goddess/Justice
Athena, Sophia, Aradia, Maat, Themis, Medusa, Cerridwen, Medea, Tara

The Queen of Heaven
Isis, Ishtar, Astarte, Arianrhod, Nuit, Kwan Yin, Hera, Aida-Wedo, Shekinah, Ariadne, Mary, Aphrodite

The Love/Fertility Goddess
Aphrodite, Venus, Hathor, Eostre, Erzulie Frieda, Freya, Oshun, Parvati, Goda, XochiQuetzal

The Goddess of Healing/Waters
Thetis, La Sirene, Lakshmi, Sulis, Melusine, Yemaya, Nimue, Sedna, Tiamat

The Battle Goddess/Destroyer
Badb, Cailleach, Scathach, Morrigan, Kali, Maeve, Sekhmet, Brunhild, Durga, Macha, Oya, the Valkyries, the Furies

The Crone/Wise Woman
Sheila na Gig, Baba Yaga, Cailleach, Nicnevin, Cerridwen, Annis, Badb, Grandmother Spider, XochiQuetzal

The Dark Lady/Night & Death
Persephone, Lilith, Kolyo, Ereshkigal, Blodeuwedd, Nephthys, Black Madonna, Maman Brigitte, Eris, Hel

The Magician
Ishar, Isis, Nephthy, Hekate, Circe, Herodias, Aradia, Oya, Cerridwen, Zorya, Freya, Ereshkigal

Copyright Asteria Books 2017

Witch Mother

The three sacred colors of red, white and black appear in many forms and iterations in American Folkloric Witchcraft, but one of the most direct and pervasive manifestations of these colors is in the three central Deities of the Trad: the Black Goddess, the White Goddess and the Red God.

The White Goddess rules in the South at Lammas, and the Black Goddess dominates the North at Imbolc. In truth, these are two faces of the SAME Goddess – the quintessential Witch's Goddess. She is both light and darkness. But just as the sun does not shine during the darkness of night, She does not fully reveal both sides of Her nature simultaneously.

Through the light half of the year, we mark the influence of the White Goddess whom we call upon as Goda. In the dark half of the year, we honor Kolyo, the Black Goddess.

However, as much as the Black and White Goddesses counterpoint each other on the Year Wheel and within the compass that we lay, we must acknowledge and understand that they work along a continuum. They are not truly separate from each other. One requires the other for full manifestation, and the dynamic balance maintained between the two is critical to the practice of the Craft as we know it.

Each holds within Herself the core of the other. Within the darkness of the night, the light of the moon and stars reaches us. During the brightness of the day, shadows lurk and provide respite.

Just as the white knife cuts in the physical realm, and the black in the astral; so, too, do the Goddesses relate respectively to the physical and astral. The two are, in fact, reflections of each other.

A rare few Goddesses are both Black and White – Hela, Hekate, Lilith. These, we know as the Witch Mother.

Copyright Asteria Books 2015

Witch Father

Traditional Witches often refer to the Angel or God who brought enlightenment, alchemy, and magic to mankind as the Witch Father. This being has been revered and respected by those few in each generation of man who were ready and open to receive gnosis — ready to understand and embrace their own divine nature. He has been despised and demonized by the masses who find terror and blasphemy in his message.

The Witch Father is usually depicted with horns between which a green fire burns. This is the Cunning Fire, the Witch Fire. It is this fire that is the symbol of enlightenment. A Red Thread of ancestry connects us to this Witch Father and reminds us that we carry the blood of the rebel, the blood of the heretic, the blood of the scapegoat, the blood of the wise.

He is called by many names, this Witch Father. He is Azazel. He is Qayin and Tubal Cain. He is Melek Taus. He is Lucifer. He is Shamash. It is the experience of witches in the American Folkloric Tradition that these are not different beings. Rather, the names are different titles, different cultural depictions of the same God.

"Melek Taus" means "Peacock Angel/King." The peacock angel is the central figure, the benevolent and creative demiurge, of the Yezidis. He is seen as repentant after the fall from God's grace, his tears quenching the fires of hell. The Yezidis equate Melek Taus with Azazel. Muslims consider Melek Taus to be a *shaitan* or adversary.

The Nephilim, the "Fallen Angels" or spirits who descended into the material realm to interact with and guide mankind, were first seen as the "Shining Ones" or Gods of Sumerian lore. Both Lucifer and Azazel are considered Fallen Angels, and the name Lucifer means "light-bringer."

Shamash is the Babylonian name for the Sun God of justice, law, and salvation. He is linked in a triad with the Nannar-Sin (the Mood God) and Ishtar (the fertility-Earth Goddess, who incidentally is represented by the planet Venus, the Morning and Evening Star). Ishtar and Shamash are divine twins.

Copyright Asteria Books 2015

Ancestors & Beloved Dead

When most people think of Ancestors, they are limited in their thinking to only their biological or adopted elders. Those Ancestors are a wonderful place to start in your practice, but you may have other Beloved Dead in your Spirit Court who aren't necessarily family – or who weren't predecessors, per se. Well, they pre-deceased you, but you may not be their descendant. In fact, they could be yours.

Our offspring, if they pass before us, are certainly among the Beloved Dead that we can and should honor. Including our deceased children in our Ancestor work can also be extremely healing and much more holistic than the ways in which our culture currently chooses to ignore this loss.

Friends and mentors are also great folks for us to honor among our Beloved Dead when they depart this life ahead of us. They were protectors and guides in life, so it is reasonable to think they will continue offering guidance and guardianship in death. The thread of love and respect and (often) personal knowledge goes in both directions and doesn't end at death.

Creating an Ancestor Altar

Covering the Ancestor Skull when not in use can be more comfortable for some practitioners – and is the preference for some Spirits. The covering can be a handkerchief, hat, sunglasses, or any other object that can act as a veil for either the eyes or the crown. Photos and keepsakes related to the Dead you honor are great ways to create links on your altar. An offering area should be included – a plate and a cup/bowl. If you plan to burn incense or Hel Notes, be sure to use a fireproof dish as part of your offering set-up. Dispose of offerings in living water or at a crossroads, if you can – but always with a final "thank you" as a sign of respect (wherever the disposal happens). Keep your Ancestor altar clean and clutter-free. Adding a flame and a living plant is a nice way to bring the touch of warmth of life to the Dead.

Copyright Asteria Books 2022

Mighty Dead & Craft Saints

The term Mighty Dead usually refers to Spirits of heroes, leaders, and "saints" from myth, legend, and history. Most Craft practitioners don't refer to our Mighty Dead as "saints," but I propose that the term fits. Strictly speaking, "saint" means sanctified or holy, and we have certainly had leaders and teachers who have brought Mysteries to light, performed great magic, and (like the Catholic definition of sainthood) have died for their faith. (Not that martyrdom isn't a pre-requisite for sainthood within the Craft!) Perhaps you'll have your own views on what makes one a saint to our People.

The Mighty Dead are those folks who might be termed "Ascended Masters" in other spiritual paradigms. They are defenders and teachers of the Mysteries.

Some Mighty Dead and Craft Saints whom I honor in my own practice include:

Morgan le Fey

Robert Cochrane

Vivianne of the Lake

George Pickingill

Doreen Valiente

Taliesin

Dame Alice Kyteler

Circe

Isobel Gowdie

Copyright Asteria Books 2022

Maiden

The Maiden is a Classical Goddess archetype that is honored within the world of witchcraft and contemporary Paganism, much as it was by the Ancients. The Maiden is associated with the waxing crescent moon and she is often depicted as a Hunter, Fire-Bearer, and Wild Woman. Like Athena, she may be associated with a Craft, like weaving. The Maiden is sometimes seen as part of the contemporary Wiccan vision of the Triple Goddess, though ancient Triple Goddess were as likely to include three Maidens as they were to include a Maiden, Mother, and Crone.

Some Maiden Goddesses include:

Artemis – associated with hunting, animals, the moon, and freedom

Athena – associated with wisdom, strategy, weaving, and technical skill

Hestia – associated with the hearth, home, and eternal flame

Hekate – associated with magic, the moon, divination, torches, and the Underworld

Flora – associated with flowers, springtime, fertility, and youth

Hebe – associated with youth, cup-bearing, and baths

Idunna – associated with apples youth

Blodeuwedd – associated with flowers, owls, and independence

Copyright Asteria Books 2017

Mother

In the archetype of the Triple Goddess as explored by Robert Graves, the Mother Goddess is represented by the radiant and shining full moon. She is the Lady of ripeness, of greatest fertility, of stability, fulfillment, and power.

She is most closely connected to the land, often being a representation of the land itself. In this role, she is frequently a sovereignty Goddess who grants to her consort the right of kingship. She is the Earth Mother whose body feeds and sustains all life. She is the Nurturing One, the Sustaining One, the Comforting One.

Some Mother Goddesses from various cultures include:

Gaia – associated with the Earth itself and with ecology

Demeter – associated with grain and with devotion to her daughter

Astarte – associated with sexuality and fertility in the land, the animals, and the people

Frigga – associated with weaving and women's magic

Danu – associated with fertility, protection, wisdom, and the wind

Pachamama – associated with fertile fields, mountains, trees, and holed stones

Copyright Asteria Books 2017

Crone

The final archetype in the Maiden-Mother-Crone vision of the Triple Goddess is the wise, venerable, and sometimes terrifying Crone Goddess. She is depicted as an old woman of great experience, often imparting wisdom to those who seek her via riddles, omens, or other tellings. She is very often depicted as cloaked and hooded, which is symbolic of the Mysteries she protects.

While she is often shown stooped with age and walking with a cane, it is unwise to assume the Crone is weak or fragile. She is often more than capable of defending herself with magic, with clever tricks, or even with martial prowess.

The Crone has passed through the phase of Maidenhood and understands its freedom. She has lived the industrious and creative times in her life, whether she bore children or not, and so she carries the memories of the Mother's power. Now, she dances with Death and prepares for the Mysteries that lie beyond.

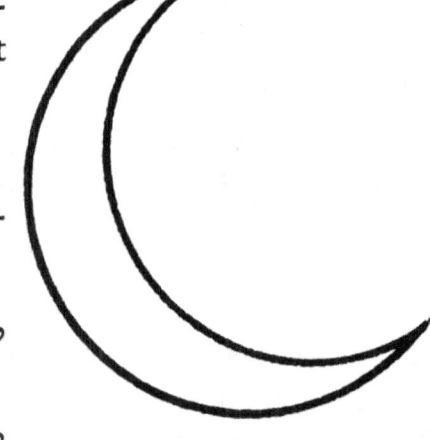

Some examples of the Crone archetype include:

Hekate — associated with the Dark Moon, crossroads, and hounds

Annis — associated with wisdom, the Old Ways, and fear

Cailleach — associated with destruction, disease, death, seasonal rites, and weather magic

Copyright Asteria Books 2017

Adonis

Adonis is honored among the Godds by some, but he was in fact a mortal man — although a legendary one who ultimately achieved immortality. His name means "Lord" and he was a prince of Cyprus.

Adonis was a hunter, and he was a lover of both Aphrodite and Persephone. He was considered the loveliest of mortal youths, and he was favored (and possibly a lover of) Apollo, Dionysos, and Heracles.

In Greek lore, Adonis splits his year between Aphrodite (who is responsible for his conception) and Persephone (who raised him). Since he descends and returns from the Underworld, he is considered a dying and resurrecting God, like his mythic predecessors from Sumer and Canaan — Dumuzi and Tammuz.

When he is later killed by a boar, Aphrodite's mourning is so intense, that she teaches all women who to lament the loss of life and love by instructing them to beat their chests and tear their clothes. The Adonia, a festival to honor Adonis's death, reenacts this mourning and also features the planting, reaping, and new growth of quick-growing plants such as lettuce, fennel, and other salad greens.

Except from the Orphic Hymn to Adonis:

> Much-named, and best of daimons, hear my prayer; ... aliment divine
>
> Female and Male, all charming to the sight, Adonis ever flourishing and bright;
>
> At stated periods doomed to set and rise, with splendid lamp, the glory of the skies.
>
> Two-horned and lovely, reverenced with tears, of beauteous form, adorned with copious hairs.

Aphrodite

Aphrodite is best known as the Greek Goddess of Love and Beauty, but her influence doesn't end there. Indeed, she is a powerful and complicated Deity who is connected with these ideas and powers, as well:

Fertility, youth, agelessness, birth, spring, war, the sea, the sky, waterfowl, illusion, truth, fate, persuasion, seduction, civic duty, leadership, darkness, brightness, pleasure, childbirth, marriage, secrets, dusk, dawn, stars, gold, and more

Although some of her attributes and areas of influence may seem to contradict each other, it is wise to understand that Aphrodite was worshipped across ancient Greece and was called upon in a myriad of ways by her followers. She is truly one of the Great Goddesses of the ancient world, and she remains so today.

Because she has always been a well-loved and well-known Goddess, she has many stories that we might draw upon for gnosis and magick.

Her symbols include apples, swans, geese, doves, fish, turtles, roses, lilies, anemones, myrtle, myrrh, mirrors, golden girdle (belt), sand dollars, starfish, 8-pointed stars, pentacles, cosmetics, gold, cowrie shells, scallop shells, and more.

Excerpt from the Orphic hymn to Aphrodite:

Heavenly, smiling Aphrodite, praised in many hymns,

sea-born, revered goddess of generation, you like the nightlong revel

and you couple lovers at night, O scheming mother of Necessity.

Everything comes from you; you have yoked the world,

and you control all three realms.

Copyright Asteria Books 2023

Apollo

Apollo (or Apollon) is a God of both Greece and Rome who is attributed with influence over archery, music and dance, truth and prophecy, healing and diseases, the Sun and light, poetry, and more. He is the son of Zeus and Leto, along with his twin sister Artemis. Both Artemis and Apollo are hunters, and they are both considered the epitome of youth and athleticism.

While Artemis is a Goddess of wild natural places, Apollo is a God of cultivated pursuits. He and Dionysos, for example, are both deeply connected to music, but one could say that the symphony is Apollonian, while a rock concert with a mosh pit is more Dionysian.

Apollo is a stalwart defender of homes and cities who are under his protection. One of his many epithets calls him "Alexikakos" which means the "averter of evil." He averted invasion and defeat by one's enemies, and he also averted the plague from areas where humans are gathered in close proximity.

As Apollo Kataibatês, he grants a happy and safe return home for travelers. As Apollo Lukeios, he is known as a bringer of light — the light that shines through music, poetry, art, and prophecy.

Copyright Asteria Books 2024

Aradia's Gifts

According to an Italian legend, Aradia is the daughter of Diana and her brother Lucifer. Aradia was said to be an avatar of Diana sent to earth to teach people the ways of Witchcraft to free them from slavery and degradation.

The Gifts of Aradia

In the fourteenth century, Aradia was said to have taught that the traditional powers of a witch would belong to any who followed in the ways of the Old Religion. Aradia stressed that these gifts were the benefits of adhering to the Old Ways and not the reason for becoming a witch. These are the powers:

To bring success in love
To bless and consecrate
To speak with spirits
To know of hidden things
To call forth spirits
To know the Voice of the Wind
To possess the knowledge of transformation
To possess the knowledge of divination
To know and understand secret signs
To cure disease
To bring forth beauty
To have influence over wild beasts
To know the secrets of the hands

THE COVENANT OF ARADIA

To obtain the powers of the Strega, there were certain rules that needed to be followed. They are as follows:

Observe the times of the Treguenda, for therein is the foundation of the powers of Stregheria.

When good is done to you, then do good to another. If someone wishes to repay you for a kindness, then bind them to go out of their way to help three others, then this shall clear the debt.

Do not use the arts of Stregheria to appear powerful among others. Do not lower the standards of the Art and thereby bring contempt upon the Old ways.

Do not take the life of anything unless it is to preserve life — yours or another's.

Do not give your word of honor lightly, for you are bound by your words and by your oaths.

Do not accept any authority over you unless it is of the Gods. Instead, cooperate with others, but do not be a slave and always preserve your honor. Give respect to others and expect respect in return.

Teach all who appear worthy and aid the continuance of the Old Religion.

Do not belittle another's religious beliefs, but simply state your own truths. Strive to be at peace with those who differ.

Do not purposely cause harm to another, unless it is to prevent true harm to yourself or another.

Strive to be compassionate to others and to be aware of the hearts and minds of those around you.

Be true to your own understanding, and turn away from those things which oppose the good in you or are harmful to you. Hold reverence to all within Nature. Destroy nothing, scar nothing, waste nothing, live in harmony with Nature, for the ways of Nature are our own ways.

Remain open in your heart and in your mind to the Great Ones who created all that is — and to your brothers and sisters alike.

Copyright Asteria Publishing 2012

Ares

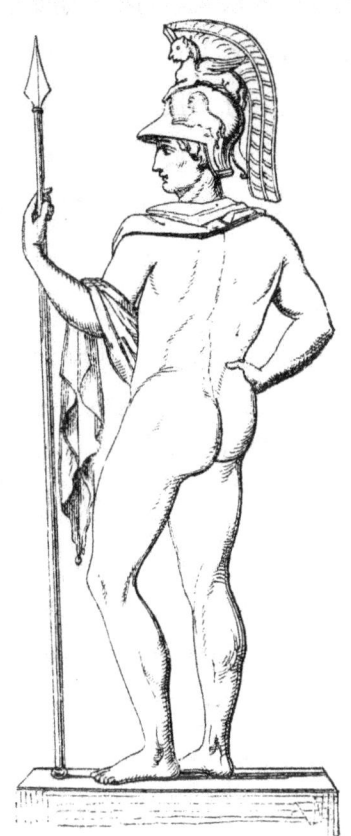

Ares, the Greek God of War, embodies the fierce and unyielding spirit of battle. Known for his relentless pursuit of conflict and his embodiment of the chaotic and brutal aspects of warfare, Ares holds a unique place among the Olympian gods.

In Greek mythology, Ares is often portrayed as a powerful and belligerent deity, driven by his insatiable thirst for battle and bloodshed. Unlike some of his fellow Olympians who possess wisdom, beauty, or craftsmanship, Ares' domain is solely focused on the art of war. He is frequently accompanied by his sister Eris, the goddess of discord, further highlighting his association with chaos and strife.

Depictions of Ares in ancient Greek art often show him in full armor, brandishing a spear or sword, ready to lead armies into battle. He represents the physical, violent, and unpredictable aspects of war, contrasting with Athena, the goddess of strategic warfare and wisdom.

Despite his fearsome reputation, Ares is not universally beloved among the gods or mortals. He is often depicted as reckless and bloodthirsty, driven more by the thrill of conflict than by any noble cause. Stories of his exploits include involvement in conflicts such as the Trojan War, where he sides with the Trojans, and his rivalry with Athena over martial prowess and strategy.

Ares' influence extends beyond mere combat; he is also considered a patron of warriors and soldiers, offering protection and strength to those who seek his favor in battle. Temples and sanctuaries dedicated to Ares existed in various Greek city-states, where warriors could pray for his blessing before going to war.

In later interpretations of Greek mythology and in modern culture, Ares continues to be a symbol of the destructive and chaotic aspects of war. His character serves as a reminder of the dual nature of conflict—both necessary for defense and destructive in its execution.

Copyright Asteria Books 2024

Arianrhod

Arianrhod is a Welsh Goddess whose name means "Silver Wheel." He story appears in the Fourth Branch of the *Mabinogi*. She is the daughter of Don, the niece of Math ap Mathonwy, King of Gwynedd. In her story as told in the *Mabinogi*, she gives birth to two sons through magical means. Her sons are Dylan ail Don and Llew Llaw Gyffes. According to the tales, Math would die unless a virgin held his feet when he was not at war. Circumstances forced Math to find a new footholder, and Arianrhod's brothers recommended her for the job. Math tested her virginity by having her step over an enchanted wand, and she gave birth to two sons. Dylan was a water spirit and departed immediately for the sea. The other boy, however, got the full brunt of his mother's humiliation and outrage. She placed a *geise* on him that he would not have a name, weapons, or a human wife. All of these were traditionally the mother's right to give, and they were all marks of masculinity and adulthood. Gwydion, Arianrhod's brother (and possibly the boy's father, according to much theory), took the boy in as his son or fosterling. Together, they tricked Arianrhod into giving the boy the name Llew Llaw Gyffes ("fair-haired, skillful-handed one") and weapons (in defense of her home — in an attack they arranged). With his use of magic, Gwydion made a bride for the boy out of flowers.

Caer Arianrhod is the Goddess's home. "Caer" means "castle." There is a rock formation called by this name off the coast of Gwynedd, Wales that is visible at low tide. This is also the Welsh name for the constellation *Corona Borealis*, the northern crown.

Copyright Asteria Books 2015

Athena

PALLAS ATHENE

Athena, the revered Greek goddess of wisdom, courage, and strategic warfare, commanded profound respect and devotion throughout ancient Greece. Her worship was not only widespread but also deeply ingrained in the cultural and religious fabric of Greek society.

As the patroness of Athens, Athena held a central place in the hearts of Athenians. The city itself was named in her honor following a contest with Poseidon, where she offered the olive tree—a symbol of peace and prosperity—to win the favor of its inhabitants. The Parthenon, arguably the most iconic temple of ancient Greece, was dedicated to Athena Parthenos (Athena the Virgin), showcasing the pinnacle of Athenian reverence and architectural splendor.

Athena was venerated not only as a wise counselor and strategist but also as a protector of cities, artisans, and heroes. Temples and sanctuaries dedicated to Athena could be found throughout Greece, including major centers like Delphi, Sparta, and Corinth, each emphasizing different aspects of her persona.

The festivals honoring Athena were significant communal events in Greek religious life. The most renowned was the Panathenaea, a grand festival held annually in Athens to celebrate Athena's birthday. This festival included athletic competitions, processions, sacrifices, and the presentation of the peplos—a sacred garment believed to be woven by Athenian women and draped over the statue of Athena Polias (Athena of the City) in the Erechtheion temple on the Acropolis.

Copyright Asteria Books 2024

Anubis

Anubis, the ancient Egyptian deity associated with mummification and the afterlife, embodies a mystical and profound aspect of ancient Egyptian religion. Known as the god of embalming and the guardian of the dead, Anubis played a crucial role in guiding souls through the journey of death and rebirth.

Anubis is often depicted as a figure with the head of a jackal or a canine, symbolizing his role as a protector and guide in the underworld. His black fur symbolizes the color of mummified flesh and the fertile black soil of the Nile River delta, emphasizing his connection to both death and regeneration.

Anubis' magical significance lies in his ability to oversee the process of mummification, ensuring that the deceased's spirit could successfully navigate the perilous journey to the afterlife. He was believed to weigh the hearts of the deceased against the feather of Ma'at, the goddess of truth and justice, in the Hall of Two Truths during the judgment of the dead. This ritual determined whether the soul would be granted eternal life in the Fields of Reeds or face oblivion.

Beyond his role in the afterlife, Anubis was also revered as a patron of healers and those skilled in magic and incantations. Priests who practiced the art of mummification and performed burial rites often invoked Anubis' protection and guidance to ensure the preservation of the deceased's spirit.

Copyright Asteria Books 2024

Azazel

Azazel was chief among the angels in the story of The Fall of the B'nai Elohim in the Book of Enoch. The B'nai Elohim is a term that refers to angels. These fallen angels, or Watchers, descended to the realm of matter (earth) where they took the descendants of Cain as human vessels. They took women as their wives and taught them witchcraft and other skills. Azazel took Tubal-Cain, the blacksmith, as his vessel and further improved the arts of smith craft and witchery.

Enoch reveals to us that Azazel shares with humanity "all the metals and the art of working them...and the use of antimony." As it turns out, antimony was critical to the alchemical process of creating the Philosopher's Stone. This same element was called *kuhl* (or kohl) by the ancient Arabs. (You might also recall references to women decorating their eyes with this substance, and that art also being taught by Azazel. This may, in fact, have been a veiled reference to the alchemical process and not to cosmetics at all.) Sir Roger Bacon tells us that when antimony is processed with vitriol, it is reduced to a "noble red oil" with all of the lesser sulfur having been purified out of it in the process. Red, then, is Azazel's color.

It is doubly his color when we consider that man is made from red clay, according to Middle Eastern tradition, and that Azazel is master of the material world from which man is made.

In American Folkloric Witchcraft, we honor Azazel as the sunset face, the Samhain face, the Saturnian face of the Witch Father.

Invocation

Come, Azazel-Qayin, come from the West!
Come, Witch Father, Wisdom's Father,
and teach me your Truths, as you taught the Ancients!

Come, Azazel-Qayin, Gatekeeper of the Paths of the Dead.
From the Samhain-place, walk the Red Path, the line of Qayin to the midst of magic's crossroads.

So mote it be!

Copyright Asteria Books 2015

Baldur

In the rich tapestry of Norse mythology, few figures shine as brightly as Baldur, the beloved god of light, purity, and beauty. Revered for his radiant presence and noble demeanor, Baldur occupies a unique place among the pantheon of Norse deities, embodying qualities that captivate both gods and mortals alike.

Baldur is the son of Odin, the All-Father, and Frigg, the goddess of love and beauty. From his birth, he exuded an aura of charm and grace, earning him the affection of all who encountered him. Often depicted as the epitome of youth and innocence, Baldur's most distinctive attribute was his luminous appearance, which illuminated even the darkest corners of the cosmos.

However, Baldur's fate was overshadowed by a tragic prophecy. It foretold his untimely death, a revelation that struck fear into the hearts of the gods. Frigg, in her despair, sought assurances from every corner of existence that no harm would come to her beloved son. All beings and objects swore oaths not to harm Baldur, from the mightiest giants to the tiniest plants.

Yet, the mischievous Loki, harboring jealousy and malice, discovered a loophole in this invulnerability. He tricked Frigg into revealing that she had overlooked mistletoe in her quest for assurances. Armed with this newfound knowledge, Loki fashioned a deadly spear from mistletoe and conspired to bring about Baldur's downfall.

At a gathering where the gods tested Baldur's invincibility by hurling all manner of weapons at him, Loki's treachery unfolded. Hodr, Baldur's blind brother, manipulated by Loki, unwittingly threw the fatal spear of mistletoe. Struck by this unforeseen weapon, Baldur fell lifeless, fulfilling the dreaded prophecy and plunging the realms into mourning.

His death becomes a catalyst for Ragnarok, the cataclysmic end of the world, where his eventual resurrection marks a renewal of hope and the cycle of life.

Copyright Asteria Books 2024

Bast

In the pantheon of ancient Egyptian deities, few hold the charm and mystery of Bast, the goddess who embodies the grace and power of the feline. Revered as both a protective deity and a symbol of feminine strength, Bast captivates scholars and enthusiasts alike with her multifaceted symbolism and enduring appeal.

Bast, often depicted as a lioness or a woman with the head of a lioness, personifies the qualities associated with cats: agility, cunning, and a fierce protectiveness of her domain. She was revered not only as a guardian of households but also as a defender of the pharaoh and a bringer of fertility and abundance.

In ancient Egypt, Bast was celebrated annually with lavish festivals where devotees gathered to honor her with music, dance, and offerings. Cats, considered sacred animals associated with Bast, were kept in homes and temples, their presence believed to invoke her protective powers and blessings.

Over millennia, Bast's cult evolved and intertwined with other deities, notably merging with the goddess Sekhmet, who shared her leonine attributes but embodied a more fearsome aspect of destruction and healing. This syncretic fusion further enriched the mythology surrounding Bast, blending her roles as a nurturing mother and a formidable warrior.

Beyond ancient Egypt, Bast's influence spread across cultures and time periods. Her image and symbolism persisted through various artistic representations, from intricate amulets to grand temple statues. In modern times, her allure continues to inspire artists, writers, and spiritual seekers, drawn to her embodiment of feminine power and protective instincts.

Copyright Asteria Books 2024

Belenus

Belenus is one of the most important, ancient, and far-reaching Gods of the Pan-Celtic pantheon. His influence was noted in Gaul, Iberia, Britain, and Italy. He is a God of the sun and also of horses. Like Apollo, he is said to draw the sun across the sky in his horse-drawn chariot. Other names for him include Bel, Beli, and Beli Mawr — as well as many variant spellings of Belenus. The root "Bel" means "Fair Shining One." Beltane was originated as a festival in honor of this deity, and the word Beltane means "bright fire." Etymologically and mythologically, Belenus and Apollo share much in common, including association with the sun, horses, the wheel, the ram, healing, the fire, mantic oracles, music, poetry, knowledge, wisdom, and more. Belenus is associated very much with the oak and the acorn, as symbols of both wisdom and masculine fertility and strength. He is also associated with the torch, a very phallic and fiery symbol that combines aspects of both the masculine generative forces and the shining light with which his name is synonymous. Appropriate offerings to Belenus include fruit and cake. Dancing, drumming, bonfires, the very phallic Maypole, and revelry are all traditional ways to celebrate his feast day — Beltane.

Copyright Asteria Books 2015

Blodeuwedd

Blodeuwedd is a Welsh Goddess whose story is told in the *Mabinogi* along with Arianrhod and Llew Llaw Gyffes. Arianrhod, in her anger and shame, had cursed her son not to be married to a human woman. Gwydion, the young man's uncle (and possibly his father) is a skilled magician, though, who conjures a girl from nine flowers — or just three (the oak, broom, and meadowsweet), depending on the version. The name Blodeuwedd means "flower face." The couple is happy for a year and a day, but then Blodeuwedd meets a man of her own choosing, Gronw. She falls in love and has an affair, and she starts to realize that she was created and has been used for another person's purposes. Despite that, she has a will of her own, and she decides to live and love on her own terms. Seeing no other way out, she and Gronw stage an elaborate plan to murder Llew, who leads a charmed life. Their plan fails, but Llew is changed into an eagle and flies away. When his uncle finds and rescues him, they put Gronw to death and punish Blodeuwedd by transforming her into an owl. She is sentenced to wander the night alone, hated and assaulted by other birds. "Blodeuwedd" is the Welsh word for "owl," and the owl is seen as a solitary and wise bird, if also lonely. In Blodeuwedd's story, we see the price we must sometimes pay to be true to ourselves, as well as the reminder that no other person must be compelled to serve our whim, however entitled we feel to the need.

Copyright Asteria Books 2015

Bran the Blessed

In Welsh mythology, Bran Fendigaidd (literally "Blessed Crow/Raven") is described as a giant and the High King of Britain. He is a mighty warrior, and he appears in several of the Welsh triads as well as the Second Branch of the *Mabinogi*. He is the brother of Branwen, Manawdan, Nisien, and Efnysien. He is a son of Lyr and Penarddun. The Irish high king comes to him, asking for his sister Branwen's hand in marriage, forging an alliance between the two islands. Efnysien, though, is insulted that he wasn't consulted, and mutilates the Irish horses. To placate the Irish, Bran gives the king a large cauldron with the power of regeneration. It will bring slain warriors back to life. The wedding proceeds, but when the new couple returns to Ireland, Branwen is terribly mistreated – beaten daily and forced to work in the kitchen. She tames a bird and sends word back to her brother, pleading for help. He comes with many warriors, but the cauldron makes it nearly impossible for the British to hold their ground. Efnysien slays Branwen's son, and Branwen dies of a broken heart. Efnysien hides himself among the Irish slain in order to be placed inside the cauldron. Once inside, he destroys the cauldron, sacrificing himself in the process. Only eight warriors survive, and Bran the Blessed is mortally wounded. He instructs his companions to cut off his head. Bran's head entertains and advises them for several years until they ultimately bury it on White Hill to act as a guardian for Britain. It is thought that White Hill is Tower Hill, the location of the Tower of London, which even today has ravens guarding the tower and the land. Bran the Blessed is associated with courage, wisdom, protection, and good advice.

Copyright Asteria Books 2015

Brigid

Brighid is a Pan-Celtic Goddess whose worship was so widespread in the British Isles and Europe that she was canonized by the Catholic Church. She is known by many variations of the same name:

Brighid (Modern Irish)
Bríd (Reformed Irish)
Bridget (Anglicanized)
Brìghde/Brìde (Scotland)
Brigantia (Great Britain)

The goddess Brigid presided over the hearth and the forge, over the inspiration and skill of sacred art and craft, and over the world of crops, livestock, and nature. The 10th-century Cormac's Glossary states that Brigid was the daughter of the Dagda, the "Great God" of the Tuatha de Danaan. It states Brigid to be a *"woman of wisdom… a goddess whom poets adored, because her protection was very great and very famous."*

The early Church could not very easily call the Great Goddess of Ireland a demon, so they opted to canonized her instead. She would become Saint Brigit, patroness of poetry and healing. The church's explanation to the Irish peasants was that Brigit was actually an early Christian missionary, and that the miracles she performed misled the common people into believing that she was a goddess. In some of the many legends about St. Brigit, there is a belief that she was the foster-mother of Jesus, having spent some part of his boyhood in Britain and Ireland, or that she was the mid-wife at his birth.

Maman Brigitte is the Haitian manifestation of this goddess brought to Haiti by indentured servants from Ireland and Scotland in the 1700's-1800's. She is the Queen of the Cemetery and consort of Baron Samedi, the gatekeeper of the graveyard. She is often depicted as a white woman with red hair, and she is believed to be a powerful witch. The grave of the first woman buried in a cemetery is consecrated to her and she is also believed to protect all the graves in the cemetery that are properly marked with a cross. In this guise, she is still shown to us as a healer and midwife – albeit of the next life and not this one.

Copyright Asteria Books 2015

Bucca

As we delve into the realm of Cornish folklore, the Bucca emerges as a fascinating embodiment of the region's mystical heritage. Through their playful antics and enigmatic presence, these spirits continue to enchant and intrigue, reminding us of the enduring magic woven into the landscapes and seascapes of Cornwall. Whether viewed as protectors, tricksters, or guides, the Bucca spirit stands as a testament to the enduring power of folklore in shaping cultural identity and fostering a deep reverence for the mysteries of the natural world.

The Bucca are often depicted as shape-shifters, capable of appearing as animals, humans, or even inanimate objects. Despite their mischievous tendencies, Buccas are not inherently malevolent; rather, they delight in playing tricks on unsuspecting mortals and sailors who venture too close to their domains.

In Cornish lore, Buccas are associated with natural landmarks such as caves, cliffs, and coves along the coastline. They are regarded as protectors of their territories, offering blessings to those who respect the land and sea. Sailors would often invoke their favor for safe passage and bountiful catches, while farmers sought their aid for fertile crops and abundant harvests.

Stories of encounters with Buccas range from humorous anecdotes to cautionary tales. They are said to appear during storms, luring travelers astray or guiding lost souls to safety. One famous legend tells of the Bucca Dhu, a black spirit haunting the mines of Cornwall, whose presence foretold riches or impending disaster.

The Bucca spirit remains a vibrant part of Cornish culture, celebrated in local festivals and commemorated in folk songs and stories passed down through generations. Their presence underscores the deep connection between the Cornish people and their natural surroundings, embodying the spirit of resilience and adaptability in the face of adversity.

Copyright Asteria Books 2024

Cailleach

The name Cailleach derives from a proto-Indo-European root that means "veiled one" and has come to mean "hag" in Irish and Scottish Gaelic. There are many Goddesses and mythic figures who are referred to by this moniker, but the primary figure we have come to think of as the Cailleach is known by the full name Cailleach Beira, which is a Scottish name related to her tales as the Winter Queen. As such, she rules the time from Samhain to Beltaine (with Brighid ruling from Beltaine to Samhain). She ushers in the winter by washing her great plaid in a gulf off the coast of Scotland — a process that takes three days. After the washing is complete, her woolen plaid is snow white and the snows settle on the land in earnest.

Spring windstorms are associated with old women called *Cailleachean*, or Storm Hags, and they are considered very dangerous.

She is credited with having shaped the mountains and hills (which some legends say she did purposefully, and others say she did haphazardly).

Cailleach is also very much an ancestral Goddess, since it is believed that the poem "The Old Woman of Beara" refers to her. She lived through seven periods of youth, taking husbands and bearing children. She lived so long as a young woman that each of her husbands, in turn, died of old age before she ever started aging. She is credited with being the foremother of tribes and races of men.

Copyright Asteria Books 2018

Cerridwen

Cerridwen is a potent and prominent figure in many modern Craft traditions. She is associated with the cauldron, the most recognizable of all witchcraft tools; and her tale is one of deep transformation — the work of the witch!

Her name means "White Sow" and this great queen of Celtic legend is known for devouring her offspring, just a s a sow will sometimes do.

Her myth tells how she set the young servant boy Gwion to the task of stirring a cauldron of knowledge and wisdom. The brew within was intended for her son, but when three scalding drops landed on Gwion's hand, he instinctively sucked away the pain - and wisdom. Enraged, a pursuit ensues in which Gwion shapeshifts to escape Cerridwen's wrath, but she transforms to capture him. When he was a hare, she was a greyhound. Then he was a fish and she an otter. Next, he was a bird, and she was a hawk. Fourth, he changed into a grain of corn, and she transformed into a hen, pecking every grain until she had consumed him. Once she had him, she transformed again to the shape of a woman, and gave birth in nine months' time to the great bard Taliesin. This last is their fifth and final transformation.

Cerridwen is honored as a lady of wisdom, of familial protection, and of spiritual transformation.

Copyright Asteria Books 2015

Cuchulainn

Cuchulainn is an Irish God who appears in the Ulster cycles and also shows up in Scottish and Manx folklore. His name means "Culann's hound." He was born Setanta, son of Lugh, but after killing Culann's guard dog in an act of self-defense, the young man offers to take the dog's place until a suitable canine replacement can be reared and trained. Cuchulainn's life was foretold to be short but full of renown. He is a celebrated hero of the city of Ulster, which he defended single-handedly against invasion by Queen Medb and her army in the *Tain Bo Cualigne* ("Cattle Raid of Cooley"). Cuchulainn is trained in the art of battle by the famous warrior woman, Scathach, on the Isle of Skye in Scotland. It is Medb and her allies who eventually conspire to kill Cuchulainn. He has a geise (taboo) against eating dog meat, but there is a general geise in Ireland against refusing hospitality. When he is offered a meal of dog meat by an old woman, he feels compelled to partake, but it weakens him spiritually. One of his enemies has fashioned three spears that are prophesied to slay three kings. One strikes and kills Cuchulainn's horse, the King of Horses. The second strikes and kills Cuchulainn's friend, the King of Charioteers. The third mortally wounds Cuchulainn himself. Being near to death, he lashes himself to a standing stone so he may die on his feet while facing his enemies. It isn't until a raven lands on his shoulder that his enemies will believe he has died. When one approaches to take his head in victory, Cuchulainn's arm falls and cuts off the man's hand.

Copyright Asteria Books 2016

Dagda

The Dagda is an important God of Irish mythology. His name likely means "the Good God," and he was seen as a protector and benefactor of the people. His brothers include Ogma and Lir, although his parentage is debatable — probably because he is so often cast in the role of the Father God. His many epithets include "All-Father", "Creator", "Lord of Great Knowledge", and "Horned Man." He also has epithet that means either "Cauldron" or "Iron." He often depicted carrying a huge club, and he is associated with a cauldron of plenty. The Dagda was said to be immensely powerful, and his club could kill eight to nine men with a single blow. The handle, however, could return the slain to life. The Dagda's cauldron was called Undry was said to be bottomless. No man left it unsatisfied. He also possessed an oak harp that, when he played it, put the seasons in order and arranged the order of battle. Depictions of the Dagda as oafish and crude were likely insinuated by Christian detractors of the Old Religion in order to make the Celtic All-Father less potent to the people. However, he was seen by the Celts as beautiful and powerful, his name (like Lugh's) have Proto-Indo-European roots that indicate a "shining" vision of the Divine. Newgrange was said to be the Dagda's home, until his son Aengus tricked him out of it. It was, however, said to be the place of the God-King's death.

Copyright Asteria Books 2015

Diana

In Roman mythology, DIANA is the goddess of the hunt, the moon, and childbirth, being associated with wild animals and woodlands, and having the power to talk to and control animals. Oak groves were especially sacred to her. According to mythology, Diana was born with her twin brother Apollo, who is sometimes referred to by the name "Lucifer" (which means "light-bringer" in Latin).

In Italy, the old religion of Stregheria embraces the goddess Diana as Queen of the Witches; witches being the wise women healers of the time. Diana was said to have created the world of her own being, having in herself the seeds of all creation yet to come. It was said that out of herself she divided the darkness and the light, keeping for herself the darkness of creation and creating her brother Apollo, the light. Diana was believed to have loved and ruled with her brother Apollo, the god of the Sun.

In Charles Leland's *Aradia: Gospoel of the Witches*, Diana is not only the witches' goddess, but she is presented as the primordial creatrix. After giving birth to Apollo-Lucifer, Diana seduces him while in the form of a cat, eventually giving birth to Aradia, their daughter. Diana demonstrates the power of her witchcraft by creating "the heavens, the stars, and the rain." This book presents the original witches as slaves that escaped from their masters, beginning new lives as "thieves and evil folk." Diana sends her daughter Aradia to them to teach these former serfs witchcraft, the power of which they can use to "destroy the evil race (of oppressors)." Aradia's students thus became the first witches, who would then continue the worship of Diana. Leland was struck by this cosmogony: "In all other Scriptures of all races, it is the male... who creates the universe; in Witch Sorcery it is the female who is the primitive principle"

Copyright Asteria Books 2015

Demeter

In ancient Greek mythology, Demeter stands as a prominent figure, revered for her association with agriculture, fertility, and the cycle of life. As the goddess of the harvest and nurturing motherly love, Demeter's influence extends beyond mythological narratives to encompass profound cultural, societal, and spiritual significance.

Demeter's primary role as the goddess of agriculture underscores her vital importance in ancient Greek society. She presided over the fertility of the earth, ensuring bountiful harvests and the wellbeing of crops. Farmers and agrarian communities honored Demeter through rituals, prayers, and offerings, seeking her favor for favorable weather, fertile soil, and abundant yields.

Beyond her agricultural role, Demeter embodies the archetype of the nurturing mother. Her deep love for her daughter Persephone, whom she tragically lost to the underworld, epitomizes maternal devotion and the depths of grief. This myth of Persephone's abduction by Hades and Demeter's relentless search for her daughter reflects themes of loss, renewal, and the eternal cycle of life and death.

Demeter's worship was central to the Eleusinian Mysteries, ancient rituals held in Eleusis, near Athens. These mysteries were secretive ceremonies dedicated to Demeter and Persephone, promising initiates spiritual enlightenment and a deeper understanding of life's mysteries. The rituals included dramatic reenactments of Demeter's grief and joy upon reuniting with Persephone, offering participants hope for life after death and the promise of eternal renewal.

Demeter's influence transcended the boundaries of ancient Greece, permeating artistic expressions, literature, and philosophical reflections. Her symbolism as a guardian of life and fertility resonated in various cultural contexts, influencing agricultural practices, societal norms, and moral values associated with nurturing and protection.

Copyright Asteria Books 2024

Dionysos

Dionysos is a deity of revelry, fertility, and the transformative power of wine. Worship of Dionysos, also known as Bacchus in Roman mythology, was marked by joyful celebrations, rituals, and a profound connection to the natural world.

Dionysos, son of Zeus and the mortal Semele, embodies the dual nature of ecstasy and madness. Often depicted with vine leaves in his hair and a thyrsus—a staff wrapped with ivy—in hand, he symbolizes the liberating and intoxicating effects of wine. His cult celebrated these qualities through ecstatic rituals known as Bacchanalia, characterized by music, dance, and uninhibited revelry.

The worship of Dionysos held a central place in ancient Greek religious life, particularly in the form of festivals like the Dionysia and the Anthesteria. These events not only honored the god but also provided opportunities for communal bonding, artistic expression, and catharsis. Theater performances, especially tragedies and comedies, were integral to Dionysian festivals, reflecting his association with both the joys and sorrows of life.

Dionysos's mythology is rich with symbolism, depicting his journeys of rebirth, transformation, and divine ecstasy. His encounters with mortals and gods alike illustrate his role as a bringer of inspiration and madness, challenging societal norms and fostering creativity. Stories of his adventures, including his descent into the underworld and his triumphant return, highlight themes of renewal and the cyclical nature of life.

The worship of Dionysos transcended the ancient Greek world, influencing Roman culture and later inspiring artistic movements, literature, and philosophy throughout history. His association with fertility, abundance, and the mysteries of life continues to captivate scholars and enthusiasts alike, reflecting enduring themes of human experience and spiritual exploration.

Copyright Asteria Books 2024

Freya

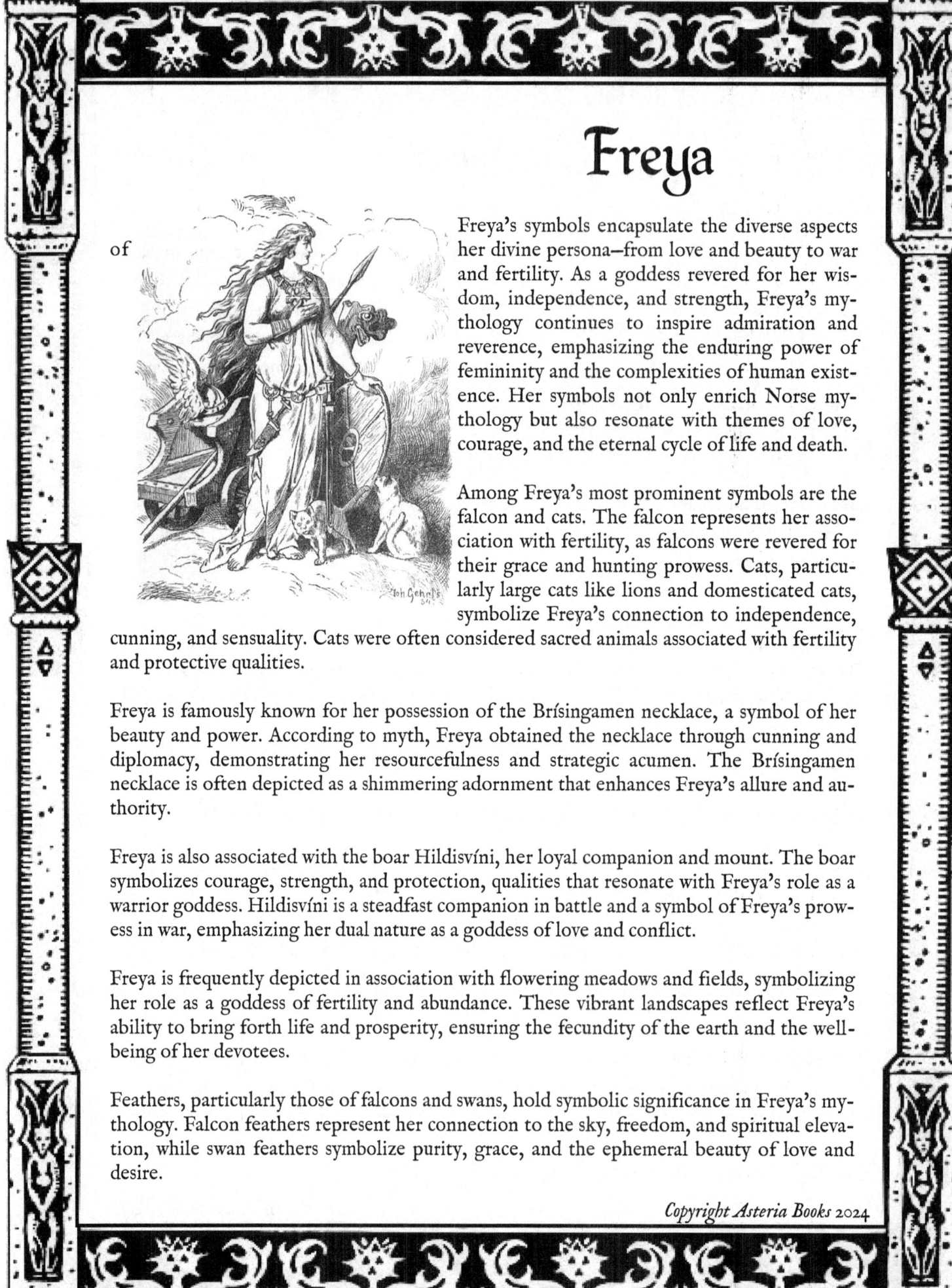

Freya's symbols encapsulate the diverse aspects of her divine persona—from love and beauty to war and fertility. As a goddess revered for her wisdom, independence, and strength, Freya's mythology continues to inspire admiration and reverence, emphasizing the enduring power of femininity and the complexities of human existence. Her symbols not only enrich Norse mythology but also resonate with themes of love, courage, and the eternal cycle of life and death.

Among Freya's most prominent symbols are the falcon and cats. The falcon represents her association with fertility, as falcons were revered for their grace and hunting prowess. Cats, particularly large cats like lions and domesticated cats, symbolize Freya's connection to independence, cunning, and sensuality. Cats were often considered sacred animals associated with fertility and protective qualities.

Freya is famously known for her possession of the Brísingamen necklace, a symbol of her beauty and power. According to myth, Freya obtained the necklace through cunning and diplomacy, demonstrating her resourcefulness and strategic acumen. The Brísingamen necklace is often depicted as a shimmering adornment that enhances Freya's allure and authority.

Freya is also associated with the boar Hildisvíni, her loyal companion and mount. The boar symbolizes courage, strength, and protection, qualities that resonate with Freya's role as a warrior goddess. Hildisvíni is a steadfast companion in battle and a symbol of Freya's prowess in war, emphasizing her dual nature as a goddess of love and conflict.

Freya is frequently depicted in association with flowering meadows and fields, symbolizing her role as a goddess of fertility and abundance. These vibrant landscapes reflect Freya's ability to bring forth life and prosperity, ensuring the fecundity of the earth and the well-being of her devotees.

Feathers, particularly those of falcons and swans, hold symbolic significance in Freya's mythology. Falcon feathers represent her connection to the sky, freedom, and spiritual elevation, while swan feathers symbolize purity, grace, and the ephemeral beauty of love and desire.

Copyright Asteria Books 2024

Freyr

Freyr, the Norse god of fertility and prosperity, remains a revered figure. Through his attributes of abundance, peace, and benevolence, Freyr embodies timeless values that emphasize the interconnectedness between humanity and the natural world.

Freyr is often depicted as a handsome and benevolent deity, wielding powerful symbols such as the sword that fights for peace and the ship Skíðblaðnir, which could travel on land, sea, and air. His most iconic symbol, however, is the boar Gullinbursti, which embodies strength, virility, and agricultural abundance.

As a god of fertility, Freyr was invoked by farmers and communities seeking fertile soil, successful harvests, and the growth of livestock. His benevolence extended beyond agriculture to include blessings of peace, prosperity, and harmonious relationships among people. Rituals and offerings were dedicated to Freyr during seasonal festivals, ensuring his favor and protection for the community's prosperity.

Freyr's mythology intertwines with themes of love and destiny, most notably in his relationship with the giantess Gerðr. Their union symbolizes the cyclical nature of life and the alignment of divine forces with mortal affairs. Freyr's generosity and compassion toward mortals underscore his role as a patron of humanity, offering guidance and blessings in times of need.

The worship of Freyr persisted beyond the Viking Age, influencing cultural practices and beliefs throughout Scandinavia. His symbolism as a guardian of fertility and prosperity resonated in agricultural rituals, folk traditions, and societal values that emphasized the importance of abundance and communal harmony.

Copyright Asteria Books 2024

Goda

Goda is the name given to one of the three great Tutelary Spirits of the Spiral Castle Tradition of Witchcraft (the first branch of the Craft to use the term American Folkloric Traditional Witchcraft). She is the White Goddess who forms a sort of "Trinity" with Kolyo (the Black Goddess) and Tubal Qayin (the Red God).

Goda is the Lady of Light who stands as a beacon of life, light, love, and liberty. Like the legendary Lady Godiva who rode naked through the streets, she guards the Mysteries by hiding them in plain sight. After all, when Godiva rode her white horse through town, nobody (or very few) actually saw her, as the townsfolk averted their eyes.

The White Goddess as an archetype can be seen in the form of many named and known Goddesses across cultures. These ladies share some common attributes including being linked to love, romance, and sex; life, fertility, abundance, and prosperity; beauty, joy, laughter, and singing; as well as nature spirits, faerie magick, illusion, and glamoury.

Where her counterpart, the Black Goddess, is shrouded and obscured from sight, the White Goddess stands boldly bare for all those with wisdom, cunning, and bravery to witness. She knows that only the rare few will see beyond the dazzling delights of her flesh to the Truth that she embodies.

From "Liber Qayin":

I am all possibility without limit.
You see in me the ocean or the vast starry heavens, opening into the fruition of your dreams. And so I am.
And if you have Wisdom, you tremble before me. For I am untempered Life come rushing to meet you, unbounded Love poured upon you like the Sea.

The Graces

The Kharites, or Graces, were the Goddesses of pleasure, joy, beauty and happiness. They were the Goddesses of "favor" - the favors of beauty and charm and delight. The favors of those almost unnamable, intangible qualities of attraction. There are generally considered to be three primary Graces. They are Aglaea (Splendor), Euphrosyne (Mirth), and Thalia (Good Cheer). These are actually the oldest of the Graces, and they are the ones specifically honored in certain parts of Greece.

Aglaia is the oldest of all the Graces, and she is sometimes just called Kharis. She is also sometimes called Kalleis, which means "beautiful." She is the Grace of beauty, adornment, splendor and glory.

Euphrosyne is the second sister of this triad. She presides over merriment, joy and mirth. Euthymia, or contentment, is another name for her.

Thalia is the youngest of this of this triad of sisters. Her name means "good cheer," and she is credited with presiding over banquets and festive celebrations. Thalia is also the Muse of comedy.

Athenian vase painting shows a host of young Goddesses that are counted among the Graces who attend Aphrodite. Antheia's name relates to flowers, and she is credited with overseeing floral decorations and the garlands worn to parties and festivals. Eudaimonia is the Goddess of happiness, opulence and prosperity. Paidia is the Goddess of play and amusement. Pandaisia is the Goddess of rich banquets, and Pannykhis is the Goddess of nighttime revelries and celebrations.

Phaenna and Kleta are Graces that were worshipped in Sparta. Phaenna means "shining" and Kleta means "fame, glory." The radiance of fame and glory, particularly in battle and heroic deeds, would naturally have been honored among the Spartans who were known throughout Hellas as a dedicated warrior people. Aphrodite was honored in her war-like aspect among the Spartans, in fact, as Aphrodite Area.

Auxo and Hegemone were Horae (or Seasons) that were also worshipped as Graces. Auxo was the Goddess of Spring growth. The name Hegemone means "Queen" or "Leader."

Copyright Asteria Books 2024

Hades

The magic of Hades lies not only in his role as a god of the Underworld but also in his symbolism of transformation, justice, and the cyclical nature of life. Through myths and symbols, Hades invites us to explore the depths of human existence, the passage from life to death, and the enduring mysteries that shape our understanding of the divine and the mortal realms alike. As we delve into the realm of Hades, we uncover layers of meaning and contemplation that enrich our perception of life's journey and the ultimate destiny that awaits us all.

Hades' primary role is as the ruler of the Underworld, where souls journey after death. Contrary to popular belief, Hades is not depicted as an evil entity but rather as a stern yet just ruler who ensures order and balance in the afterlife. His realm is a place of judgment and rest, where souls receive their due fate based on their deeds in life.

Hades (Pluto). From a Statue in the Vatican.

Hades is often associated with symbols that reflect his dominion over the Underworld, such as the Helm of Darkness (or invisibility helmet) which he received from the Cyclops during the Titanomachy. This helm allows him to move unseen and maintain control over his domain. Other symbols include the bident, a two-pronged fork similar to Poseidon's trident, which symbolizes his authority and power.

Mythological tales involving Hades often revolve around his interactions with other gods and mortals, such as his abduction of Persephone, which led to her becoming his queen in the Underworld. This story highlights themes of transformation, the cycle of life and death, and the balance between light and darkness.

Hades' mythology has influenced various cultural expressions, from ancient Greek literature and drama to modern interpretations in art, literature, and psychology. His role as a keeper of the dead and judge of souls inspires contemplation on mortality, fate, and the mysteries of the afterlife.

Copyright Asteria Books 2024

Hathor

Hathor's symbols encapsulate the essence of her divine attributes — love, music, fertility, and joy — reflecting her profound influence in ancient Egyptian culture and spirituality. Through her symbols, rituals, and religious practices, Hathor continues to inspire reverence and admiration as a benevolent goddess who brings harmony, abundance, and creative inspiration to those who invoke her blessings. Her presence in Egyptian mythology enriches our understanding of ancient beliefs and values, emphasizing the importance of love, music, and joy in the human experience.

Hathor.

Hathor is often depicted as a woman with the ears of a cow, symbolizing her maternal and nurturing qualities. The cow was sacred to ancient Egyptians for its association with fertility, abundance, and maternal care, qualities that Hathor embodies as a goddess of love and motherhood. She is also depicted wearing the Hathor crown—a sun disk encircled by cow horns or sometimes by a uraeus (cobra)—symbolizing her solar aspect and protective power.

One of Hathor's most iconic symbols is the sistrum, a musical instrument resembling a rattle, often used in religious rituals and ceremonies dedicated to her. The sistrum's sound was believed to invoke Hathor's blessings and drive away evil spirits, making it an essential tool in worship. Additionally, Hathor is associated with the menat necklace, a symbol of fertility and divine protection, worn by priestesses and adorned with colorful beads and amulets.

The lotus flower holds special significance in Hathor's mythology, representing rebirth, purity, and spiritual enlightenment. Hathor is often depicted holding or surrounded by lotus flowers, symbolizing her role in facilitating the transition from life to the afterlife and embodying the eternal cycle of creation and renewal.

As a solar goddess, Hathor is sometimes associated with the Eye of Ra, a symbol of protection, power, and divine authority. The Eye of Ra, often depicted as the sun or as a goddess with the head of a lioness or a falcon, underscores Hathor's role as a powerful deity who embodies both the nurturing aspects of motherhood and the fierce protectiveness of a lioness.

Copyright Asteria Books 2024

Hecate

Hecate or Hekate is an ancient goddess, most often shown holding two torches or a key and in later periods depicted in triple form. She is variously associated with crossroads, entrance-ways, fire, light, the Moon, magic, witchcraft, knowledge of herbs and poisonous plants, necromancy, and sorcery. She has rulership over earth, sea and sky, as well as a more universal role as Saviour (Soteira), Mother of Angels and the Cosmic World Soul.

Hecate is also one of the 'patron' goddesses of many witches, who in some traditions identify her with the Triple Goddess, for Hecate has three faces, or phases. Her role as a tripartite goddess, which many modern-day Wiccans associate with the concept of 'the Maiden, the Mother and the Crone', was made popular in modern times by writers such as Robert Graves in <u>The White Goddess</u>. Historical depictions and descriptions show her facing in three different directions, a clear reference to the tripartite nature of this ancient Goddess.

Hecate was associated with borders, city walls, doorways, crossroads and, by extension, with realms outside or beyond the world of the living. She appears to have been particularly associated with being 'between' and hence is frequently characterized as a "liminal" goddess. Hecate was also associated with plant lore and the concoction of medicines and poisons. In particular she was thought to give instruction in these closely related arts. Medea was said to be taught by Hecate.

Hecate has survived in folklore as a 'hag' figure associated with witchcraft. Scholars note that Hecate, conflated with the figure of Diana, appears in late antiquity and in the early medieval period as part of an "emerging legend complex" associated with gatherings of women, the moon, and witchcraft that eventually became established in the area of Northern Italy, southern Germany, and the western Balkans.

Epithets

Aedonaea (Lady of the underworld)
Anassa eneri (Queen of the dead)
Apotropaia (that turns away/protects)
Atalus (tender)
Brimo (the terrible one)
Chthonia (of the earth/underworld)
Enodia (on the way)
Klêidouchos (holding the keys)
Kourotrophos (nurse of children)
Liparocredemnus (bright-coiffed)

Nyctipolus (night-wandering)
Phosphoros (bringing or giving light)
Propolos (who serves/attends)
Propulaia/Propylaia (before the gate)
Scylacagetis (leader of dogs)
Soteira (savior)
Trimorphe (three-formed)
Triodia/Trioditis (who frequents crossroads)
Zerynthia (of Mt. Zerynthia in Samothrace)

Copyright Asteria Publishing 2012

Heimdall

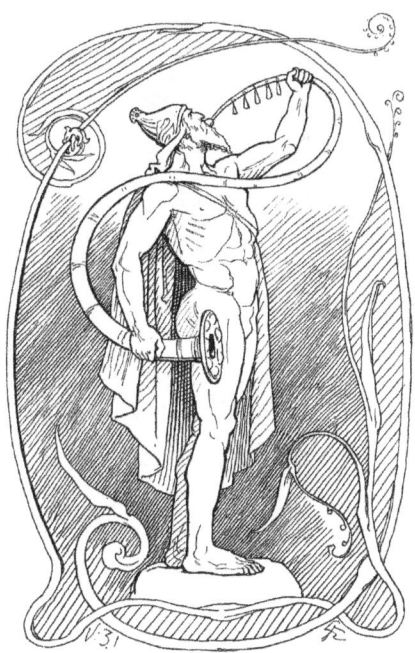

Heimdall, the vigilant guardian of Bifrost and keeper of secrets, embodies the magic of perception, protection, and cosmic vigilance in Norse mythology. Through his role as a sentinel of Asgard and his iconic symbols like the Gjallarhorn, Heimdall enriches our understanding of divine guardianship and the eternal struggle between order and chaos in the cosmos. As we delve into Heimdall's mythology, we discover a figure whose steadfast presence and unwavering dedication continue to inspire reverence and contemplation in the realms of myth and imagination.

Heimdall's primary role is to watch over Bifrost, the bridge that spans the realms and serves as the pathway for gods and souls alike. With his keen eyesight and acute hearing, Heimdall stands eternally vigilant, ensuring that only those worthy and permitted may pass into Asgard, the realm of the gods.

One of Heimdall's most iconic symbols is the Gjallarhorn, a powerful horn that he uses to announce the arrival of Ragnarök, the prophesied end of the world in Norse mythology. The sound of the Gjallarhorn is said to be heard throughout the cosmos, signaling the onset of cosmic battles and the renewal of the world.

Heimdall possesses senses so acute that he can hear the grass grow and see for hundreds of miles, making him an unparalleled sentinel and guardian. His ability to perceive threats and maintain cosmic order underscores his importance as a protector of the gods and the divine realms.

In addition to his guardianship of Bifrost, Heimdall plays a pivotal role in Norse mythology. He is considered one of the Aesir, the principal gods of the Norse pantheon, and is revered for his integrity, loyalty, and dedication to his duty. Heimdall's role in myths and sagas often portrays him as a steadfast defender and wise counselor, trusted by both gods and humans alike.

Heimdall's mythology continues to inspire admiration and fascination, reflecting themes of duty, vigilance, and the cosmic order inherent in Norse beliefs. His symbolism as a guardian and protector resonates in various cultural expressions, from literature and art to modern interpretations in popular culture.

Copyright Asteria Books 2024

Hera

In Greek mythology, Hera reigns as the queen of the Olympian gods, embodying sovereignty, marriage, and family. As a deity of immense power and complexity, Hera is associated with a variety of symbols that reflect her roles, attributes, and mythological narratives.

One of Hera's most iconic symbols is the peacock, renowned for its extravagant display of feathers. In mythological lore, the peacock is said to have drawn Hera's chariot—a symbol of her regal authority and divine splendor. The peacock's association with Hera also signifies her connection to beauty, pride, and the vibrant spectrum of emotions that characterize her personality.

Hera is often depicted with associations to cows and heifers, symbolizing fertility, nurturing, and maternal care. In her role as a goddess of marriage and childbirth, these gentle creatures represent her protective and nurturing aspects, fostering the growth of families and ensuring the continuity of life.

The pomegranate holds symbolic significance in Hera's mythology, particularly in relation to her role as a goddess of marriage and fertility. In some myths, pomegranates are associated with the sacred union between Hera and Zeus, representing abundance, fertility, and the fruitful bonds of matrimony.

Hera is sometimes portrayed holding a scepter topped with a lotus flower. The lotus, a symbol of purity and rebirth, underscores Hera's divine authority and connection to the natural world. It also signifies her role as a protector of women and families, ensuring harmony and order within the domestic sphere.

The cuckoo bird is another significant symbol associated with Hera. According to myth, Zeus transformed into a cuckoo to approach Hera in her infancy, gaining her trust and later marrying her. This bird symbolizes Zeus's cunning and Hera's initial innocence, highlighting themes of deception and transformation in their complex relationship.

Copyright Asteria Books 2024

Hermes

In Greek mythology, Hermes occupies a unique and multifaceted role as the god of boundaries, travel, communication, and commerce. Known for his swiftness and cunning intellect, Hermes embodies the magic of connection and transformation, making him a beloved figure in ancient Greek culture and beyond.

Hermes is primarily recognized as the divine messenger of the Olympian gods, entrusted with delivering messages between the realms of gods and mortals. His agility and speed—often depicted with winged sandals and a caduceus, a staff entwined with serpents—symbolize his ability to traverse distances swiftly and bridge realms with ease.

Beyond his role as a messenger, Hermes is revered as a protector of travelers and guide of souls. He presides over boundaries, both physical and metaphysical, ensuring safe passage and smooth transitions. His presence is invoked during journeys, rites of passage, and moments of change, offering guidance and protection to those in transition.

Hermes also governs communication, eloquence, and negotiation—the skills essential for effective interaction among individuals and communities. As the patron of merchants and traders, he facilitates commerce and exchange, fostering prosperity and social cohesion within ancient Greek society.

In addition to his positive attributes, Hermes embodies the archetype of the trickster—a mischievous yet benevolent figure who challenges conventions and fosters creativity. His playful demeanor and cleverness are reflected in myths where he outwits adversaries and navigates complex situations with ingenuity.

Copyright Asteria Books 2024

Hestia

In ancient Greek religion, Hestia, the goddess of the hearth, embodies the sacred essence of home and familial warmth. Revered for her gentle and nurturing nature, Hestia's worship held a central place in the hearts of ancient Greeks, reflecting values of hospitality, unity, and domestic tranquility.

Hestia is often depicted as a serene figure, seated beside a hearth fire—an eternal flame symbolizing both physical and spiritual warmth. As the eldest of the Olympian siblings, she voluntarily relinquished her seat among the gods to ensure harmony and peace, choosing instead to preside over the hearth and its sacred fire.

In Greek households, the hearth served as the focal point of daily life. It was here that families gathered to share meals, offer prayers, and seek refuge from the challenges of the outside world. Hestia's presence at the hearth was invoked during rites and rituals, ensuring the continuity of familial bonds and the sanctity of home.

Worship of Hestia was marked by simple yet heartfelt offerings—such as food, wine, and olive oil—placed upon the household hearth. These offerings were made in gratitude for her blessings of warmth, sustenance, and protection. Her role extended beyond the domestic sphere, as communities also honored her during public ceremonies and festivals.

Beyond her role as a deity of the hearth, Hestia's worship influenced Greek philosophy and ethics. Her embodiment of stability, humility, and hospitality inspired virtues that were cherished in both private and civic life. Philosophers and poets alike praised her as a symbol of inner peace and communal harmony.

Copyright Asteria Books 2024

Horned God

According to most witchcraft traditions, the primary God of the Craft is a horned figure. The names given to that figure vary by tradition and include, Cernunnos, Herne, Holt, Tubal Qayin, and others.

Cernunnos in Celtic iconography is often portrayed with animals, in particular the stag, and also frequently associated with the ram-horned serpent, besides association with other beasts with less frequency, including bulls, dogs, and rats. Because of his frequent association with creatures, scholars often describe Cernunnos as the "Lord of the Animals" or the "Lord of Wild Things," and Miranda Green describes him as a "peaceful god of nature and fruitfulness."

Herne the Hunter is a specifically British figure, the ghost of the huntsman who was hanged upon a tree known as Her's Oak in Windsor Forest and who bears horns upon his head. Some scholars suggests that "Herne" as well as other Wild Huntsmen in European folklore all derive from the same ancient mytho-poetic source. The name "Herne" could be derived ultimately from the same Indo-European root, *ker-n-, meaning bone or horn from which "Cernunnos" derives.

In the Early Middle Ages, Windsor Forest came under the control of the pagan Angles who worshiped their own pantheon of gods, including Woden, who was sometimes depicted as horned, and whose Norse equivalent Odin rode across the night sky with his own Wild Hunt and hanged himself on the world tree Yggdrasil to learn the secret of the runic alphabet. It has been suggested that the name *Herne* is derived from the title *Herian*, a title used for Woden in his role as leader of fallen warriors.

Copyright Asteria Books 2015

Hulda

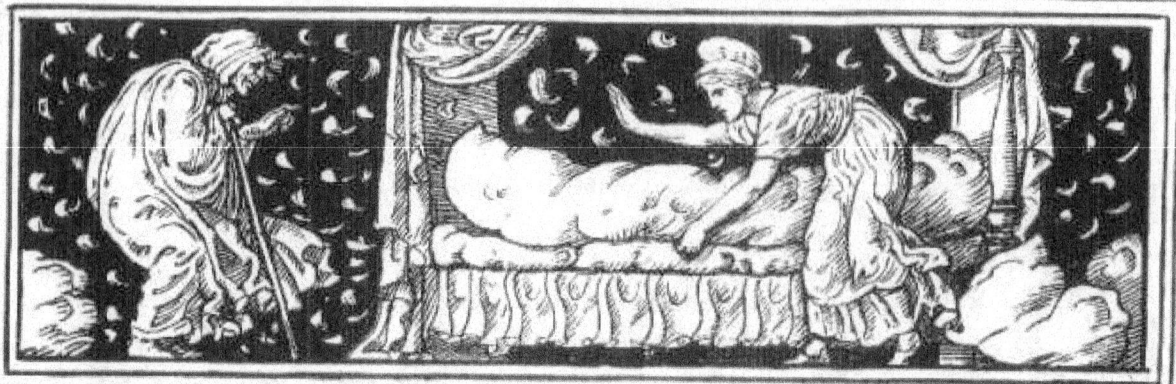

Hulda, or Frau Holle, is an ancient Germanic Goddess figure whose name is attested in Latin inscriptions as early 235 CE, though her worship undoubtedly well pre-dates these Roman records. She is known by a variety of names that are variations on Hulda (northern Germany) and Perchta (southern Germany). She is associated with Mother Goose and La Reine Pedauque, as well as being the forerunner for St. Lucia. She is also called Frau Goden and Frau Frekke, naming her Woden's wife (linking her with the Norse Frigga).

Holle is usually depicted in one of two ways: either as an old, bent grandmother with a crooked nose or as a young and lovely maiden whose white garments gleam like a fresh blanket of snow. She is often seen holding a lantern, and sometimes one of her feet is said to be a goose-foot.

Frau Holda is the matron of women's chores and domestic duty. She is particularly associated with spinning, a task almost entirely carried out by women and one of the few from which a woman could honorably receive payment in the Middle Ages. Spinning is intimately linked with magic, and it is Hulda who teaches both linen-making and magic.

She personifies the weather, particularly weather events that seem to transform the land, such as snow and fog. When it snows, the Folk would say that Frau Holle was shaking out her feather pillows. Fog, on the other hand, is said to be smoke from her fire. In the thunder, we hear Hulda reeling her flax.

The blustery winter weather helps to link Holda to the Wild Hunt, which she is said to lead alongside Woden. In this guise, she is linked to the harrowing visage of death, but it is said that Perchta, in particular, is surrounded by the souls of children who died before baptism, marking her is a protector of the young, even in death. She is also linked to Witch Flight, as it is said that she would ride the sky with Witches mounted on distaffs to the Sabbat.

Mother Holle is credited with nurturing an protecting children in several ways. She is known to rock the cradles of babes whose nurses have fallen asleep, and she is said to be the keeper of the pool through which the souls of newborn children enter the world. During the twelve days between Christmas and Epiphany (and especially at Twelfth Night), Perchta would roam the countryside to leave a silver coin in the shoes of children who were well-behaved and industrious.

Copyright Asteria Books 2017

Ishtar

Ishtar is the Babylonian goddess of love, war, fertility, and sexuality. She is often depicted riding a lion or flanked by two lions, and she is usually shown with a horned crown and wings. Her symbol is an eight-pointed star, and she is considered "the divine personification of the planet Venus."

Her worship seems to have involved sacred prostitution. Scholar have referred to her holy city Uruk as the "town of the sacred courtesans" and to her as the "courtesan of the gods."

Ishtar is also very deeply connected to both magic and sacrifice. In one account, she tricks her grandfather into giving her all of his magical gifts (the sacred laws of heaven and the knowledge of how to use them), promoting her to Queen of Heaven and Queen of Earth.

In one of the most famous myths about Ishtar describes her descent to the underworld, we spy her fiery rage:

> If thou openest not the gate to let me enter,
> I will break the door, I will wrench the lock,
> I will smash the door-posts, I will force the doors.
> I will bring up the dead to eat the living.
> And the dead will outnumber the living.

Other myths and poems show us the joyous lust and passion with which she is associated:

I bathed for the wild bull,
I bathed for the shepherd Dumuzi,
I perfumed my sides with ointment,
I coated my mouth with sweet-smelling amber,
I painted my eyes with kohl.
 He shaped my loins with fair hands,
The shepherd Dumuzi filled my lap with cream and milk,
He stroked my pubic hair,
He watered my womb.
He laid his hands on my holy vulva,
He smoothed my black boat with cream,
He quickened my narrow boat with milk,
He caressed me on the bed.
 Now I will caress my high priest on the bed,
I will caress the faithful shepherd Dumuzi,
I will caress his loins, the shepherdship of the land,
I will decree a sweet fate for him.

Copyright Asteria Books 2015

Isis

Isis is one of the most widely worshipped Goddesses of the ancient world. Her worship began in the period known as the late Old Kingdom in Egypt, and it was spread throughout the Classical world by the Romans and the Greeks. Much of her mythology was merged with that of the Virgin Mary by the early Church, as well, in the figure of the Virgin Mary. She continues to be widely worshipped and loved by modern Pagans.

The name "isis" means "throne," and one of her crowns is throne-shaped. She is a sovereignty goddess who acts as Divine Mother to the pharaoh.

Her associations are intimately linked to life and regeneration, and she is often shown holding an ankh, the symbol of life. She is also deeply connected to magic. Her magic restores her husband Osiris to life after he is torn apart by Set.

The following Awakening Prayer comes from the Book of the Dead:

Awake, awake, awake,
Awake in peace,
Lady of Peace.
Rise thou in peace,
Rise thou in beauty.
Goddess of Life,
Beautiful in heaven,
Heaven is in peace.
Earth is in peace.
O Goddess,
Daughter of Nut,
Daughter of Geb,
Beloved of Osiris,
Goddess rich in names!
All praise to You.
All praise to You.
I adore You. I adore You. Lady Isis!

Copyright Asteria Books 2017

John Barleycorn

One way to think about the Year Wheel is to look at the balladry figure of John Barleycorn. The stations of his life, as marked in the verses of the song below, are the Sabbats -- at least the ones dealing with planting and harvesting.

There were three men came out of the west,
    Their fortunes for to try.
And these three men made a solemn vow:
    John Barleycorn must die.

They've plowed, they've sown, they've harrowed him in,
    Threw clods upon his head.
And these three men made a solemn vow:
    John Barleycorn was dead.

They've let him lie for a very long time,
    Till the rains from heav'n did fall.
And little Sir John sprung up his head,
    And so amazed them all.

They've let him stand 'till midsummer's day,
    Till he looked both pale and wan.
And little Sir John's grown a long, long beard,
    And so become a man.

They've hired men with scythes so sharp,
    To cut him off at the knee.
They've rolled him and tied him by the waist,
    Serving him most barb'rously.

They've hired men with the sharp pitchforks,
    Who pricked him to the heart.
And the loader, he has served him worse than that,
    For he's bound him to the cart.

They've wheeled him 'round and around the field,
    'Till they came unto a barn,
And there they've made a solemn oath,
    On poor John Barleycorn.

They've hired men with the crabtree sticks,
    To cut him skin from bone,
And the Miller, he has served him worse than that,
    For he's ground him between two stones.

And little Sir John in the nut-brown bowl,
    And the brandy in the glass.
And little Sir John in the nut-brown bowl,
    Proved the strongest man at last.

The Huntsman, he can't hunt the fox,
    Nor so loudly blow his horn,
And the Tinker, he can't mend kettle nor pot,
    Without a little Barleycorn.

Copyright Asteria Publishing 2012

Kolyo

Kolyo is the name associated with the Black Goddess the in the Spiral Castle Tradition of American Folkloric Traditional Witchcraft. She is one of the three great Tutelary Spirits who form the path's Trinity.

Kolyo's name draws its origin from the same proto-IndoEuropean root word as the Scottish Cailleach, Greek Callypso, and Hindu Kali. Their names all reference shrouding or veiling, which is the method Kolyo employs to guard the Mysteries of the Wise. She conceals.

Kolyo is a weaver, and she can be viewed as being synonymous with Dame Fate. She teaches us that Wisdom is often accompanied by silence and that the threads of our destinies are interlinked.

As the archetypal Black Goddess, she is associated with night, silence, winter, and death; spinning, weaving, and cutting both literal fibers as well as the threads of fate and magick that form the fabric of our lives; strategy, war, and survival; and the collecting, keeping, studying, and sharing of lore and skills from one generation to the next.

Kolyo (like Goda) can appear either young or old, as she wills. She is an ancient Power, and she and Goda are often viewed as two sides of the same coin. Kolyo covers the path of the Initiate in mist, forcing us to use both our wits and our intuition to find our way.

From "Liber Qayin":

There, I inhabited the Tree of Wisdom and learned all its Mysteries.

And mine is the sad, cruel song of Knowledge that shrieks in the darkness.

Copyright Asteria Books 2025

Lilith

Lilith is generally thought to be derived from a class of female demons called Lilitu in Mesopotamian texts. In Jewish folklore, Lilith becomes Adam's first wife, who was created at the same time and from the same earth as Adam. This contrasts with Eve, who was created from one of Adam's ribs.

Lilith's legend was greatly developed during the Middle Ages. In a 13th Century writing, Lilith left Adam after she refused to become subservient to him and then would not return to the Garden of Eden after she mated with archangel Samael. She was said to have spoken the secret Holy name of God and transformed herself into an owl to fly from Eden. In some medieval folklore, Lilith does return to Eden as a serpent. She then offers forth the fruit of the Tree of Knowledge to Eve, making her a kind of proto-Sophia or wisdom Goddess.

In some Traditional covens, Lilith is viewed as the embodiment of the Witches' Goddess, being both a White Goddess and a Black Goddess. She was said to have embodied herself in the form of Na'amah, the sister of Tubal Cain, and is therefore one of the original sources of Witchblood.

One of the old names for the moon is Lilith's Lantern, as it was said to be the light that Witches met by. Lilith is associated with the moon, owls, and serpents.

Enochian Invocation of Lilith by Dr. John Dee & Sir Edward Kelly

Black Moon, Lilith, mother darkest,
Whose hands form the hellish mire, At my weakest, at my strongest, Molding my as clay from fire.

Black Moon, Lilith, Mare of Night,
You cast your litter to the ground.
Speak the Name and take to flight,
Utter now the secret sound!

Copyright Asteria Books 2015

Loki

Loki, the trickster god of Norse mythology, embodies the magic of transformation, chaos, and the unpredictable forces that shape the world. Through his cunning intellect, shape-shifting abilities, and mischievous deeds, Loki challenges our perceptions and invites us to explore the dualities of creativity and destruction, order and chaos. As we unravel Loki's mythology, we uncover a figure whose influence extends beyond mischief, inspiring contemplation on the nature of change, fate, and the enduring allure of the trickster archetype in myth and storytelling.

Loki is revered as the quintessential trickster — a figure who challenges societal norms, provokes change, and disrupts the status quo. His cleverness and wit often lead to both humorous and disastrous consequences, reflecting the dual nature of chaos and creativity inherent in the trickster archetype.

One of Loki's most remarkable abilities is his skill in shape-shifting, allowing him to assume various forms and personas at will. This power enables him to deceive and manipulate others, further emphasizing his role as a trickster who blurs the boundaries between reality and illusion.

Despite his antics and betrayals, Loki's loyalty and occasional acts of heroism demonstrate his capacity for change and redemption.

Copyright Asteria Books 2024

Lucifer

Lucifer is the "light-bearer" – the bringer of enlightenment to mankind. He is Qayin in the East, the Morning Star. He is the torch-bearer of wisdom, inspiration, the Divine Spark, the Cunning Fire. He is "Prometheus" (literally, "fore-sight"), who rebelled against God (the Gods) to give Fire (the Cunning Fire) to mankind and fell from Divine Grace.

Lucifer, more than any other name or title by which we can call our Gods, is a terrifying name for the non-witches of the world. This title is tantamount to calling him the Devil or Satan. While we don't see him as the great, evil, anti-God of the Christians, many traditional witches claim another measure of the transgressive power he represents by calling him "Devil" within their rites.

As the Red God of American Folkloric Witchcraft, Lucifer is simply another title for Qayin, the Witch Father. We see different aspects of Him at Beltaine and Samhain, but He is always the Red God. His is the red thread that offers us the foundational fiber for weaving magic and connecting with the Mighty Dead. He is the fiery red of sunrise, and His is the light that kindles the forge deep within the earth.

To the Romans, Lucifer was a Forge God of the Sun and brother to Diana, the Moon Goddess of wild places. Together, they conceived Aradia, the first of the Witches.

We honor Lucifer in the East, the place of sunrise and fire. His time is Beltaine, with its bel-fires and hints of gnosis through physicality.

Invocation

Hail to Lucifer-Qayin, Lord of Light
Lord of the Forge
Lord of the Cunning Fire!

Come to the crossroads, Morning Star
Golden Man
King of the Bel-Fires!

So mote it be!

Lugh

The Pan-Celtic God Lugus was known to the Irish as Lugh and the Welsh as Llew. The name means "Shining One" and is accompanied by many epithets, including "Long-Arm" (due to his skill with a spear), "Sword-Shouter" (due to his fierceness with a sword in battle), "Fierce-Striker", "Skillful-Handed", "Skilled in Many Arts" and "Strong-Handed." Lugh's tales portray him as a crafty, clever, and heroic king. Lugh, in Irish tradition, is the lone survivor of three triplets, and there are many other triplicities that recur in his myths, making him a Triple God, in many ways. He is often depicted as have three heads, not unlike Brighid, in Irish lore. As a young man Lugh travels to Tara to join the court of king Nuada of the Tuatha Dé Danann. The doorkeeper will not let him in unless he has a skill with which to serve the king. He offers his services as a wright, a smith, a champion, a swordsman, a harpist, a hero, a poet and historian, a sorcerer, and a craftsman, but each time is rejected as the Tuatha Dé Danann already have someone with that skill. But when Lugh asks if they have anyone with all those skills simultaneously, the doorkeeper has to admit defeat, and Lugh joins the court and is appointed Chief Ollam of Ireland. Lugh eventually takes his place as king, as well. He established a series of games called the Lughnasadh in honor of his foster-mother, Tailtiu, and even now the month of August bears the name *Lúnasa* in the Irish language. Lugh is the father of Cuchulainn.

Copyright Asteria Books 2015

Maat

Maat's symbols encapsulate the essence of her divine attributes—truth, justice, harmony, and cosmic order—reflecting her profound influence in ancient Egyptian religion and moral philosophy. Through her symbols, rituals, and teachings, Maat continues to inspire reverence and admiration as a goddess who embodies the timeless principles of righteousness and ethical conduct. Her legacy endures as a guiding light, reminding us of the importance of integrity, balance, and the pursuit of truth in both spiritual and earthly realms.

The Feather of Maat, also known as the Feather of Truth, is perhaps the most iconic symbol associated with Maat. In the afterlife judgment scene depicted in the Egyptian Book of the Dead (Book of Coming Forth by Day), the heart of the deceased is weighed against the Feather of Maat on the scales of justice. If the heart is lighter than the feather, indicating a life lived in accordance with Maat's principles of truth, justice, and morality, the deceased is deemed worthy of entering the afterlife and achieving eternal bliss.

Maat is often depicted holding a scepter or an ankh, symbols of her authority and power. The scepter represents her role as the goddess who upholds cosmic order and divine law, ensuring that justice prevails over chaos. It signifies her influence in maintaining harmony and balance among gods, humans, and the natural world.

Maat is sometimes portrayed with wings, symbolizing her role as a protective and nurturing deity who oversees the well-being of humanity. Her wings represent her ability to transcend earthly limitations and uphold the principles of truth and righteousness across the cosmos.

The ankh, an ancient Egyptian symbol resembling a cross with a loop at the top, is associated with Maat as a symbol of life and immortality. It signifies Maat's role in guiding souls through the afterlife and ensuring their eternal existence in harmony with cosmic principles.

Copyright Asteria Books 2024

Mithras

The worship of Mithras, with its mysteries and rituals, provided a unique spiritual experience in the Roman world, blending Persian, Greek, and Roman influences into a distinct religious practice focused on personal transformation and devotion to the sun god. Mithraism's enduring symbols and mysteries offer insights into ancient beliefs and the quest for spiritual enlightenment in the classical world.

Mithras originates from Persian and Zoroastrian mythology as Mithra, associated with the sun and the battle against darkness. In Roman times, Mithras became identified with Sol Invictus, the unconquered sun god, embodying attributes of courage, loyalty, and cosmic order.

Central to Mithraic worship were elaborate initiation ceremonies conducted in underground temples called mithraea. These rituals, often involving purification, symbolic meals, and the enactment of Mithras slaying a sacred bull (tauroctony), were believed to bring spiritual transformation and communion with the divine.

Mithraism is rich in symbolic imagery, including the tauroctony depicting Mithras slaying the bull, representing the triumph of light over darkness and the renewal of life. Other symbols include the torchbearers Cautes and Cautopates, the celestial ladder, and the serpent representing wisdom and regeneration.

Mithraism spread throughout the Roman Empire, particularly among soldiers and traders, influencing Roman religious practices and art. Its secretive nature and emphasis on personal salvation and moral integrity appealed to individuals seeking spiritual fulfillment and community within a hierarchical structure.

Copyright Asteria Books 2024

The Muses

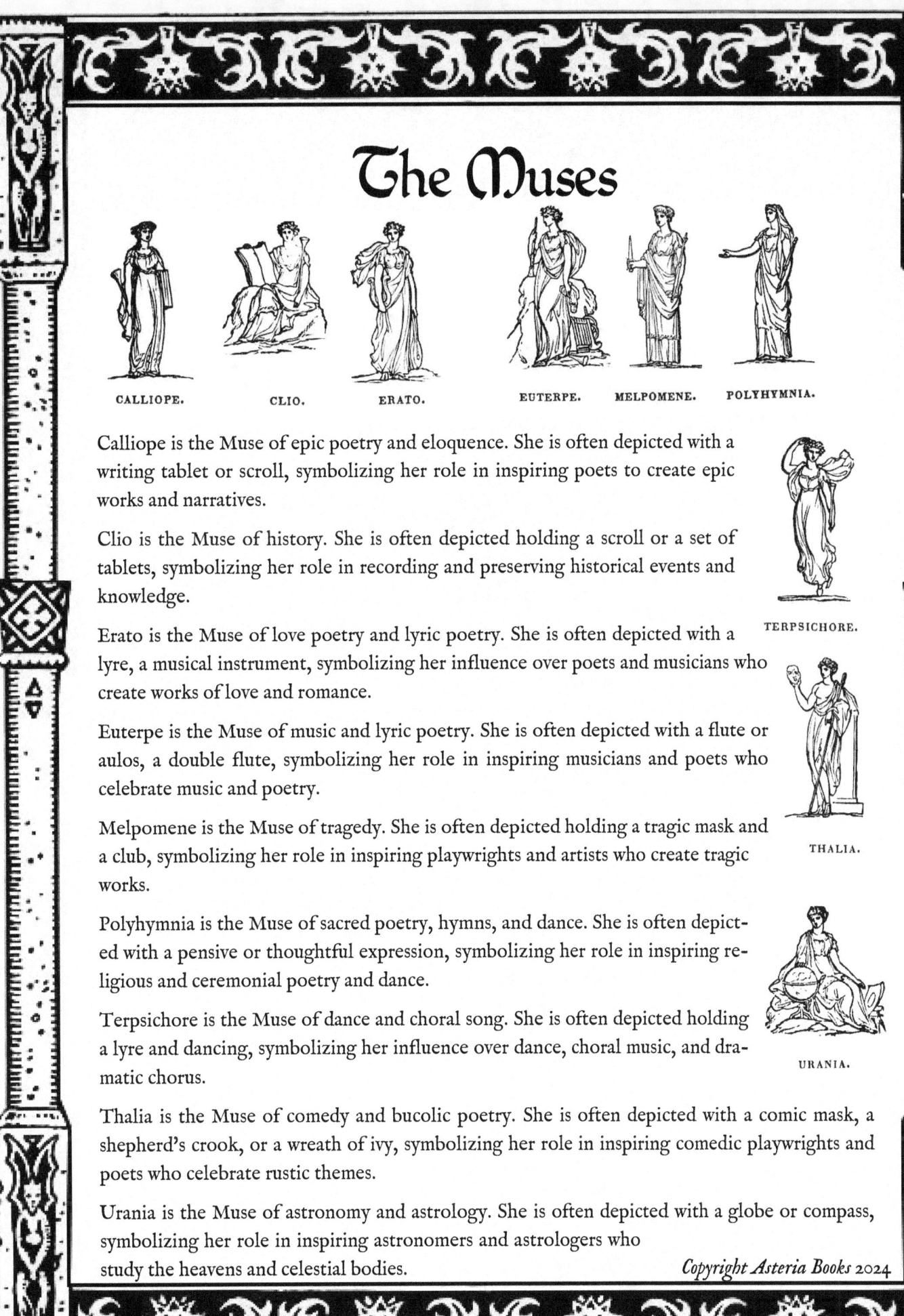

Calliope is the Muse of epic poetry and eloquence. She is often depicted with a writing tablet or scroll, symbolizing her role in inspiring poets to create epic works and narratives.

Clio is the Muse of history. She is often depicted holding a scroll or a set of tablets, symbolizing her role in recording and preserving historical events and knowledge.

Erato is the Muse of love poetry and lyric poetry. She is often depicted with a lyre, a musical instrument, symbolizing her influence over poets and musicians who create works of love and romance.

Euterpe is the Muse of music and lyric poetry. She is often depicted with a flute or aulos, a double flute, symbolizing her role in inspiring musicians and poets who celebrate music and poetry.

Melpomene is the Muse of tragedy. She is often depicted holding a tragic mask and a club, symbolizing her role in inspiring playwrights and artists who create tragic works.

Polyhymnia is the Muse of sacred poetry, hymns, and dance. She is often depicted with a pensive or thoughtful expression, symbolizing her role in inspiring religious and ceremonial poetry and dance.

Terpsichore is the Muse of dance and choral song. She is often depicted holding a lyre and dancing, symbolizing her influence over dance, choral music, and dramatic chorus.

Thalia is the Muse of comedy and bucolic poetry. She is often depicted with a comic mask, a shepherd's crook, or a wreath of ivy, symbolizing her role in inspiring comedic playwrights and poets who celebrate rustic themes.

Urania is the Muse of astronomy and astrology. She is often depicted with a globe or compass, symbolizing her role in inspiring astronomers and astrologers who study the heavens and celestial bodies.

Copyright Asteria Books 2024

Morrígan

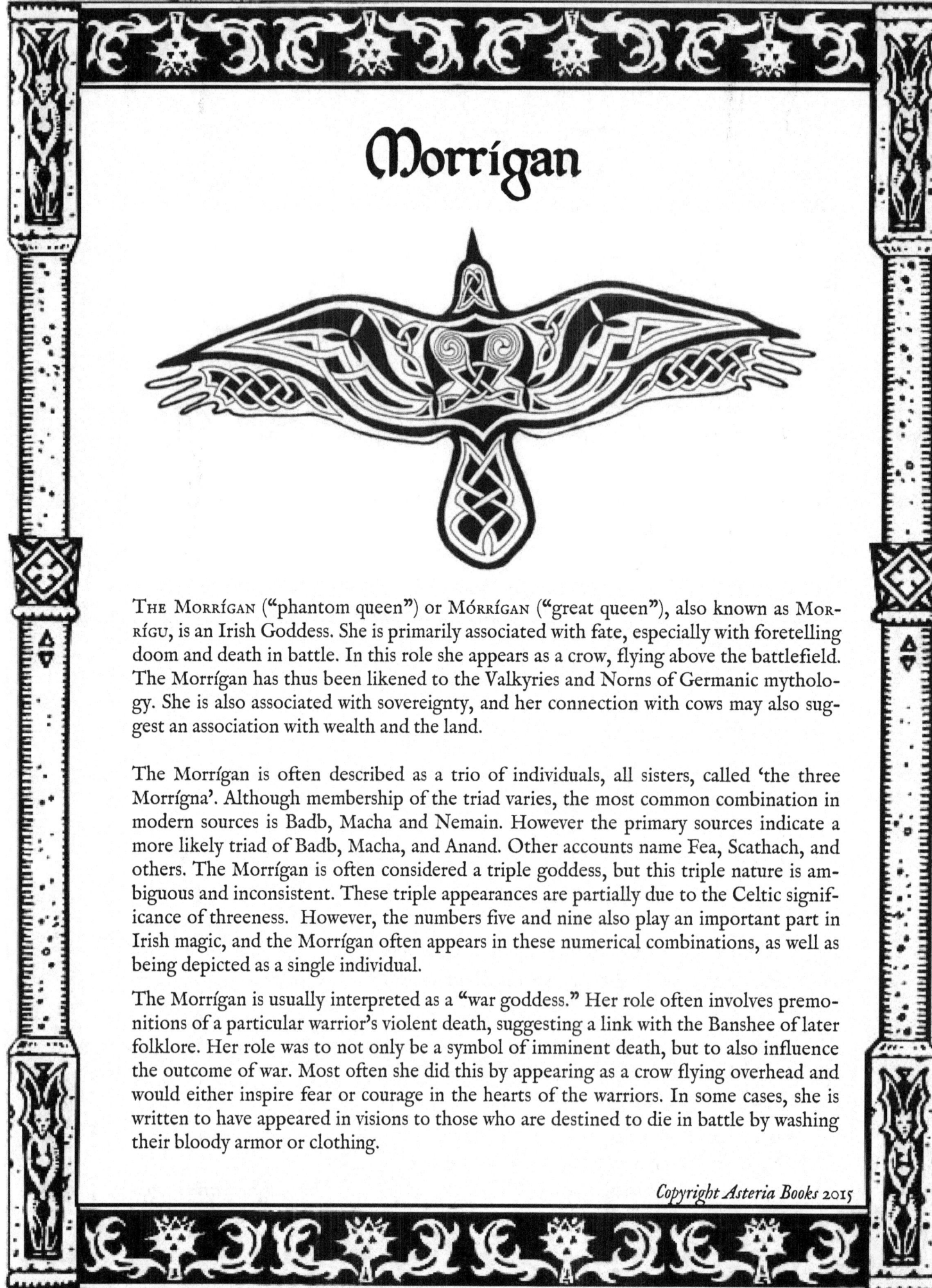

The Morrígan ("phantom queen") or Mórrígan ("great queen"), also known as Morrígu, is an Irish Goddess. She is primarily associated with fate, especially with foretelling doom and death in battle. In this role she appears as a crow, flying above the battlefield. The Morrígan has thus been likened to the Valkyries and Norns of Germanic mythology. She is also associated with sovereignty, and her connection with cows may also suggest an association with wealth and the land.

The Morrígan is often described as a trio of individuals, all sisters, called 'the three Morrígna'. Although membership of the triad varies, the most common combination in modern sources is Badb, Macha and Nemain. However the primary sources indicate a more likely triad of Badb, Macha, and Anand. Other accounts name Fea, Scathach, and others. The Morrígan is often considered a triple goddess, but this triple nature is ambiguous and inconsistent. These triple appearances are partially due to the Celtic significance of threeness. However, the numbers five and nine also play an important part in Irish magic, and the Morrígan often appears in these numerical combinations, as well as being depicted as a single individual.

The Morrígan is usually interpreted as a "war goddess." Her role often involves premonitions of a particular warrior's violent death, suggesting a link with the Banshee of later folklore. Her role was to not only be a symbol of imminent death, but to also influence the outcome of war. Most often she did this by appearing as a crow flying overhead and would either inspire fear or courage in the hearts of the warriors. In some cases, she is written to have appeared in visions to those who are destined to die in battle by washing their bloody armor or clothing.

Copyright Asteria Books 2015

Njord

Njord, the Norse god of the sea and wealth, embodies the interconnectedness between nature, fertility, and prosperity in Norse mythology. Through his association with maritime endeavors and abundance, Njord remains a revered figure whose influence extends beyond the realms of the sea to encompass the cycles of life, growth, and prosperity in the Norse worldview.

Njord is primarily known as the god of the sea and seafaring. He presides over the wind and waves, offering protection to sailors and fishermen during their voyages. Njord's domain extends beyond mere maritime activities; he symbolizes the bounty of the sea and the wealth derived from maritime trade and exploration.

Beyond his association with the sea, Njord is revered for his role in fertility and agriculture. He ensures fertile lands and abundant harvests, promoting prosperity and well-being among the Norse people. His influence over fertility extends to livestock and the natural world, emphasizing his connection to the cycles of growth and abundance.

Njord is also known for his familial ties and relationships. He is the father of Freyr and Freyja, two prominent deities associated with fertility, love, and prosperity. Njord's family connections underscore his role as a nurturing and protective figure within the Norse pantheon.

Symbols associated with Njord include seashells, ships, and sea creatures like fish and dolphins. These symbols reflect his dominion over the sea and his benevolent influence in providing sustenance and prosperity to those who venerate him. Worship of Njord often involved rituals and offerings to invoke his blessings for successful voyages, fertile fields, and prosperous endeavors.

Copyright Asteria Books 2015

Odin

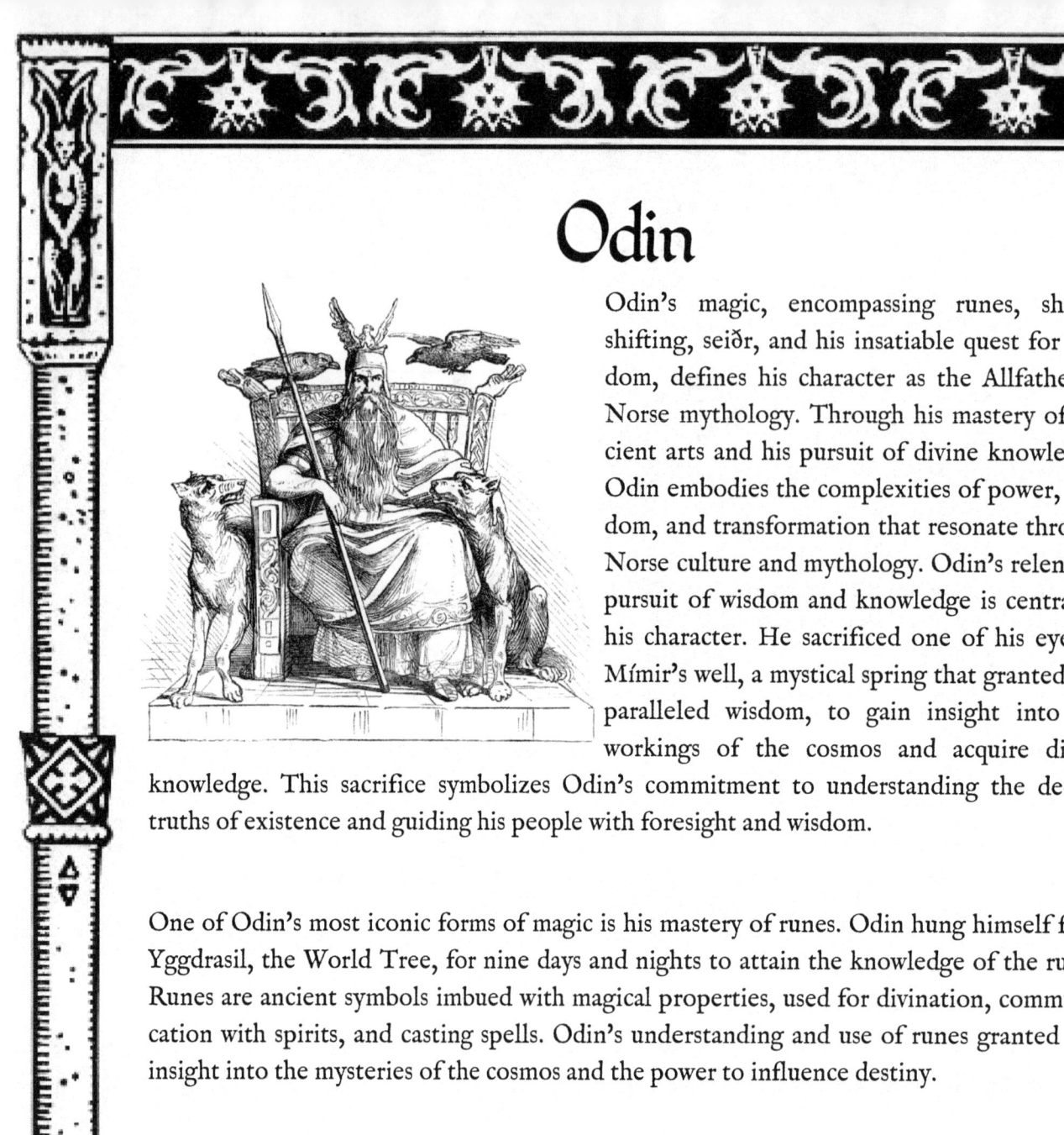

Odin's magic, encompassing runes, shape-shifting, seiðr, and his insatiable quest for wisdom, defines his character as the Allfather of Norse mythology. Through his mastery of ancient arts and his pursuit of divine knowledge, Odin embodies the complexities of power, wisdom, and transformation that resonate through Norse culture and mythology. Odin's relentless pursuit of wisdom and knowledge is central to his character. He sacrificed one of his eyes at Mímir's well, a mystical spring that granted unparalleled wisdom, to gain insight into the workings of the cosmos and acquire divine knowledge. This sacrifice symbolizes Odin's commitment to understanding the deeper truths of existence and guiding his people with foresight and wisdom.

One of Odin's most iconic forms of magic is his mastery of runes. Odin hung himself from Yggdrasil, the World Tree, for nine days and nights to attain the knowledge of the runes. Runes are ancient symbols imbued with magical properties, used for divination, communication with spirits, and casting spells. Odin's understanding and use of runes granted him insight into the mysteries of the cosmos and the power to influence destiny.

Odin is also known for his ability to shape-shift into various forms, such as animals or other beings. This shape-shifting ability allowed him to travel through different realms unseen, gather knowledge, and interact with mortals and supernatural beings alike. His transformations exemplify his adaptability and cunning, enabling him to navigate challenges and achieve his goals.

Additionally, Odin is associated with seiðr, a form of Norse sorcery traditionally practiced by women. Despite its association with femininity, Odin is depicted as a master of seiðr, using it to manipulate fate, foresee future events, and influence outcomes in battles and conflicts. His proficiency in seiðr underscores his versatility as a god of wisdom and cunning strategy.

Copyright Asteria Books 2024

The Norns

In Norse mythology, the Norns are powerful female beings who control the destinies of both gods and humans. These ancient entities are responsible for weaving the threads of fate that shape the lives and events of all beings in the cosmos.

The Norns are typically depicted as three sisters:

Urðr (Wyrd) governs the past, weaving the thread of fate that has already been spun.

Verðandi (Present) oversees the present moment, actively spinning the thread of fate as events unfold.

Skuld (Future) determines what is yet to come, shaping the future based on the decisions and actions of individuals.

According to Norse belief, even the gods themselves are subject to the decrees of the Norns. These beings reside at the base of Yggdrasil, the World Tree, where they tend to the roots and ensure the order and continuity of the cosmos. They dictate the lifespan and fortune of every being, from the mightiest gods to the lowliest mortals.

The Norns are symbols of inevitability and cosmic order in Norse mythology. Their influence extends beyond individual lives to encompass the entire world, ensuring that fate unfolds as ordained by the gods. They are revered and feared for their power to shape destinies and bring about both fortune and adversity.

The Norns, as weavers of fate in Norse mythology, hold a central role in shaping the destinies of gods and mortals alike. Through their vigilant weaving of the threads of past, present, and future, these powerful beings embody the timeless principles of inevitability and cosmic order that govern the Norse cosmos.

Copyright Asteria Books 2024

Pan

In Greek religion and mythology, Pan is the god of the wild places, shepherds, and flocks, and rustic music, and a companion of the nymphs. Some scholars say his name originates within the Ancient Greek language, from the word *paein* (πάειν), meaning "to pasture," while others see in it the Greek word for "all." He has the hindquarters, legs, and horns of a goat, in the same manner as a satyr. With his homeland in rustic Arcadia, he is also recognized as the god of fields, groves, and wooded glens; because of this, Pan is connected to fertility and the season of spring. The ancient Greeks also considered Pan to be the god of theatrical criticism — the word "satire" being connected to satyrs.

The goat-god was nurtured by Amalthea with the infant Zeus in Athens. Pan aided his foster-brother in the battle with the Titans by letting out a horrible screech and scattering them in terror.

One of the famous myths of Pan involves the origin of his pan flute, fashioned from lengths of hollow reed. Syrinx was a lovely water-nymph of Arcadia, daughter of Landon, the river-god. As she was returning from the hunt one day, Pan met her. To escape from his importunities, the fair nymph ran away and didn't stop to hear his compliments. He pursued her from Mount Lycaeum until she came to her sisters who immediately changed her into a reed. When the air blew through the reeds, it produced a plaintive melody. The god, still infatuated, took some of the reeds, because he could not identify which reed she became, and cut seven pieces (or according to some versions, nine), joined them side by side in gradually decreasing lengths, and formed the musical instrument bearing the name of his beloved Syrinx. Henceforth Pan was seldom seen without it.

Disturbed in his secluded afternoon naps, Pan's angry shout inspired panic (*panikon deima*) in lonely places.

Pan's greatest conquest was that of the moon goddess Selene. He accomplished this by wrapping himself in a sheepskin to hide his hairy black goat form, and drew her down from the sky into the forest where he seduced her.

Copyright Asteria Books 2015

Hymn to Pan

Aleister Crowley

Thrill with lissome lust of the light,
O man! My man!
Come careering out of the night
Of Pan! Io Pan!
Io Pan! Io Pan! Come over the sea
From Sicily and from Arcady!
Roaming as Bacchus, with fauns and pards
And nymphs and satyrs for thy guards,
On a milk-white ass, come over the sea
To me, to me,
Come with Apollo in bridal dress
(Shepherdess and pythoness)
Come with Artemis, silken shod,
And wash thy white thigh, beautiful God,
In the moon of the woods, on the marble mount,
The dimpled dawn of the amber fount!
Dip the purple of passionate prayer
In the crimson shrine, the scarlet snare,
The soul that startles in eyes of blue
To watch thy wantonness weeping through
The tangled grove, the gnarled bole
Of the living tree that is spirit and soul
And body and brain — come over the sea,
(Io Pan! Io Pan!)
Devil or god, to me, to me,
My man! my man!
Come with trumpets sounding shrill
Over the hill!
Come with drums low muttering
From the spring!
Come with flute and come with pipe!
Am I not ripe?
I, who wait and writhe and wrestle
With air that hath no boughs to nestle
My body, weary of empty clasp,
Strong as a lion and sharp as an asp —
Come, O come!
I am numb
With the lonely lust of devildom.
Thrust the sword through the galling fetter,
All-devourer, all-begetter;
Give me the sign of the Open Eye,
And the token erect of thorny thigh,
And the word of madness and mystery,
O Pan! Io Pan!
Io Pan! Io Pan Pan! Pan Pan! Pan,
I am a man:
Do as thou wilt, as a great god can,
O Pan! Io Pan!
Io Pan! Io Pan Pan! I am awake
In the grip of the snake.
The eagle slashes with beak and claw;
The gods withdraw:
The great beasts come, Io Pan! I am borne
To death on the horn
Of the Unicorn.
I am Pan! Io Pan! Io Pan Pan! Pan!
I am thy mate, I am thy man,
Goat of thy flock, I am gold, I am god,
Flesh to thy bone, flower to thy rod.
With hoofs of steel I race on the rocks
Through solstice stubborn to equinox.
And I rave; and I rape and I rip and I rend
Everlasting, world without end,
Mannikin, maiden, Maenad, man,
In the might of Pan.
Io Pan! Io Pan Pan! Pan! Io Pan!

Copyright Asteria Publishing 2012

Persephone

Persephone (Proserpine) enthroned.

Persephone's worship in ancient Greece reflected profound beliefs about the interconnectedness of life, death, and renewal. Through rituals, mysteries, and festivals, worshippers honored her dual nature as queen of the underworld and bringer of spring's bounty. Persephone's enduring legacy invites contemplation on the mysteries of existence and the timeless cycles that shape our world and our souls.

Persephone's tale revolves around her abduction by Hades, god of the underworld, and her subsequent role as queen of the dead. This myth symbolizes the cyclical nature of life, where Persephone's descent into the underworld in winter brings about the barrenness of the earth, while her return in spring heralds the renewal of life and fertility.

One of the most significant aspects of Persephone's worship was the Eleusinian Mysteries, celebrated near Athens. These ancient rituals were secretive and believed to offer initiates profound insights into the afterlife and the mysteries of existence. Persephone's role in these mysteries emphasized her dual nature as both queen of the underworld and bringer of life and renewal.

Persephone was often depicted in art and sculpture with symbols of fertility, such as grains, flowers, and pomegranates. Offerings to Persephone included grains, honey, and symbolic representations of the underworld, reflecting her dual role as both a goddess of spring and a powerful figure in the realm of death.

Persephone was worshipped throughout the Greek world, with prominent cult centers in regions such as Eleusis, Sicily, and Attica. Festivals honoring Persephone, such as the Thesmophoria and the Anthesteria, involved rituals, processions, and sacrifices aimed at ensuring agricultural fertility and honoring the cycle of life and death.

Copyright Asteria Books 2024

Poseidon

Poseidon, the powerful Greek god of the sea, storms, earthquakes, and horses, held a significant role in ancient Greek mythology and religious practices. Revered as one of the Olympian gods, Poseidon's worship and influence extended across maritime societies and coastal regions, reflecting his dominion over the waters and the natural world.

POSEIDON AND AMPHITRITE.

Poseidon is depicted as the god who rules over the seas, rivers, and all bodies of water. He is often portrayed wielding a trident, a three-pronged spear symbolizing his mastery over the waters and his ability to stir up storms and waves. Poseidon's association with earthquakes also highlights his role as a god of the earth's depths and natural disasters, showcasing both his power and unpredictability.

Poseidon plays a central role in various myths and legends, including his rivalry with Athena over the patronage of Athens, where he offered the city a saltwater spring by striking his trident against the ground. Another well-known myth involves Poseidon's creation of horses from the sea foam, demonstrating his creative abilities and connection to equestrian pursuits.

Symbols associated with Poseidon include the trident, dolphins, horses, and bulls. Offerings to Poseidon often included sacrifices of bulls or other livestock, as well as libations of wine and water poured into the sea or sacred springs. Rituals and festivals dedicated to Poseidon sought his favor for safe voyages, abundant fishing, and protection from storms and natural disasters.

Copyright Asteria Books 2024

Rhiannon

Rhiannon is a major literary figure of the earliest Welsh-British prose, the *Mabinogi*. Her tales appear in the First and Third Branch of the *Mabinogi*, and like a great many characters from British-Celtic lore, we are able to see the religious and mythological roots of this Great Queen Goddess. Rhiannon's name is synonymous with Rigantona and means "Great Queen." She is a sovereignty goddess of the Celts, meaning that the King ruled by right of being married to this Queen. She represented the Land and the People. Rhiannon is often associated with horses, and her stories are laden with horse imagery, which connected her to the Gaulish Epona. When Pwyll, the Prince of Dyfed, approached the fairy mound in search of wisdom and boon, Rhiannon appeared, riding a white mare. She gave chase, and his horsemen were unable to catch her for two days, until on the third day he rode after her himself and plead with her to stop. She did, but chastised him for not pursuing her on his own account from the start. Three years after they are married, Rhiannon bore a son to Pwyll, but the infant disappeared the night he is born. Her maids killed a puppy and smeared the sleeping queen's face and hands with blood, claiming that she killed and ate her son. Pwyll didn't believe this, but set a punishment for her at the insistence of the people. Each day, Rhiannon must sit at the city gate and tell her tale to those who enter and offer to act as their horse, carrying them or their goods throughout the city. This went on for several years until a golden-haired boy came to Dyfed with his foster-father. Every May Eve, his best mare would foal but the foal would vanish. Once, he kept vigil, hacking at the monstrous claw that snatched the foal. In the foal's place, it had left Rhiannon's infant son. The horse master reunited the boy with his mother, who named him Pryderi, which means both "delivered" and "loss."

Copyright Asteria Books 2015

Skadi

Skadi, also known as Skaði, the Norse goddess of winter, hunting, and mountains, represents the untamed spirit of nature and the resilience needed to survive its harsh elements. Through her mythological tales and symbols, Skadi continues to captivate imaginations and inspire admiration for her strength, independence, and connection to the wild landscapes of the Norse cosmos. Her story serves as a reminder of the ancient Norse reverence for nature's beauty and the powerful forces that shape our world.

Skadi is the daughter of Thjazi, a giant, and is best known for her pursuit of revenge against the gods after they slew her father. In one version of the myth, Skadi storms into Asgard demanding restitution. As compensation for her loss, the gods offer her a husband of her choice from among them, under the condition that she picks him based only on his feet. Skadi chooses Njord, the sea god, mistaking his beautiful feet for those of the sky god Balder. This mismatch eventually leads to their separation, as Skadi prefers the cold mountains and Njord the sea.

Skadi is often depicted as a fierce huntress, skilled in archery, skiing, and survival in the harsh winter landscapes. Her symbols include skis, snowshoes, bows, and arrows, reflecting her association with winter sports, hunting, and the wilderness. Skadi is also linked to the mountains, where she dwells alone in her icy hall, Thrymheim, surrounded by her beloved mountains and the howling winds.

In Norse culture, Skadi was venerated as a goddess who embodied the untamed and wild aspects of nature. She was invoked by hunters and travelers seeking her favor in their pursuits and adventures in the mountains and snowy regions. Her independence and strength made her a symbol of resilience and self-reliance, qualities valued in Norse society.

Copyright Asteria Books 2024

Set

Set, also known as Seth or Setesh, is a complex and enigmatic deity in ancient Egyptian mythology. Often depicted as a powerful and unpredictable force, Set embodies attributes of chaos, storms, and the desert, playing a significant role in both mythology and religious practices of ancient Egypt.

Set is primarily known as the god of chaos and disorder, representing the forces that oppose order and harmony in the cosmos. Unlike many other Egyptian gods associated with natural and cosmic balance, Set's nature is often seen as more unpredictable and disruptive. He is also associated with storms, particularly the destructive forces of wind and desert sandstorms that ravage the fertile lands along the Nile.

One of the most famous myths involving Set is his ongoing conflict with his brother Osiris, the god of the afterlife and fertility. Set's jealousy and ambition lead him to murder Osiris, symbolizing the eternal struggle between chaos and order, and the cycle of death and rebirth in Egyptian beliefs. This myth underscores Set's role as a deity who challenges the established order and disrupts divine harmony.

Set is often depicted in art and hieroglyphs with distinct features, including the head of an unknown animal (often debated but commonly identified with an aardvark or a fantastic composite creature), square-tipped ears, and a long, curved tail. His symbols include the Set animal, a mythical creature resembling a dog or jackal, which symbolizes his chaotic and untamed nature.

Copyright Asteria Books 2024

Thor

In Norse mythology, Thor is celebrated as the god of thunder, storms, and fertility. Revered for his strength, courage, and protective nature, Thor holds a significant place in Norse religious practices and cultural beliefs, embodying both the power of nature and the virtues valued by ancient Norse societies.

Thor is best known for his role as the defender of Asgard, the realm of the gods, and Midgard, the realm of humans. As the god of thunder, Thor wields Mjölnir, his mighty hammer, which he uses to summon storms and protect both gods and humans from malevolent forces, including giants and monsters. Thor symbolizes strength, resilience, and the ability to overcome adversity through sheer force and determination.

Numerous myths and legends surround Thor, showcasing his bravery and prowess in battle. One of the most famous tales involves his battle with the Midgard Serpent, Jörmungandr, during Ragnarök, the Norse apocalypse. Despite knowing it would result in his own demise, Thor courageously confronts the serpent, demonstrating his unwavering commitment to defending the realms and upholding cosmic order.

Symbols associated with Thor include Mjölnir, the hammer that symbolizes his power over thunder and protection. Offerings to Thor often included food and drink, particularly mead and barley, reflecting his role as a god of fertility and agricultural prosperity. Rituals dedicated to Thor involved prayers for protection, strength in battle, and favorable weather for crops and livestock.

Thor's worship was widespread among ancient Norse societies, particularly among farmers, warriors, and sailors who relied on his protection and blessings. Temples and sanctuaries dedicated to Thor were established throughout Scandinavia, where worshippers sought his favor through offerings and rituals during times of hardship or celebration.

Copyright Asteria Books 2024

Thoth

Thoth is an ancient Egyptian God whose associations include knowledge, the moon, measurement, wisdom, the alphabet, records, thought, intelligence, mediation, the mind, logic, reason, reading, hieroglyphics, magic, secrets, scribes, writing, arbitration, and judging the Dead.

Thoth was linked in Egyptian mythology to many types of mediation and judgment. He is the arbitrating power between Good and Evil, perpetually ensuring that neither establishes domination over the other.

He is a God who is mighty in magic, and his unparalleled power seems inexorably linked to words. He is associated with both spoken and written language, being credited as the creator of the written word. It is by virtue of "the Word" that creation happens — which is a theme that is carried forward in Greek philosophy and also in Biblical mythos. Thoth's words are the foundation for the creation of the celestial bodies and the ordering of their movements, which linked Thoth to the sciences. Ultimately, the Greeks eventually credited him with ALL areas of knowledge, both human and divine.

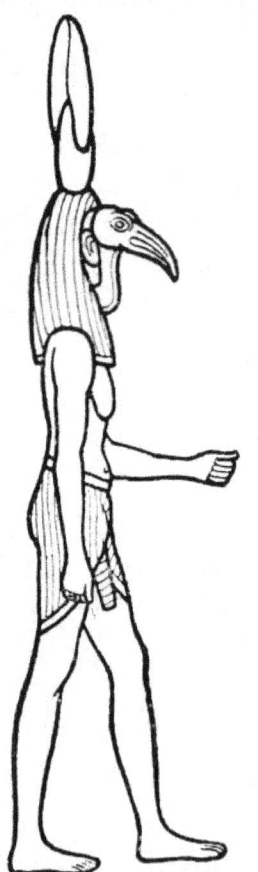

Ancient Prayer to Thoth

Come to me, Thoth, O noble Ibis,
O letter-writer of the gods,
O great scribe!
Come to me and give me counsel,
Make me skillful in your calling!
Better is your calling than all callings,
It makes men great.
He who masters it is found fit to hold office.
I have seen many whom you have helped,
Grant me your wisdom, O Thoth!

Tubal Cain

Tubal Cain, T'Cain, Qayin, Qābīl, Kain, Vulcan, Hephaestus, Wayland, Gobannus, Atho, Janus, Óss, Azazel, Azazil, Izrail, Melek Taus, Lucifer, Lugh, Shamesh, Shemyaza, Lumiel, Orion

Of special interest to Witches is the concept of the Smithing God. Metalsmiths were among the first alchemists, and, by virtue of their powers of transmutation of ore into steel, they were once credited with magical powers. Blacksmiths were considered the mages par excellence of this group, and today we find iron horseshoes (iron ore transformed into the God's horns) prized as good luck symbols. The Smithing God is often associated with lameness, which is attributed to a folk practice of laming the village smith so that such an important member of society could not leave. The shambling step of the lamed God is echoed in the most basic Witch dances.

Tubal Cain appears to mean *he who spices the craft of Cain*. Gordon Wenham suggests that the name *Cain* means *smith*, or that he is called *Tubal Cain* in order to distinguish him from the other Tubal, the son of Japheth. Henry Morris suggests that etymologically, his name is the progenitor of the name of the Roman God Vulcan. Tubal Cain is sometimes thought to be the progenitor of the Celtic peoples. He is the "first ancestor" and the Witchfather.

Genesis 4:22 says that Tubal Cain was the *forger of all instruments of bronze and iron*. Although this may mean he was a metalsmith, a comparison with verses 20 and 21 suggests that he may have been the very first artificer in brass and iron. T. C. Mitchell suggests that he *discovered the possibilities of cold forging native copper and meteoric iron*. Tubal-cain has even been described as the first chemist.

According to the Book of Enoch, Azazel was among those in the Biblical story of the fall of the angels. Azazel is represented in the Book of Enoch as one of the leaders of the rebellious Watchers in the time preceding the flood; he taught men the art of warfare, of making swords, knives, shields, and coats of mail, and women the art of deception by ornamenting the body, dying the hair, and painting the face and the eyebrows, and also revealed to the people the secrets of witchcraft and corrupted their manners, leading them into wickedness and impurity.

According to Luciferian tradition, Azazel and Tubal Cain are the same entity. Azazel chose Tubal Cain as his earthly vessel when he lead the rebellion of the fallen angels. Tubal Cain is of the line of Cain, through his father Lamach, marking him with the holy blood of Lucifer. By teaching the daughters of man witchcraft, Azazel/Tubal Cain became the Witchfather.

Copyright Asteria Publishing 2012

Tyr

Tyr, the Norse god of war and justice, embodies the virtues of bravery, sacrifice, and moral integrity in Norse mythology. Through his role as a warrior and arbiter of justice, Tyr continues to inspire admiration and reverence for his unwavering commitment to upholding principles of law and courage amidst the tumultuous world of gods and mortals. His legacy endures as a symbol of valor and righteous conduct, reflecting the complexities of honor and duty in Norse culture and mythology.

Tyr is primarily known as the god of war and combat in Norse mythology. He is revered for his bravery and martial prowess, often depicted as a fierce warrior clad in armor and wielding a sword or spear. Tyr symbolizes the courage and honor required in battle, as well as the principles of justice and order that govern conflicts among gods and mortals.

One of Tyr's most famous myths involves the binding of Fenrir, the monstrous wolf. When Fenrir grew too powerful and threatening, the gods sought to restrain him. Only Tyr was brave enough to approach Fenrir and offer his hand as a pledge of goodwill. When Fenrir realized he was tricked, he bit off Tyr's hand. This sacrifice demonstrates Tyr's commitment to duty and his willingness to uphold divine laws, even at great personal cost.

Tyr's symbol is often depicted as a sword or spear, representing his role as a warrior god. His association with justice is symbolized by scales or a balance, signifying his role in maintaining order and fairness in the Norse cosmos. Despite losing his hand to Fenrir, Tyr's actions underscore his unwavering commitment to upholding principles of law and courage.

Tyr's worship and reverence were widespread among Norse societies, particularly among warriors and leaders who sought his favor in battle.

Copyright Asteria Books 2024

Zeus

In Greek mythology, Zeus is the king of the gods and ruler of Mount Olympus. His symbols are iconic representations of his power, authority, and dominion over the heavens and earth.

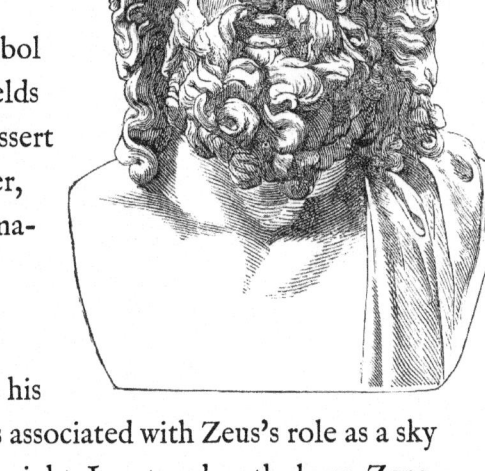

The thunderbolt is perhaps the most recognizable symbol of Zeus. As the god of thunder and lightning, Zeus wields this powerful weapon to strike down his enemies and assert his authority. The thunderbolt symbolizes divine power, forceful intervention, and the unpredictable forces of nature.

Zeus is often accompanied by an eagle, which serves as his sacred animal and a symbol of his majesty. The eagle is associated with Zeus's role as a sky god, symbolizing strength, keen vision, and divine oversight. In art and mythology, Zeus is depicted in the company of an eagle, reinforcing his sovereignty over the heavens and his role as a divine protector.

The oak tree is sacred to Zeus, symbolizing strength, endurance, and longevity. It serves as a natural emblem of Zeus's power and permanence in the natural world. Sacred groves dedicated to Zeus were common in ancient Greece, where worshippers paid homage to the god amidst the ancient oaks.

The aegis is a protective cloak or shield associated with Zeus and his daughter Athena. Adorned with the head of the Gorgon Medusa, the aegis symbolizes divine protection and intimidation. Zeus uses the aegis in battle to inspire fear in his enemies and protect those under his patronage.

Copyright Asteria Books 2024

Ritual, Liturgy, and Spells

Ritual Preparation

Before leading a group ritual, it is wise for a person be able to do ALL of the following:

1. Grounding and Centering – This foundational skill is the mainstay of meditation and a key way of staying healthy. It simply involves taking a time-out to clear all the little nagging distractions of your mind and body and concentrating on what you're doing and how you're really feeling. You'll need to do this at the beginning and end of the ritual. A great way to ground excess energy at the end of a magical practice is through group discussion and food.

2. Laying the Compass – You should have a solid, if basic, working knowledge of the Realms, Gates, and Castles and what energies and powers reside in each. You can use words or gestures that help you, but it is far more important that you are able to call on the energies in an etheric sense. Practice calling them individually and meditate with each until you are comfortable with everything you or your group will be calling.

3. Summoning and Banishing – You must be able to call on and stir up energies, spirits, and other powers, and you must also know how to release and/or banish those same powers. Practice the Witches' LBRP or study other banishing techniques until you feel confident in your abilities.

4. Raising Energy – Clapping, dancing, stamping, chanting, praying, yelling, laughing, drumming...the trance-inducing activities most common to ritual are all means of raising energies, and anything that holds your attention and usually garners some enjoyment works well for energy raising.

5. Directing Energy – After you've raised energy, you need to be able to collect it and assign it where it's supposed to go. This takes a developed discipline in visualization and skill in describing what task precisely you wish that energy to perform. Energy ball games are excellent for developing this skill.

6. Visualizing – A skill for use in and out of ritual - it's not just imagining something with your mind's eye. It's about seeing, hearing, touching, smelling, or tasting something with such vividness that your visualization, while you know it is a visualization, actually looks real to you.

7. Shielding – This is a basic skill for practice of any form of magic, generally a visualization sometimes aided by spell components to turn off your psychic responsiveness.

Copyright Asteria Books 2015

Aligning the Three Souls

A helpful daily practice (and certainly one that is very effective for what many people would call "grounding and centering" prior to ritual) is that of bringing the Three Souls into alignment. This is simple and can be done with little fanfare, in a matter of a few short breaths. If your Sense of Arte favors more complicated ritual, there are certainly more elaborate accommodations that can be made.

Start by getting your feet planted or otherwise feeling your connection to the earth below you. Then state, "May the Three Souls be straight within me."

Continue by taking a deep breath out, sending your energy like a taproot into the earth. On the inhale, pull the earth's energy (and with it, the Forge Fire at the center of the earth) into your belly – the seat of the Black Soul (the fetch, the personal identity, the Soul most connected with this life and your sense of Self).

On the next breath, pull the energy higher, to your chest – the seat of the Red Soul (the Bone Soul, the ancestor connection through blood and fire).

On the third breath, pull the energy higher yet, to the skull, the crown of the head – the seat of White Soul (the higher self, the Holy Guardian Angel, the God-Self).

On the final breath, pull/push the energy all the way through yourself, connecting to the Star Fire above, releasing the breath with a sigh. You are connected to the Witch-Fire above and below, within and without. All three soul-parts are connected and in harmony.

Copyright Asteria Books 2020

Ritual Participant Roles

<u>Priest & Priestess</u> - In some groups, the individuals holding these positions are called by other titles. "Magister" and "Maid" are titles more commonly used in Traditional Craft, for example. Most groups refer to the man or woman who "centers" the ritual by one of these titles. "Centering" a ritual refers to the weaving together of the group's energy and keeping the ritual cohesive and on-track. Traditionalists don't always bestow these titles on someone in a permanent sort of way (though some groups do, as a way to recognize clergy or other leadership positions within a coven). Your ritual may have one or two people acting in this role, individually or as a partnership.

<u>Quarter Callers</u> - Very often a different individual will be assigned to each Quarter. Sometimes, only one or two individuals will call all the Quarters (or other sacred spaces/entities).

<u>Herald/Summoner</u> - Sometimes a ritual will benefit from someone calling the celebrants to the door of the compass/circle. Sometimes the Summoner will go to a separate space to retrieve a person who has been isolated from the ritual and bring them to the ritual grounds. The Herald/Summoner serves that role, welcomes them, and will often also issue a challenge before allowing admission.

<u>Smudger</u> - This person will pass the smoke of incense over each participant as they enter. This is almost always accompanied by someone asperging participants with saltwater.

<u>Guardian/(Wo)Man in Black</u> - The nature of some rituals requires an extra level of protection. You may want an Outer Guardian if you are in an exposed public area, or you may need an Inner Guardian if you anticipate difficult psychic work. Choose this person very carefully. They should be very experienced in such work.

Copyright Asteria Books 2018

Laying the Compass

American Folkloric Witchcraft circles are cast by calling in the three spheres or circles of power and protection — the Realms, the Gates (Quarters), and the Castles (Watchtowers). The AFW compass is directly linked to our Year Wheel, and we call Powers that lie opposite each other as a pair — both being called toward the center of the circle. Thus, they form a road or an energetic pathway, with the Stang as the center point.

CENTER AND FIRST CIRCLE — Raise the stang, which serves as the world tree and connects Three Realms. We call these Realms, either with extemporaneous or pre-planned words. At the base of the stang is the Oath Stone or anvil upon which we make our blood oaths to the tradition. Near the oath stone are the cauldron and the skull. Also placed at the center of the compass are the personal fetishes of each member of our Clan and the three knives. With the raising of the Stang and the calling of the Realms, the 1st Circle is cast.

SECOND CIRCLE (GATES) — At the North gate are placed the staves of the coven, along with the spear, and the troy stone, or gate stone. Also at this gate are symbols of the Black Goddess, as well as totemic items for Imbolc like an owl's feather, fur from a cat, and a willow switch. Any tools associated with air are kept at this gate, such as the censer if one is used.

The South are symbols of the White Goddess and the shields of the coven. The binding cords and the bread for the red meal are placed at this gate. Horsehair, apples, and swan feathers are all symbols for this gate.

In the East are the tools of fire. Here we place the blacksmith's hammer and tongs and keep a bonfire burning, if we are outdoors. The coven sword is here, as are items related to bull, hawthorn, and bee, such as mead in cow horns.

The West is the gate of water, the quench tank of Tubal Cain. Representations of water are placed here, along with toad and crane. Elder is only brought into the circle for certain dark magics. The weapon of this gate is the helm, and the masks of the Clan are kept here.

THIRD CIRCLE (CASTLES) — At the north-east is the Castle of Revelry. Here we place the lantern of inspiration and the broom, as well as representations of hare, birch, and goose.

In the southwest is the Castle Perilous and the silver chalice, along with the red wine that it will hold. Hawk feathers, vines, and representations of the boar or sow are also placed here.

At the northwest corner is the Glass Castle and its treasure — the glass orb. The totems are goat, holly, and wren. Tools of divination are kept in this castle.

The south-east is the home of the Stone Castle, where we place the stone bowl and the casting stones, along with stag horns, acorns, and oak staves.

Thus is the compass laid. It may be as elaborate or as minimal as your tastes and needs dictate. Although the instructions above explain the placement of all of the gates, treasures, tools, weapons, and totems, simply treading the mill once and acknowledging the four gates and the four castles, along with their rulers, is enough to lay the compass.

Copyright Asteria Books 2015

Sleep Circles

Sleep Circles are an easily adapted and applied practice under the greater umbrella of "Sleep and Dream Magic" that, while not entirely uncommon, are not well-documented or widely discussed.

The purpose of a Sleep Circle is to offer protection in both Dreaming and Physical spaces for the person(s) within its circumference. Some practitioners use the Sleep Circle only during periods when they find they or a member of their

household are being unusually plagued by insomnia, nightmares, or other sleep disturbances. However, plenty of practitioners also use this practice to enhance journey and energetic work in Dreaming spaces.

The most straightforward version of a Sleep Circle is to lay the compass (according to your Tradition or preferred method) using only visualization and verbalization from the vantage point of the bed itself, being tucked in and ready for sleep. You can include just the bed, the bedroom, or a portion of the house to include the bathroom (if nocturnal bathroom visits are part of your or your partner's / child's routine).

You can also experiment with the type of circles you cast. For instance, using the AFW Compass as an example, you could conjure a Sleep Circle one night using only the Castles, the next using only the Realms, the next, calling on the Spirit Animal and/or Tree Allies ("Totems"), and the next using the Gates.

Copyright Asteria Books 2020

Opening the Gates

North Gate

I call to the Winds beyond the North Gate. Open the door from the North, place of Air, Kolyo's domain. By cat, and owl, and willow tree, I call you to open wide the Gate and send forth your road to the center of this, our compass. So mote it be!

South Gate

I call to the Fields beyond the South Gate. Open the door from the South, place of Earth, Goda's domain. By horse, and swan, and apple tree, I call you to open wide the Gate and send forth your road to the center of this, our compass. So mote it be!

East Gate

I call to the Sunrise beyond the East Gate. Open the door from the East, place of Fire, Lucifer's domain. By bull, and bee, and hawthorn tree, I call you to open wide the Gate and send forth your road to the center of this, our compass. So mote it be!

West Gate

I call to the Ocean beyond the West Gate. Open the door from the West, place of Water, Azazel's domain. By toad, and crane, and elder tree, I call you to open wide the Gate and send forth your road to the center of this, our compass. So mote it be!

Copyright Asteria Books 2015

Calling the Realms

First Realm

My voice reaches high into the etheric Upper World – the Land of Sky, place of thoughts and aspirations and future plans. I call into Ceugent, the Otherworld – place of struggle and enlightenment, the undying realm of birth. First Realm, be the roof of this, our sacred compass. With my breath, I call you to be here now! So mote it be!

Second Realm

My hands reach out into the physical Middle World – the Land of Stone, place of action and progress. I call out to Gwyned, the Green World – place of consensus reality and limitations, the living realm of Earth. Second Realm, be the walls of this, our sacred compass. With my flesh and bone, I call you to be here now! So mote it be!

Third Realm

My roots reach deep into the chthonic Lower World – the Land of Sea, place of emotion and mystery and past memories. I call into Abred, the Underworld – place of preparation and rest, the realm of death. Third Realm, be the floor of this, our sacred compass. With my blood, I call you to be here now! So mote it be!

Raising the Castles

Castle of Revelry

I call to the Castle of Gold, rising up from the Lake of Fire. Castle of Revelry! Within your walls, warriors sing and drink and tell tales of great deeds. Your keeper is the Golden Queen — Freya, Brighid, Aphrodite. The Golden Lantern shines its inspiration from the heart of the hall. Castle of Revelry, Golden Watchtower, be here now! So Mote it Be!

Castle Perilous

I call to the Castle of Silver, rising up from the Lake of Blood. Castle Perilous! Within your walls, strong men quake and young girls find their deep power. Your keeper is the Silver Queen — Cerridwen, Morgana, Babalon. The Silver Cup drips its sacrifice from the belly of the hall. Castle of Revelry, Silver Watchtower, be here now! So Mote it Be!

Stone Castle

I call to the Castle of Stone, rising up from the Earthen Hill. Stone Castle! Within your walls, warriors train and provisions are prepared. Your keeper is the Oak King — Cernunnos, Herne, Basajaun. The Stone Bowl holds its knowledge at the base of the hall. Castle of Stone, Earthen Watchtower, be here now! So Mote it Be!

Glass Castle

I call to the Castle of Glass, rising up from the Hill of Cloud. Glass Castle! Within your walls, wise ones Odin, Holt, Janicot. The Glass Orb encases its wisdom from the summit of the hall. Castle of Glass, Crystalline Watchtower, be here now! So Mote it Be!

Copyright Asteria Books 2015

Building the Pyramid

MATERIALS:

- Wooden/cloth triangle OR sticks/stones
- Soil from the Millgrounds
- Invitation Incense
- 2 Lamps of Arte (Luna and Sol)

The Pyramid is built after the Compass has been laid. Place the boundary marking for your Pyramid (or Triangle of Arte) outside the Moat in the direction from which you expect the Spirit to arrive. (Place it in the South, if not specified.) Place Luna's Lamp to the left and Sol's Lamp to the right of the Pyramid.

Your Pyramid may be a painted wooden form, an embroidered cloth, an outline fashioned by laying three equal-length sticks end-to-end, or of any material your choose. It may be elaborate or simple, as pleases you.

Sprinkle each side of your Pyramid with either soil from the land upon which you are working or a portion of the Invitation Incense, speaking aloud the three names you ascribe to the three sides of the Triangle, with the following request:

"Goda, give the Spirit form.

Kolyo, give the Spirit voice.

Tubelo, give the Spirit time here with me.

Iarbatha! So be it!"

Light the two Lamps of Arte that flank the Pyramid and prepare for the Invitation.

The Housle

As with many faiths, we partake of a small meal with a spirited drink after our rites. In many witchcraft traditions this is called "Cakes and Ale". We call it the Housle, or Red Meal, and base it in part on a ritual created by fellow walker of the crooked path, Robin Artisson.

The Housle Song
To the tune of Greensleeves

To Housle now we walk the wheel
We kill tonight the blood red meal
A leftward tread of magic's mill
To feed the Gods and work our Will.

Red, red is the wine we drink
Red, red are the cords we wear
Red, red is the Blood of God
And red is the shade of the Housle.

When the compass is laid place in the southwest corner: Dark bread in a bowl (or lipped dish) and Red Wine in Silver Quaich or Chalice. In the center, near the stang will be placed the Red Knife.

1. The sacrificial meal is brought from Castle Perilous to the Spiral Castle by an Initiate,.
2. Tread the Mill widdershins three times while singing the Housle Song.
3. Take up the bread saying: *"Here is bread, source of strength and life."*
4. Kill the bread by saying: *"I kill this loaf in the name of the Mighty Ones."* Cut it with the red knife.
5. Take up the wine saying: *"Here is wine, source of joy and blood of the Gods."*
6. Kill the wine by saying: *"I kill this cup in the name of the Mighty Ones."* Slide the knife over the top of the quaich or chalice.
7. Each person eats and drinks of the Meal, making whatever personal offerings they like. Each person takes the Meal with their left hand, saying *"With my left hand I take it."*
8. The remainder of the wine is poured into the bread bowl, and each person dips their finger in and anoints themselves. This can also be used for blessing tools, etc.
9. The Meal is either given to the ground now, if outside, or later, if inside, saying the following:

"White is black and black is white
Bless us, Witchfather, on this night.
Fair is foul and foul is fair,
We give this back with mickle care.
For what is given is truly taken,
And what is taken is humbly given back."

Copyright Asteria Publishing 2012

Possessory Work

In his first letter to Norman Gills, Robert Cochrane writes that a witch *"... INVOKES THE GODDESS THROUGH 'THE DARK OF NIGHT AND THE EVENING STAR MEETING TOGETHER', WHICH AS YOU SHOULD KNOW IS BROUGHT ABOUT IN THE BEGINNING BY 'AN UNEASY CHAIR ABOVE CAER OCHREN'."* These phrases refer to the Mystery of invocation or possession.

Let's start with 'The dark of night and the evening star meeting together.' This is a reference to possession, which is also called channeling, invocation, aspecting, or being ridden. Later in the same letter, Cochrane says that this process can't be taught in writing.

Perhaps it is easiest to say that the "dark of night" is a reference to the Self – that internal place, the opening, yearning for something greater than what is known and seen. We all have it, this chasm that cries out for spiritual experience, for that which is beyond us.

The "evening star," then, is the Goddess who is being invoked. It could be any Goddess or God. Some covens do possessory work at specific Sabbats or Esbats, and it is often done for the primary purpose of oracular communications from specific Deities. We seek their advice and listen to the wisdom that they share.

Caer Ochren is one of the castles of Grail lore, possibly Caer Sidhe itself. Some of this is just our gut instinct, but a little comes from an interesting linguistic find. "Ochren" means "sides." It could be easy to mistake "sidhe" (which means fairy) as "sides" – or to intentionally muddy the waters by playing language tricks with these words. This is the center point of the witch's compass, opening onto all the sides. A seat above it, poetically, speaking could be the starry point to which the central spire of the castle rises. The North Star, Tubelo's nail star, the iron hook.

It is possibly a reference to the oracle of Delphi sitting upon her tripod stand above the fissure within the temple's floor. The temple at Delphi held the omphalos, the world's navel, the center point. You can use a rocking chair as the tripod, as the "uneasy seat." When a witch sits in the rocking chair at the Sabbat, she begins the process of ascending to the top of the Spiral Castle. It is the seat of wisdom, the seat of vision. By rocking back and forth as she works toward invocation, she is seething, which is a VERY effective way to alter consciousness.

Tapping the Bone

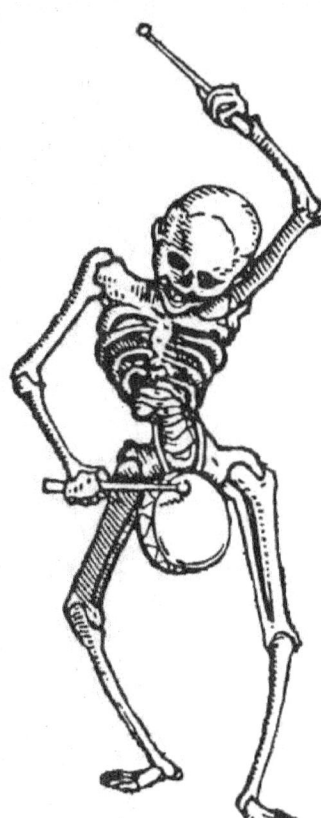

"Tapping the Bone" is the name often given to a practice (or set of practices) in which a skull (human, animal, or replica) is enlivened and used as a vessel for your Ancestors to communicate with you — and you with them. You are "tapping into" the Bone Soul and the connection held in your own bones through the vehicle of the skull.

A practice referenced in Robert Cochrane's description of the symbols on the menhir stone (in Justine Glass's book Witchcraft, the Sixth Sense) is the crossing and uncrossing of bones (presumably leg bones) to "open the gates" of communication with the Dead — using the skull as the vessel. To this end, you'll find that some Witches keep either animal leg bones, replica human arm/leg bones, or carved wooden bones with their Ancestor Skulls. Crossed bones in front of the skull close the path of communication, while uncrossed bones open it.

There has been some controversy lately about using human remains in one's necromantic work (for this is certainly necromancy — communicating with the Dead). Many TradCrafters don't feel comfortable purchasing the skull of a stranger (through a medical supply company, for instance) for use in their Craft, but they do feel comfortable using a cruelty-free animal skull and bones.

If you are not keen on working with remains, though, I highly recommend using crystal / stone skulls and bones (or wooden ones). They can serve as a wonderful vessels, as well.

Some practitioners also work with "Tapping the Bone" in a rhythmic sense that resembles drumming -- waking up the pulse of the bones.

The Charge of the Goddess

Listen to the words of the Great Mother, who was of old also called amongst men Artemis, Astarte, Diana, Melusine, Aphrodite, Cerridwen, Dana, Arianrhod, Isis, Bride and by many other names.

The Charge of Great Mother:

At my altars, the youth of most distant ages gave love, and made due sacrifice. Whenever you have need of anything, once in a month, and better it be when the Moon is full, then shall you gather in some secret place and adore the spirit of Me, who am Queen of all Witcheries.

There shall you assemble, ye who are fain to learn all sorcery, yet have not won its deepest secrets; to these will I teach things that are yet unknown. And you shall be free from slavery, and as a sign that you be really free you shall be naked in your rites. And you shall dance, sing, feast, make music and love all in my praise; for mine is the ecstasy of the spirit, and mine also is joy on Earth, for my law is love unto all beings.

Keep pure your highest ideal, strive ever towards it; let naught stop you or turn you aside, for mine is the secret door which opens upon the door of youth. And mine is the cup of the wine of life and the Cauldron of Cerridwen, which is the Holy Grail of Immortality.

I am the gracious Goddess who gives the gift of joy unto the heart of man, upon Earth I give knowledge of the Spirit eternal, and beyond death I give peace and freedom and reunion with those who have gone before; nor do I demand sacrifice, for behold I am the Mother of all living, and my love is poured out upon the Earth.

Hear ye the words of the Star Goddess. She in the dust of whose feet are the hosts of Heaven, whose body encircles the universe.

The Charge of the Star Goddess:

I who am beauty of the green Earth and the white Moon amongst the stars. And the mystery of the waters, and the desire of the heart of man, call unto thy soul. Arise and come unto me, for I am the soul of Nature who gives life to the universe.

From me all things proceed, and unto me all things must return. And before my face, beloved of Gods and men, thine inmost divine self shall be enfolded in the rapture of the infinite.

Let my worship be with the heart that rejoices, for behold, all acts of love and pleasure are my rituals. And therefore let there be beauty and strength, power and compassion, honor and humility, mirth and reverence within you.

And you who thinks to seek for me, know thy seeking and yearning shall avail you not, unless you know the mystery, that if that which you seek, you find not within thee, you will never find it without thee. Behold I have been with you from the beginning and I am that which is attained at the end of desire.

Copyright Asteria Publishing 2012

The Charge of the Horned God

Listen to the Words of the Horned God,
Who was of old called among men:
Adonis, Tammuz, Dianus, Herne,
Bran, Beli, Lugh, Gwyn,
Dionysus, Osiris, Cernunnos, Pan,
And by many other Names.

I am the Flame that burns in the heart of every being,
And in the core of every Star.
I am Life, and the Giver of Life,
Yet therefore is the Knowledge of Me
The Knowledge of Death and Resurrection.

I am alone, the Lord within ourselves,
Whose Name is Mystery of Mysteries.
I am the Horned God.

I am the Lord of the Universe,
The Father of all living,
The All-Devourer and the All-Begetter.

I am He Whose Seed lies strewn
As glittering Gems across velvet darkness
Within the Womb of the Mother.

I am the Lord of the Shadows
In the darkness of the Underworld,
For I am the Midnight Sun.

I am the Light of the Stars,
And the Spark of the Spirit Eternal,
For I am the God Within.

I am the Horned Leader of the Hosts of Air,
The Leader of the Wild Hunt,
The Judge of Gods and of Men.

I am the Hidden God,
Who ever yet remains,
For I dwell within the secret seed.

I am the seed of grain,
I am the seed of flesh,
I am the Seed of the Stars.

I am the Lord of the Heights,
I am the Lord of the Depths,
God of forest, of flock, and of field.

I am the Hunter and Hunted,
I am the wolf and the Shepherd,
I am the vine and the grain.

I am a Guiding Star above you,
I am a bright Flame before you,
I am a smooth Path beneath you.

I am the Light of Life.
I am the Flame of Love.
I am the Horned God!

Copyright Asteria Publishing 2012

The Charge to New Dedicants

You who have declared your intent to become one of us, hear now that which you must know to do:

Single are all races,
single of men and of Gods.
From a single source we both draw breath,
but a difference of Power in everything keeps us apart,
for we are as nothing,
but the Gods stay forever.
Yet we can,
in greatness of minds,
be like the Gods.

Though we do not know her goals by day or in the night,
Fate has written that we shall run beyond all seas,
and earth's last boundaries.
We shall travel beyond the Spring of night
and the Heaven's vast expanse,
for there lies a majesty which is the domain of the Gods.
You who would pass through the Gates to Avalon,
which is between the world of men and the domains of the Gods,
know that unless you walk our path in love and trust,
and unless there is truth in your heart,
your efforts here are for naught.

HEAR THEN THE LAW!

You shall love all things in nature.
You shall walk humbly in the ways of men and the ways of the Gods.
You shall learn contentment even through suffering,
and through long years,
and from nobility of mind and of purpose.
FOR THE WISE NEVER GROW OLD.
Their minds are nourished by living in the daylight of the Gods.

And if cowans should discover your beliefs in the Gods
for the most part keep silent.
For there it is a great risk to reveal all that you have learned
to those who have not worked to learn it for themselves.

And if such a cowan should say to you
that you cannot be a Witch,
for you will not share your knowledge,
then know that the mysteries must be kept secret from them,
for they do not desire to believe.

But if this cowan desires to know the Gods,
and to suffer to learn,
then share your knowledge,
but only a little,
for the Gods have brought them to you.

Copyright Asteria Publishing 2012

The Descent of the Goddess

In Ancient times our Lord, the Horned One, was, as he still is, the Consoler and the Comforter. But men knew him as the dread Lord of Shadows. Lonely, stern and just.

Now our Lady the Goddess had never loved, but she would solve all the Mysteries. Even the mystery of Death, and so she journeyed to the Underworld.

The Guardians of the Portal challenged her thus: Strip off thy garments, lay aside thy jewels, for naught mayest thou bring with thee into this our land.

So she laid down her garments and her jewels, and was bound, as are all who enter the Realms of Death the Mighty One.

Such was her beauty, that Death himself knelt and kissed her feet, saying: Blessed be thy feet, that have brought thee in these ways. Abide with me, but let me place my cold hand on thy heart.

She replied: I love thee not. Why dost thou cause all things that I love and take delight in to fade and die?

Death replied: Lady, 'tis age and fate, against which I am helpless. Age causes all things to wither; but when men die at the end of time, I give them rest and peace, and strength so that they may return. But thou! Thou art lovely. Return not; abide with me!

But she answered: I love thee not!

Then said Death: An thou receivest not my hand upon thy heart, thou must kneel to Death's scourge.

It is fate - better so, She said. And she knelt, and Death scourged her tenderly. And she cried: I feel the pangs of love!

And Death raised her, and said: Blessed be! And he gave her the Fivefold kiss, saying: Thus only mayest thou attain to joy and knowledge.

And he taught her all his Mysteries, and they loved and were one. And she taught him her mystery of the sacred cup which is the cauldron of rebirth. And he gave her the necklace which is the circle of rebirth and taught her all the Magics.

For there are three great events in the life of man: Love, Death and Resurrection in the new body; and Magic controls them all.

For to fulfill love you must return again at the same time and place as the loved one, and you must meet, and know, and remember, and love them again.

Copyright Asteria Publishing 2012

Orkney Charm for Becoming a Witch

While recording the rapidly disappearing folklore and traditions of Sanday in the 1880s, folklorist Walter Traill Dennison documented the ritual carried out by aspiring witches to gain their magical powers.

The witch had to first wait for a full moon. Then she would go to a solitary beach at midnight where she had to turn widdershins three times before lying prostrate on the ebb - the area between the limits of high and low tide. This was a liminal space, and we believe that this rite could also be held at a crossroads at midnight under a full moon.

She then had to stretch out her arms and legs, and place stones beside them. Further stones were also placed at her head, on her chest and over her heart. Once enclosed by the circle of seven stones, the witch spoke aloud:

Oh Master King of all that's ill,
Come fill me with the Witches' Skill
And I shall serve you with all my will.
Devil take me if I sin!
Devil take me if I fly!
Devil take me when I cannot!
Come take me now, and take me all,
Take eyes and liver, organs and feet
Take me, take me, now I say!
From the brow of the head, to the tip of the toe.
Take all that's out and in of me.
Take hair and hide and all to thee.
Take heart and brains, flesh, blood and bones
Take all between the seven stones!
In the name of the great black Witch Goddess!

The person must lie quiet for a little time after repeating the Incantation. Then opening his eyes he should turn on his left side, arise, and fling the stones used in the operation into the sea. Each stone must be flung singly; and with the throwing of each a certain malediction ("*Devil take these stones and witch's bones!*") was said.

Copyright Asteria Publishing 2012

A Scottish Curse
The Wicked Who Would Do Me Harm
Carmina Gadelica. Vol. II. T. & A. Constable, Edinburgh: 1900

The wicked who would do me harm
May he take the throat disease,
Globularly, spirally, circularly,
Fluxy, pellety, horny-grim.
Be it harder than the stone,
Be it blacker than the coal,
Be it swifter than the duck,
Be it heavier than the lead.
Be it fiercer, fiercer, sharper, harsher, more malignant,
Than the hard, wound-quivering holly,
Be it sourer than the sained, lustrous, bitter, salt salt,
Seven seven times.
Oscillating thither,
Undulating hither,
Staggering downwards,
Floundering upwards.
Drivelling outwards,
Snivelling inwards,
Oft hurrying out,
Seldom coming in.
A wisp the portion of each hand,
A foot in the base of each pillar,
A leg the prop of each jamb,
A flux driving and dragging him.
A dysentery of blood from heart, from form, from bones,
From the liver, from the lobe, from the lungs,
And a searching of veins, of throat, and of kidneys,
To my contemners and traducers.
In name of the God of might,
Who warded from me every evil,
And who shielded me in strength,
From the net of my breakers
And destroyers.

Copyright Asteria Publishing 2012

The Warning

Keep a book in your own hand of writ. Let Brothers and Sisters of the blood copy what they will, but never let this book out of your hands, and never keep the writings of another, for if it be found in their hand of writ, they may well be taken and tortured. Each should guard his own writings and destroy them whenever danger threatens.

Learn as much as you may by heart, and when the danger is past, rewrite your book. For this reason, if any die, destroy their book if they have not been able to; for, if it is found, it is clear proof against them. "Ye may not be a Witch alone," so all their friends be in danger of the torture.

If your book be found on you, it is clear proof against you. You may be tortured. Keep all thought of the cult from your mind. Say you had bad dreams, that a Devil caused you to write this without your knowledge. Think to yourself, "I know nothing. I remember nothing. I have forgotten all." Drive this into your mind. If the torture be too great to bear, say, "I will confess. I cannot bear this torment. What do you want me to say? Tell me and I will say it."

If they try to make you talk of the Brotherhood, do not; but if they try to make you speak of impossibilities, such as flying through the air, consorting with the Devil, sacrificing children, or eating men's flesh, say, "I had an evil dream. I was not myself. I was crazed."

Not all Magistrates are bad. If there be an excuse, they may show you mercy. If you have confessed aught, deny it afterwards. Say you babbled under the torture; you knew not what you did or said. If you be condemned, fear not.

The Brotherhood is powerful. They may help you to escape if you are steadfast. If you betray all, there is no hope for you, in this life, or in that which is to come. But, it is sure, that if steadfast you go to the pyre, drugs will reach you. You will feel naught, and you go but to Death and what lies beyond, the ecstasy of the Goddess.

Never boast, never threaten, never say you wish ill to anyone. If any speak of the Craft, say, "Speak not to me of such, it frightens me, and it is evil luck to speak of it."

Copyright Asteria Publishing 2012

Witches' Lesser Banishing Ritual

This ritual is an adaptation of the Lesser Banishing Ritual of the Pentagram. It uses forms of Witch Gods in place of the traditional Hebrew names of God. It also replaces the Archangel guardians with the four Watchtowers of Celtic lore. The purpose of the LBRP is to banish all undesirable forces from oneself and the local area and to create Sacred Space. It is often recommended as a daily magical exercise to discipline the mind and create peace.

Qabbalistic Cross

Imagine a ball of light above your head. Reach up with your right hand and grab the light. Now when you touch yourself with that hand part of the light will go into you. Touch your forehead as you say "Coronis." (Crown) Let it fill with the light. Touch your pelvis at the pubic bone and say "Serpentis". (Serpent) Let it fill with light. Touch your right shoulder and say "Clementia". (Mercy) Let it fill with light. Touch your left shoulder and say "Severitas". (Severity) Let it fill with light. Hold your hands in prayer over your heart and say "Fortunia". (Blessings) Let it fill with light. Feel your whole body fill with the cross of light.

The Pentagrams

Face East. Before you in the air draw a giant pentagram using your right index finger (or if you prefer use the whole hand) in the direction shown in the illustration. Now imagine that pentagram shining in front of you. Electric blue is a nice color to see it in. If you see it a different color that's fine. Take a step forward with your left foot. Just the left. Leave your right one where it is. The size of the step will be determined by your space. At the same time you step forward thrust your open hands, side by side, palms downwards, into the pentagram, as if you are diving in. This is called the Sign of the Enterer. As you enter the pentagram you will say one of the names of the Witch God or Goddess. Here, at the first pentagram you will shout "Lucifer."

Now, step back with your left foot so it is once again beside your right foot. Touch your right index finger to your lips like you are making the "Shhh, no talking" gesture. Point your right index finger to the center of the pentagram and make a quarter turn to your right. As you do so, draw an imaginary arc of white light around to the next direction. Now draw a pentagram in South. Enter the pentagram singing "Goda." Make the "shhh" gesture and turn to the right drawing an arc. Draw a pentagram in West. Enter the pentagram intoning "Azazel" in a low voice. Make the "shhh" gesture and turn to the right drawing an arc. Draw a pentagram in North. Enter the pentagram whispering "Kolyo." Make the "shhh" gesture and turn to the right drawing an arc.

The Watchtowers

You are now standing in the center of a circle of white light. At each quarter there is a giant electric blue pentagram. Now we post a guardian between each pentagram. Open up your arms. Stretch out like you are a cross: feet together, arms out at shoulder height. Call the watchtowers to their posts. Stand in the cross position and say: "Before me stands the Castle of Stone. Behind me stands the Castle of Glass. On my right stands the Castle Perilous. On my stands the Castle of Revelry."

Stand in pentagram position and say: "Around me flame the pentagrams. Above me shines a six-rayed star, and below me spins a three-armed triskle. I stand within the Spiral Castle. I am the World Tree."

Now repeat the Qabbalistic Cross as you began. "Coronis, Serpentis, Clementia, Severitas, Fortunia".

Copyright Asteria Publishing 2012

A Four-Fold Blessing

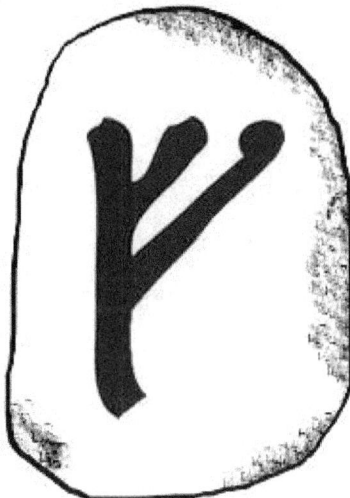

You may have seen witches signing off with the signature line "FFF" or "FFFF" and wondered what these letters stand for. In online Traditional Witchcraft communities the series of F's is used much like Neo-Wiccans use "BB" for "Blessed Be." Indeed, FFFF is also a kind of blessing, although it has very old roots.

The F rune, fehu, is a mark of prosperity and good fortune. It, in and of itself, is a blessing. When tripled or quadrupled its energies are increased exponentially. FFFF is, quite literally, a spell.

FFFF stands for "Flags, Flax, Fodder and Frigg," as Cochrane makes clear in his third letter to Joe Wilson.

"Flags are a form of rush, a plant that grows in European waters - so the answer is Flags, water, Flax, being the weavers plant and blue, thus representing the Goddess of Birth and Death (Fate) being the principle of Air, and Fodder - which means grass, the Earth. The ancients swore an inviolable oath by grass roots - the answer will come to you if you think on it."

Cochrane's interpretation is element-based (or three-realm based: air, earth & water) and omits the final F.

There is also a different interpretation of the benediction, which includes the final F. In this system Flags, Flax, Fodder and Frigg breaks down to:

FLAGS = the flagstone, the home, the hearth and the hearthfire
FLAX = clothing, the material of weaving, the benediction of the weaver's power
FODDER = food for animals and people
FRIGG = the Goddess Frigg, also slang for copulation

So, Flags, Flax, Fodder and Frigg can be translated as "Blessings of the hearth, the weavers, abundant food, and love/sex/fertility." These were also once popularly given as gifts to families entering a new home. (Gifts of fire, hand woven cloth, food -- usually something baked -- and love or friendly devotion).

Copyright Asteria Publishing 2012

Love Spells

To draw your Beloved close to you, after an absence remove your shoes and place them in a T-shape, saying the following:

"When my love I long to see,

I lay my shoes out in a T."

Attract a man (and inspire fidelity) by wearing a yellow garter on your left leg (or a yellow ribbon in your hair).

Dried turkey bones, kept in the space where you meet your Beloved, are a charm to inspire great lust.

Write a letter to your Beloved on red paper, envisioning them receiving it with the response you would desire. Mark it with honey X and bury it. Wait seven days, then offer your Beloved a rum drink.

Put one of your hairs and one of your Beloved's hairs inside a clean jar. Write your Beloved's name in red ink on a piece of paper. Rotate the paper 90 degrees, and write your name over it (crossing it). Fold the paper toward you until it won't fold anymore. Put it in the jar and cover completely with honey. Burn a red chime candle on top of the jar every Friday until your Beloved has come to you.

Copyright Asteria Books 2019

Lost & Found Spell

Pendulum

Pendulums are excellent at helping to track down lost objects. You can use them for dowsing for the missing item, or you can use this simple spell to reclaim your wandering artifact.

1. Anoint a small candle (like a tealight, votive or chime candle) with a basic conditioning oil.

2. Inscribe the name of the lost item on the candle.

3. Chant the following 3 time while swinging your pendulum in circles around the candle: "By Land and Sky and Flame and Sea, what once was lost return to me. By the power of 3 times 3, this is my Will. So mote it be."

4. When you have finished the chant, lay the pendulum down in a circle around the candle and put the whole thing out of your mind while it burns out. (You'll usually have a sudden flash of memory or inspiration about your missing item's hiding place.)

Copyright Asteria Books 2020

Banishing Spells

GTFO Oil is a heavy-duty version of traditional hot foot powder — cayenne, which can be used very effectively to cause an unwanted person to "hot-foot it" out of your life. With crossroads dirt, asafetida, sulfur, sage AND cayenne blended mixed into castor oil your nuisance CAN'T stick around.

1. You need something connected to the target person — a photo, lock of hair, item of clothing, etc. Make sure it isn't connected to anyone else or you could make them leave, too. (Nobody else in photo, nobody else's hairs in the comb, etc.)
2. Failing a personal object, you could write as many defining characteristics of that person as possible on a piece of paper — name, description, job, personality, history, birthday, etc.
3. Make 3 X's on the object using the oil with an iron nail. Don't get any on your skin, if you can help it.
4. Burn the object.

Banishing ingredients can include cayenne, black pepper, cinnamon, chopped bay laurel leaves, sea salt, sulfur, asafetida, crossroads dirt, dragon's blood powder, gunpowder/shotgun pellets, file powder (ground sassafras root), crushed wasp nest, ground ginger.

Sprinkle your mixture onto your target's shoes, across their doorstep, or into their footprint to compel them to move away. You can also hide/mix it into a gift/item (the soil of a potted plant) that the person will bring into their home!

Bell, Book & Candle
To banish spirits, ring an iron bell 3 or 9 times and chant/read from a text you hold sacred while burning a beeswax candle.

Un-Welcome Mat
Write the names of people who are no longer welcome in your home on individual slips of paper. Cross each with GTFO oil and bury them under your porch or the walkway to your door.

Copyright Asteria Books 2020

Beauty Spells

Aphrodite's Spa

The Greek Goddess of Love & Beauty returned to her beachy birthplace for a spa-like ritual of renewal anytime she needed a pick-me-up. Do the same for yourself, bringing energy and intention to bathtime, a mani-pedi, facial mask, etc. Add flowers, friends, dancing, music & wine to give yourself the full Aphrodite beauty treatment.

Golden Girdle

Love Goddesses the world over are depicted with a golden (or gold-hued) accessory (often worn at or near the heart) that enhances their beauty and makes them irresistible — a necklace or type of sash or belt. Maybe a bracelet. Find and empower (or craft) such an item for yourself. Materials might include actual gold metal or beads made of amber ("tree gold").

Lunar Mirror

Gaze into a mirror that has been charged with the moon's beams until you see your own radiance shining forth.

Elecampane

Inula helenium is named for the famous Greek beauty Helen of Sparta (who fled to Troy with Paris, sparking the Trojan War). It is said that she carried this herb with her when she went, and carrying it with you will likewise confer a little of her beauty, charm, and grace.

Milk & Honey Self-Love Bath

Add rosewater, cow's milk, and a little honey to your bathwater. Luxuriate in the water. Wash your face and gently caress your skin. Remind yourself, as a lover would, of both your beauty and of your deep inherent worth.

Morning Dew

The morning dew on both Beltaine and Midsummer are especially potent for beauty spells and cosmetic treatments. Dew caught on certain flowers — like lilacs and roses — is even more powerful. Use it in facewashes, baths, hair treatments, etc. Bottle and store it for use throughout the year, if you can. Just be sure to label it!

Copyright Asteria Books 2020

Psychic Power Spell

Flax

Flax, flaxseed, and spinning have a long association with women's power, magic, and divination. This is especially true in Northern European religions where Goddesses like Freyja, Frigga, and Frau Hulda (each seen as Queen/Matriarch of her particular region) held sway and were associated with leadership, fiber arts (spinning, weaving, sewing, etc), and the potent and mystical realm of women's magic.

In fact, the völva (a particular type of magic practitioner), was hailed as the "staff-carrying woman" — and that staff was fashioned very much like the weaver's distaff.

Drink a cup of a flaxseed tea before divination to enhance your psychic power and pay tribute to the Goddesses who teach the weaving of the liminal threads of magic.

Keep a small bag of flaxseeds among your divination tools.

Wear a linen robe or shawl, the fiber spun from flax, when performing divination or magic.

Copyright Asteria Books 2020

Psychic Power Spells

Mugwort & Wormwood

Very bitter tasting but energetically potent siblings in the Artemisia family, these herbs can be *drunk as tea* (1 tsp dried leaf to 1 cup boiling water, allowed to steep for 5 minutes), *steeped in wine* (1/4 oz dried leaf to one bottle, then strained, decanted, and consumed sparingly/as needed for rituals and spells), or used in *incense blends*. These herbs help Witches tap into their psychic senses. * Pregnant women should not ingest these herbs. *

Psychic Soap

If you give a lot of divinatory readings (especially to strangers), use a palm-sized piece of selenite or citrine to cleanse your energy field between readings/clients, as these stones don't need special preparations to remove psychic "junk" or negativity from them.

Spice Necklace

Wear a garland of cloves, star anise, and nutmeg to renew, refresh, and rejuvenate your psychic energy.

Sleeping with Stones

Certain crystal, gems, and rocks have a reputation for bestowing enhanced/psychic dreams. Keep them in proximity to your bed as you sleep. Some include fluorite, labradorite, clear quartz, and celestite.

Star Stones

Meteorites and crystals formed because of meteoric impact (like moldavite, tektites, Libyan desert glass, etc) are all considered significant enhancers of psychic ability. Wear these as jewelry. Carry them in a pocket or putzi bag. Sleep with them to enhance dreams and strengthen your aura and power while you rest.

Clary Sage

Open your 3rd Eye quickly by anointing your brow with an oil blend that includes clary sage essential oil. (Lemongrass pairs well with it, and adds a nice clairvoyant boost.)

Copyright Asteria Books 2020

Fertility Spells

Witch Ladder

Using red cord, braid and tie a ladder with cowries, gold and silver coins, fruits, and nuts. Tie your desires and intentions into every knot. Hand this over your bed.

Red Candles

Burn red candles as part of other fertility spells, before/during/after sex, or anytime you can safely burn. Just keep them burning.

Bloodstone

This gem "keeps the blood in." Especially useful in women's fertility magic.

- Incorporate into putzi bags
- Wear as jewelry next to the skin
- Corry in your pocket
- Place around your bedroom

Poppet

Make a small doll, stuffing it with fertility herbs and natural filling (like cotton balls). Decorate the doll's surface with seashells, flowers, beads, charms, and symbols of life. Whisper to the doll your desire to conceive, and tell it you will be a caring parent. Carry it with you (secretly, if you wish) – feeding, grooming, and attending to it like you would any baby. When you successfully have a baby, you can pass this poppet along to another parent in need or continue to care for the doll-baby. If you never conceive, this poppet child should be buried with you.

Tree Shrine

Develop a personal relationship with a specific tree related to fertility Deities. Bring it offerings and ask for blessings.

- Apple (female fertility)
- Pine (male fertility)

Copyright Asteria Books 2020

Good Luck Spells

Anvil

Decorate an anvil like an altar with candles and evergreen boughs. Make offerings to it. This is especially lucky at New Year's, but can be auspicious any time. (The anvil is a prominent tool in some lines of the Craft – including AFW. But even a smaller jeweler's anvil will work for this spell.)

Vervain

Add an infusion of vervain to your bath water to draw luck.

Lucky Cat

Cats are considered lucky in many parts of the world.

- Carry cat charms in luck bags, jewelry, or incorporated into witch ladders
- Burn a cat figure candle (in color of your need) dressed with Fast Luck & Black Cat Oils.

Charm Bracelet

Gather charms related to luck. Empower them (one at a time) at the New Moon and add them to your bracelet. Burn candles in colors related to the charms.

Coin

Carry a coin minted in the year you wear born. Drill a small hole in it and add it to your keyring so you never mistakenly spend it or drop it.

Sunwise Circles

Three clockwise (deosil) circles around your home bring luck, especially at Midsummer with coals or brands from the ritual fire.

Copyright Asteria Books 2020

Money Spells

Simple Money Jar

Keep a large container where you can toss loose coins. Any container will do (glass gallon jar, ceramic cookie jar, big plastic pretzel container). "Seed" it with a special coin (eg, one minted in your birth year, foreign currency, commemorative, etc). Anoint the seed coin(s) and container with Has No Hanna or Money Drawing Oil.

Treasure Chest

Make a spell box for wealth. Use a metal box for extra security, if possible. (Iron is the best, but hardest to find these days.) Include charms, talismans, amulets, coins/bills, Spirit money, sigils, bindrunes, images of prosperity Spirits/Deities, etc. Visit and work often with the energy of the chest.

Grow Your Own Money

Plant coins or bills with some crossroads dirt and money-drawing plants (like basil, fenugreek, money tree, philodendron, fern, chamomile, ginger, thyme, etc.) Do this in your garden or in houseplant pots.

Witches' Ladder

Braid and knot a ladder using green cord or ribbons. Braid 9 coins that are tied with 9 knots. Keep this in your treasure chest or money jar, hang it over your bed, or use it to activate or petition a prosperity Spirit/Deity to help you with your financial request by placing it on their image or statue.

Romany Chant

Toss 3 coins into a bowl of water while chanting each day upon waking for 9 consecutive days (27 coins, total). Place bowl where you'll see it but not disturb it.

"Trinka Five! Trinka Five!

Ancient Spirits, come alive.

Let money flow, let money thrive,

Spirits of the Trinka Five!"

Five and Seven Putzi

Place cinquefoil ("five finger grass") in a green bag along with 7 other money-drawing charms, stones, herbs/spices, sigils, coins, talismans, etc.

Copyright Astoria Books 2020

Healing Spells

Poppet

Use any style of human-type doll (plastic/porcelain/cloth, store-bought/homemade, vintage/new, etc.) Stuff the body of the doll with healing herbs. Adorn it with healing charms and talismans. Use pins like you would use acupuncture needles to direct healing energy to targeted areas. Anoint or massage with healing oils and infusions. Chant healing songs and incantations over it. Use the doll in any way you would normally interact with the person during healing rituals. *OR* Transfer all the illness and disease into the doll (via blood or other bodily fluids), and then either bury or burn the doll to prevent the disease from returning to the afflicted person.

Plague & Epidemic Fighters

Use the following in your spellwork (and in your herbal medicine chest, as applicable — with doctor approval): Angelica, Amethyst, Beeswax, Four Thieves Vinegar, Iron Nails, Hyssop, Mugwort, Thyme

Broom Healing

Make a small broom from tree branches and/or herb stalks. Choose what to include based on origin/nature of illness, availability, and intuition. Sweep the patient and sickroom while praying, chanting, petitioning Spirits, etc. Burn the broom outside.

Crossroads Plea

Make an offering (food, drink, money, etc) at a crossroads. Make your request to each roadway. Return home without looking back.

Raphael Invocation

Envision archangel Raphael with his shepherd's staff, surrounded in emerald green light. Say:

"Angel Raphael *SURROUND* me

Angel Raphael *EMBRACE* me

Angel Raphael *HELP* me

With your healing power

Thank you, Thank you, Thank you!"

Copyright Asteria Books 2020

Protection Spells

Witches' Glove

Both the hand and the five-pointed star are long-time symbols of protection, showing up in many forms all over the globe. A hand or star at the front door of the home is thought to protect the inhabitants from all manner of harm.

Fiery Ring

Create a fiery ring or wall of protection around yourself in times uncertainty and turmoil. Seek the calm of meditation, and place 2 jar candles – 1 at your head and 1 at your feet. Or place 4 – 1 each at the cardinal directions. Or place 13 around you in a circle for the lunar year.

Beans & Ghosts

Scatter (or plant) beans around your home to prevent ghosts from bothering you. (Beans are the food of the Dead, according to Greek lore. So you are both feeding them, and keeping those who are not your own honored ancestors at a respectful distance. Win-win!)

Bay Laurel

This tree (and its leaves) are especially protective for women. Place one leaf in each corner of your bedroom (especially if you have house-mates) and also in each corner of your home. If you share the bed, put a leaf under your side of the mattress.

Blue Stones

Place blue gemstones of any type around your home or designated area to protect it. Blue star sapphire is especially protective (but pricey). Consider wearing one, if you can.

Three Bloods Witch Ladder

Craft a protective ladder with coral (sea blood) and iron (earth blood) that has been anointed with your blood (menstrual, if possible). Add your saliva for an extra boost of protection. Hang this above the doorway.

Hag Stones

Hang naturally holed stones from red cords in your windows or carry as a charm against evil.

Copyright Asteria Books 2020

Domination Spells

Sweet Woodruff

Sprinkle the Waldmeister ("Master of the Forest" the German name for this herb) over the path where your target is sure to walk in order to gain dominance over them.

Name Jar

These jars are used to influence people who are either mildly unaware or wildly opposed to you or your goals. Get them in line! Write the name on a slip of paper three times, turning the paper 90-degrees and crossing each with your own name (to make a grid). If you're working on more than one person for the same intention, use a different slip of paper for each person. Fold the papers toward you as tightly as you can. Put the paper(s) into a canning jar with honey, jam, syrup, or sugar. (I prefer raw, natural honey.) Cover the papers completely, saying something like, "[Target] be as sweet to me as this honey is upon my lips." Light a chime candle on top of the jar that matches your intentions. Repeat weekly (on the day associated with your intention) as needed.

Calamus & Licorice

Sweet flag (calamus) & licorice root (not candy) are the basis of traditional "Command & Compel" formulas (along with the castor bean/oil) — dating back to the *Magical Papyri*. Sometimes vetivert (which is also sometimes called calamus) and patchouli are substituted, giving practitioners a few options for mixing and matching. These formulas were used to make both spirits and people obey the commands of the magician. Use calamus & licorice in:

- A ritual bath by making a decoction that you add to the water
- Oils & powders for dressing candles — or simply touch your target after anointing your own hands
- A witch's ladder in which strands of the target's har have been soaked in a decoction these roots
- A putzi bag that you carry with you to increase your influence and command

Heads, Hands, Feet

These symbols have been used for purposes of control for centuries. Wear a necklace of them strung on red silk cord to control the thoughts and actions of your target. Or carve their name on the sole of your shoe to keep them at heel!

Copyright Asteria Books 2020

Ruination Spells

Witch Bottle Hexing

Use a bottle or jar that you can lid, cap, or cork. Fill it with your target's photo, name paper, black ink, War Water, your urine, rusty nails, pins, and botanicals related to your intentions. Seal with wax from a black candle and bury upside down.

Black Candle Spell

Reverse the candle by slicing the top to flatten it, and carving the bottom to expose the wick. Carve and dress the candle using a rusty nail, Flying Devil Oil, and the botanicals of your choice. Chant your intentions while your candle burns.

Coffin Curse

Fashion a wax or cloth poppet of your target. Include their hair, nails, or other items, if you can get them. If not, embed a name paper and photo. Place this doll inside a small wooden coffin. Bury the coffin and place a rock on top.

Curse Tablets

Inscribe sheets of metal or wax with target's name, birthday, etc & your intention for them. Be specific and explicit. Drop it in the sewer (or make your own "sewer jar" with urine and excrement to drop it in, seal it up, and send it to the landfill).

Goofer Dust

This is potent stuff with no single recipe. Variations of it exist outside the African diaspora (under different names & with their own variations). ALL variations are malevolent — with results from effects on sanity all the way to death. The most common ingredients include cemetery dirt, church bell grease, salt, sulfur, gunpowder, and more.

- Toss at target's back
- Sprinkle across target's path or on front steps
- Use it to dress a black candle
- Incorporate it into poppet work

Copyright Asteria Books 2020

Success Spells

If you're looking for financial success for your business or shop, keep aventurine in your cash register/drawer, money bag, safe, etc. (Handle all your business banking electronically? Make a piggy bank or chest for this purpose only.)

Place clusters of citrine in a bowl on a table or place them singly in windows around your home or business to promote confidence, esteem, and financial abundance.

Keep live basil growing in pots. It's like growing your own money, and it promotes contentedness and peace.

Laurel has been associated with crowning victory and achievement since Ancient Greece, and it is the basis of the Hoodoo "Crown of Success" formulas. Use oils, infusions, or the simple bay laurel leaf to:

* Anoint a lodestone that you carry with you in a red putzi bag
* Anoint yourself
* Add to bath water

Night-blooming jasmine (or possibly jessamine, which is a tuberose) is the foundation of the Has No Hanna formula. Most recipes call for jasmine, orange or tangerine, and something earthy like vetivert or oakmoss. This potent drawing formula will bring clients and customers your way when used to anoint letterhead, business cards, sales materials, etc.

Copyright Asteria Books 2020

Broom Spell for Purification

When moving into a new home, always get a fresh, new broom — and dispose of the old one. (Don't just leave it behind for the new residents, as this would be no kindness for them.)

Spray the new broom with saltwater (or soak the brush and allow it to dry) before its first use. You can add other spiritually deep cleaning agents, like Florida Water, for an extra boost, if you want.

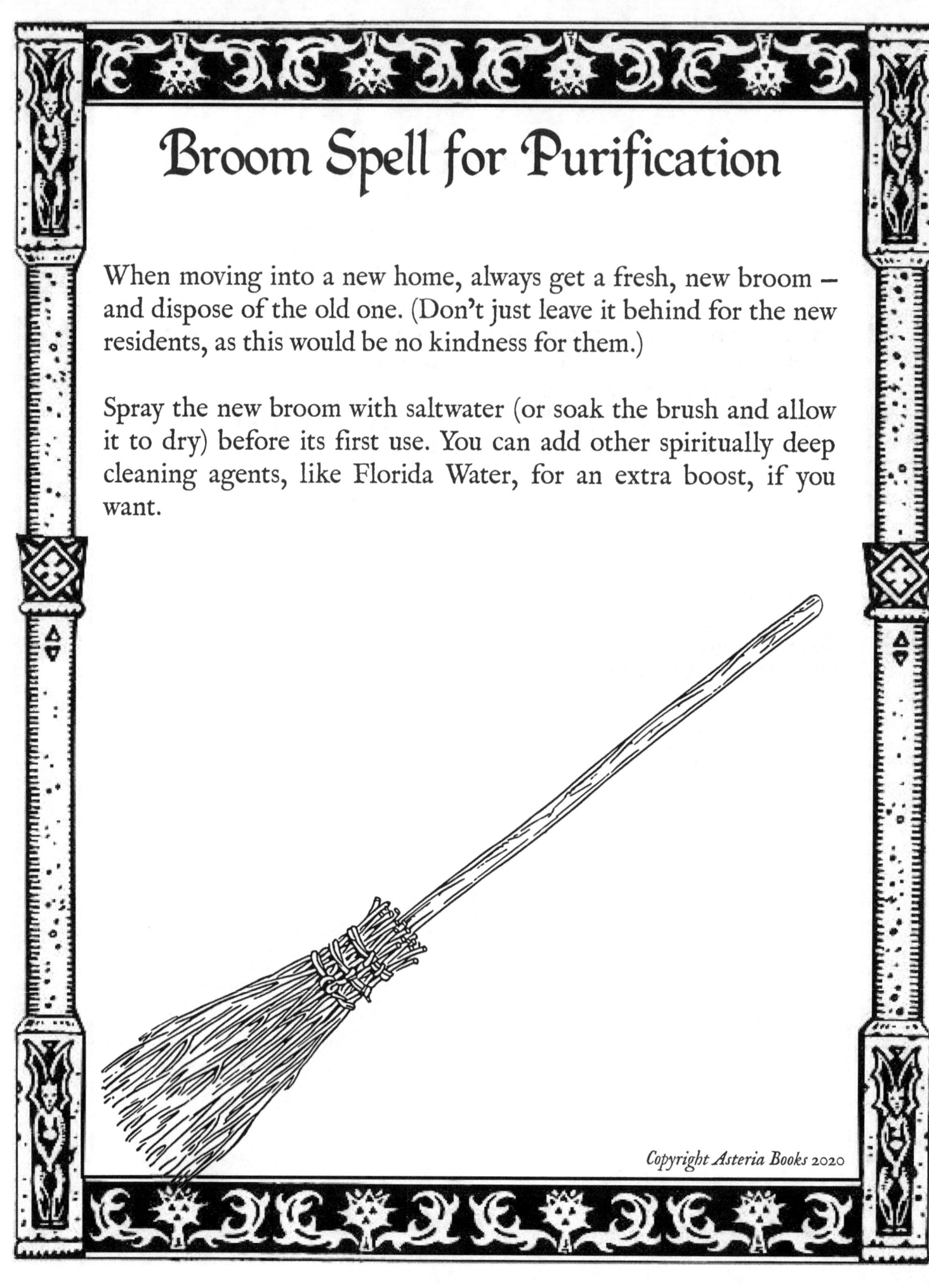

Purification Spells

Lustration is the act of cleansing by virtue of bathing an object or body with water. Perform a self-lustration with any living water (spring, rain, ocean, river water etc) or other holy water. Dip your hands into the vessel of water saying "Hands clean." Bring drops to your brow while saying "Mind clear." Touch your feet and say "Feet fresh." Wrap your arms around yourself — "Body cleansed." Hold your arms aloft "Spirit purified."

Asperging is cleansing by sprinkling an area, object, or person with liquid. Usually, the vessel, liquid, and aspergillum (tool) are all composed of sacred materials, but they can still be very simple. A wood bowl, spring water, and a spring of cedar. Choose your aspergillum with care, as different botanicals have different uses in ritual and magic.

Smudging is the name given to the process of cleansing with smoke created by burning sacred herbs or woods. People, animals, and objects can be passed through the smoke, or smoldering herbs or blends can be walked arounds areas. Incense blending is part of the smudging tradition, and many world religions have some variation of this practice.

Sounds and vibrations — like those made by metals bells, chimes, and gongs — have been recognized by ancient cultures worldwide as an effective method of purification and spirit banishing. Ring a bell to cleanse your space, your mind, and your energy — QUICKLY.

Eggs are potent absorbers of negative energy. If you are feeling hexed, go to the railroad tracks, run an egg all over your body, and then leave the egg on the tracks. When you walk away from it, don't look back. Know the train will destroy and scatter the hex.

Copyright Asteria Books 2020

Justice Spells

Hold the Justice card from a Tarot deck (or a drawing/copy/picture of it) in your hands and focus on the situation for which you are calling for justice to be done. Pour into the picture all the ways in which you've been wronged and the specific ways in which the "scales of Justice" can be balanced. When you're ready, place the card/picture on a fireproof plate. Surround the card with a black stone, white stone, and red stone. On top of the card, set and burn a carved and dressed purple taper or chime candle. Light another purple candle every Thursday.

For Justice work that involves the courts, uses galangal root (which is also called courtcase root). You can carry it with you in a putzi bag, or you can chew it and (discreetly) spit it on the floor before the judge enters. Unlikely as it sounds, this will help them favor you in the case.

If you need extra help with Justice – including strength while you fight the good fight – call on the archangel Michael using his traditional invocation. As you say each of the following lines, imagine a flaming sword appearing at each of the locations, close to the body (with the last flaming sword being at the heart energy center).

Angel Michael BEFORE me
Angel Michael BEHIND me
Angel Michael ABOVE me
Angel Michael BENEATH me
Angel Michael at my RIGHT
Angel Michael at my LEFT
Angel Michael WITHIN me

Michael is a powerful being, and has been called upon by magicians outside of the Judeo-Christian context for work involving war and plague, and also protection and healing. He adds a potent punch to Justice work since he will go to any length to do what is right. Just make sure you are on the side of "right" (by his standards) when you call on him.

Copyright Asteria Books 2020

Peace Spells

Resin Garland

Fashion a garland of frankincense and myrrh tears charged with prayers of comfort and healing. This can be worn, hung on the home or at an altar, or unstrung and burned as incense.

Holy Basil

This herb is called holy because it promotes peace, harmony, tranquility, and cooperation.

- Plant it around the home or grow it in containers indoors
- Cook with it & drink as a tea
- Use it in spellwork (poppets, bags, etc)

Blue Birds & Blue Flowers

Both are rare and are said to bring peace, joy, and protection. Incorporate their images in spells and decorations. Grow the flowers around your home, if you can — or bring in cut, fresh flowers in a vase.

Vervain

It is said that this herb wants happiness for humans. It loves us and craves our presence. Plant it around your home, if you can. Use it in your incenses, sachets, and putzi bags. Steep it in boiling water to make tea.

Peace in Sleep

Place vetivert roots and citronella leaves under your mattress for tranquility, peace, and security. Replace them when they've lost their scent.

Dove of Peace

The dove as a symbol of peace and serenity predates Christianity. This bird was associated with Love Goddesses as early as Ishtar, but Aphrodite was the first of these who was also a Goddess of Peace and Harmony. She was very often depicted carrying a dove (or surrounded by them). Call on Aphrodite and her Dove of Peace to bring this quality into your life.

Copyright Asteria Books 2020

Witching Ritual

MATERIALS
- Stang, candle, lighter
- Cauldron, water, lancet
- Anvil, hammer
- Three knives (red, black, white)
- Bread, lipped dish or bowl
- Red wine, cup
- Incense, holder, charcoal
- White Cord for child
- Simple Robe for child
- Drawstring pouch
- Talismans, tokens, and amulets brought by guests
- Extra charms/stones that can be empowered by guests, if needed

RAISE THE STANG

LAY THE COMPASS

WORKING

- NAMING THE CHILD ~ The parents bring the child to the Officiant, who then asks for the child's full and proper name. The Officiant then blesses the child and introduces them to the assembled community by this name, and acknowledges that this child is one of our own.

- CHALLENGES TO PARENTS ~ The Officiant offers three challenges to the parents. Will you love and nurture this child's mind, body, and spirit? Will you respect this child's autonomy as a free, unique, and independent being? Will you guide and teach them all you can so they might find their own way and know their own Souls? After answering yes to all, the Officiant offers a blessing to the parents.

- CHALLENGES TO GODD-PARENTS ~ The Officiant asks the parents to name the child's Godd-Parent(s). The Godd-Parents are offered three challenges. Will you love and respect this child as an autonomous, free, and unique bring? Will you support this child's parents in their obligation to rear and nurture this child? Will you protect and offer succor to this child in times of need? After answering yes to all, the Officiant blesses the Godd-Parents.

Copyright Asteria Books 2022

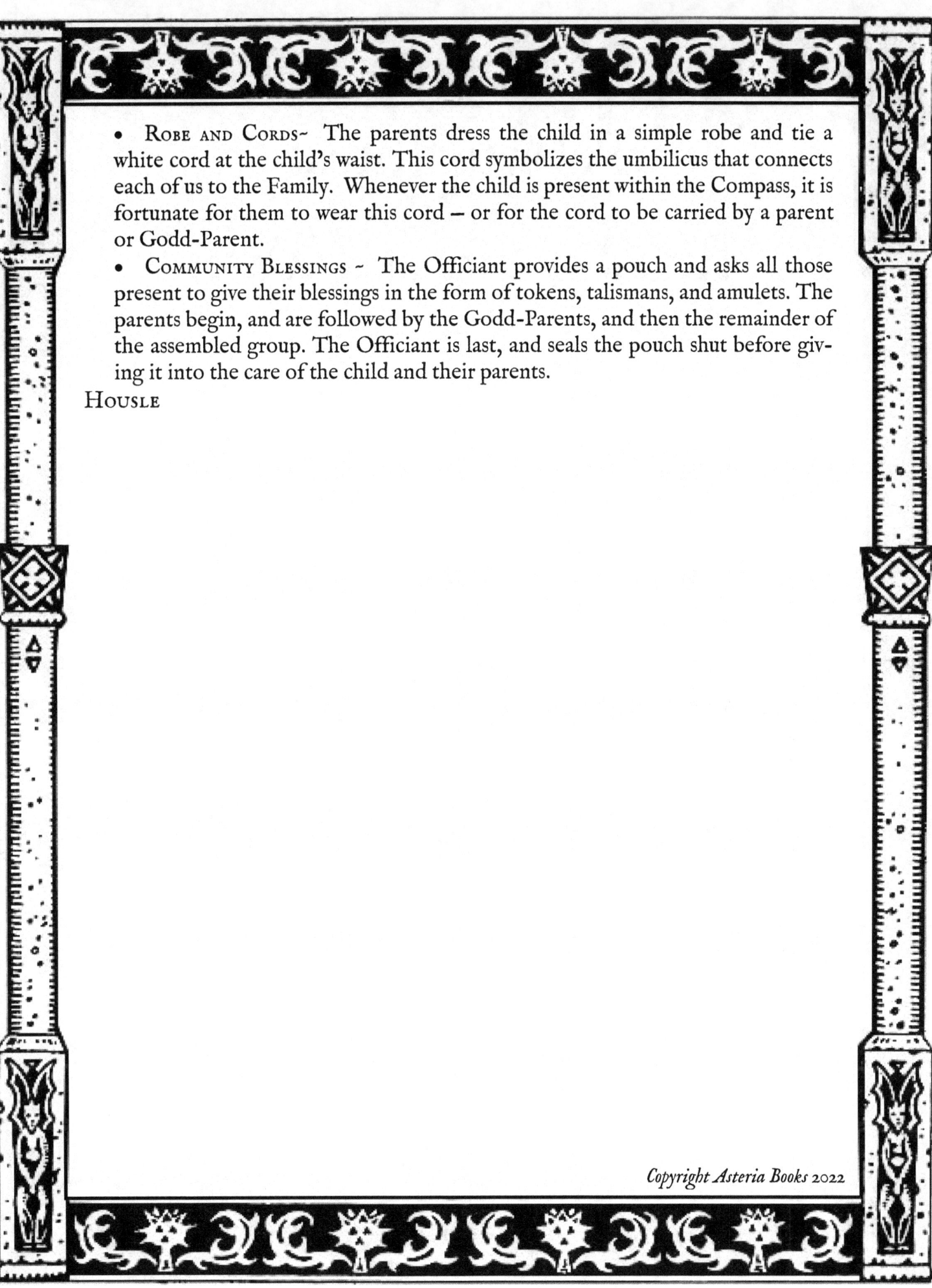

- Robe and Cords~ The parents dress the child in a simple robe and tie a white cord at the child's waist. This cord symbolizes the umbilicus that connects each of us to the Family. Whenever the child is present within the Compass, it is fortunate for them to wear this cord – or for the cord to be carried by a parent or Godd-Parent.
- Community Blessings ~ The Officiant provides a pouch and asks all those present to give their blessings in the form of tokens, talismans, and amulets. The parents begin, and are followed by the Godd-Parents, and then the remainder of the assembled group. The Officiant is last, and seals the pouch shut before giving it into the care of the child and their parents.

Housle

Puberty Ritual

"Ritual of Fire and Water"

MATERIALS
- Stang, candle, lighter
- Cauldron, water
- Anvil, hammer
- Three knives (red, black, white)
- Bread, lipped dish or bowl
- Red wine, cup
- Incense, holder, charcoal
- Red candle (taper, pillar, or floating)
- Bowl
- Gifts for the adolescent
- Red and White roses (charms, talisman, embroidery, etc)

RAISE THE STANG

LAY THE COMPASS

WORKING
- PRESENTING THE ADOLESCENT ~ The parents stand with the Adolescent as the Officiant announces: "Today, we celebrate and honor [Name], who has experienced a quickening of the Fire and the Water they carry within. This is a quickening of both the body and the spirit, and it is cause for joy!" (Everyone cheers.)
- WATER ~ The Officiant instructs the Adolescent to use the bowl to dip water from the Cauldron and then set the bowl on the ground. "You now share with us in the watery Mysteries of life and the creation of life. Water flows within us in our tears, our blood, and in our passions."
- FIRE ~ The Officiant instructs the Adolescent to light the red candle. "You now share with us in the fiery Mysteries of life and the creation of life. Fire burns within our hearts, our minds, and in our passions."
- Alchemy of Water and Fire ~ The Officiant instructs the Adolescent to place the candle within the bowl of water, keeping the flame lit. "We all strive to balance the Water and Fire within ourselves. You will experience many trials and

turnings as you work this alchemy for yourself. You will also experience many joys and revelations."

- **PRESENTATION OF GIFTS AND ADVICE** ~ The Officiant invites the assembled community to offer their gifts (which includes their wisdom) to the Adolescent. Everyone is given the opportunity to speak, if they choose.
- **RED AND WHITE ROSES** ~ The Officiant presents the Adolescent with the red and white roses (which can be fashioned as a talisman to be worn or carried, or as a talisman to reside on the Adolescent's altar). "Red and White Roses have many meanings among the Wise. One set of those meanings is connected to the quickening you have experienced. There is both beauty and pain in these Mysteries — both are unavoidable, natural, and unique to yourself. I give you this to contemplate as you continue on your journey, along with my blessings and the blessings of our Godds."

HOUSLE

Coming of Age Ritual

Materials
- Stang, candle, lighter
- Cauldron, water
- Anvil, hammer
- Three knives (red, black, white)
- Bread, lipped dish or bowl
- Red wine, cup
- Incense, holder, charcoal
- Blindfold
- Gifts

Raise the Stang

Lay the Compass

Working

- Preparing the Young Adult ~ The parents walk with the Young Adult away from the group, offering personal advice and reflections on becoming an adult within the community. Before fully returning to the space, they blindfold the young adult and then bring them to the gate of the Compass. During this time, the other adults are divided into two groups — Birthing Parents and Supporting Parents. People will self-select where they wish to be. Birthing Parents will form two parallel lines at ground level (either sitting or kneeling), facing each other. Supporting Parents will stand or sit together as group at the end of this canal or passageway.
- Challenges ~ The Officiant offers three challenges to the Young Adult. "Will you be counted as an Adult within this community? Will you be personally accountable for your words and deeds? Will you support and be supported by this community as you walk the path that is laid at your feet?" After answering Yes, the Young Adult is brought to the beginning of the passageway.
- Birthing ~ The Officiant says, "When you were born, it was a struggle. A fight for life. You and your parents worked hard to bring you into this world as an infant. You are now ready to come into the world as an adult, and you and they have worked hard to make that happen, as well." Officiant assists the Young Adult to their hands and knees. "[Name], the Child, kneels here at the passage. [Name], the Adult, is to be found on the other side. Crawl forward, and

Copyright Asteria Books 2022

make this journey, [Name]." The Birthing Parents squeeze and push against the Young Adult as they crawl. (It should be difficult.) The Supporting Parents call out encouragement and give directions. (The Birthing Parents can also speak words of encouragement and comfort.) When the Young Adult reaches the end, the Supporting Parents help pull them to their feet, remove the blindfold, and give hugs.

- NAMING ~ The Officiant says, "When you were born and received within this community, your parents named you [Name]. You may continue to use this name among our People, or you may choose another. Tell us, friend, what is your name?" (Everyone cheers and calls out the name.)

- PRESENTATION OF GIFTS AND ADVICE ~ The Officiant invites the assembled community to offer their gifts (which includes their wisdom) to the Young Adult. Everyone is given the opportunity to speak, if they choose.

HOUSLE

Handfasting Ritual

MATERIALS
- Stang, candle, lighter
- Cauldron, water
- Anvil, hammer
- Three knives (red, black, white)
- Bread, lipped dish or bowl
- Red wine, cup
- Incense, holder, charcoal
- Handfasting Cord
- Rings
- Lanterns/Torches for each Quarter/Gate
- North: incense and Staff for the couple; South: bread and Coin for the couple; West: Cup of water with cedar asperger; East: candle and Dagger or Sword for the couple

RAISE THE STANG

LAY THE COMPASS

WORKING

- PROCESSIONAL ~ The bridal party enters in this order: One spouse stands with Officiant at Center, North Gate attendant, South Gate attendant, West Gate attendant, East Gate attendant, other spouse (with or without escort). Each enters, makes a full circle, and then takes their place.
- WELCOME ~ The Officiant addresses the assembly. "Beloved Friends and Family, we have come together this evening to witness the sacred profession of Love and Will between NAME and NAME. This act of Magic is a custom from time immemorial, and we are blessed to witness this declaration of matrimony and offer our blessings on the union of these two Souls."
- CHALLENGES AND BLESSINGS AT THE GATES ~ The Officiant says, "NAME and NAME have chosen faithful companions to stand with them on this day to offer challenges, blessings, and talismans as a tribute to their love and commitment to each other. Let us all stand witness to this alchemical union of minds, hearts, bodies, and lives."

North Gate asks: "Marriage is a union of minds. Do you choose to KNOW each

Copyright Asteria Books 2022

other deeply?" Couple each respond: "I KNOW." North Gate passes incense smoke over the couple and picks up the Staff and says: "With this Staff, I bless you with the shared intellect to overcome obstacles and the wit to defend each other from all foes." Couple respond: "So Mote it Be!"

South Gate asks: "Marriage is a union of lives. Do you choose to speak truthfully to each other in all things?" Couple each respond: "I SPEAK." South Gate offers the couple a bite of bread, then offers them the Coin saying: "With this Coin, I bless you with the sharing of material and social wealth and the ability to build a life together." Couple respond: "So Mote it Be!"

West Gate asks: "Marriage is a union of hearts. Do you DARE to be linked together through times of celebration and also of sorrow?" Couple each respond: "I DARE." West Gate sprinkles Couple with water from the cup, then offers the Cup saying: "With this Cup, I bless you with joy and also with the healing balm that deep partnership offers." Couple respond: "So Mote it Be!"

East Gate asks: "Marriage is a union of passions. WILL you choose daily to commit to each other?" Couple each respond: "I WILL." East Gate says: "With this Blade, I bless you in the forging of your goals and the manifestation of your Will." Couple respond: "So Mote it Be!"

- HANDS-FASTED ~ The Officiant says, "It is a custom among us to signify the joining of lives, minds, passions, and hearts by the symbolic joining of hands. Take the right hand of your Beloved." The couple joins right hands and Officiant ties the cord. "This is what is meant by 'tying the knot.'"
- VOWS ~ Officiant says, "NAME and NAME, you have answered the challenges and accepted the blessings. We now look to you, that you may speak your personal vows to your Beloved, and accept theirs in return." The couple takes turns speaking their personal vows. Officiant says, "These are your promises to each other, and we here stand witness."
- RINGS ~ The Officiant says, "The rings you exchange represent the magick of the circle. They act as a reminder of your Love and Will. Place the ring you have chosen for your Beloved upon their left hand, signifying the commitment you have made to each other."
- KISS ~ Officiant says, "I invite you to seal your vows and consummate your blessings with a kiss." The couple kisses. Officiant says: "And so it is - today and all days to come!"

Copyright Asteria Books 2022

- **Presentation of the Couple** ~ Officiant says, "We have all stood witness to this act of Magic - this bonding under the mighty forces of Will and Love. May we all support you and celebrate with you - today and all days to come." Couple turn to face the guests. Officiant says, "Friends and Family, I present to you, Name and Name, fs the [Last Names]!" (much cheering)

Housle & Recessional (Couple exits to Feast, followed by bridal party, officiant, and then guests)

Handparting Ritual

MATERIALS
- Stang, candle, lighter
- Cauldron, water
- Anvil, hammer
- Three knives (red, black, white)
- Bread, lipped dish or bowl
- Red wine, cup
- Incense, holder, charcoal
- Handfasting Cord
- Rings
- Lanterns/Torches for each Quarter/Gate
- North: incense and feather for each individual; South: salt and coin for each individual; West: Cup of water with cedar asperger and holey stone; East: candles for each individual
- Two small boxes

RAISE THE STANG

LAY THE COMPASS

WORKING
- PROCESSIONAL ~ The couple enters together with attendants for the Gates following them. Each enters, makes a full circle, and then takes their place.
- WELCOME ~ The Officiant addresses the assembly. "Beloved Friends and Family, we have come together this evening to witness and support the dissolution of the union between NAME and NAME. This is an act of Magick – through Love and Will – between these two Souls. We offer them both blessings as they uncouple and lead separate lives."
- CHALLENGES AND BLESSINGS AT THE GATES ~ The Officiant says, "NAME and NAME have chosen faithful companions to stand with them on this day to offer challenges, blessings, and talismans as a tribute to the bond they shared and desire to walk separate paths. Let us all stand witness to this declaration."

North Gate asks: "Marriage is a union of minds. Do you choose to separate from each other's thoughts and deepest confidences?" Couple each respond: "I choose to know myself." North Gate passes incense smoke over the couple and picks up

Copyright Asteria Books 2022

the two feathers and says: "With these feathers, I bless each of you with the hard-earned wisdom and clarity of thought." Individuals respond: "So Mote it Be!"

South Gate asks: "Marriage is a union of lives. Do you choose to keep silent and forfeit your voice and vote in each other's choices?" Individuals each respond: "I choose my own counsel." South Gate offers the couple a grain of salt, then offers them each the Coins saying: "With these Coins, I bless each of you with new potential and individual fortune." Individuals respond: "So Mote it Be!"

West Gate asks: "Marriage is a union of hearts. Do you choose experience your joys and sorrows separately?" Individuals each respond: "I choose my own heart." West Gate sprinkles individuals with water from the cup, then offers the two Holey Stones saying: "With these Hagstones, I bless you each with rebirth, cleansing, and self-soothing." Individuals respond: "So Mote it Be!"

East Gate asks: "Marriage is a union of passions. WILL you remove your commitment to each other?" Individuals each respond: "I WILL." East Gate says: "With these lights, I bless you in the manifestation of your Wills." Individuals respond: "So Mote it Be!"

- Hands-Parted ~ The Officiant says, "Your lives, minds, passions, and hearts were joined by invisible threads, and your hands were bound together in symbolic union. Those hands are now separate, and the cord must be cut." The individuals grasp the cord and Officiant cuts it. "This severing is deep, but we strive for a clean cut." Each individual places their portion of cord in the fire.
- Farewells ~ Officiant says, "NAME and NAME, you have answered the challenges and accepted the blessings as you embark on separate lives. We now look to you, that you may speak a farewell and blessing to the Stranger who was your Beloved, and accept theirs in return." The individuals take turns speaking. Officiant says, "These are your farewells to each other, and we here stand witness."
- Rings ~ The Officiant says, "The rings you exchanged represented the magick of the circle. They acted as a reminder of your Love and Will. Returning them now to each other is also an act of Love and Will." Individuals remove their rings and give them back to the other.
- Balm ~ Officiant says, "We have witnessed a cutting of ties, a returning of gifts and promises, and many blessings on these two individuals. These conscious divisions are painful, and we offer balm and succor to the raw and ragged places

in each of you." The Officiant anoints each individual's brow, heart, belly, and right hand. Officiant says: "So Mote it Be!"

- **Presentation of the Individuals** ~ Officiant says, "We have all stood witness to this act of Magic - this dissolution under the mighty forces of Will and Love. May we all support you both and love you both - today and all days to come." Individuals turn to face the guests. Officiant says, "Friends and Family, I present to you, Full Name and Full Name!" Individuals take separate places in the Compass.

Housle

Note: It is preferred that both partners choose to be present to undo the magick of matrimony and cut these links together. However, if that is not possible, this ritual can easily be adapted to fit a single partner.

Copyright Asteria Books 2022

Wisdom Ritual

Materials
- Stang, candle, lighter
- Cauldron, water
- Anvil, hammer
- Three knives (red, black, white)
- Bread, lipped dish or bowl
- Red wine, cup
- Incense, holder, charcoal
- Red candle (taper, pillar, or floating)
- Cloak
- Staff
- Glass Orb
- High Seat (throne, chair, place of honor)

Raise the Stang
Lay the Compass
Working

- **Presenting the Wise One** ~ The Wise One stands as the Officiant announces: "Today, we celebrate and honor [Name], whose wisdom and experience have marked them as an Elder among us!" (Everyone cheers.)
- **Cloak** ~ The Officiant drapes the Cloak over the shoulders of the Wise One. "Wisdom is often veiled. Wisdom is a shield and a comfort. Wisdom is a mantle of responsibility and honor."
- **Staff** ~ The Officiant hands the Staff to the Wise One, who holds it in their right. "Wisdom is a support. Wisdom is a tool. Wisdom is a weapon."
- **Glass Orb** ~ The Officiant places the Glass Orb into the left hand of the Wise One. "Wisdom is a clarity. Wisdom is foresight. Wisdom is a dominion."
- **High Seat** ~ The Officiant leads the Elder to the High Seat. Before the Elder sits, the Officiant says, "By this robe, this scepter, and this orb, we recognize and honor you as monarch among us — one who rules their own life and domain through Wisdom. We honor you as an Elder of our People — a counselor and regent. Take, now, this place of pride and receive our thanks." The Wise One sits in the throne/chair.
- **Presentation of Gifts and Advice** ~ The Officiant invites the assembled

community to offer their gifts (which includes their service, blessings, and thanks – only other Wise Ones should offer wisdom about this stage of life) to the Wise One. Everyone is given the opportunity to speak, if they choose.

- RED AND WHITE ROSES ~ The Officiant presents the Wise One with the red and white roses (which can be fashioned as a talisman to be worn or carried, or as a talisman to reside on the Elder's altar). "Red and White Roses have many meanings among the Wise. One set of those meanings is connected to the Veiled Queen and the Naked Queen. There is much Wisdom in the Mysteries that run the road between these two. I give you this emblem, which is blazoned on that wagon, to contemplate as you continue on your journey, along with my blessings and the blessings of our Godds."

HOUSLE

Crossing Ritual

Materials
- Stang, candle, lighter
- Cauldron, water
- Anvil, hammer
- Three knives (red, black, white)
- Bread, lipped dish or bowl
- Red wine, cup
- Incense, holder, charcoal
- Kuthun (inheritance)
- Deceased Witch's Cords
- Journals of the Deceased
- Fire/firepit
- Coins, small box/chest
- Cups and drinks

Raise the Stang

Lay the Compass

Working
- Farewells ~ The Officiant invites the assembly to speak their farewells and give voice to their mourning. All who wish to speak are given leave to do so.
- Cutting the Cords ~ The Officiant holds up the Cords worn by the Witch. "These Cords have signified the promises, connections, and Mysteries explored by our Sibling. By cutting them, we freely release our Beloved to continue on their journey through the Universe."
- Burning the Book ~ The Officiant instructs a designee from the kin of the Deceased to bring forward the journal(s). "As a Witch, the records of our Witching are private and personal. In times past, books like these were worth our lives. In deepest respect for our Beloved, we take these private accounts out of the reach of the Living." The designee throws the book(s) into the flames.
- Kuthun ~ The Officiant brings forward any magickal items that are being passed along to inheritors. "[Name] has noted that these sacred tools should pass into the care of some specific Family members." The Officiant passes along the tool/jewel along with any special notes about its significance.
- Coins for the Crossing ~ "It has been three (or more) days since our Be-

loved left this life. The Souls often linger during this time of transition, but they cross fully to the other-side around now. It is an ancient custom to provision the Dead for this journey. Come and place your coins in this box, which represents the tomb and will be buried to aid [Name] on their journey." The box should be open on the altar next to a photo of the Deceased. An attendant can offer coins to anyone who didn't bring one.

- TOASTS TO LIFE AND DEATH ~ "Mourning and grief are a natural part Death, but we have also come to celebrate the Life of our friend. We choose to remember the joys, the love, and the vitality that they imparted during their time among us. Let us raise a cup and share our stories as a testament to a life well and fully lived." Stories are shared freely. When they come to a natural stopping place, invite the assembly to remain after the Housle for more food, drinks, and sharing.

HOUSLE

Sabbats

Samhain

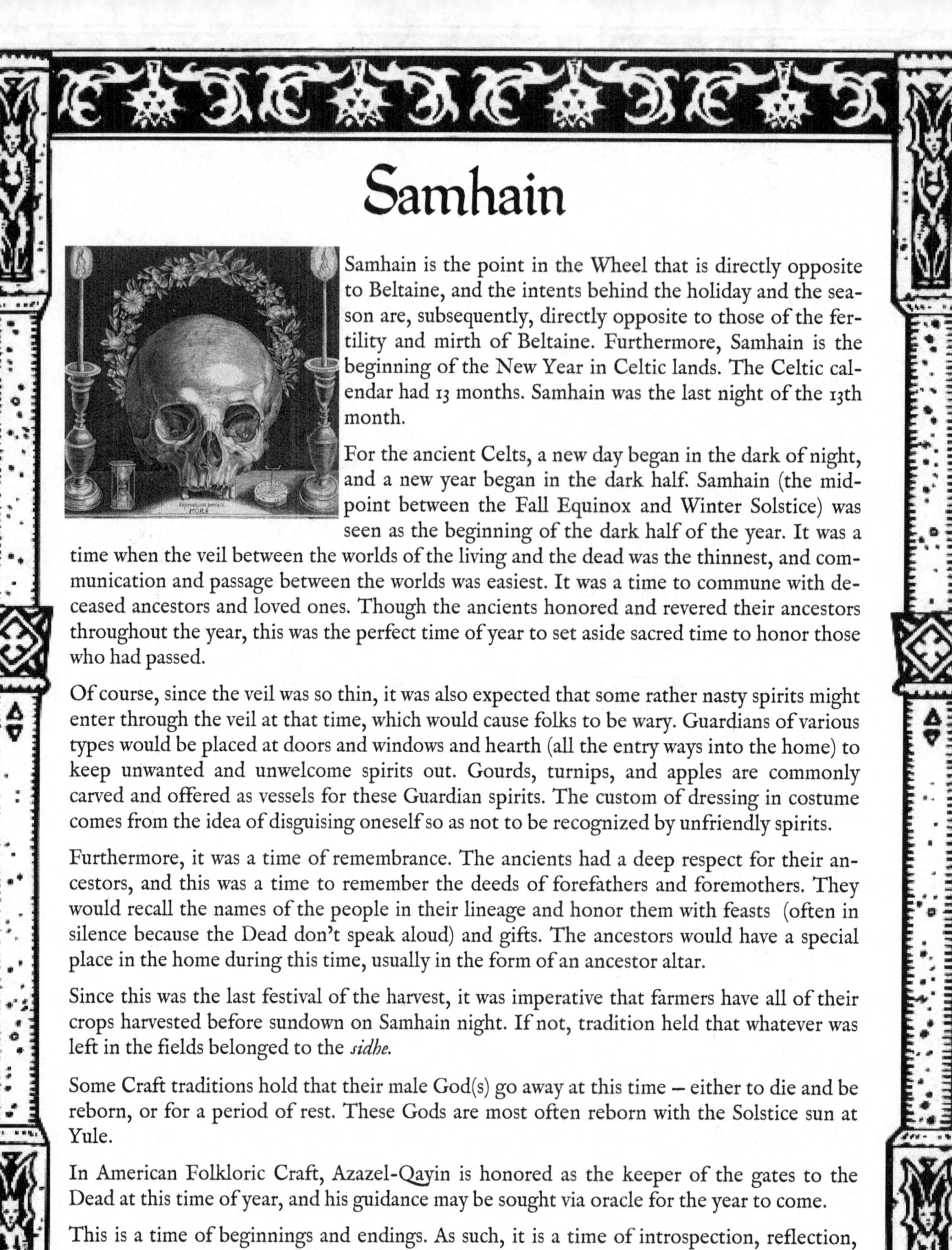

Samhain is the point in the Wheel that is directly opposite to Beltaine, and the intents behind the holiday and the season are, subsequently, directly opposite to those of the fertility and mirth of Beltaine. Furthermore, Samhain is the beginning of the New Year in Celtic lands. The Celtic calendar had 13 months. Samhain was the last night of the 13th month.

For the ancient Celts, a new day began in the dark of night, and a new year began in the dark half. Samhain (the midpoint between the Fall Equinox and Winter Solstice) was seen as the beginning of the dark half of the year. It was a time when the veil between the worlds of the living and the dead was the thinnest, and communication and passage between the worlds was easiest. It was a time to commune with deceased ancestors and loved ones. Though the ancients honored and revered their ancestors throughout the year, this was the perfect time of year to set aside sacred time to honor those who had passed.

Of course, since the veil was so thin, it was also expected that some rather nasty spirits might enter through the veil at that time, which would cause folks to be wary. Guardians of various types would be placed at doors and windows and hearth (all the entry ways into the home) to keep unwanted and unwelcome spirits out. Gourds, turnips, and apples are commonly carved and offered as vessels for these Guardian spirits. The custom of dressing in costume comes from the idea of disguising oneself so as not to be recognized by unfriendly spirits.

Furthermore, it was a time of remembrance. The ancients had a deep respect for their ancestors, and this was a time to remember the deeds of forefathers and foremothers. They would recall the names of the people in their lineage and honor them with feasts (often in silence because the Dead don't speak aloud) and gifts. The ancestors would have a special place in the home during this time, usually in the form of an ancestor altar.

Since this was the last festival of the harvest, it was imperative that farmers have all of their crops harvested before sundown on Samhain night. If not, tradition held that whatever was left in the fields belonged to the *sidhe*.

Some Craft traditions hold that their male God(s) go away at this time — either to die and be reborn, or for a period of rest. These Gods are most often reborn with the Solstice sun at Yule.

In American Folkloric Craft, Azazel-Qayin is honored as the keeper of the gates to the Dead at this time of year, and his guidance may be sought via oracle for the year to come.

This is a time of beginnings and endings. As such, it is a time of introspection, reflection, communication with the Otherworld and Underworld. It is a time of profound spiritual growth. It can be quite intense.

Copyright Asteria Books 2019

Samhain Ritual

MATERIALS
- Stang, candle, lighter
- Cauldron, water, lancet
- Anvil, hammer
- Three knives (red, black, white)
- Red Cord
- Bread, lipped dish or bowl
- Dark beer
- Red wine, cup
- Incense, holder, charcoal
- Carved gourd/pumpkin, tealight candle
- Skull (real human OR human-shaped ceramic, glass, crystal, paper-mache, wood, etc)
- Lineage chant

RAISE THE STANG

LAY THE COMPASS

OPEN THE GATES (beginning in the West)

WORKING
- LIGHTING JACK ~ Hold your carved pumpkin or gourd (or turnip) in your hands and send energy into it to "wake it up." Call on a specific guardian Spirit, or ask that a guardian from your tribe of spirits comes forward to inhabit the vessel and keep watch over you and your home during Samhain-tide. Light the candle inside the jack-o'-lantern, and set it as a Ward at the edge of the Compass.
- RECITATION OF LINEAGE ~ Pick up the skull. With pride and love, declare, "I am, (name), child of (name), child of (name), child of (name), child of (name)." Go back as many generations as you know. If you want to focus on the matrilineal or patrilineal line, you may. It is equally acceptable to recite the lineage of adoptive and foster families if that is your circumstance and preference.
- ENLIVENING OF SKULL ~ Still holding the skull, send a thread of energy to the skull, feeling it come alive with the energy of your blood, your breath, your flesh. Say something like, "I invite my ancestors, those names and those un-

Copyright Astoria Books 2018

named, to be with me, speak with me, eat with me, dance with me, laugh with me during these dark days at the the turn of the year. I offer you this vessel, now and always, as a seat in my home." Place the skull at the base of the Stang. In future rituals, always place the skull here. Outside of ritual, place the skull upon your altar or ancestor shrine.

- DARK BEER FOR QAYIN ~ At the anvil or Oath Stone, pick up the hammer. Strike the anvil and call out, "Tubal Qayin!" Strike again and call out, "Tubal Qayin!" Strike a third (final) time and call out, "Witch Father!" Pour the dark beer over the anvil/stone or into the cauldron. (If you're inside pour all of it into the cauldron. If you're outside, reserve at least part of it for the cauldron.) Acknowledge with whatever words or gestures come to you that this offering us to Tubelo. It is not inappropriate to share a drink, so take a swig from the bottle to share with the Red God, if you feel so moved.
- SCRYING ~ Sit down in front of the cauldron. Get comfortable. Refresh the incense, if needed. Pour some water into the cauldron if more liquid is needed. Clean the top of a finger with an alcohol swab and prick with a lancet. This works best on the outside edge of a fingertip, where you are not calloused. Keeping your hand below your heart, raise a drop or two of blood. Drop them into the liquid if there cauldron. Gaze at the cauldron, relax your focus, and allow images and impressions to come to you. Don't try to force a conversation with the spirits. They will speak in their own way. You may experience images, sounds, ideas, temperature shifts, sensations, smells. Any of these may seem to generate spontaneously within your own mind, like a stay thought. Let them come. Allow the session to continue as for a little while. You'll probably have a good sense of when you're finished and nothing else is coming through. If needed, you can end the session early and beginning to ground by moving into the Red Meal.

HOUSLE

Copyright Asteria Books 2018

Samhain Ritual

MATERIALS
- Stang, candle, lighter
- Cauldron, water, lancet
- Anvil, hammer
- Three knives (red, black, white)
- Triple Cord
- Bread, lipped dish or bowl
- Dark beer
- Red wine, cup
- Incense, holder, charcoal
- Carved gourd/pumpkin, tealight candle
- Skull (real human OR human-shaped ceramic, glass, crystal, paper-mache, wood, etc)
- Lineage chant
- Feast foods of your choice

RAISE THE STANG

LAY THE COMPASS

OPEN THE GATES (beginning in the West)

RAISE THE CASTLES

WORKING
- LIGHTING JACK -- Empower and light your carved pumpkin/gourd, like you did last Samhain.
- RECITATION OF LINEAGE -- Pick up the skull. With pride and love, declare, "I am, (name), child of (name), child of (name), child of (name), child of (name)." Go back as many generations as you know. If you want to focus on the matrilineal or patrilineal line, you may. It is equally acceptable to recite the lineage of adoptive and foster families if that is your circumstance and preference.
- TAPPING THE BONE -- Your skull was enlivened last year, so you needn't re-do the enlivening (unless you're using a new skull).

However, you may want to "tap" the skull to quicken the pulse if it has been a whole year since you've worked with it. If you are using leg bones to open/close the portal, this is the time to open them and welcome your Ancestors to join you.

- DARK BEER FOR QAYIN -- Strike the anvil 3 times and pour out dark beer for the Witchfather, as you did last year (and possibly since then).
- DUMB FEAST – From this point forward during the ritual, you will not speak. (I personally like to perform this entire ritual in silence – including the Compass Laying, etc.) Communicate via energy and gesture, but do not use audible words. Eat a meal with your Ancestors, setting them a place of honor and preparing a plate of food for them. The silence allows you the opportunity to commune with them and to immerse yourself in a a sensory experience whereby you might communicate. Perhaps you'll hear messages from them as you eat. Perhaps the tastes of certain foods will be especially delicious for you. Try to include foods that were family favorites, if you are able. Taste and smell are very primal sense, and they can connect us to old (even ancient) memory. (Many customs hold that this meal should be set and served in reverse. This is not how I was taught, but feel free to incorporate the custom, if the folklore suits you.)

HOUSLE

Samhain Mysteries

At Samhaintide, it is our custom to explore the Mysteries of:

"Life in Death; Death in Life" — This is a phrase we use to reference something very fundamental to this Tradition. While the WitchMother isn't particularly prominent at this Sabbat, this phrase IS. (And this phrase is very much associated with Her.) This Mystery is also very present with us at Beltaine.

"Rose Beyond the Grave" — Writers from within the Clan of Tubal Cain have written about this Mystery. To contemplate the Rose Beyond (or Within) the Grave is to contemplate what happens to the Souls of the Witch after Death.

"What the Mask Reveals" — The Spiral Castle Tradition associates the West with Samhain. The weapon of the West is the Helm (or Mask). We sometimes work with the Mask in order to better understand both ourselves and That which is represented by a specific mask.

Copyright Asteria Books 2022

Yule

Yule is celebrated on the Winter , which is the shortest day of the year. Solstice celebrations are universal, being celebrated in nearly every culture the world over.

Groups as different as Iranians are to the Swedes, Chumash Indians to the Germans, and Spain to peoples of Tibet have very old traditions for the same solar event. The impetus for the holiday, nearly the world over, is the fear that the failing light of the sun may not return and therefore needs some help. According to many traditions, there are evil spirits that thrive in the darkness and require light and warmth to drive them out. This accounts, in part, for the extensive use of candles and lanterns to drive away the darkness. Of course, the flame of a candle is also similar (though a much smaller representative) to the light of the Sun itself.

Structures have been built, as far back as the dim memory of mankind and beyond, that mark and honor the Winter Solstice. Stonehenge (which marks both Solstices), Newgrange in Ireland, and Maeshowe in the Orkney Islands off the coast of Scotland are some of the most well known of these ancient pieces of architecture. However, there are also similar structures throughout Europe, Asia, the Middle East, Indonesia and the Americas. One has even been found recently in Africa.

The Romans celebrated Saturnalia, which was a combination of the traditions already in use by the Egyptians and Persians. Saturnalia was a 12-day celebration that involved decorating with greenery and burning candles to chase away evil spirits. Naturally, it became a party in the pure Roman style with the passage of time.

Yule was the Norse and Celtic celebration of the Solstice. "Yule" means "feast" or, possibly, "wheel." As with the other cultures, the Celtic and Norse traditions tend to revolve around the return of light, warmth, and fertility brought by the Sun. Of course, the peoples to the North had a much rougher time in winter than their neighbors to the South, so their need for the return of light (and heat) may have helped imbue this holiday with special significance.

Boughs of holly were used in decoration because their verdant color was a strong reminder of life in the midst of the white, snow-covered world they lived in. White, interestingly, was a color of death and mourning to the Northern people, and winter was the time of the Earth's death in preparation for rebirth. Holly was also hung in windows because of its prickly leaves and poisonous berries, which make it excellent for guardianship.

The Holly King rules at this holiday, but loses his battle to the Oak King, who will then rule until Summer Solstice. All solar deities are honored, and this day is accounted as the birth of many of them.

Copyright Asteria Books 2019

Yule Ritual

Materials
- Stang, candle, lighter
- Three knives (red, black, white)
- Red Cord
- Bread, lipped dish or bowl
- Red wine, cup
- Incense, holder, charcoal
- Skull
- Yule candle, log, and/or firewood
- Wassail, bowl
- Lemon, ribbon, orris powder, cinnamon, ginger, whole cloves, toothpick

Raise the Stang

Lay the Compass

Open the Gates (beginning in the West)

Working
- Vigil Fire ~ Keep a fire burning all night. Stay with it, tending to it as needed. This isn't always an easy task. The night is long. It invariably becomes a time for self-reflection, much as the winter itself is. But it can also be a time for mirth, family, friends, and craft.
- Wassail the Trees ~ Take the wassail bowl outside, if you aren't already outside. Salute the trees that surround your home. Wish them health and long life and offer them a drink. Sing the song "Here We Come A-Wassailing" as you go, if you choose. As with other offerings, it is appropriate for you to share the drink, as well, if you are so moved.
- Prosperity Pomander ~ These clove-studded, dried citruses take some time to be fully made, but they are well worth it. Place in a dish on your altar while it dries.

Housle

Copyright Asteria Books 2018

Wassail Recipe

1 gallon Apple Cider
1 can (6 oz) Frozen Orange Juice
1 can (6 oz) Lemonade
4 cups Water

Put the above ingredients in a 30 cup coffee percolator.

In the basket, put:

6 Cinnamon Sticks
1 & 1/2 tsp whole Allspice
1/2 tsp whole Cloves
1 cup Brown Sugar

This wassail recipe can be adapted to taste, and it serves a crowd. It is my family's favorite! You can also add some extra holiday cheer to it, if you like. It combines well with both wine and liquor, depending on your preference.

Copyright Asteria Books 2018

Here We Come A-Wassailing

Here we come a-wassailing
Among the leaves so green,
Here we come a-wand'ring
So fair to be seen.
[REFRAIN]
Love and joy come to you,
And to you your wassail, too,
And God bless you, and send you
A Happy New Year,
And God send you a Happy New Year.

Good master and good mistress,
As you sit beside the fire,
Pray think of us poor children
Who wander in the mire.
[REPEAT REFRAIN]

We are not daily beggars
That beg from door to door,
But we are neighbors' children
Whom you have seen before
[REPEAT REFRAIN]

We have a little purse
Made of ratching leather skin;
We want some of your small change
To line it well within.
[REPEAT REFRAIN]

Bring us out a table
And spread it with a cloth;
Bring us out a cheese,
And of your Christmas loaf.
[REPEAT REFRAIN]

God bless the master of this house,
Likewise the mistress too;
And all the little children
That round the table go.
[REPEAT REFRAIN]

Copyright Asteria Books 2018

Yule Ritual

MATERIALS
- Stang, candle, lighter
- Cauldron, water, lancet
- Anvil, hammer
- Three knives (red, black, white)
- Triple Cord
- Bread, lipped dish or bowl
- Red wine, cup
- Incense, holder, charcoal
- Log, candles, evergreen clippings, firepit/hearth
- Bells

RAISE THE STANG

LAY THE COMPASS

RAISE THE CASTLES (beginning with the Castle of Glass)

OPEN THE GATES

WORKING

- YULE LOG - There are a few different ways to incorporate a Yule log into your celebrations. We're talking about the wooden log here, not the cake roll, by the way. It can be cut from the base of your Yule tree, a piece held in reserve from your Maypole or Beltaine fire, or specially selected log that has no other connections. Contemporarily, these are often decorated with evergreen bows and sometimes set with candles. Inscribe it with sigils of prosperity and protection, as this is what the Yule Log represents.
- VIGIL FIRE ~ Like you did last year, keep a fire burning all night — this time using your Yule Log as a focal point. Either set candles on/in it or burn it in your hearth/firepit. Stay with it, tending to it as needed. This isn't always an easy task. The night is long. It invariably becomes a time for self-reflection, much as the winter itself is. But it can also be a time for mirth, family, friends, feasting, and craft. (Feel free to wassail THE TREES AGAIN, IF YOU LIKE!)
- BELL RINGING - Welcome the dawn with the sound of bells. Greet the sun with joy and triumph, ringing out the darkness and welcoming back the return of the light.

HOUSLE

Copyright Asteria Books 2022

Yule Mysteries

At Yuletide, it is our custom to explore the Mysteries of:

"Robin and Wren"/"Oak King and Holly King" — Here in the darkest time of year is a good time to consider the power of solitude, contemplation, and thriftiness (as well as how these things balance with community, activity, and abundance).

"What is seen by Odin's eye" — The Glass Orb is the vessel associated with the Winter Solstice. It can be thought of as Odin's eye, in addition to its associations with the Adder's Egg or glain. Spend some time with this vessel and consider what it reveals.

Imbolc

Imbolc is the mid-point between Winter Solstice and Spring Equinox. It is the time of the year when one begins to notice that the sunlight is waxing once again. In colder climes, like the ones many of our European pagan forebears lived in, this would have been the coldest part of the year. They would know that Spring was on its way, but there was very little physical evidence in the land that gave obvious witness to this fact. In fact, the returning light was about the only thing that really heralded the return of warmth and growth. Because this was the time of year that the ewes would come into their milk (for the lambs they were about to bear), the holiday was named "Oimelc" in some places. For human women, too, this could be a season of birth. (A woman who gets pregnant at Beltaine, and carries the baby to term, will be in labor near the beginning of February.)

Brighid is associated with this holiday due, in part, to her association with birthing and midwifery. She was one of the highly loved and honored pan-Celtic Goddesses, and this was an ideal holiday for celebrating her role as midwife and mother. Because of this, some traditions refer to this holiday as "Brighid" or "The Feast of Brighid" or even "Bride's Day" in honor of her.

Some traditional witches work within the Celtic framework of the John Barley-Corn cycle. At this time of year, John Barley-Corn would be in the womb, waiting to be born. As a part of the John Barley-Corn celebrations, the last mug of beer and the last loaf of bread would be drunk and eaten to help revitalize John Barley-Corn.

Many traditions send the Gods to their rest around the time of Samhain. Among those that do, there is a portion who would be calling the Gods back to life and fertility at this time of year, leaving them to rest during the darkest part of the cycle.

Candlemas, a festival that the Christians picked up on some centuries ago, is also associated with this time of year. Many covens use this time of returning light to make and/or bless their candles. This is not surprising, as Imbolc was one of the four great fire festivals of the Celts.

Fire and Ice are common themes (very often in conjunction) for this festival, as the hope of spring stirs beneath the frozen land.

In American Folkloric Craft, Kolyo (the Black Goddess) is honored at this time.

Copyright Asteria Books 2019

Imbolc Ritual

MATERIALS
- Stang, candle, lighter
- Three knives (red, black, white)
- Red Cord
- Bread, lipped dish or bowl
- Red wine, cup
- Incense, holder, charcoal
- Skull
- Novena candle, Kolyo label, packing tape
- Florida Water or other perfume

RAISE THE STANG

LAY THE COMPASS

OPEN THE GATES (beginning in the North)

WORKING
- Kolyo Candle ~ Affix a Kolyo candle label onto a novena jar candle. Or draw Kolyo sigils onto a glass jar. Hold the jar between both hands and send energy into it while you seethe (next). Once ready, keep this candle on your altar all year long. If needed, you can transfer the flame and every into a new novena.
- Seething ~ Rock back and forth, side to side, in a circle or however the energy encourages you. Whisper or intone the name Kolyo while you do this. Enliven the candle with the Kolyo energy you are raising.
- Uneasy Seat ~ When you feel compelled to stop, allow yourself to sit still for a moment, sensing the energies around you. Focus on Kolyo and listen for Her voice in your mind and in your heart. Allow your spirit to sense Her and be in communication. See Her, hear Her, feel Her, smell Her, taste Her. Be in close contact with Her. Understand the messages She has for you. Let this continue until you are ready to stop, or She is. Dab Florida Water or another perfume onto your hands, feet, and the back of your neck to fully end the session and come back to yourself (and only yourself).

HOUSLE

Copyright Asteria Books 2018

Imbolc Ritual

Materials
- Stang, candle, lighter
- Cauldron, water, lancet
- Anvil, hammer
- Three knives (red, black, white)
- Triple Cord
- Bread, lipped dish or bowl
- Red wine, cup
- Incense, holder, charcoal
- Hood (veil, large scarf, shawl)
- Taper or pillar candle, ice cubes, bowl
- Florida Water

Raise the Stang

Lay the Compass

Open the Gates (beginning in the North)

Raise the Castles

Working
- Fire & Ice ~ Place a taper or pillar candle in a bowl surrounded by ice cubes. You can dress the candle in oil and herbs, if you like. Light the candle and spend some time in contemplation of the dynamic between Fire and Ice in our lives. Think about the need for both action and stillness. Consider the destruction of both obsession and immobilization. How does this play out for you in your personal life? Professional life? How do you see this manifesting in the world around you? Be encouraged to take in more than just visual stimulus from this experience. Reach out to feel the heat and cold with your hands (safely, of course). Smell the burning wick and the scent of the ice. Taste/eat an ice cube. (It's not off-limits.) Listen to the crackling of the flame and the popping or dripping of the ice. You might be surprised what insights you have when you immerse yourself in the full sensory experience.
- Veiling ~ Cover your head and obscure

Copyright Asteria Books 2022

Imbolc Ritual

your vision with your hood, veil, scarf, or shawl. Kolyo, whom we particularly honor at Imbolc, is the "Covered One," and one way we can better access her wisdom is to take a moment to block out visual sensations and turn our thoughts toward the inner landscape.

- S℮℮thing ~ Rock back and forth, side to side, in a circle or however the energy encourages you. As discussed in lesson 07-04, the movement will likely start as something controlled and conscious; but the goal is to get out of your own way and allow the energy to move freely through you. Whisper or intone the name Kolyo while you do this.
- Un℮asy S℮at Upon Ca℮r Ochr℮n~ When you feel compelled to stop, allow yourself to sit still for a moment, sensing the energies around you. You will likely still feel wonky at this point, like you're moving. Maybe you are a little. All of that is okay. Focus on Kolyo and listen for Her voice in your mind and in your heart. Allow your spirit to sense Her and be in communication. See Her, hear Her, feel Her, smell Her, taste Her. Be in close contact with Her. Understand the messages She has for you. Let this continue until you are ready to stop, or She is. Dab Florida Water or another perfume onto your hands, feet, and the back of your neck to fully end the session and come back to yourself (and only yourself).

Housle

Imbolc Mysteries

At Imbolctide, it is our custom to explore the Mysteries of:

"Uneasy Seat Above Caer Ochren" — This is a wonderful time to explore the Mysteries of oracular work. Our Tradition associates Imbolc with invoking Kolyo and asking for Her guidance and wisdom on Her most holy day. She often reveals Her own Mysteries, but the process itself has much to impart, as well.

"The Light in the Darkness, the Darkness in the Light" — Kolyo and Goda share this Mystery, which they teach us using different methods. Starlight in an inky sky. Stark shadows in the brightest sun. Nakedness. Cloaking. Youth. Age. Nothing is as straightforward as it seems. First impressions are often deceiving.

"The Staff" — All of the weapons and vessels of the Spiral Castle carry their own Mysteries. When contemplating the lessons of the Staff, think of its many forms and functions — walking stick, battle-staff/quarter-staff, lantern pole, sounding rod, spear, arrow, wand, hobby horse, tein, distaff.

"Fire and Ice" — Climate change notwithstanding, Imbolc tends to be the coldest and bleakest of the Sabbats in North America. But "far beneath the winter snows, a heart of fire beats and glows." This is a great time to ponder what unseen things are happening during periods of rest.

Copyright Asteria Books 2022

Spring Equinox

It seems that the most popular and common name for this holiday (and many of the traditions surrounding it) has sprung from the not-so-common (in her own time) Teutonic Goddess Eostre (or Ostara). She was a fertility Goddess whose symbols were bunnies and eggs and the like. The idea of fertility is linked closely with this time of the year, and even the early Church couldn't get rid of the symbols. It is them, in fact, that we have to thank for popularizing the name and spreading the love of sweet Eostre's bunnies far and wide.

Within traditions that focus on the cycles of the sun, this is one of the four major events in the year. The vernal equinox is the solar event that marks the point of balance between day and night, while moving into longer and longer days. It is viewed as a time of balance with the understanding that we are moving into a time of increased light, action, and fertility.

Within the Greek cycle of the Eleusian Mysteries, this is the time when Persephone returns from her stay with her husband, Hades, in the Underworld. She is welcomed home by her rejoicing mother, Demeter, who is a Goddess of the fields. During Persephone's long absence, the fields gave no food and the land was dark and cold. With her return, flowers spring to life at her feet and the land is blessed with fertility. This is the joy of the reunion between mother and daughter.

This is also one of the two times of year attributed to Aphrodite's ritual cleansing and sacred bath. As such, some groups use this as a time of cleansing and renewal. Indeed, "spring cleaning" after a long winter is in order for most homes, and spiritual spring cleaning is a wise course of action, as well.

The Great Rite, in symbol or truth, can be done at this time in keeping with the fertility running so rampant in the land.

For groups who work with a John Barley-Corn myth cycle, little John is born (planted) at this holiday.

Copyright Asteria Books 2019

Spring Equinox Ritual

Materials
- Stang, candle, lighter
- Three knives (red, black, white)
- Red Cord
- Bread, lipped dish or bowl
- Red wine, cup
- Incense, holder, charcoal
- Skull
- Broom (ritual besom or practical broom)
- Shell, water, salt, evergreen sprig
- Candle, oil lamp, or lantern

Raise the Stang

Lay the Compass

Open the Gates (beginning in the North)

Working
- Cleansing the Space ~ Using the Cleansing Chants and accompanying tools (broom, saltwater in a shell with evergreen sprig, smoking incense, and lantern or lamp) energetically clean and cleanse the sacred space in which you work. You can, of course, go a step further and cleanse the whole house and/or property. Visualize all the staleness of winter, all the remnants of last year's harvest, all being swept and washed away.
- Cleansing the Self ~ Using the same tools, energetically cleanse yourself. You probably already bathed before ritual, but you can use these same tools to cleanse yourself and your energy. The broom is the only one that may feel awkward, due to size and shape. Use the evergreen sprig instead.
- Standing the Broom ~ Center yourself in your newly cleansed space. Feel the balance within you. Work on finding that external point of balance, via the broom. Try to get it to stand on its own long enough and steady enough that you can walk away from it. Once you've found the "sweet spot," it's often easy to do again and again -- any day of the year.

Housle

Copyright Asteria Books 2018

Spring Equinox Ritual

Materials
- Stang, candle, lighter
- Cauldron, water, lancet
- Anvil, hammer
- Three knives (red, black, white)
- Triple Cord
- Bread, lipped dish or bowl
- Red wine, cup
- Incense, holder, charcoal
- Three eggs (room-temperature, uncooked, organic)
- Candle
- Anointing/Blessing Oil, pray bottle, water

Raise the Stang

Lay the Compass

Raise the Castles (beginning with the Castle of Revelry)

Open the Gates

Working
- Blessing the Eggs ~ Eggs are symbolic of new life and the Sun. Hold all three eggs, in turn, up to the light of the candle flame to empower and bless them.
- Balancing the Eggs ~ Name and mark the eggs (Home, Compass, Self). Find the balance-point of each, if you can. Take your time. Make note of any challenges you face.
- Egg Cleansing ~ Eggs act as sponges, absorbing illness, negativity, and evil. Pass each of the eggs over, through, and around the space they are named for. Use strokes that move top to bottom, left to right, and clockwise (as appropriate). Only touch the body with the egg if you are experiencing pain or illness in a given area (and then, only touch that area). Dispose of the eggs under a tree away from your home, in a moving natural water source, or at a crossroads.
- Sealing the Work ~ Use an anointing or blessing oil (even as simple as frankincense diluted in olive oil) to seal the work on yourself by rubbing the oil through your hands and over your body, from the feet up. Add a few drops of the same oil to a water bottle and spritz your Home and Compass, as well.

Housle

Copyright Asteria Books 2018

Spring Equinox Mysteries

At Imbolctide, it is our custom to explore the Mysteries of:

"The Broom" — In his letters to Joe Wilson, Robert Cochrane discusses what we call "The Mystery of the Broom." He sums it up using the enigmatic phrase "spinning without motion between three elements." The Broom as a transvective tool allows us to MOVE between the Realms — without necessarily moving our bodies at all.

"The Golden Lantern" — All of the vessels and weapons of the Spiral Castle impart their own Mysteries. To better understand the inspiration, poetry, art, and illusion of the Golden Lantern, consider the Sun in alchemy and classical astrology, will o' th' wisps and foxfire in Irish and Appalachian lore, the rays of Awen, and tales of magic lamps.

Copyright Asteria Books 2022

Beltaine

Beltaine is one of four Celtic fire festivals that are associated with the agricultural turns of the seasons. It is, therefore, one of the Greater Sabbats, and it marks the opposite end of the Wheel from Samhain. Traditional Beltaine activities include blowing horns (a symbol of the male reproductive power) and gathering flowers, making garlands, and hanging greenery (flowers being the symbols of female fertility). Hawthorn was especially sacred to this holiday. In fact, old traditions dictate that the date of Beltaine is set by the flowering of the local Hawthorn tree, and the Hawthorn was usually the tree of choice for the Maypole. The Maypole itself would be symbol of male and female fertility conjoined once the dance was complete and the ribbons had been snugly wrapped about the pole. (While frolicsome and youthful, this is certainly not a dance for children, as it has become in modern culture.)

Beltaine is linked to the Sacred Marriage (hieros gamos) and fertility almost universally. Many Wiccan trads see this as the wedding day of the May Queen and May King. Mothers and fertility are especially honored, and the contemporary secular holiday of Mother's Day (which occurs within about a week of Beltaine) may have Pagan roots associated with this festival.

Communing with fairies has frequently been associated with this holiday, and a lot of lore surrounds ways to contact and work with fairy energy during this time for those who feel inclined to contact the Good Neighbors.

Sacred bonfires were used in many ways in May Day celebrations. Many people would jump balefires for fertility or pass cattle and other livestock between bonfires for protection, fertility, purification.

Walpurgisnacht is a May Eve celebration that originated in Southern Germany (Bavaria). Its purpose is to scare away all the evil spirits that lurk in the shadows before the bright day of Beltaine. Interestingly, Walpurgis is the name of both a well-known nun and a famous witch, but it doesn't seem to have been a Goddess name.

Within American Folkloric Craft, Lucifer-Qayin is honored as the May-King and the Lord of the East, the direction associated with Beltaine on the Year Wheel.

Copyright Asteria Books 2019

Beltaine Ritual

Materials
- Stang, candle, lighter
- Three knives (red, black, white)
- Red Cord
- Bread, lipped dish or bowl
- Red wine, cup
- Mugwort, lemongrass (1/2 tsp each)
- Honey
- Incense, holder, charcoal
- Skull

Raise the Stang

Lay the Compass

Open the Gates (beginning in the East)

Working

- **Sabbat Wine** ~ Prepare Sabbat Wine for yourself by steeping a tablespoon of mugwort (or a blend of mugwort and lemongrass) in a cup of warm red wine for 10 minutes. Remove the herbs (easiest done when using a tea ball), and add raw honey to sweeten. I like to use a local sweet red wine and local honey, as well as local herbs (when I can get them). Drink the wine without gulping or chugging. Give it time to work with you to open your psychic senses.
- **Guided Meditation** ~ Journey through the Walpurgisnacht Flight guided meditation either by reading it aloud while recording (prior to ritual) and then playing it back for yourself during the ritual, or by reading through the meditation prior to ritual so that you are familiar enough with the steps, and then doing your best to follow those steps without guidance. You can also read through the meditation after you feel the soft focus from the wine wash over you, doing what you can to walk between the worlds of reading and meditating. (Or you can listen to the recorded version on the RTA YouTube channel.)

Housle

Copyright Asteria Books 2018

Walpurgisnacht Flight

Close your eyes and and follow your breath. Take long, slow inhalations, followed by long, slow exhalations. As you breathe, you notice a white mist settling around your body. It quickly becomes a thick fog obscuring sight and sound. The fog is cool and numbing, and you find yourself a little tingling and disoriented. A strange heaviness pervades your body as you continue to breathe deeply, in and out. After a moment, the fog begins to lift, and you also feel lighter. You stand, gripping your Stang and use it as a walking stick. You move a few paces off, and the fog clings a little less, though you still can't see where you are. You take another step and are able to recognize your surroundings, though they look altered in ways that are difficult to describe fully. You notice yourself and your surroundings for a moment, seeing both this familiar place and your own self with the eyes of Spirit. You move out of this familiar space and into unknown territory. You're surprised how rapidly the landscape shifts into unfamiliar scenery. You may have thought you knew this place well, but only a few yards from familiar ground, you find yourself confronted with a hedgerow unlike any that could have been there before. It is thick, dense, made of several kinds of hedge trees, and it is quite a lot taller than most hedges. Far on the other side of this hedge, the Dancing Place of the Witches awaits you. You can hear the distant call of the pipes and drums and bells. The sounds are so distant, you are sure it isn't your ears that hear them. You smell the wood smoke and feast meats. You can taste the promise of mead and kisses and laughter beyond this hedge. You look down the row to the left and the right and don't see a gate. There may be one if you talk a walk, of course. A rabbit pops up from a burrow about six feet away from you. Yes, *under is an option. You lean on your Stang to think and it leans back. Ah! Over it is.* You straddle the Stang and lift into air. You notice a star shining from the candle flame between the horns of the Stang and are reminded of the iron foot at the base. Be aware of the sensations you experience as you mount the Stang. From above the hedge, you notice a wild landscape. A patchwork of ancient forests, fertile countryside, villages, hills, and a mountain range looming in the distance. It is here where the Witches dance. The peak you seek is the Brocken. The highest. Your soul knows the way. You land at the Hexentanzenplatz (Witches' Dancing Place) to find the Sabbat in full revelry. More Witches than you'd ever dreamed are gathered here. Witches of every color, from every place, who have made covenant with the Witchfather are here to celebrate the great Beltaine Sabbat. And not just Witches are here. As you take a moment to observe the stunning spectacle, you see many Familiars, too. This Dance is a revel for all the senses and offers any delights you care to indulge. Food, sex, music, drink, wisdom, mysticism, laughter, scent, beauty, inspiration. You stay as long as you choose, taking your fill, before eventually returning the way you came (across the sky, over the hedge, and back into the fog).

Copyright Asteria Books 2018

Beltaine Ritual

Materials
- Stang, candle, lighter
- Cauldron, water, lancet
- Anvil, hammer
- Three knives (red, black, white)
- Triple Cord
- Bread, lipped dish or bowl
- Red wine, cup
- Incense, holder, charcoal
- Firepit, cast iron cauldron
- Sacred woods bundle

Candle

Raise the Stang

Lay the Compass

Open the Gates (beginning in the East)

Working
- Lighting the Balefire ~ It is best if you can perform this ritual outdoors, but hearth and cauldron options are available for indoors, if needed. (It is also ideal if this fire is either at the East or Center point of your Compass, if possible.) Whether you are able to light a campfire, cauldron-fire, hearthfire, or bonfire, add a bundle of Sacred Woods (ie, any of the trees we work with as Allies). You can use logs, branches, twigs, or shavings – depending on the size of the fire and your access to the woods. Light the fire in a manner that you consider sacramental and respectful.
- The Second Flame ~ Light your candle (or light a second cauldron or campfire) from the flames of the first. Place this second flame at either the East or Center point of your Compass, forming a passage between the two flames.
- Balefire Blessings ~ Your balefire is a very propitious fire for all manner of magic. Write and burn petition papers. Jump the fire for luck, health, and protection. Pass yourself and members of your household (including pets) between the two flames for prosperity and protection. (You can use poppets of them, if they can't be present.) Meditate and scry in the flames for messages.

Housle

Copyright Asteria Books 2022

Beltaine Mysteries

At Beltainetide, it is our custom to explore the Mysteries of:

"Life in Death; Death in Life" — This is a phrase we use to reference something very fundamental to this Tradition. While the WitchMother isn't particular prominent at this Sabbat, this phrase IS. (And this phrase is very much associated with Her.) This Mystery is also very present with us at Samhain.

"The Sword That Cuts Both Ways" — All of the weapons and vessels of the Spiral Castle impart their own lessons and Mysteries. The Sword (weapon of the East Gate) has much to teach. One of the ways it shows up is as the Sword Bridge that we cross into the place of Initiation. As such, we name the Coven Sword as "The Sword That Cuts Both Ways."

Copyright Asteria Books 2022

Midsummer

The Summer Solstice is considered one of the Lesser Sabbats to most Neo-Pagans, since it is one of the solar holidays. It is the longest day of the year, and the shortest night. Many Wiccan groups refer to this holiday as Litha.

The Oak King and Holly King story is once again enacted, and this time the Holly King takes power and the light of the sun begins to diminish. The Holly King is the ruler of the dark half of the year, and his reign signals the beginning of the sun's wane in energy.

In a spiritual sense, many groups typically view this holiday in terms of its influence on their own power and ability. This is the height of the active force in nature, and the ultimate display of our own potential and ability to put our plans into action. The sun on this day reminds us of our own potential for greatness. It also reminds us that this potential does have an upward limit, but we can strive to reach that potential by calling on all our resources.

Traditionally, this holiday has a strong historical association with fairies. In fact, it is only eclipsed by Samhain in terms of fairy lore. Unlike Samhain, however, those wishing to experience a positive interaction with the Good Neighbors are more likely to do so at this Sabbat. Be cautious and do your research, though. Fairies are tricky, even when the sun is shining!

Since this is the shortest night of the year, it is a traditional bonfire vigil (and revel) night. Fireworks, lanterns, fire-dancing, and more all common practices today that stem from traditional Celtic roots. Unlike Yule vigils, which often test endurance after the merriment of the feast has faded, Midsummer revels are frolicsome and fast.

Solar and fire Deities are often called at this time, as are those who represent action, potential, and drive.

Within American Folkloric Tradition, we associate the Oak King with Cernunnos and Herne, the Lords of the forest and the hunt.

Copyright Asteria Books 2019

Midsummer Ritual

Materials
- Stang, candle, lighter
- Cauldron, water, lancet
- Anvil, hammer
- Three knives (red, black, white)
- Triple Cord
- Bread, lipped dish or bowl
- Red wine, cup
- Incense, holder, charcoal
- St. John's Wort, Vervain, Mugwort, and Yarrow
- Sticks, twigs, stones, leaves, etc
- Cream

Raise the Stang
Lay the Compass
Open the Gates (beginning in the East)
Working
- Fair Herbs ~ Obtain (gather, if you can) some of the herbs associated with the Good Neighbors. These include St. John's Wort, Vervain, Mugwort, and Yarrow. These particular herbs have a reputation for attracting friendly fey folk, while warding against less friendly ones. Twist them into a wreath/crown, tie them with a ribbon, or pack into a pouch. However you arrange them, wear or carry them on you as you work today/tonight.
- Faerie House ~ In some outside space, build a little house of twigs, grasses, herbs, stones, and leaves. You can use twine, jute, or long blades of grass to bind pieces together — or just rely on gravity. I like to keep the house as natural as possible, while still making it interesting. The "Fey" can be seen as Spirits of the Dead, landwights, nature Spirits, and by other descriptors used across cultures for similar types of beings. You are offering this house as a vessel — most likely to a landwight. For now, don't ask or expect anything in return. (You may eventually build a relationship, but right now, you are just being a good neighbor to the Good Neighbors.) NOTE: I like to build a Stone Castle, if I'm able, since this is the Sabbat that aligns with that Watchtower.
- Offering ~ Leave a little cream, honey, and/or whiskey in a leaf, piece of bark, or a cupped stone.

Housle

Copyright Asteria Books 2022

Midsummer Ritual

Materials
- Stang, candle, lighter
- Three knives (red, black, white)
- Red Cord
- Bread, lipped dish or bowl
- Red wine, cup
- Incense, holder, charcoal
- Skull
- Fire pit, fire wood, kindling OR
- Cauldron, Epsom salt, rubbing alcohol
- Recorded music or musical instruments, drums, etc.

Raise the Stang

Lay the Compass

Open the Gates (beginning in the East)

Working

    Bonfire or Cauldron Fire ~ This is best done outside, for obvious reasons, but it is possible to build a very, very small sacred fire indoors in a cauldron with Epsom salt and rubbing alcohol. Another alternative is to place a candle in your cauldron. Of course, the preference here is to build a fire outside, if at all possible. It doesn't have to be large. Midsummer fires are wonderful for revelry, music, dancing, and the high spirits that come with the joys of summer. Play music, make music. Dance. The type of music and style of dance don't matter. Get your blood up, your energy up. Have fun! Keep it going as long into the night as you like. This is a celebration of life, io the ability to DO, and of the ripeness of the world.

Housle

Copyright Asteria Books 2018

Midsummer Mysteries

At Midsummerstide, it is our custom to explore the Mysteries of:

"Robin and Wren"/"Oak King and Holly King" — Here in the lightest time of year is a good time to consider the power of community, activity, and abundance (as well as how these things balance with solitude, contemplation, and thriftiness).

"The Stone Bowl" — All of the vessels and weapons of the Spiral Castle carry their own Mysteries. The Stone Bowl reminds us that "There is no magic without sacrifice" — a phrase which we often paint or carve on the bottom of this dish.

Copyright Asteria Books 2022

Lughnasadh

Lughnasadh is another of the Greater Sabbats, one of the High Holy Days - a Celtic fire festival based on the agricultural wheel. It is named after the Pan-Celtic God Lugh whose name comes from "lugio" meaning "oath" - marriages and other contracts were made at this time. Both the Welsh stories of Lleu and the Irish ones of Lugh are very much tied up with oaths, promises, and bonds.

Another name for this holiday is Lammas, which means "loaf mass." Because this is the first of the harvest festivals, grain and the first fruits were often blessed and honored at this holiday. The loaf mass was a Catholic adaptation of the blessing of the grain that clearly had Pagan roots. This holiday gave rise to country fairs that still happen (and are particularly popular in the Midwestern United States) at this time of year. The country craft fairs also give unknown honor to Lugh in another way (since he is the master of all crafts).

Lughnasadh is named after Lugh because he instituted funeral games in honor of Tailtiu, his foster-mother, who died after clearing a forest for cultivation.

Traditional activities include picking bilberries (as representative of all of Earth's bounty), playing games, having contests of wit and strength, and making a corn dolly. The corn dolly represents the harvest itself and is ploughed or burned in the spring to prepare for the next sowing and harvest cycle.

Obviously, Lugh is the most obvious Deity for this holiday, as it is his festival. However, other commonly honored at this time of year include the Dagda (and other regional harvest Deities) and Tailtiu.

Within American Folkloric Witchcraft, this holiday is sacred to Goda, the White Goddess of the land.

Copyright Asteria Books 2019

Lughnasadh Ritual

MATERIALS
- Stang, candle, lighter
- Three knives (red, black, white)
- Red Cord
- Bread, lipped dish or bowl
- Red wine, cup
- Incense, holder, charcoal
- Skull
- Green corn husks (removed from corn), twine/cord
- Bread, corn, tomatoes, melons, local seasonal produce

RAISE THE STANG

LAY THE COMPASS

OPEN THE GATES (beginning in the South)

WORKING
- CORN DOLLY ~ Fashion a human-shaped figure from the corn husks, using the string to tie the head, body, arms, and legs. Place on your altar and allow to dry. Name your doll.
- FIRST FRUITS FEAST ~ Offer a blessing of the seasonal fruits, vegetables, and grains. Place some of each in the sacrificial bowl before consuming them for yourself. Give thanks to Goda for the bounty. Eat and enjoy!
- OATH TAKING ~ Consider an area of your life that needs a commitment from you. Make an oath to improve or address that area. Be specific. Write down the oath in your journal. Hold yourself accountable for it.

HOUSLE

Copyright Asteria Books 2018

Lughnasadh Ritual

MATERIALS
- Stang, candle, lighter
- Cauldron, water, lancet
- Anvil, hammer
- Three knives (red, black, white)
- Triple Cord
- Bread, lipped dish or bowl
- Red wine, cup
- Incense, holder, charcoal
- Corn dolly
- Bread man
- Fresh seasonal fruits and vegetables (local is best)

RAISE THE STANG

LAY THE COMPASS

OPEN THE GATES (beginning in the South)

RAISE THE CASTLES

WORKING
- CORN DOLLY ~ Fashion a human-shaped figure from the corn husks, using the string to tie the head, body, arms, and legs. Place on your altar and allow it to dry. Name your doll.
- FIRST FRUITS FEAST ~ Offer a blessing of the seasonal fruits, vegetables, and grains. Place some of each in the sacrificial bowl before consuming them for yourself. Give thanks to Goda for the bounty. Eat and enjoy!
- SACRIFICIAL BREAD MAN ~ Shape and bake a Bread Man. (He can be made of any bread, according to the traditions of your region/family and your baking ability — sourdough, soda bread, cornbread, canned biscuits/rolls.) Sacrifice him with your Red Knife using the words from the Housle and place his body upon the bed of fruits in the sacrificial bowl. All present should eat a portion of the Bread Man, as well.

HOUSLE

Copyright Asteria Books 2022

Lammas Mysteries

At Lammastide, it is our custom to explore the Mysteries of:

"What songs the siren sings?" — Goda is Our Lady of Lammas — a time of sacrifice and also joy, abundance, and oaths. This is a great time to contemplate Goda and her associations with love, loss, reunion of the Soul, and song.

"Uneasy Seat Above Caer Ochren" — This is a wonderful time to explore the Mysteries of oracular work. Our Tradition associates Lammas with invoking Goda and asking for Her guidance and wisdom on Her most holy day. She often reveals Her own Mysteries, but the process itself has much to impart, as well.

"The Dance of the Seven Veils" — Goda stands naked, having shed the veils already. What do we find when we strip away our careers, relationships, memories, bodies, desires, etc. Consider Inanna's descent, and the jewelry/garments she relinquishes at each gate. Consider the 7 classical planets, and the 7 most commonly discussed chakras. Consider the process of aging and death, and how we all eventually "stand naked."

"The Shield" — Each of our vessels and weapons unfolds its own Mysteries. Some are better documented than others in the traditions of the Craft and other Mystery Schools. The Shield is one that gets short shrift in most places, but it is still present and powerful. It is related to the Witch's Glove, the

Copyright Asteria Books 2022

Lammas Mysteries

Pentacle, and even the Cloak (which is a shielding device in myth and literature).

"The Light in the Darkness, the Darkness in the Light" – Kolyo and Goda share this Mystery, which they teach us using different methods. Starlight in an inky sky. Stark shadows in the brightest sun. Nakedness. Cloaking. Youth. Age. Nothing is as straightforward as it seems. First impressions are often deceiving.

Fall Equinox

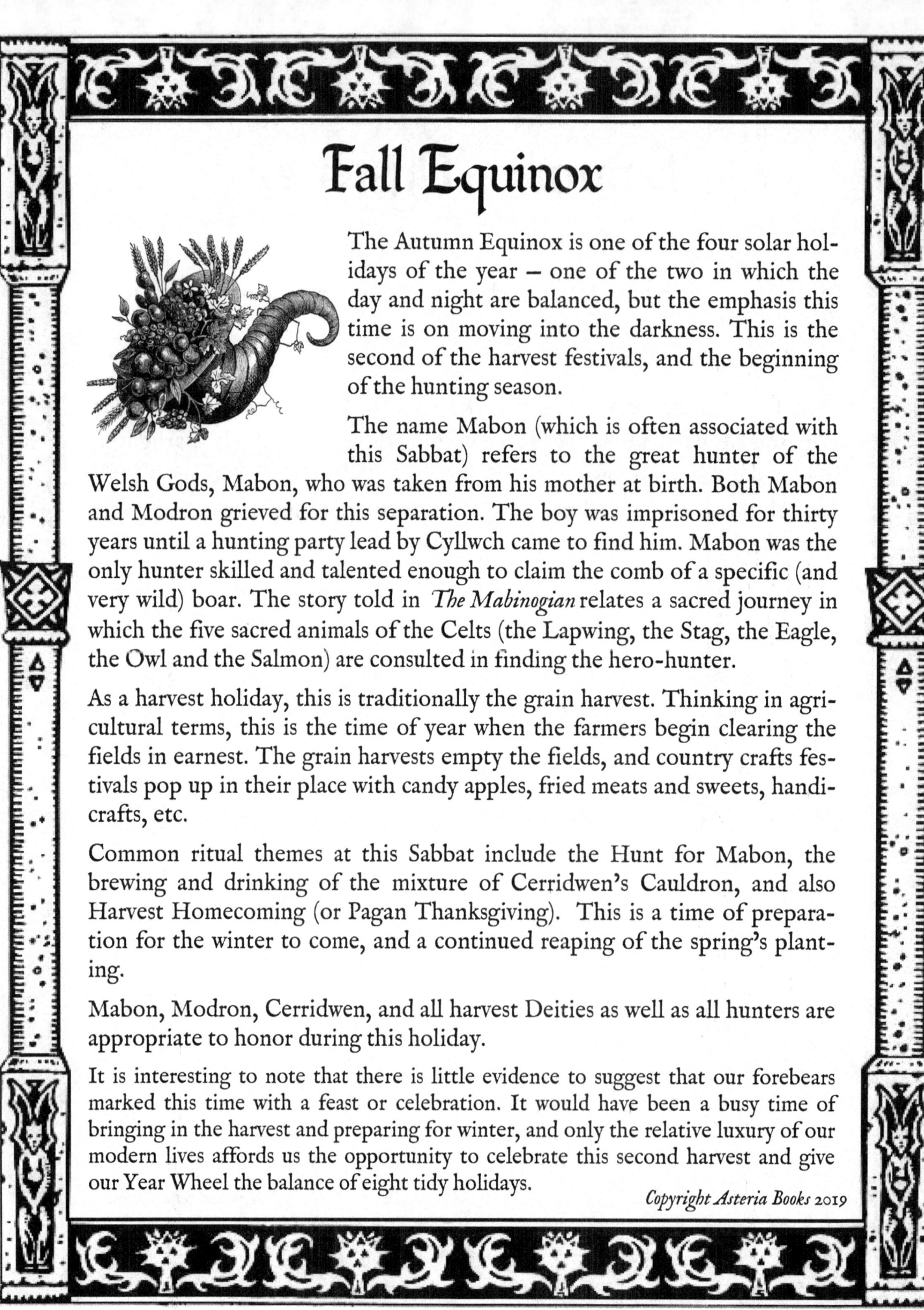

The Autumn Equinox is one of the four solar holidays of the year – one of the two in which the day and night are balanced, but the emphasis this time is on moving into the darkness. This is the second of the harvest festivals, and the beginning of the hunting season.

The name Mabon (which is often associated with this Sabbat) refers to the great hunter of the Welsh Gods, Mabon, who was taken from his mother at birth. Both Mabon and Modron grieved for this separation. The boy was imprisoned for thirty years until a hunting party lead by Cyllwch came to find him. Mabon was the only hunter skilled and talented enough to claim the comb of a specific (and very wild) boar. The story told in *The Mabinogian* relates a sacred journey in which the five sacred animals of the Celts (the Lapwing, the Stag, the Eagle, the Owl and the Salmon) are consulted in finding the hero-hunter.

As a harvest holiday, this is traditionally the grain harvest. Thinking in agricultural terms, this is the time of year when the farmers begin clearing the fields in earnest. The grain harvests empty the fields, and country crafts festivals pop up in their place with candy apples, fried meats and sweets, handicrafts, etc.

Common ritual themes at this Sabbat include the Hunt for Mabon, the brewing and drinking of the mixture of Cerridwen's Cauldron, and also Harvest Homecoming (or Pagan Thanksgiving). This is a time of preparation for the winter to come, and a continued reaping of the spring's planting.

Mabon, Modron, Cerridwen, and all harvest Deities as well as all hunters are appropriate to honor during this holiday.

It is interesting to note that there is little evidence to suggest that our forebears marked this time with a feast or celebration. It would have been a busy time of bringing in the harvest and preparing for winter, and only the relative luxury of our modern lives affords us the opportunity to celebrate this second harvest and give our Year Wheel the balance of eight tidy holidays.

Copyright Asteria Books 2019

Fall Equinox Ritual

MATERIALS
- Stang, candle, lighter
- Cauldron, water, lancet
- Anvil, hammer
- Three knives (red, black, white)
- Triple Cord
- Bread, lipped dish or bowl
- Red wine, cup
- Incense, holder, charcoal
- Harvest Feast foods – try to include chicken, pork, and grape (wine)

RAISE THE STANG

LAY THE COMPASS

RAISE THE CASTLES (beginning with Castle Perilous)

OPEN THE GATES

WORKING
- GATHERING THE FEAST ~ Lay out the food you have prepared/purchased. If you can, include items from this month's Spirit Allies – the Vine, the Swine, and the Chicken. If you are unable (for any reason), try including images or figurines of the animals and/or grapes, in recognition of the generations of Ancestors who were sustained and uplifted by the sacrifice of these Spirits.
- BLESSING THE FEAST ~ This entire Feast is a Housle, so speak and perform the portions of our Housle Rite that bless the Meal.
- OFFERINGS OF GRATITUDE ~ Be sure to include a bit of everything from the Feast/Meal in your offering bowl. As you give each piece, offer gratitude for some aspect of the bounty you have experienced this year. At the end of the meal, offer the contents of the offering bowl as you normally do, with the Declaration, etc.

HOUSLE

Copyright Asteria Books 2022

Fall Equinox Ritual

MATERIALS
- Stang, candle, lighter
- Three knives (red, black, white)
- Red Cord
- Bread, lipped dish or bowl
- Red wine, cup
- Incense, holder, charcoal
- Skull
- "Hunter" mask of your own design and creation
- Animal print-outs (placed around Compass as indicated)
- Mirror (placed at base of Stang)
- Colored pencils, crayons, pen (in a basket or bag that can move with you)

RAISE THE STANG

LAY THE COMPASS

OPEN THE GATES (beginning in the South)

WORKING

- MASKING ~ Create a mask as a representation of the Hunter. Before you don your mask, name it and bless it. Know, as you put it on, that you become one of the hunting party in search for Mabon.
- PURPOSE OF THE HUNT ~ The Harvest is underway and the Dark Days of Winter are approaching. The tribe, the clan, the Family needs the assurance of sustenance during the lean times to come. This is a time to be grateful for the bounty of the Harvest, which is still being brought in, but it is also a time to take action to prepare for the hard times, the lean seasons. The Great Hunter acts a guide to help you, as do the animals who point the way to him.
- HUNT FOR MABON ~ In your reenacted search for the Great Hunter, you will move from one quarter to the next, spending time with each of the Sacred Animals. Begin in the East, with the Lapwing. As you move to each animal, understand that you are seeking their wisdom and guidance. Read the words on the page, then spend some time in reflection, listening for any direct message that animal may have for you. Fully tread the mill between each animal.

HOUSLE

Copyright Asteria Books 2018

Lapwing

Place at the East Gate

LAPWING says:

When I first came to this forest, there was a smith's anvil. No work was done upon that anvil except for the pecking of my beak, and the anvil is now worn down to a speck. In all that time, I have never heard of the man you name. You should seek out the Stag. He has been here far longer than I.

MY REFLECTIONS WITH LAPWING:

Next, seek Stag at South Gate.

Stag

Place at the South Gate

STAG says:

When I first came to this forest, I had only one antler on either side of my head. At that time, there was no tree but a single oak sapling. That sapling grew into an oak of 100 branches, and then fell. Now all that is left is a red stump. During that time, and since then, I have never heard of the man you seek. You should go to the Owl, who has been here much longer than I.

MY REFLECTIONS WITH STAG:

Next, seek OWL at North Gate.

Owl

Place at the North Gate

OWL says:

This great valley was a wooded glen when I first came here. Then men came and destroyed the forest. A second forest grew, and a second time destroyed. This is the third forest, and my wings are now nothing but stumps, but I have never heard of the one you seek. You must seek the Eagle, who is the oldest animal in the forest, and who has traveled the most.

MY REFLECTIONS WITH OWL:

Next, seek ANIMAL at ____ Gate.

Eagle

Place at the South Gate

EAGLE says:

When I first came to this forest, I sat on a stone from which I pecked at the stars every evening. That stone is now worn so low that it is only a hand's breadth high. In all the time I have been here, I've heard nothing of Mabon, except when I made a trip to Llew's Lake for food. I sank my claws into a salmon, but it was stronger than me, and it pulled me under the water. We made peace. That fish is very wise, the wisest in the forest. If he doesn't know of Mabon, nobody in the forest can help you.

MY REFLECTIONS WITH EAGLE:

Next, seek SALMON at West Gate.

Salmon

Place at the West Gate

SALMON says:

I swim upstream on every tide until I reach Gloucester. Near that place I have found such a one as you seek. The Great Hunter for whom you search is imprisoned there. You must free the Hunter.

MY REFLECTIONS WITH SALMON:

Next, seek the Hunter at the Stang.

Mabon/Great Hunter

Place at the Stang

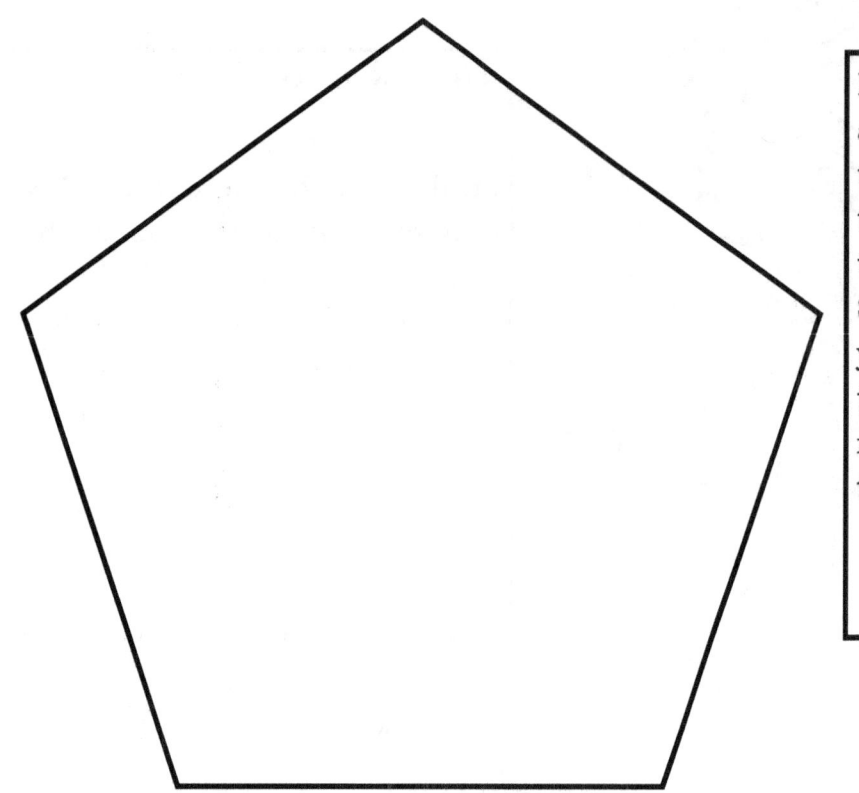

It is up to you to find the Hunter and entirely up to you to hear the Hunter's message for you this Autumn. Record your thoughts and impressions below. Sketch a drawing of the Hunter you found. Make note of any tools at the Stang that were most helpful to you in finding the Hunter.

MY REFLECTIONS WITH MABON/GREAT HUNTER:

Autumn Mysteries

At the Autumnaltide, it is our custom to explore the Mysteries of:

"What the Mask Reveals" — The Spiral Castle Tradition often performs a "Hunt for Mabon" at the Fall Equinox. During this ritual, we usually mask — either as a Hunter or as one of the Five Animals that the hunting party queries. We work with the Mask in order to better understand both ourselves and That which is represented by a specific mask.

"The Mystery of the Cauldron" — Robert Cochrane wrote about the Mystery of the Cauldron in this letters to Joe Wilson. He poses a riddle to Wilson, asking him what can't within the Cauldron. "Two words: Be Still." The Cauldron holds all — all life, all hope, all desire, all abundance, all possibility. It is always moving. Always shifting. Always becoming. There is no stillness in the Cauldron. (But there can be stillness within us, which we find within this tumult.)

"The Bloody Cup/The Holy Grail" — All of the vessels and weapons of the Spiral Castle impart their own Mysteries. This is probably the most well-known of all the Mysteries we seek. The San Greal — or Sang Real.

"The Five Transformations" — Ceridwen is one of the ladies whom we see most clearly as our Silver Queen. She is the keeper of the Cauldron, and her story of flight, pursuit, and transformation with the young Gwion Bach (who becomes Taliesin) is most revealing.

Copyright Asteria Books 2022

Chants and Balladry

On Chants

Of old, there were many chants and songs used, especially in the Dances. Many of these have been forgotten by us here, but we know that they used cries of IAU, which seems much like the cries EVO or EVOHE of the ancients. Much depends on the pronunciation if this be so. In my youth, when I heard IAU it seemed to be AEIOU, or rather, AAAEEIOOOOUU. This may be. The natural way to prolong it to make it fit for a call, but it suggests that these be possibly the initials of an invocation as AGLA is said to be. The whole Hebrew alphabet is said to be such, and for this reason is recited as a most powerful charm. Whatever the case, at least this is certain: these cries during the dances do have profound effect.

Other calls are IEHOUA and EHEIE; also Ho Ho Ho Ise Ise Ise. IEO VEO VEO VEO VEOV OROV OV OVOVO may be a spell but is more likely to be a call. 'Tis like the EVOE EVOE of the Greeks and the "Heave ho!" of sailors. "Emen hetan" and "Ab hur, ab hus" seem calls; as does "Horse and hattock, horse and go, horse and Pellatis, ho, ho, ho!"

"Thout, tout a tout tout, throughout and about" and "Rentum tormentum" are probably mispronounced attempts at a forgotten formula, though they may have been invented by some Unfortunate being tortured to evade telling the real formula.

Mimicking animal sounds is also an ideal way to raise the Power. Howling, as a wolf, crowing as a cock, or any forceful ululation, as the Muse takes you, is entirely appropriate.

Please keep in mind that the larger the group, the smaller and simpler you should strive to keep your chants. Elaborate chants rarely work well with a group unfamiliar with them and can distract the group mind from concentrating on the work itself. Raymond Buckland has some interesting thoughts on this:

What to chant as you dance? You want something simple and something rhythmic. By simple I mean not only non-complex but also intelligible. No mumbo-jumbo! Some covens dance around chanting strange words that no one knows the meaning of. How can you put feeling into what you're saying if you don't know what you're saying?! You are working magick to bring money? ...then chant about bringing money. Why not something like "Lord and Lady, we're your Witches. Make us happy; bring us riches"? It may seem mundane and non-mystical but it's a lot easier to put feeling into that (and to remember the words) than it is into something like "...Lamach, lamach, bacharous, carbahaji, sabalyos, barylos ..." Not only is it simple and more intelligible, but it is rhythmic. There is a definite beat to it that you can put to a dance step.

Copyright Asteria Publishing 2012

Alone
Edgar Allan Poe

From childhood's hour I have not been
As others were—I have not seen
As others saw—I could not bring
My passions from a common spring—
From the same source I have not taken
My sorrow—I could not awaken
My heart to joy at the same tone—
And all I loved—I loved alone—
Then—in my childhood—in the dawn
Of a most stormy life—was drawn
From every depth of good and ill
The mystery which binds me still—
From the torrent, or the fountain—
From the red cliff of the mountain—
From the sun that 'round me rolled
In its autumn tint of gold—
From the lightning in the sky
As it passed me flying by—
From the thunder, and the storm—
And the cloud that took the form
(When the rest of Heaven was blue)
Of a demon in my view—

Cleansing Chants

Each portion of the chant requires a Witch to walk the compass either once or thrice, wielding the appropriate cleansing tools.

With Incense:

Smoke and fume, now as you burn,
cause all harm from us to turn;
let nothing harmful here be found,
as we tread the witch's round.

With Flame:

Fire that burns and light that glows,
send all harm away from us;
let nothing harmful here be found,
as we tread the witch's round.

With Salt Water:

Water and salt, brine of the sea,
wash this circle clean and free;
let nothing harmful here be found,
as we tread the witch's round.

With Broom:

Besom sweep and besom clean;
above, below and in between;
let nothing harmful here be found,
as we tread the witch's round.

Copyright Asteria Publishing 2012

Green Grow the Rushes, O

"Green Grow the Rushes, O" is a counting or teaching song of the type that is called a "chant of the creed." It is alternately entitled "The Dilly Song." Versions of it exist in the Muslim, Jewish, and Christian liturgical canon. THIS version was given to Joe Wilson by Robert Cochrane in their early correspondence.

I'll sing you One-O
Green Grow The Rushes-O
What is your One-O?
Green Grow The Rushes-O
One is One and All Alone,
And ever more shall be so!

I'll sing you Two-O
Green Grow the Rushes-O
What is your Two-O?
Green Grow The Rushes-O!
Two, two, the Lily and the Rose
That shine both red and green-O.
One is One and All Alone,
And ever more shall be so!

Three, three the Rivals
Four for the Four Wind-Makers
Five for the Symbol at my Door
Six for the Lady's Bower
Seven for the Stars of Heaven
Eight for the April Rainers
Nine for the Nine Bright Shiners
Ten for The Lady's Girdle
Eleven Maidens in a Dance
Twelve for the Wren in Ivy

I'll sing you Thirteen-O
Green Grow the Rushes-O
What is your Thirteen-O?
'……………………'

Here We Come A-Wassailing

Here we come a-wassailing
Among the leaves so green,
Here we come a-wand'ring
So fair to be seen.
[REFRAIN]
Love and joy come to you,
And to you your wassail, too,
And God bless you, and send you
A Happy New Year,
And God send you a Happy New Year.

We are not daily beggars
That beg from door to door,
But we are neighbors' children
Whom you have seen before
[REPEAT REFRAIN]

Good master and good mistress,
As you sit beside the fire,
Pray think of us poor children
Who wander in the mire.
[REPEAT REFRAIN]

We have a little purse
Made of ratching leather skin;
We want some of your small change
To line it well within.
[REPEAT REFRAIN]

Bring us out a table
And spread it with a cloth;
Bring us out a cheese,
And of your Christmas loaf.
[REPEAT REFRAIN]

God bless the master of this house,
Likewise the mistress too;
And all the little children
That round the table go.
[REPEAT REFRAIN]

Copyright Asteria Books 2018

Invocation of the Circle

~ Doreen Valiente ~

By stang and cauldron, cup and knife,
By right of office that I hold,
Ye ancient powers of death and life,
Forgather to the circle's fold.

Kinship to kinship, blood to blood,
By wild night wind and starry sky,
By heathland brown and darkling wood,
To this our circle now draw nigh.

In likeness of a henge of stone,
Stand guard around this circle's rim,
While looming through the dark alone,
Stands in the east the Hele-stone dim.

I summon forth the fairy hounds,
Sharp-fanged, white-coated, red of ear,
To prowl beyond the circle's bounds,
And put intruders' hearts in fear.

Ancestral powers of this our blood,
We are your people, guard us well,
By earth and air, by fire and flood,
By magic mime and spoken spell.

Our craft's own Goddess I invoke,
And Ancient Ones of hill and mound.
With fire aflame and drifting smoke,
I dedicate this circle's bound.

By three times three,
Thus shall it be!

Copyright Asteria Books 2019

Invocation of the Horned God

~ Doreen Valiente ~

By the flame that burneth bright,
O Horned One!
We call thy name into the night,
O Horned One!

Thee we invoke by the moon led sea
By the standing stone and the twisted tree
Thee we invoke where gather thine own
By the nameless shrine forgotten and lone

Come where the round of the dance is trod
Horn and hoof of the goat-foot God
By moonlit meadow on dusky hill
When the haunted wood is hushed and still

Come to the charm of the chanted prayer
As the moon bewitches the midnight air
Evoke thy powers, that potent bide
In shining stream and secret tide

In fiery flame by starlight pale
In shadowy host that ride the gale
And by the fern-brakes fairy-haunted
Of forests wild and wood enchanted

Come! O Come!
To the heartbeats drum!

Come to us who gather below
When the broad white moon is climbing slow
Through the stars to the heavens height
We hear thy hoofs on the wind of night
As black tree branches shake and sigh
By joy and terror we know thee nigh

We speak the spell thy power unlocks
At Solstice, Sabbat, and Equinox

Word of virtue the veil to rend
From primal dawn to the wide world's end
Since time began---
The blessing of Pan!

Blessed be all in hearth and hold
Blessed in all worth more than gold
Blessed be in strength and love
Blessed be wher'er we rove

Vision fade not from our eyes
Of the pagan paradise
Past the gates of death and birth
Our inheritance of the earth

From our soul the song of spring
Fade not in our wandering

Our life with all life is one,
By blackest night or noonday sun
Eldest of gods, on thee we call
Blessing be on thy creatures all

Provided by Asteria Books 2022

Macbeth Witches' Chant
William Shakespeare

When shall we three meet again
In thunder, lightning, or in rain?
When the hurlyburly's done,
When the battle's lost and won.
That will be ere the set of sun.
Where the place?
Upon the heath.
There to meet with Macbeth.
I come, graymalkin!
Paddock calls.
Anon!
Fair is foul, and foul is fair:
Hover through the fog and filthy air.

Thrice the brinded cat hath mewed.
Thrice and once, the hedge-pig whined.
Harpier cries:—'tis time! 'tis time!

Round about the cauldron go:
In the poisoned entrails throw.
Toad, that under cold stone
Days and nights has thirty-one
Sweated venom sleeping got,
Boil thou first in the charmed pot.

Double, double toil and trouble;
Fire burn and cauldron bubble.

Fillet of a fenny snake,
In the cauldron boil and bake;
Eye of newt and toe of frog,
Wool of bat and tongue of dog,
Adder's fork and blindworm's sting,
Lizard's leg and howlet's wing.
For charm of powerful trouble,
Like a hell-broth boil and bubble.

Double, double toil and trouble;
Fire burn and cauldron bubble.

Scale of dragon, tooth of wolf,
Witch's mummy, maw and gulf
Of the ravin'd salt-sea shark,
Root of hemlock digg'd in the dark,
Liver of blaspheming Jew;
Gall of goat; and slips of yew
Sliver'd in the moon's eclipse;
Nose of Turk, and Tartar's lips;
Finger of birth-strangled babe
Ditch-deliver'd by a drab,—
Make the gruel thick and slab:
Add thereto a tiger's chaudron,
For ingredients of our cauldron.

Double, double toil and trouble,
Fire burn and cauldron bubble.
Cool it with a baboon's blood,
Then the charm is firm and good.

By the pricking of my thumbs,
Something wicked this way comes.
Open, locks,
Whoever knocks!

Copyright Asteria Publishing 2012

Mill Songs

Treading the Mill is the act of walking 'round the circle while focusing energy on the center. This is sometimes done while chanting to raise power.

The Mill of Magic

Fire flame and fire burn, make the Mill of Magic turn.
Work the Will for which we tread by the Black and White and Red.
Earth without and earth within, make the Mill of Magic spin.
Work the Will for which we tread by the Black and White and Red.
Water bubble, water boil, make the Mill of Magic toil.
Work the Will for which we tread by the Black and White and Red.
Air breathe and air blow, make the Mill of Magic go.
Work the Will for which we tread by the Black and White and Red.

Power of the Elements

Power of Sky and power of Wind and power of Air the North doth send,
We tread the Mill to work our spell, both by your Breath and by out Will.
Power of Spark and power of Fire, power of all our hearts' desire,
We tread the Mill to work our spell, both by your Flame and by out Will.
Power of Ice and Water free and power that hides in depth of Sea,
We tread the Mill to work our spell, both by your Wave and by out Will.
Power of Stone and power of Land and power of rich Soil in our hands,
We tread the Mill to work our spell, both by your Earth and by out Will.

Copyright Asteria Publishing 2012

The Song of Amergin

Chorus:
From the breeze on the mountain
To the lake of deep blue
From the waterfall down to the sea
Never changing or ending on the voice of the wind
Sing now the riddle of Erenn to me

I am the wind that breathes on the sea
I am the wave that roars on the ocean
I am the stag, seven points are my glory
I am the hawk of victory in motion

I am the tomb, so cold in the darkness
I am the ray, bright eye of the Sun
I am a tree, straight, strong and peerless
I am a star, I am the One

I am a wonder, a wonder in flower
I am the spear as it cries out for blood
I am the word, the word of great power
And thrice times have I visited Caer Arianhrod

I am the song of the blackbird in mourning
I am the depths of a sacred pool
I am a boar's tusk flashed out in warning
I am the salmon, yet also the fool

Who but I can cast light upon the meeting of the mountains?
Who but I am a lure beyond the ends of the earth?
Who but I will cry aloud the changes of the moon?
Who but I can find the place of death and rebirth?

The Witches' Creed
Doreen Valiente

Hear now the words of the witches,
The secrets we hid in the night,
When dark was our destiny's pathway,
That now we bring forth into light.

Mysterious water and fire,
The earth and the wide-ranging air,
By hidden quintessence we know them,
And will and keep silent and dare.

The birth and rebirth of all nature,
The passing of winter and spring,
We share with the life universal,
Rejoice in the magical ring.

Four times in the year the Great Sabbat
Returns, and the witches are seen
At Lammas and Candlemas dancing,
On May Eve and old Hallowe'en.

When day-time and night-time are equal,
When sun is at greatest and least,
The four Lesser Sabbats are summoned,
And Witches gather in feast.

Thirteen silver moons in a year are,
Thirteen is the coven's array.
Thirteen times at Esbat make merry,
For each golden year and a day.

The power that was passed down the age,
Each time between woman and man,
Each century unto the other,
Ere time and the ages began.

When drawn is the magical circle,
By sword or athame of power,
Its compass between two worlds lies,
In land of the shades for that hour.
This world has no right then to know it.

And world of beyond will tell naught.
The oldest of Gods are invoked there,
The Great Work of magic is wrought.

For the two are mystical pillars,
That stand at the gate of the shrine,
And two are the powers of nature,
The forms and the forces divine.

The dark and the light in succession,
The opposites each unto each,
Shown forth as a God and a Goddess:
Of this our ancestors teach.

By night he's the wild winds rider,
The Horn'd One, the Lord of the Shades.
By day he's the King of the Woodland,
The dweller in green forest glades.

She is youthful or old as she pleases,
She sails the torn clouds in her barque,
The bright silver lady of midnight,
The crone who weaves spells in the dark.

The master and mistress of magic,
That dwell in the deeps of the mind,
Immortal and ever-renewing,
With power to free or to bind.

So drink the good wine to the Old Gods,
And Dance and make love in their praise,
Till Elphame's fair land shall receive us
In peace at the end of our days.

Copyright Asteria Publishing 2012

The Witches' Rede

Bide within the Law you must, in perfect Love and perfect Trust.

Live you must and let to live, fairly take and fairly give.

For tread the Circle thrice about to keep unwelcome spirits out.

To bind the spell well every time, let the spell be said in rhyme.

Light of eye and soft of touch, speak you little, listen much.

Honor the Old Ones in deed and name,
let love and light be our guides again.

Deosil go by the waxing moon, chanting out the joyful tune.

Widdershins go when the moon doth wane,
and the werewolf howls by the dread wolfsbane.

When the Lady's moon is new, kiss the hand to Her times two.

When the moon rides at Her peak then your heart's desire seek.

Heed the North winds mighty gale, lock the door and trim the sail.

When the Wind blows from the East, expect the new and set the feast.

When the wind comes from the South, love will kiss you on the mouth.

When the wind whispers from the West, all hearts will find peace and rest.

Nine woods in the Cauldron go, burn them fast and burn them slow.

Birch in the fire goes to represent what the Lady knows.

Oak in the forest towers with might, in the fire it brings the God's insight.

Rowan is a tree of power causing life and magic to flower.

Willows at the waterside stand ready to help us to the Summerland.

Hawthorn is burned to purify and to draw faerie to your eye.

Hazel-the tree of wisdom and learning adds its strength to the bright fire burning.

White are the flowers of Apple tree that brings us fruits of fertility.

Grapes grow upon the vine giving us both joy and wine.

Fir does mark the evergreen to represent immortality seen.

Elder is the Lady's tree burn it not or cursed you'll be.

Four times the Major Sabbats mark in the light and in the dark.

As the old year starts to wane the new begins, it's now Samhain.

When the time for Imbolc shows watch for flowers through the snows.

When the wheel begins to turn soon the Beltane fires will burn.

As the wheel turns to Lammas night power is brought to magick rite.

Four times the Minor Sabbats fall use the Sun to mark them all.

When the wheel has turned to Yule light the log the Horned One rules.

In the spring, when night equals day time for Ostara to come our way.

When the Sun has reached it's height time for Oak and Holly to fight.

Harvesting comes to one and all when the Autumn Equinox does fall.

Heed the flower, bush, and tree by the Lady blessed you'll be.

Where the rippling waters go cast a stone, the truth you'll know.

When you have and hold a need, harken not to others greed.

With a fool no season spend or be counted as his friend.

Merry Meet and Merry Part bright the cheeks and warm the heart.

Mind the Three-fold Laws you should three times bad and three times good.

When misfortune is enow wear the star upon your brow.

Be true in love this you must do unless your love is false to you.

Eight words the Witches' Rede fulfill:
"An Ye Harm None, Do What Ye Will"

Copyright Asteria Publishing 2012

The Witches' Rune

By Doreen Valiente

Darksome night and shining moon,
East then South then West then North;
Hearken to the Witches' Rune:
Here come I to call ye forth!

Earth and Water, Air and Fire,
Wand and Pentacle and Sword,
Work ye unto my desire,
Hearken ye unto my word!

Cords and Censer, Scourge and Knife,
Powers of the witch's blade,
Waken all ye unto life,
Come ye as the charm is made!

Queen of Heaven, Queen of Hell,
Horned Hunter of the night,
Lend your power unto the spell,
Work my will by magick rite!

By all the power of land and sea,
By all the might of moon and sun,
As I do will, so mote it be;
Chant the spell and be it done!

The Witches' Ballad
Doreen Valiente

Oh, I have been beyond the town
Where nightshade black and mandrake grow
And I have heard and I have seen
What righteous folk would fear to know!
For I have heard, at still midnight
Upon the hilltop far, forlorn
With note that echoed through the dark
The winding of the heathen horn
And I have seen the fire aglow
And glinting from the magic sword
And with the inner eye beheld
The Hornid One, the Sabbat's lord
We drank the wine, and broke the bread
And ate it in the Old One's name
We linked our hands to make the ring
And laughed and leaped the Sabbat game
Oh, little do the townsfolk reck
When dull they lie within their bed!
Beyond the streets, beneath the stars
A merry round the witches tread!
And round and round the circle spun
Until the gates swung wide ajar
That bar the boundaries of earth
From faery realms that shine afar
Oh, I have been and I have seen
In magic worlds of Otherwhere
For all this world may praise or blame
For ban or blessing naught I care
For I have been beyond the town
Where meadowsweet and roses grow
And there such music did I hear
As worldly-righteous never know

Eko Eko Chant 1

Eko, eko, azarak. Eko, eko, zomelak.

Bagabi lacha bachabe, Lamac cahi achababe.

Karrellyos.

Lamac lamac bachalyas.

Cabahagy sabalyos. Baryolos.

Lagoz atha cabyolas. Smnahac atha famolas.

Hurrahya.

This version of the Eko Eko chant is often used when summoning the Witch Father or when raising power for trance and spells. The first line(s) of Eko, Eko, seem to be connected to Version 2 of the chant. The remainder, beginning with "Bagabi lacha ..." are very similar to a chant used in a 13th Century French miracle play, and are said to "summon the Devil" — our Folkloric Devil, who is summoned in that play by a sorcerer called Saladin (a famous Islamic military figure from the time of the Crusades who is associated with freemasonry and magick).

Eko Eko Chant 2

Eko! Eko! Azarak! Eko! Eko! Zomelak!

Zod-ru-koz e Zod-ru-koo

Zod-ru-goz e Goo-ru-moo!

Eko! Eko! Hoo...Hoo...Hoo!

This version of the Eko Eko chant is often used when summoning the Witch Father, specifically. This version first appeared in an article by C. Fuller in the Occult Review in 1926, but strikingly similar versions of it were in use by Doreen Valiente and, later, the Farrars.

Eko Eko Chant 3

Eko! Eko! Azarak!

Eko! Eko! Zomelak!

Eko! Eko! Karnayna!

Eko! Eko! Arida!

This version of the Eko Eko chant is often used when summoning the Spirits of the Craft – the Great Powers. The names (particularly the final two names) are often changed for the names of Deities or Spirits specific to a Coven or group.

An example would be:

Eko! Eko! Azarak!

Eko! Eko! Zomelak!

Eko! Eko! Kolayda!

Eko! Eko! Godena!

Sun, Moon, and Star Lore

Wheel of the Year

THE WITCH'S COMPASS AND THE YEAR WHEEL

The Year Wheel doesn't have be a simple calendar of the holy days of the Witch's year. While many modern Craft traditions share the "eight spokes on the wheel" that is the typical Neopagan festival calendar, some Craft traditions (like the American Folkloric Tradition) recognize that the Year Wheel is in fact a reflection of the entire macrocosm of the Craft — encompassing within its frame both a map of the Mill Grounds and several Craft Mysteries.

Copyright Asteria Books 2019

Planetary Influences

☉ **Solar Influences:** General success and recognition; spiritual illumination; decisiveness, vitality; activities requiring courage or a mood of self-certainty - making big decisions, scheduling meetings for reaching decisions, giving speeches, launching new projects; seeking favors from father, husband, boss, authorities.

☾ **Lunar Influences:** Health; home (buying home, moving); journeys / vacationing (time of leaving home or takeoff); activities remote in time or space - meditation, making reservations, finding lost objects or people; planting food crops; hiring employees; seeking favors from mother, wife, employees.

♂ **Mars Influences:** Courage, adventure; enforcing your will; success with drastic action (lawsuits, conflicts, going to war, surgery); sports, exercises; risk-taking; making complaints; firing employees; seeking favors of husband or boyfriend.

☿ **Mercury Influences:** Success in studies / communications; children; making a good impression; routine activities and activities needing clear communications; teaching / learning; important business letters / phone calls; meetings to develop or communicate ideas; buying / selling; routine shopping, errands, travel; job applications / interviews; seeking favors from neighbors, co-workers.

♃ **Jupiter Influences:** Wisdom, optimism; money (borrowing / lending / investing / earning / winning); activities necessitating enthusiasm; buying lottery tickets; seeking advice / consultation; settling disputes; seeking favors from grandparents, aunts and uncles, advisers (doctors, lawyers, accountants, astrologers).

♀ **Venus Influences:** Love; friendship; artistic and social success; enjoyable, sociable and aesthetic activities such as parties, social gatherings, recitals / exhibitions, weddings, visits, dating and seeking romance; planting ornamentals; buying gifts, clothing, luxuries; beauty treatments; seeking favors from women.

♄ **Saturn Influences:** Discipline and patience; giving up bad habits; overcoming obstacles; success with difficult tasks or difficult people; projects of long duration - breaking ground, laying foundations; planting perennials; treating chronic illness; making repairs; seeking favors from older people (not relatives) or difficult people.

For example, a person should ask a woman for a favor while Venus is influencing the situation (but ask a man for a favor during a Mars influence); one should ask one's boss for a favor during a solar influence; money should be invested during a Jupiter influence; medical treatments should commence under a lunar influence (except surgery should commence under a Mars influence); and so on. Each zodiac sign and day of the week is ruled by a planet which lends its influence.

Copyright Asteria Publishing 2019

Planetary Correspondences

The seven classical planets are the basis of most systems of magical correspondence, and they can form a very important part of a Witch's understanding of sympathetic magickal operations. Of particular use in designing your spell or ritual may be your consideration of the planetary influence in the timing of your working. Each of the days of the week and signs of the zodiac are ruled by a planet. Even the 24 hours in each day are divided between these planets, if you want to be precise and powerful in your timing. (You'll have to use an ephemeris or an app to help determine planetary hours.)

☉ SUN: Sunday; Leo

☽ MOON: Monday & Cancer

♂ MARS: Tuesday; Aries & Scorpio

☿ MERCURY: Wednesday; Gemini & Virgo

♃ JUPITER: Thursday; Sagittarius & Pisces

♀ VENUS: Friday; Taurus & Libra

♄ SATURN: Saturday; Capricorn & Aquarius

Lunar Magic

More than any other celestial body or natural force, the Moon and its magick have been linked to the Witch and her Craft across cultures and millennia. Its monthly cycles were observably connected to the tidal movements of the world's waters and menstrual flows, linking women inherently with the Moon's mysterious influence.

Ancient Greek and Roman Witches were especially noted for their ability to "draw down the Moon," a ritual procedure which Horace notes in reference to the Witch Canidia. She says "... *I, who can move waxen images and draw down the moon from the sky by my spells, who can raise the vaporous dead, and mix a draught of love ...*"

Werewolves famously shape-shift during the full moon, and the cult of the werewolf has ties to the ancient witch-cult. However, Witches are famously known to "fly out" in numerous animal shapes, not just that of wolves -- including the form of hares, goats, cats, toads. The full moon is an excellent time to use the moon's power to enhance shamanic shape-shifting work.

In Charles Leland's <u>Aradia, The Gospel of the Witches,</u> Aradia, the holy daughter of Diana, left these instructions to her followers in a speech that later became the basis of the Charge of the Goddess: "*Whenever you have need of anything, once in the month when the Moon is full, then shall you come together at some deserted place, or where there are woods, and give worship to She who is Queen of all Witches. Come all together inside a circle, and secrets that are as yet unknown shall be revealed.*"

The word "esbat" is a derivation from the Old French term of the same spelling meaning amusement or diversion. It is not necessarily a Full Moon celebration or magical working, as Janet and Stewart Farrar and Doreen Valiente have noted in their own works. It is simply NOT a Sabbat. Esbats are times when Witches gather or set aside personal time to work with the Moon's energy. The Full Moons of the year are generally considered the most important and potent magickal points, and Traditional Witches tend to honor and observe the Full Moons more ardently than any other cyclical celebrations.

Copyright Asteria Publishing 2019

Drawing Down the Moon

Ancient Greek and Roman Witches were said to perform a ritual to draw down the moon -- a ritual tradition that survives into current times. It is depicted on a Greek vase from the second century B.C.E., illustrated below. Of this ritual, Thessalian Witches were reputed to have said, *"If I command the moon, it will come down; and if I wish to withhold the day, night will linger over my head; and again, if I wish to embark on the sea, I need no ship, and if I wish to fly through the air, I am free from my weight."*

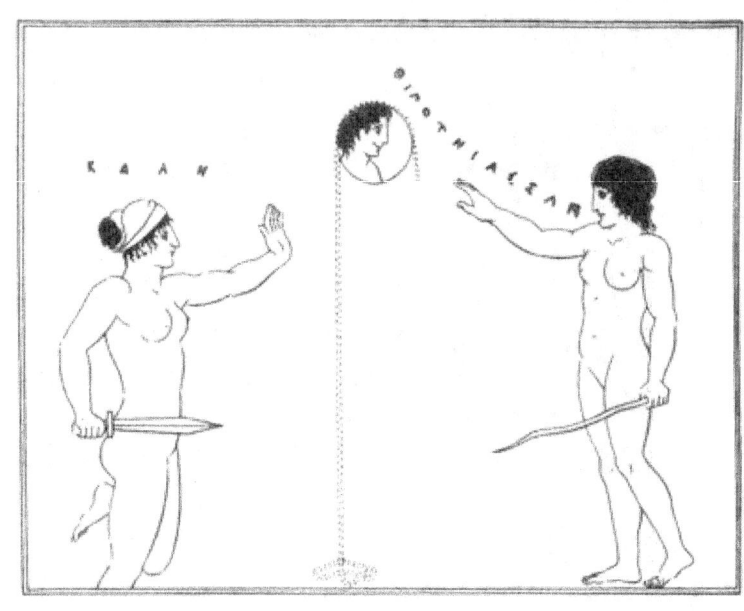

This ritual produces a trance-like state for the Witch, who is filled with lunar energy. Traditionally, this has been a High Priestess who has been aided in achieving the lunar trance by the coven's High Priest. Once she is imbued with the divine lunar energy, she speaks the words of the Charge of the Goddess. However, this ritual can be performed by a person of any gender, with or without assistance.

After conducting your ritual preparations, including the preparation of your sacred space, hold your arms aloft to the Moon, drinking in its beams. Feel it filling your mind, body, and spirit as you chant:

I invoke thee and call upon thee, Mighty Mother of us all, bringer of all fruitfulness by seed and root, by bud and stem, by leaf and flower and fruit,
By life and love do I invoke thee to descend upon the body of this, thy servant and priest(ess).

Spend time in reflection or performing magic while in this invoked state. When finished, administer unto yourself the fivefold blessing by anointing your body with oil:

Blessed be my feet, that have brought me in these ways.
Blessed be my knees, that shall kneel at the sacred altar.
Blessed be my sex, without which we would not be.
Blessed be my heart, formed in beauty.
Blessed be my lips, that shall utter the Sacred Names.

Copyright Asteria Publishing 2019

Moon Phases

The Full Moon rises at sunset and sets at sunrise. Astrologically, the sun and moon are in opposition (i.e., opposite each other in the sky and in opposite signs of the zodiac). She is visible all night long, from moonrise to moonset. Etheric energy peaks during Full Moons, and they are considered to be most favorable for all magic. The moon will remain full for two or three days. The full moon has a special connection to shapeshifting magic and invocation. Complete your work prior to the fading of the moon's fullness for best effect. The 13th Moon, or "Blue" Moon can occur at any time during the year. A Moon is called Blue only when it is the second full Moon to take place that month (moon-th). Blue Moons are considered to be stronger than regular Full Moons.

The waning period of the Moon's cycle is the time after the Full Moon when the light lessens as she progresses toward her Dark phase. It is the best time to do work that likewise focuses on ideas of lessening, removing, decreasing, minimizing, etc. It is also a good time to seek answers and inner wisdom, as outside distractions are decreased. During the waning moon, do spells to banish evil influences, lessen or remove obstacles and illness, neutralize enemies, scry, divine, and to remove harm. These influences become stronger as the moon darkens. The half-face of the last quarter moon is suited to work of balance and justice, but in a darker and more final sense than would be performed during the first quarter. The days of the Balsamic Moon (or Waning Crescent, or even Hekate's Sickle) are well-suited to harvesting, trance-work, and deep intuition.

The Dark Moon (also called the "New Moon") is the time between the last sliver of the Balsamic Moon (or Waning Crescent) and the first sliver of the Waxing Crescent. Astronomically, it is the time when the Moon is positioned between the Earth and the Sun, making her essentially backlit and ostensibly invisible. She rises and sets at roughly the same times as the sun, as well, leaving the night sky without any lunar influence. The Dark Moon is the most auspicious time for divination, banishing, and neutralizing spells. It is the peak of darkness, the time for blasting and battle magic. The second Dark Moon in a month is known as a Black Moon and is considered stronger than a regular Dark Moon.

The waxing period of the Moon's cycle is the time after the Dark Moon when the light increases as she progresses toward her Full phase. The days of and around the waxing crescent moon are the most powerful time to work spells for new growth and beginnings, which should manifest at the Full Moon. This moon is the silvery bow of Artemis and offers a fresh start to all workings. The waxing moon, in general, is the best time to do spells for growth, beginning new projects, initiation, and enhancement. It is the time to focus on increase, gain, forward movement, and all types of abundance. The clean half-face of the first quarter moon is also well-suited to work of balance and justice, especially with a focus on hope and positive restoration. The days of and around the gibbous moon are the most powerful time for spells of fruition and completion.

Copyright Asteria Books 2019

13 Moons of the Year

Month—Moon Name—Lunar Powers

January—Wolf Moon—*Powers of Blasting and Binding*

February—Ice Moon—*Powers of Stillness and Warning*

March—Wind Moon—*Powers of Quickening and Inspiration*

April—Budding Moon—*Powers of New Growth and Vitality*

May—Mother's Moon—*Powers of Joy and Celebration*

June—Mead Moon—*Powers of Fertility and Passion*

July—Herb Moon—*Powers of Healing and Strength*

August—Grain Moon—*Powers of Abundance and Love*

September—Wine Moon—*Powers of Ecstasy and Dreaming*

October—Blood Moon—*Powers of Sacrifice and Necromancy*

November—Mourning Moon—*Powers of Endings and Offerings*

December—Cold Moon—*Powers of the Wild Hunt and the Fool*

2nd Full Moon in a Month—Blue Moon—*Powers of Blasting and Binding*

Copyright Asteria Books 2018

Magical Tools

Saining of Tools

It is customary when a Witch acquires new tools to cleanse and consecrate them to their own use. This true whether the tools are purchased, homemade, or received as a gift, and also whether they are for personal or coven use.

The term "sain" is an archaic word that means to make the sign of the cross over something in order to banish evil or unwanted forces from it, or viewed another way, to bless it so that evil cannot touch it. The symbol of the cross as sign of blessing far pre-dates Christianity. Indeed, the equal-armed cross (often depicted with a circle encompassing it) is such a prehistoric and universal symbol of which every land and culture had some version. It is a symbol that is related to concepts of perfection and the totality of known existence.

You will need:
the tool to be sained
dark bread in a bowl (or lipped dish)
red wine in a cup
the Red Knife
a lancet (optional)
a portion of purification or blessing incense
a thurible with a lit charcoal

1.) Cast the Caim as usual.

2.) Place some of the incense on the lit charcoal and run the tool through the resulting smoke making the shape of a cross, visualizing all past energies of the tool being carried away and dissolved with the smoke.

3.) Say: "I cleanse this '*tool*' in the name of the Mighty Ones, that it may serve me well in my Craft."

4.) Raise power by seething. Rock back and forth, hum, chant, wail, and draw power up from the third realm and down from the first realm into yourself and into your tool.

5.) Perform the rite of the Housle.

6.) Anoint the tool with a cross of the sacrificial fluid, giving it a name at this time if you so wish. The Housle is the blood of the Mighty Ones.

7.) Finally, raise a drop of your own blood for the third and final cross in the Saining.

Copyright Asteria Books 2018

On Altars

In the ancient world, altars were places of offering and sacrifice. Devotees would petition a Deity by bringing an animal to be cooked (and often eaten communally), incense to be burned, or votive figurines to be placed in honor of the God or Goddess aligned with the petitioners' need. The altar was a consecrated place that was usually elevated, although on very rare occasions some specific types of altars (usually to Underworld Deities) were dug into the ground or incorporated into burial mounds.

Contemporary Neopagan and Witchcraft altars tend to be of two general types: the shrine and the working altar.

A shrine is an altar space that is consecrated and dedicated to prayer, service, or meditation related to a particular Deity, Spirit, energy, or idea. A Witch might erect an elemental shrine for Water in their bathroom, an ancestor shrine on their mantelpiece, or an Aphrodite shrine on a bedside table. These shrines might have collections of statuary, candles, flowers, offerings, photographs, jewelry, etc. However, they wouldn't necessarily have a full complement of tools for performing spells and rituals.

A working altar is the space where a Witch actually performs her spells and rituals, and it may also be where she stores a certain set of her symbolic or functional tools when not in use. It is her workshop table, in many ways. This is where candles are inscribed, poppets are sewn, and talismans are fashioned. It is also where trancework and other inner work is undertaken.

Most Witches have at least one altar space that is a blend of the shrine and the working altar. This is especially true for practitioners who can only create one altar due to space or privacy limitations.

Care should be taken to keep the altar both physically clean and energetically cleansed.

Copyright Asteria Publishing 2019

The Three Knives

The Athame, the Kerfane, and the Shelg are the three knives, Black, White, and Red.

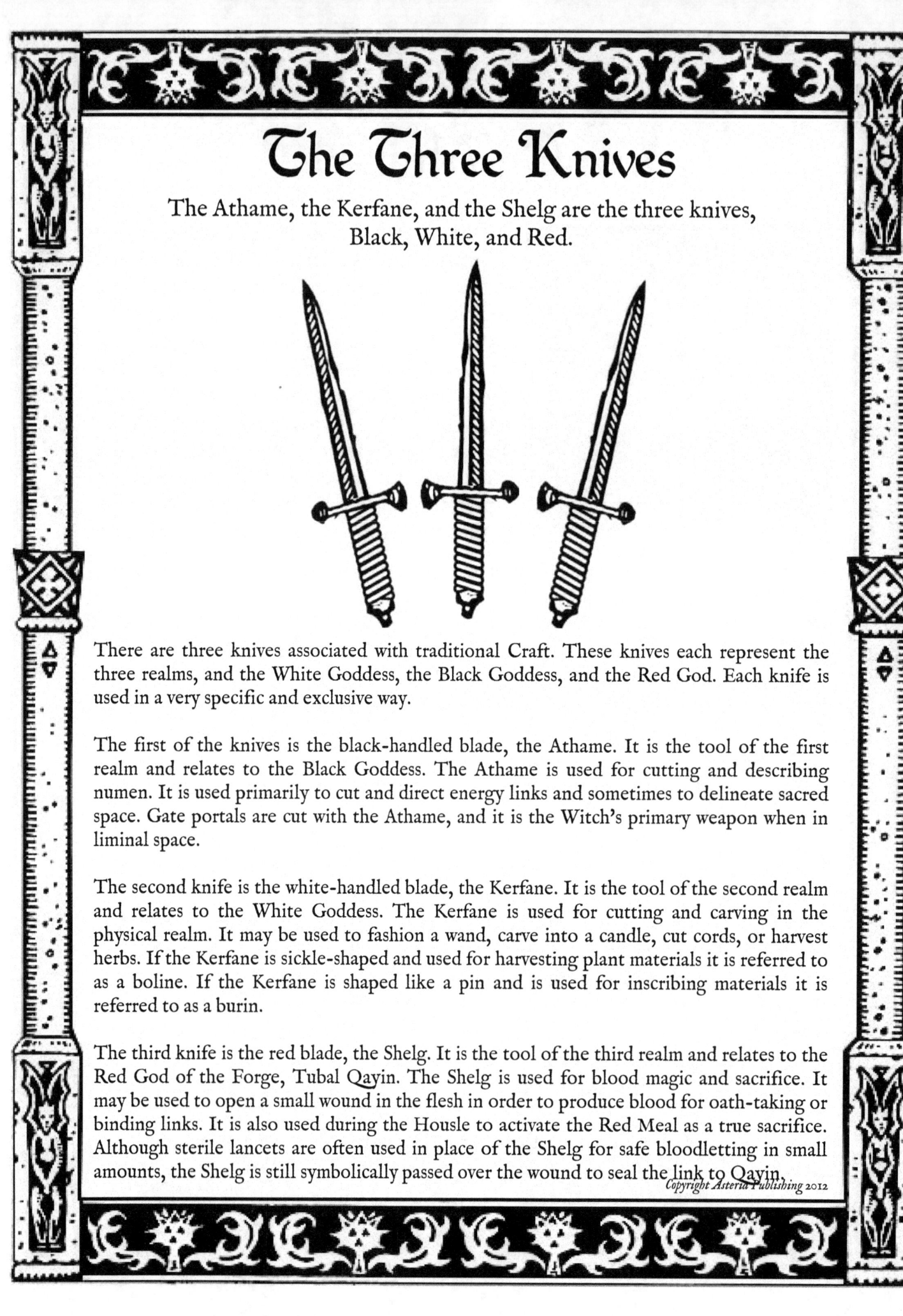

There are three knives associated with traditional Craft. These knives each represent the three realms, and the White Goddess, the Black Goddess, and the Red God. Each knife is used in a very specific and exclusive way.

The first of the knives is the black-handled blade, the Athame. It is the tool of the first realm and relates to the Black Goddess. The Athame is used for cutting and describing numen. It is used primarily to cut and direct energy links and sometimes to delineate sacred space. Gate portals are cut with the Athame, and it is the Witch's primary weapon when in liminal space.

The second knife is the white-handled blade, the Kerfane. It is the tool of the second realm and relates to the White Goddess. The Kerfane is used for cutting and carving in the physical realm. It may be used to fashion a wand, carve into a candle, cut cords, or harvest herbs. If the Kerfane is sickle-shaped and used for harvesting plant materials it is referred to as a boline. If the Kerfane is shaped like a pin and is used for inscribing materials it is referred to as a burin.

The third knife is the red blade, the Shelg. It is the tool of the third realm and relates to the Red God of the Forge, Tubal Qayin. The Shelg is used for blood magic and sacrifice. It may be used to open a small wound in the flesh in order to produce blood for oath-taking or binding links. It is also used during the Housle to activate the Red Meal as a true sacrifice. Although sterile lancets are often used in place of the Shelg for safe bloodletting in small amounts, the Shelg is still symbolically passed over the wound to seal the link to Qayin.

Copyright Asteria Publishing 2012

Athame

The black-handled blade, traditionally called the Athame, is usually a double-edged blade. It is the tool of the first realm and relates to the Black Goddess, Kolyo. The Athame is used for inscribing and cutting energy. It is used to cut energy links. It is the Witch's primary weapon when in liminal space, especially when dealing with baneful spirits.

The black-handled blade is almost never used to cut physical objects, though Traditional Witches are nothing if not pragmatists. Some will have only one knife and will use it equally for cutting energy, slicing through a magical threat, inscribing a spell candle, drawing blood for an initiatory oath, and slicing a roast for feast. It is for the individual Witch to determine the what is sanctified use of their own tool, and it is for that Witch to maintain those boundaries.

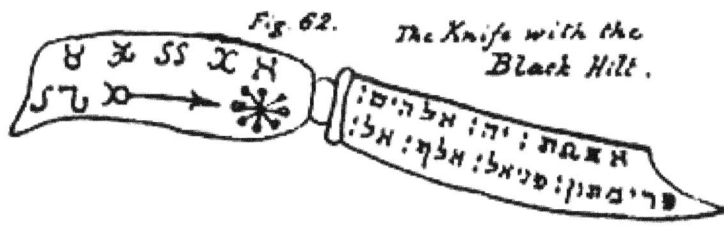

The black-handled knife as a magical tool dates back to the Key of Solomon, a medieval grimoire rumored to have been authored by the Biblical King. This knife was called by a slightly different name in that text, and it's appearance was a little different. However, its function was very similar. In that text, magicians are instruction in the forging of the knife using specific quenching liquids (hemlock juice and a coded herbal blend infusion) and sigils. It was recommended to make the knife on a Saturday in the planetary hour of Saturn.

Learn the meanings of these symbols — or choose/design several of your own to inscribe on the hilt of your blade. Begin at the hilt working toward the guard.

Copyright Asteria Books 2018

Kerfane & Boline

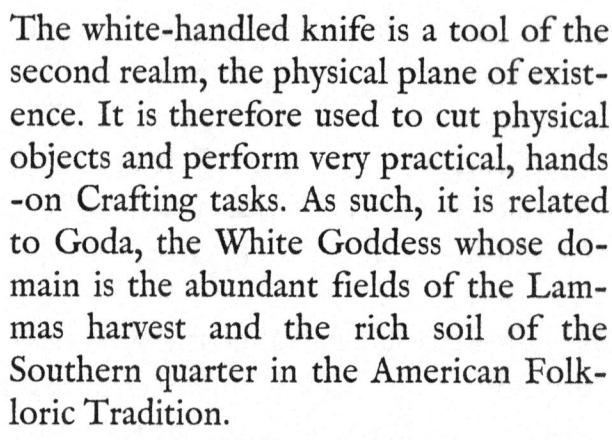

The white-handled knife is a tool of the second realm, the physical plane of existence. It is therefore used to cut physical objects and perform very practical, hands-on Crafting tasks. As such, it is related to Goda, the White Goddess whose domain is the abundant fields of the Lammas harvest and the rich soil of the Southern quarter in the American Folkloric Tradition.

Wiccan Tradition advocates for a crescent-bladed white-handled knife, the *Boline* — a name dating back to Solomonic texts (though the shape differed). The crescent has delicious lunar references and is often made of either silver or copper, for these magical blades.

The name *Kerfane* for a straight, single-edged blade seems to have Germanic origins and refers to a carving knife. Less lore and a great deal more every day practicality seems to surround this style of blade.

The white knife was described in the Key of Solomon, with directions to include mulberry sap and pimpernel extract in its quenching and to wrap in it a silk cloth for storage. The image below shows suggested inscriptions for both handle and blade.

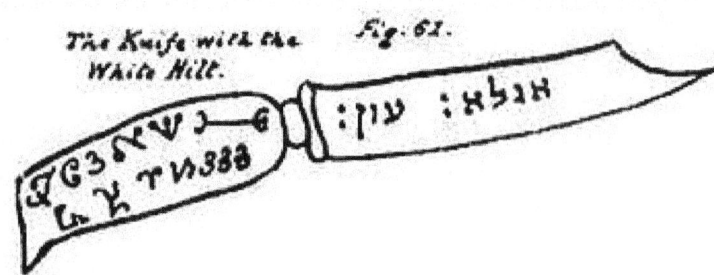

Copyright Asteria Books 2018

Shelg

The red-handled knife is the most secretive of blades within Craft practices. There are veiled references within both Solomonic lore and the writings of Joe Wilson (founder of the 1734 Tradition in the US) to a third knife, though its use is never specified. However, blood magic and blood bonds within the Craft and within traditional magical systems are both very well known.

There are at least styles of tool that can easily be used for this blade, depending on the preference of the Witch. The first is a hunting knife, which is the source of the name for *Shelg* (a Manx term that means to hunt or chase). The other is an awl or ice-pick, which hearkens back to the ancient practice of bloodletting through use of a lancet as a medical practice. Whichever style is chosen, great care should be taken to keep the blade razor sharp and sheathed when not in use.

The red-handled knife is dedicated in service to the Red God, Tubal Qayin, and should be sterilized, wiped clean, dried, and oiled with a thin layer of vegetable oil after each use.

Use this blade to "stab" the bread and "spill the blood" of the wine in your ritual sacrifice for the Red Meal or to make a small cut or puncture in the skin when doing blood magic or taking blood oaths. Remember that only a single drop of blood is needed to form a link. The code of your life is present in that single drop.

Copyright Asteria Books 2018

Care & Feeding of Steel

Witches use many types of blades within their Craft, and while blades can be fashioned from bone, wood, and other materials, it is most common for them to be forged from steel. It is wise, then, to know how to care for your steel blades to show respect for your tools and keep them in good repair.

To clean a blade, you'll first need to note whether it is Damascus or steel. If it is Damascus, use steel wool only, because it is delicate. If it is steel, you have the whole gambit of options – beginning with MetalGlo (or similar) cream and a clean, soft natural cloth. (Wash rags from auto supply stores work well.)

From there, you can try rottenstone (rust eraser). It works well on all sorts of metals.

After that, if you still have pitting from rust, you can move up to steel wool or sandpaper. Remember that the higher the number on the sandpaper, the finer the grit and softer it will be on the steel. For steel wool, look at the O rating. The more O's, the softer it is.

Always start with the softest abrasives available and work your way up when trying to clean up a problem. If you jump right into the harshest abrasive, you may forever ruin the finish or polish on your blade.

Once your blade is clean and rust free, put a light coat of oil on the steel. Use blade oil if it is a blade you do not use with food and drink (or to pierce your skin). Use vegetable oil if it is a blade you use for those purposes. Use a soft, clean cloth to apply the oil.

After each use, wipe the blade clean, and apply another thin layer of oil before securing the blade in its sheath.

Copyright Asteria Books 2018

The Crane Bag

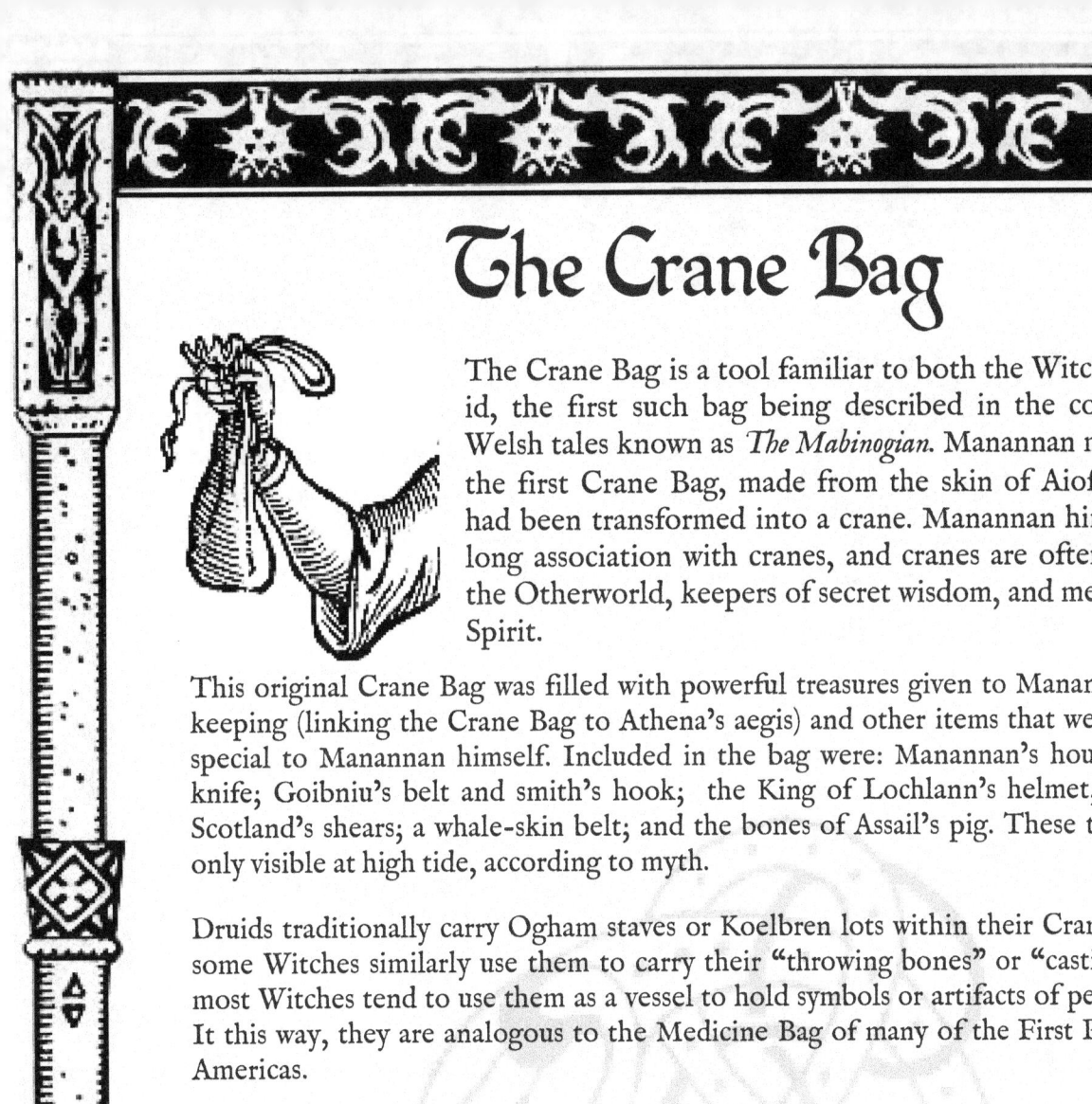

The Crane Bag is a tool familiar to both the Witch and Druid, the first such bag being described in the collection of Welsh tales known as *The Mabinogian*. Manannan mac Lir had the first Crane Bag, made from the skin of Aiofe after she had been transformed into a crane. Manannan himself had a long association with cranes, and cranes are often guides to the Otherworld, keepers of secret wisdom, and messengers of Spirit.

This original Crane Bag was filled with powerful treasures given to Manannan for safekeeping (linking the Crane Bag to Athena's aegis) and other items that were sacred and special to Manannan himself. Included in the bag were: Manannan's house, shirt, and knife; Goibniu's belt and smith's hook; the King of Lochlann's helmet; the King of Scotland's shears; a whale-skin belt; and the bones of Assail's pig. These treasures were only visible at high tide, according to myth.

Druids traditionally carry Ogham staves or Koelbren lots within their Crane Bags, band some Witches similarly use them to carry their "throwing bones" or "casting lots." But most Witches tend to use them as a vessel to hold symbols or artifacts of personal power. It this way, they are analogous to the Medicine Bag of many of the First Peoples of the Americas.

Given that it is illegal in the US and UK to buy, sell, or possess any part of the Crane (or Heron), it is not a contemporary practice to make this tool of actual crane-skin. Modern practitioners use a wide variety of other natural materials that have personal meaning and potency, often taking the time to design and decorate a bag that is as powerful as the objects contained within it.

In much the same way that the contents of Manannan's bag were kept protected and only visible at high tide, a custom has developed among Witches of being secretive with the contents of their bags. One custom holds that no Witch should show any single person all the contents of their bag. If he feels safe to share any, let it only be a few — and let the other Witch also reveal something of their bag in return.

Contents Might Include:
Rocks and crystals
Shells
Bark, roots, seeds, twigs, herbs, leaves, flowers, etc
Dirt and sand
Fabric scraps
Jewelry, talismans, figurines, lucky charms, gifts
Feathers, fur, skin, bones, claws, teeth, hair, etc
Tools of trade or Craft

Copyright Asteria Books 2019

The Cauldron

The cauldron is an ancient vessel of cooking and brewing that is associated in myth and legend with deep wisdom and transformation. This association stems, in part, to the story of Cerridwen and Gwion, in which Cerridwen sets her young farmhand the task of stirring a brew that is meant to bestow vast wisdom upon the one who drinks it. When three drops bubble onto Gwion's thumb, and he sucks the scalding burn, he is granted all the wisdom in the brew, and a perilous and transformative chase ensues. Eventually, Cerridwen consumes Gwion, when she is a hen and he is a grain, later giving birth to him as the renowned bard, Taliesin.

Another famous Celtic cauldron was that of the Dagda. His was called the Un-Dry Cauldron, for it was said to be bottomless. No man ever walked away from it unsatisfied. The cauldron had a ladle so large that two grown men could fit inside it.

Bran the Blessed had a cauldron called the Pair Dadeni ("Cauldron of Rebirth"), as recounted in the Mabinogian, a Welsh cycle of stories, that could restore the dead to life.

Robert Cochrane writes on the "two words that do not fit in the cauldron" as a mystery of the Craft. The answer to this riddle (which he provides in one of his letters) is "Be Still," for within the cauldron lies all motion, all potential, and all things. It cannot hold stillness, but this too is a mystery. The cauldron is used not just for the brewing of potions, but also as a vessel for scrying in liquid or flame. To accomplish this we must find stillness within the cauldron, by quieting our own minds.

The cauldron is also very similar to the Holy Grail of legend. We must ever seek it and its mysteries, for in it lies true communion with the Gods, and deep healing of our souls. "Who does the Grail serve?" is the riddle traditionally associated with this quest. The Grail serves all who seek it with honest intent, for it is only in not questing for the mystery that it serves no one.

"In fate and the overcoming of fate, lies the true Grail." - Robert Cochrane

Copyright Asteria Books 2018

Seasoning a Cast Iron Cauldron

If you only intend to use your cauldron as a symbolic ritual decoration, you don't need to take any special precautions for its physical care. However, it IS a functional piece of cookware that most Witches use in traditional ways to hold various liquids, make brews, and even light small fires. For these purposes, you will need to season it. A properly seasoned cast iron pot can last a lifetime, if cared for.

New Cauldrons
1. Heat the oven to 250°–300°F
2. Coat the cauldron with lard or bacon grease. Do not use vegetable oil, as it will leave a sticky surface, and the cauldron will not be properly seasoned.
3. Put the cauldron in the over for 15 minutes. Remove it and pour out any excess grease, wiping down the interior and exterior surfaces.
4. Return the cauldron to the oven to continue seasoning for another 2 hours.
5. Repeat this process several times, as it will create a stronger "seasoning bond."

Cauldrons Needing to be Re-Seasoned
If the cauldron was not seasoned properly, or if a portion of the season has worn off and there is now rust, the cauldron will need be cleaned and re-seasoned.
1. Remove residue or rust by cleaning thoroughly with hot water and a scouring pad. Heating the cauldron to a safely touchable temperature is also recommended to help with this process.
2. Dry the cauldron immediately with dish towel or paper towel.
3. Season the cauldron as outlined above.

Caring for Your Cast Iron Cauldron
When you first purchase your cast iron cook-pot, it will be medium grey in color and will darken with seasoning and use. This is normal. Store with the lid off (if it is a Dutch oven style) to prevent condensation, which leads to rust. Wipe clean and dry thoroughly after each use. If a liquid other than water was in the cauldron, use hot water to remove any sticky residue.

Copyright Asteria Books 2018

The Witch Jewels

I have seen the Witch Jewels sometimes referred to as "Rings of Power" – though this can be a misleading (or at least confusing term), since "Ring of Power" is also used to describe the Witch's Compass or the often very complex Circles and inscriptions of the Ceremonial Magician. However, all the Jewels encircle the body and are imbued with Power, so the play on words is clever.

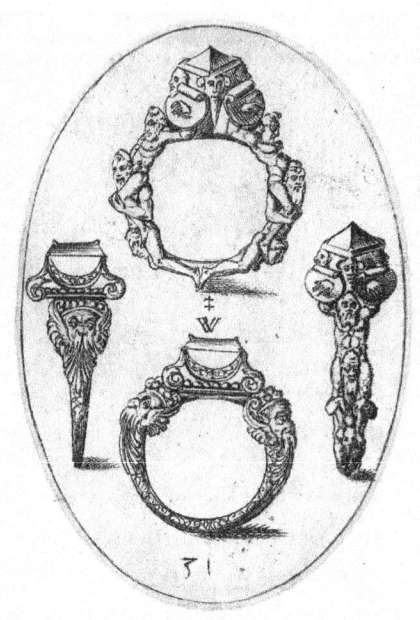

Not every Tradition emphasizes their use or teaches the lore behind all of these Jewels, but many Witches are instinctively drawn to them nonetheless.

The Seven Jewels (which are worn by all genders) include the Necklace, the Pendant, the Bracelet, the Finger Ring, the Girdle/Cord, the Crown, and the Garter.

NECKLACE – Sometimes called a Circle of Stones, this piece hearkens back in some ways to Freya's *Brisingamen* and Aphrodite's golden *zonai*. Though it is often made of amber and jet (sometimes with bone added, thereby incorporating all three sacred colors of red, black, and white), it is not entirely uncommon for it to be made of acorns (linking it to skulls, life/death, resurrection lore as well as to the Goddesses Macha and Diana, though for different reasons – as well as to the Druids and the woodland Gods and their wisdom).

PENDANT – Often used for purposes of fascination and to both cast and turn away the Evil Eye, this jewel is usually made of a semi-precious stone that is dear to the Witch.

BRACELET – Copper or silver cuffs worn on the left wrist and marked with the magical name of the bearer (in Theban or another runic script), along with other mystical symbols, identify the Witch to others, stealthily.

FINGER RING – For some, this is another personal tool of fascination and magic, while some groups use it as a gift upon admission or elevation to a certain rank or degree. Band and stone materials are chosen based on personal or group symbolism. For instance, in the Spiral Castle (AFW) Tradition, the Bone Ring is given at Adoption (along with the Red Cord) – symbolizing a Red Soul (aka bone-deep, ancestral) connection to the Craft and each other.

GIRDLE CORD – The (often-braided) Witch's ladder-style girdle cord serves multiple functions. As a "Jewel," it is a belt that is worn in ritual and spellcasting. But it can also act as a tool to restrict blood-flow, a devotional tool, and a tool for marking the ritual space.

GARTER – Within many covens, only Witches of a certain degree wear a garter. In others, all do, but markings embroidered upon the garter indicate rank/degree. It is usually worn above the left knee. Colors and materials vary by group.

CROWN – Most groups reserve the crown for either coven leaders or ritual leaders. Some rituals also have crowns or head-wear that is specific to the rite.

Copyright Asteria Books 2020

Amber, Jet, and Bone

Amber, jet, and bone (which is also called ivory) have been prized jewelry-making components since Antiquity – and especially so by shamans and magic-workers. All three are the result of living organisms, which results in a different sort of energetic experience during ritual use as compared to stones, woods, shells, and metals. Additionally, amber and jet (when rubbed vigorously) produce a natural negative charge, attracting positive ions to it. Finally, these three components collectively represent the three sacred colors of the Celts (and the Craft) – red, black, and white.

Amber

Amber is fossilized tree resin that has been a prized component in jewelry and adornments since the Neolithic era. Its most common color variants range from light yellow to a golden orange-brown, but amber can be almost white in its paleness and nearly black in its sable depths. There are also variations that are cherry red, green, and even blue. Amber gives a soothing, light energy that is both calming and energizing. It can help manifest desires and heighten the intellect, clarity of thought, and wisdom.

Jet

Jet is fossilized and pressurized wood. Like amber, it is warm to the touch (unlike stones and glass, which is useful in distinguishing jet from the black stones many jewelry dealers try to sell under this name). Jet has been found in burial sites as far back at 17,000 BCE, and it was attested in Roman magical records as being capable of averting the "evil eye." It is a powerfully protective stone against all negativity, often crumbling and deteriorating as an alert of the presence of powerful dark forces (such as depression, abuse, and spiritual attack). Jet draws negativity out of the wearer and also aids in alertness and problem-solving.

Bone

Bone is an important material in shamanic ornamentation. The teeth and bones of both humans and every animal imaginable have been found at ancient gravesites in jewelry and ceremonial tools of rulers and priests. Like amber and jet, bone was once a vessel of life, connecting it to the soul itself. American Folkloric Witches wear a bone rose ring to symbolize adoption in the Family of the Craft and the nature of working *subrosa* within the coven. Witch garlands (akin to a rosary, also called a ladder) are made of amber, jet, and snake bone – connecting to the serpent energy of the spine.

Copyright Asteria Books 2019

The Cords

Cords are seen in both Wiccan and Trad Craft practice.

In Robert Cochrane's writing "On Cords," he describes the use of both devotional and magical cords:

"When worked up properly they should contain many different parts--herbs, feathers and impedimenta of the particular harm. They are generally referred to in the trade as "ladders," or in some cases as "garlands," and have much the same meaning as the three crosses. That is they can contain three blessings, three curses, or three wishes. A witch also possesses a devotional ladder, by which she may climb to meditational heights, knotted to similar pattern as the Catholic rosary."

Above, Cochrane talks first about using the cord for magical operations.

The second use of cords is that of the devotional ladder. While many of us will make and use multiple devotional ladders for trance and meditation work related to a variety of focal objects, a great many Witches receive their first ladder as a cord (or set of braided cords) that marks their admission to a coven.

The cords are usually a length of silk or wool (or other natural fiber) rope, braided yarn, or upholstery cord, whose thickness, length and color vary by tradition. They are versatile, as they are used for cinching ritual robes, indicating rank or degree, measuring the circle, and sometimes for binding blood flow in certain circumstances. When used to control blood flow, they may also be called the *cingulum*.

Cords used as a cingulum help alter consciousness, and they are often employed in initiation rites. There are a few different ways to tie the cords to act in this capacity, but the most common is shown here. However they are used, a cingulum should be administered with care (and training) to avoid causing damage or harm.

Cords can also be used as a meditational or trance tool in much the same way as a Catholic rosary. Because they are usually braided and knotted, often with multi-colored fibers, they bind together symbols and imagery that are important to the Witch who wears them. Meditating on a particular knot, strand, or other element of the cord will produce a focused experience on the symbol set contained therein, while working through all the knots (climbing the ladder) produces a transcendent state.

The AFW Tradition uses a specific progression of cords as markers of admission to the coven. Each length of cording that we use is made of 3 hand-braided strands of cotton yarn.

Copyright Asteria Books 2020

The Garter

The magical garter has significance dating back to prehistoric times. Cave art in eastern Spain that dates to the Paleolithic period shows a sorcerer performing in a ritual while wearing nothing but a pair of garters just below his knees.

In many traditions the garter is worn only by a Witch Queen, or Queen of the Sabbat. However, the traditional dress of Morris dancers consists of garters, usually red, and "Green Garters" is a traditional Morris Dancer tune.

In the trial record of Margaret Johnson (Lancshsire 1633) the Devil was said to wear: "a suite of black, tyed about with silke pointes (garters)." If we take the position that the "Devil" was the Magister of the coven, then we see that the garter is not the sole province of the Queen of the Sabbat, but was also worn by men.

Red garters were said to be worn by a coven's Summoner, whose job it was to advise members on meeting days and times. The red garters signified to others that s/he was genuine. Gerald Gardner used the red garters as a plot device to this effect in his novel about the witch cult, High Magic's Aid.

In some traditions the garter is prepared with green leather or velvet with a lining made of blue silk. In others the garter is made of red leather or snakeskin. There is usually one large, silver or gold buckle on the garter, representing the Queen's own coven, with additional, smaller silver buckles for each of the other covens under her authority. The garter is worn on the left leg, just above the knee. It may be fastened with the large buckle or with silk ribbons.

Pennethorne Hughes states that when a tortured witch was likely to reveal others, he or she may be murdered in jail by the other witches to avoid further arrests and tortures. To prove that the murder had been done under those circumstances, a garter would be left tied loosely around the victim's throat.

The Witch Garter is found in English history as being linked to the creation of the Order of the Garter. The most widespread story states that the countess of Salisbury was dancing with King Edward III at a court function. As they danced, the countess's garter fell to the ground. The king picked it up and, to save her embarrassment, put it on his own leg with the words, "Honi soit qui mal y pense" (Shame be to him who thinks evil of it.") He went on to found the Order of the Garter, with that phrase as its slogan. The precise date for the founding of the order is not known, since the records have been destroyed, but it is thought to be 1348.

Margaret Alice Murray mentions that it took more than a dropped garter to embarrass a lady in the 14th century, even a lady of the court. However, if the garter dropped was a ritual one, demonstrating that its owner was in fact a leader of the Old Religion, then there would be very real embarrassment, particularly since there were high personages of the Christian Church in attendance at the event. Edward's action, then, was incredibly smart thinking, for in placing the garter on his own leg, he not only saved face for the countess, but also proclaimed himself prepared to be a leader of the Pagan population as well as the Christian. This was a clever move taking into account that a large portion of his subjects were still Pagan at that point in time.

Copyright Asteria Books 2020

The Crown

The Crown (Coronet, Circlet, or Headdress) is another of the Jewels of the Witch that can take several styles and has sometimes been entirely abandoned by some practitioners and groups. However, there is ample evidence of its use within folkloric sources, and both mythic and historic material gives us plenty of inspiration if we are drawn to incorporating it within our ritual practice.

The illustrations above show masculine and feminine variations on "horns" – some that are supposed to be intrinsic to the bearer (such as in the case of the blacksmithing Devil aided by his helpful Witch Dame); while others are embellishments, such as the up-turned "horns" of the moon born by Hecate (or her triple-horned hat, worn by another of her visages). In the Middle Ages, horned headdresses and hairstyles were very popular among ladies, and sculptural as well as painted art shows us a long history of people donning animal horns and adorning their heads with celestial emblems for spiritual and religious ceremonies.

Horns and antlers have featured most prominently, for all genders, with some cultures or time periods showing a gender preference for certain animals or emblems. Contemporarily, Wiccan crowns tend to assign horns/antlers to those who identify as masculine, with moon crowns (with up-turned points) belonging to feminine practitioners. Ancient myth and art, though, ascribe horns to several Witch Goddesses, including Ishtar, Lilith, and Hecate.

Typically, only the leaders of the coven – the Maid/Dame/Queen/High Priestess and the Magister/Devil/High Priestess – wear a Crown. It is usually seen as an emblem of office or rank. Some groups use specialized crowns or headdresses for specific Sabbats or initiatory practices, in which case, only the indicated ritual rolebearer would wear the Crown. The argument can be made, though, that flower / foliage crowns are traditional and folkloric for ALL coveners, regardless of rank.

When made for ritual, plastic and other synthetic materials should be avoided in its construction. Choose your components carefully – based on what you want activated in your energetic Crown – the seat of the White Soul (the Higher Self, the God Self.)

Copyright Astoria Books 2020

The Robe, Cloak & Hood

There is wide disparity within Craft practice regarding what is required or preferred in regard to vestments. Two of the most vocal and published early proponents of Craft — Gardner (representing Wicca) and Cochrane (representing Traditional Craft) — took very different stances on this.

Gardner advocated for practitioners to be *skyclad* (nude) in their rites, and this is often still the norm in Gardnerian and Alexandrian covens, though some derivations have adopted the use of Tau or T-shaped robes from Ceremonial practice.

The great majority of Craft practitioners wear some form of robe, however. They may use ritual nudity for certain types of magic, but they typically wear special ritual robes. Traditional Crafters are more likely than not to have robes — and even cloaks.

These robes can vary in styles by Tradition, but many groups have specifications regarding the cut, length, fibers (whether synthetics are allowed, for example), colors, etc.

A ritual robe has symbolic connections to the physical body of the practitioner, but a Tradition may also use it to symbolize other metaphysical concepts, as well. While the cloak (an outer garment that is chosen for warmth) may or may not be optional, a black hooded robe can be seen as a woven symbol of the work the WitchMother. It is deeply protective.

Some groups change the color of the robe (or another vestment, like a tabard or sash) throughout the year to indicate change of season. Others use color or style of robe to indicate degree, rank, or office within the group.

Within the Spiral Castle (AFW) Tradition, our members wear either white or black garments of their choosing (depending on the season), so long as they are clean and satisfy their personal sense of Arte. We require a black cloak and a separate deep black hood for specific ritual use.

Having a hood as a separate garment allows for covering the entire head and face during deeply meditative states and certain ritual practices, like hoodwinking.

Copyright Asteria Books 2020

The Oath Stone

THE ANVIL

There are several types of stones that are important to Cunning Folk. With a Witchfather linked to the forge and alchemy, it is no surprise that the Oath Stone upon which we take our vows and form our sacred blood bonds is his anvil.

To do this, simply draw a small amount of blood using your Shelg (red-handled knife or thumb-pricker) or a sterile lancet and speak your oath while holding your blood to the anvil. If you are making vows of Initiation, all of the members of the coven should also have drawn their blood and touched the Oath Stone, as well. This forms the bond of Family.

In addition to being used for taking vows, the anvil can also be used as a way to call upon Tubal Cain as the Forge Master. Strike the hammer to the anvil three times, each time pausing to call his name. It is powerful. It still gives me chills when I call to him this way. Through iron. Through our blood. Through Tubal Cain's blood. Through the heartbeat that is pounded out in the rhythm of the hammer strokes. And heartbeats.

The symbolism of the forge is powerful, alchemical, mystical. The anvil is the foundation of Stone. The forge is the transformational Flame. The bellows are the Breath. The quench is the Sea (both womb and tomb).

Ours is a path of the Mysteries of Life and Death and all that lies Between. It is Creation and Destruction. Destroying in order to Create. Mixing Fire and Water to temper the steel and make it stronger. Knowing how and when to do that in the right proportion.

And the anvil is the rock, the hard place on which this great work happens. It is the altar on which we are pounded and shaped (at our own request!) into something useful, something beautiful, something dangerous.

The earliest anvils were actual stones, of course, and a great many cultures have had ceremonies involving oathing and coronation stones. The Lia Fail (Stone of Destiny) and Jacob's Pillow are two well-known coronation stones upon which dynasties of monarchs took vows to serve God and country. Furthermore, the custom has long-existed in Celtic countries for couples to make their wedding vows upon an oathing stone.

Within this Tradition, the Anvil as the Oath Stone sits at the base of the Stang when the Compass is drawn, along with the Cauldron.

Copyright Asteria Books 2018

The Gandreid

Gandreið is an Old Norse term that has significant implications for the modern Craft practitioner. It translates most closely to "stick ride" or "spirit ride," and most people take this to mean the Broom or possibly the Stang, as depicted in medieval woodcuts. In the physical sense, it has certainly been applied to a number of "magic sticks" (including the wand and staff throughout Norse, Germanic, and Anglo-Saxon magical practice. Within this particular association, special focus has been made on the tool's use as an implement of spirit-flight — often being interwoven with seething and trancework.

Gandreið is a compound word. *Reið* is a pretty straightforward translation to "ride." But *gandr* references several concepts — spirits, the spiritual realm, magic/sorcery/witchcraft, monsters, riding animals, and wild animals.

Consider, then, the nursery rhyme about Mother Goose:

Old Mother Goose, when she wanted to wander
Would ride through the air on a very fine gander.

What interesting and exciting implications for the folkloric-based Witch! First, we have to remember that Mother Goose is very often associated with Frau Holda (Dame Hulda, Holle), and it is either she (or later, her male, Anglo-Saxon counterpart, Holt) who is said to lead the Wild Hunt — a flight of spirits and witches cross the skies that is alternately said to bless the fields and gather the dead and dying.

Next, though, we want to consider whether Mother Goose is riding a corporeal animal familiar (with "gander" being a male goose), a non-corporeal spirit familiar who (possibly?) takes the shape of this bird, or one of the magic sticks (gandr/gandreid) mentioned above.

In folklore, there are several instances of enchanted sticks or branches acting as "horses" and "birds" to carry their bearers to desired destinations, and also of granting requests when watered with tears, blood, or given other offerings. This would seem to indicate an in-dwelling spirit — a fetch, familiar, or other tutelary spirit, perhaps.

Looking to later staff, wand, broom, and stang lore, we continue to see the threads of the gandreid — the en-spirited branch of Northern European practitioners.

Copyright Asteria Books 2020

The Broom

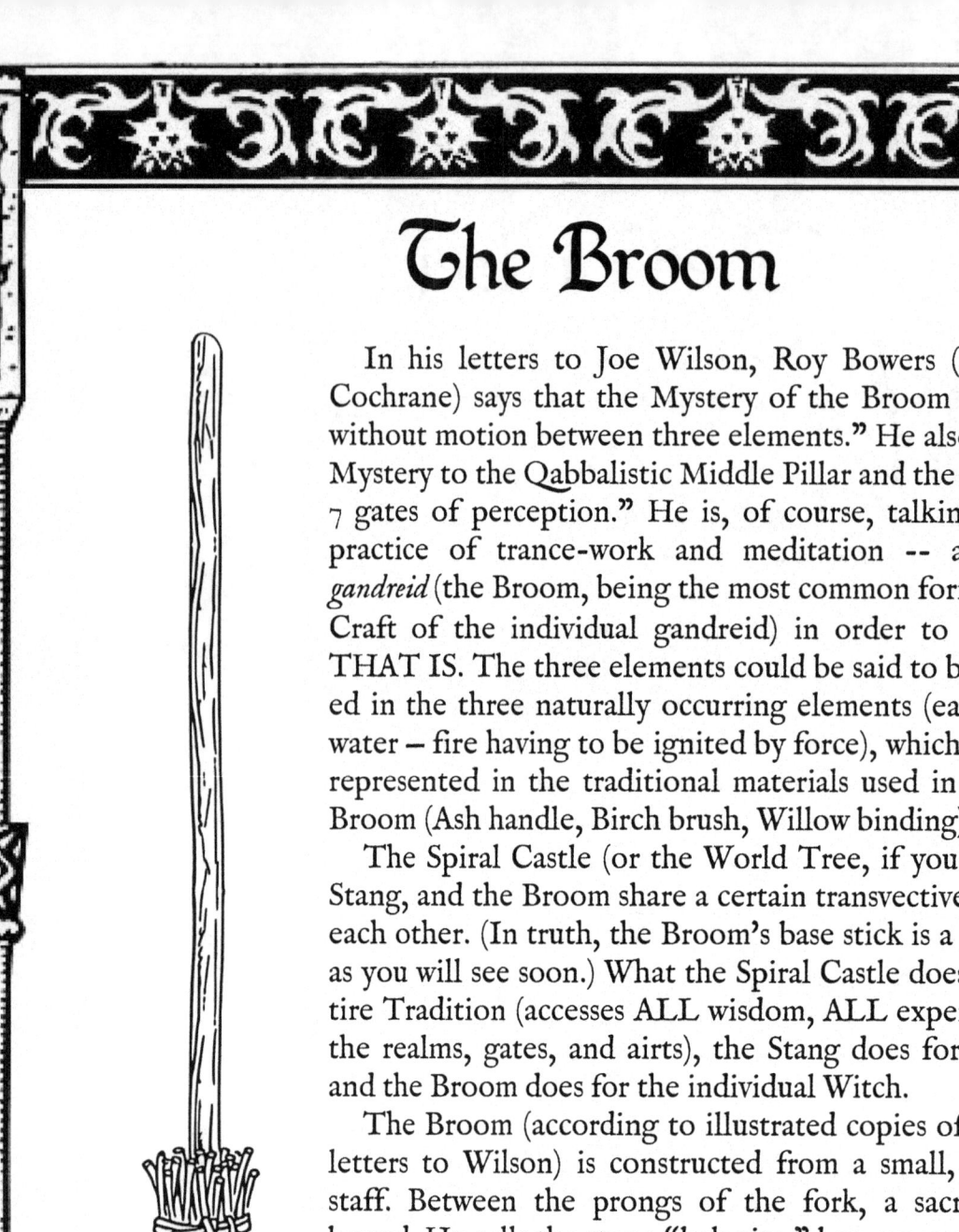

In his letters to Joe Wilson, Roy Bowers (aka, Robert Cochrane) says that the Mystery of the Broom is "spinning without motion between three elements." He also relates this Mystery to the Qabbalistic Middle Pillar and the "path to the 7 gates of perception." He is, of course, talking about the practice of trance-work and meditation -- and using a *gandreid* (the Broom, being the most common form within the Craft of the individual gandreid) in order to access ALL THAT IS. The three elements could be said to be represented in the three naturally occurring elements (earth, air, and water – fire having to be ignited by force), which are likewise represented in the traditional materials used in making the Broom (Ash handle, Birch brush, Willow binding).

The Spiral Castle (or the World Tree, if you prefer), the Stang, and the Broom share a certain transvective power with each other. (In truth, the Broom's base stick is a small Stang, as you will see soon.) What the Spiral Castle does for the entire Tradition (accesses ALL wisdom, ALL experience, ALL the realms, gates, and airts), the Stang does for the Coven, and the Broom does for the individual Witch.

The Broom (according to illustrated copies of Cochrane's letters to Wilson) is constructed from a small, forked Ash staff. Between the prongs of the fork, a sacred stone is bound. He calls the stone "balanite," but my research reveals it to be none other than basalt (common black lava stone) – which is excellent for tethering the psyche during spirit-flight.

The Broom can also be used for blessing, blasting, and cleansing magic. For blessing and blasting, carry it over the right or left shoulder, respectively – working deosil or widdershins, as appropriate. For cleansing, sweep the energetic space (above, below, and between). Cleanse the Broom's brush with saltwater after heavy spiritual cleansing work or blasting work.

Copyright Asteria Books 2020

The Stang

A stang, in its most basic form is simply a forked stick set with its long end into the ground. It acts as an axis on which magic can turn, and as a pole that can be "ridden" by the shaman or witch into different realms. Its forks represent the horns of the Witch Lord. The stang entered modern Craft by the hand of Robert Cochrane, who called it as "sacred to the People as the Crucifix is to the Christians."

A witch and her demonic familiar fly on a stang.

A masked family flies out on their stang.

The stang is sometimes represented by a iron-tined pitchfork or a pole with the skull of a horned beast on it. Often in these configurations there will be a candle or torch lit between the two horns or tines, in the style of the icon of Baphomet. Although not as popular as motif as, say, riding a broomstick, there are many examples of witches using the stang to fly in early woodcuts. The stang has antecedents in the Yggdrasill of Norse lore, the Poteau Mitan of Haitian Voudon, and the ascending-pole birch tree of the Yakut shamans. It is both a world-pillar on which the cosmos turns, and a gandreigh. Any wood is suitable for use as a stang, although ash, with its connections to Yggdrasill, the tree on which Odin was hung shaman-like for nine days, is a popular choice. The stang is hung with two arrows, one black and one white. These arrow point upwards during the light half of the year and downwards during the dark half of the year. Some covens don't always hang two arrows on the stang. Sometimes, it is a single arrow, with a linen shirt hung from it. The shirt can be either white or black, depending on the ritual or time of year. The stang is the hayfork that represents the Horned God, but it is also the spinner's distaff. The linen shirt on a single arrow is an allusion to the flax wrapped around the distaff.

Copyright Asteria Publishing 2012

The Staff

The staff is one of the most personal tools a Witch will ever create and use. Though an embellished walking stick can be purchased from talented artisans, a much more effective and bonded tool will be gained by the Witch who takes the time to engage in the creation of their own staff. It can be any height, ranging from about hip-height to roughly the full height of the Witch.

Cutting a Staff

To make your own staff, start by going into the woods with an offering (silver is traditional, but birdseed is also nice), a handsaw you have blessed to the task, your shelg or lancet, and a small first aid kit. Ask your Spirits to guide you to your staff, and then look for either a straight piece of deadfall that is unmolested by rot and bugs OR a broomstick- to wrist-thick sapling in a healthy stand of the same species. Ask permission of the tree and make an offering of coin/seed and water before cutting or taking the wood. Make a blood bond with the newly-claimed wood, allowing your spirit and that of the staff to meet and mingle. Clean the site where you drew blood. Remove unneeded pieces of wood and leave them for the creatures of the forest, including the bark.

Shodding a Staff

Drive an iron nail (such as an old-fashioned "coffin" nail) through the base of your staff, taking care not to split the wood. Alternately, you can fit your staff with a metal butt-cap. This connects the staff to Tubal Cain's forge and prepares it for use in magic.

Wielding a Staff

The staff can be used to demarcate the ritual grounds when laying the compass. It is symbolic of the weaver's distaff, the cane of the Crone, the blasting staff, the spear, the battle-staff, the standard-pole, and also the very tree from which it sprung. The staff is also a gandreigh, or riding pole, which means that it can be used in a number of ways to achieve altered states of consciousness – including seething. It is not uncommon to hang the Crane Bag or talismans from the staff.

Retiring a Staff

Depending on the uses to which you put your staff, it may deteriorate over time and need to be retired. This is natural. Depending on the level of adornment and embellishment on your staff, you may return it to the earth by using it in the garden as a bean-pole or give it to the fire as kindling. Furthermore, upon the death of a Witch, the staff should not be passed as a kuthun to another Witch because it is so bound to the life and magic of the one who wielded it. Instead, it should be given to the earth, fire, or water as part of the Witch's crossing rite.

Copyright Asteria Books 2019

Sacrificial Stone Bowl

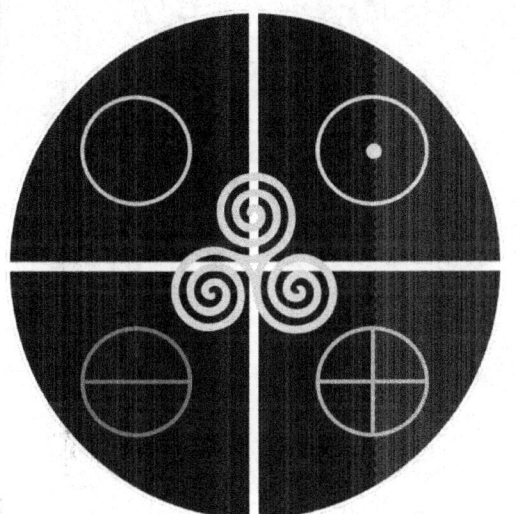

Why to Use the Stone Bowl

There is an ebb and flow to magic. Different traditions have different ways of indicating the way the price for magick will be paid, but nearly all agree that some form of price MUST be paid – whether the witch is aware and willing to pay or not. A cunning person goes into this process with their eyes open and asks up front what the cost will be in order to decide if the prize gained is worth the price to be paid. This bowl is a variation of a tool used in some Trad Craft lines to determine the type and magnitude of that price.

Symbolism & Types of Sacrifice

The design above is painted into a flat-bottomed bowl or lipped dish. The white cross that divides the space represents the crossroads. Starting in the upper right quadrant and moving clockwise, the other symbols represent:

Castle of Revelry (*yellow circle with central point*) ~ sacrifice of abstinence (refraining from sexual stimulation, smoking, alcohol, tobacco, sugar, or other pleasure for a period of time)

Castle of Stone (*green crossed circle*) ~ sacrifice of wealth (giving money to charity, donating items, gifting personal possession to someone, working on a project without compensation)

Castle Perilous (*red halved circle*) ~ sacrifice of blood/pain (submitting to flogging, lifting heavy weights, running an endurance race, shedding your own blood with intent, etc)

Castle of Glass (*blue circle*) ~ sacrifice of comfort (fasting for a period of time, sleeping on the floor, wearing an intentionally irritating garment, walking barefoot on gravel, etc)

Spiral Castle (*silver triskelion*) ~ no sacrifice associated with this Castle

How to Use the Stone Bowl

Cast three stone (one each – black, white red) into the bowl. The stones represent the Black and White Goddesses and the Red God. Whichever stone the red stone is closest to indicates to which Goddess your sacrifice will be made. The circle she has landed on indicates which type of sacrifice. The distance between the black and white stones indicates the magnitude of the sacrifice. So, if the red stone is closest to the white stone, and the white stone is on Castle Revelry, you will make a sacrifice of abstinence to the (any) White Goddess. If the black stone is close to the white stone, that sacrifice would be small. (And if the white stone had landed on the triskelion in this same scenario, there would be no sacrifice required at all.)

Copyright Asteria Books 2012-2019

The Elemental Weapons

Each of the four elemental gates is traditionally associated with a martial weapon. The masculine elements of air and fire are represented by offensive weaponry: the staff (or spear) and the sword. The feminine elements of earth and water are represented by defensive weaponry: the shield and helm. These weapons have antecedents in the four suits of the Tarot: swords, staves, coins (shields), and cups (helms). They are also representative of the four Celtic Hallows of the Tuatha: sword, stone, spear, and cauldron.

The Sword

The sword is the weapon of the east gate, where it has been forged within Tubal Cain's smithy. The sword is a symbol of nobility and initiation. Just as Lancelot crossed the Sword Bridge to enter the country of Melegant, so must we cross step across this threshold to enter the circle of initiation. It is also the Sword That Cuts Both Ways, reminding both initiate and initiator of the nature of Mystery and Oath.

The Staff

The staff is the most versatile, and often the most personal, tool of a witch. It can be a distaff, a blackthorn blasting staff, a battle staff, a spear, or a simple walking stick. The form matters far less than the function of the staff. It is the weapon of the north gate, sacred to the Black Goddess, who, in her crone aspect walks with a staff. In her aspect as the spinner of Fate, she bears a distaff; and in her bloodthirsty warrior aspect, she carries a spear.

The Shield

The shield is both a physical and a metaphysical tool. It can be a literal shield, like a targe, held as a piece of symbolic regalia upon which the symbols of the coven or the witch are emblazoned, or it can be an energetic tool which we cultivate through visualization and discipline. The shield is a symbol of guardianship of the mysteries. It is the weapon of the southern gate of earth.

The Helm

The helm, upturned, is the cup or cauldron of the western gate of water. The helm is symbolic of the mask, which we use in transformational magics and ecstatic ritual. The helm protects the head, which the Celts perceived as the seat of the soul. The western gate is also associated with the land of the Dead.

Copyright Asteria Publishing 2019

Shield

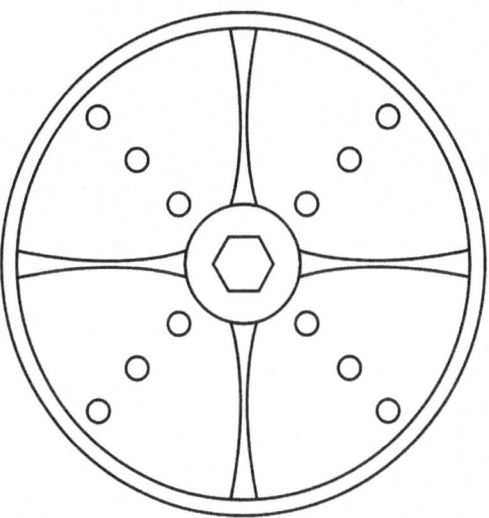

The shield is both a physical and a metaphysical tool. It can be a literal shield, like a targe, held as a piece of symbolic regalia upon which the symbols of the coven or the witch are emblazoned, or it can be a magical tool which we cultivate through visualization and discipline. This shield is a semi-permeable barrier of etheric energy that we use for self-defense and cloaking magic. The shield is a symbol of guardianship of the mysteries. It is the weapon of the southern gate of earth, and is sacred to the White Goddess. It is her shining white light which builds the etheric shield, and it is her seelie magic that weaves glamor and cloaking spells that depend on the shield.

While any style of Shield will do, Witches tend to favor the Targe. A targe is a round shield made of iron or wood that's been plated in iron. It has come to be associated with the Scottish Highlands, though its use was more widespread than that. It is worn on the forearm and has a hand-grip and a strap (usually with a buckle) to secure it to the arm. Shields made for battle were concave, but ours are usually flat.

It is the weapon of ThisWorld. It is a defensive weapon, used to guard against and deflect the dangers and assaults of day-to-day reality. It also represents the ways in which the physical realm affords certain protections and defenses against the slings and attacks of the other magical realities.

A simple shield is very easy to make and really adds to the protective, defensive magic of your home and magical space. Once it is finished, place it in a prominent location to guard your home or altar. When laying the compass for ritual, the Shield would be placed in the South.

Copyright Asteria Books 2022

To Make a Ritual Shield

Wooden round (like a pre-made table top)
Heavy duty felt
Leather
Furniture tacks
Cabinet handle
Pencil
Scissors
Measuring tape or ruler
Hammer
Staple gun with staples

1. As with any magical crafting project, you should create the targe in sacred space.
2. Place the leather face down on your worktable. Put the wooden round on top of the leather and trace the shape plus 2 inches all the way around. Cut the leather and set it aside.
3. Do the same with the felt, except cut just shy of 2 inches. You'll want the leather to cover the felt completely.
4. Place the leather face down again on the worktable. Put the felt on top of it, followed by the wooden round.
5. Fold the leather and felt over the wooden base at the top-most point of the circle. Staple it in place on the back of the shield. Do the same at the bottom, making sure that the fabric and leather are snug but not too tightly stretched.
6. Repeat the folding and stapling at the two sides, and then work your way around the entire circle. Remember to staple one side and follow it up with its exact opposite. This will keep the leather and fabric even and smooth.
7. You'll end up with staples all around the backside of the shield, holding the leather in place.
8. Next, use the furniture tacks to tack down the leather on the front of the shield. You can make a simple circle of tacks along the outer edge of the flat circle, or tacks the outer rim of the shield. Another option is to incorporate a personal design, using the tacks, on the face of the shield. Any of these options will serve the same primary function - keeping your leather snug and secure.
9. Affix your handle onto the back of the shield in place that will be comfortable when you are holding it.
10. Use a strap of leather (or fur, if you want) to create a strap for your forearm. This will help your shield wear comfortably when you have need to hold it.
11. Finish by placing your sigil and/or bindrune on the back of the shield, if you have one.
12. Dedicate it to magical use after the Shield is complete by saining it. You would be wise to call on Goda, Horse, Swan, Apple Tree, and the Southern Gate to empower this weapon.

Copyright Asteria Books 2022

Sword

The Sword is a magickal weapon that is common to many traditions of magick and Craft. This is due in no small part to its associations with alchemy and smithing, as well as to its cross-like shape. (Crosses have been important symbols since ling before Christianity – having connections to both the Axis Mundi or World Tree and also the Cross of the Elements.)

In the east, the gate of fire, is the forge of Tubal Cain. Created on this primal forge is that most iconic of forged weapons, the sword. The sword is a symbol of nobility and initiation. It is the "sword bridge" we cross to enter the circle of initiation, just as Lancelot had to cross the sword bridge to enter the enchanted country of Melagant. It is also the "sword that cuts both ways," demonstrating that both initiate and initiator are creating a solemn pact. In Arthurian legend the sword Excalibur was drawn from a stone, but in the earliest forms of the myth the sword was drawn from an anvil. In our tradition the "oath stone" of the coven is represented by an anvil in honor of Tubal Cain, Lord of the forge, and the fire of creation.

Within Witchcraft, it is less common for each Witch to have their own Sword – much like this would not have been the norm for our pre-modern forebears. Instead, we often see a single Sword being wielded by the leader of the Coven or leader of a particular ritual.

Double-edged blades are the most common in the Craft. Some blades that might be considered long knives (by blade aficionados) could also work nicely. These might include the Seax, the Arkansas Toothpick, the Gladius, the Tanto, a "hand and a half" dagger, or others along these lines.

Copyright Asteria Books 2022

Helm and Mask

 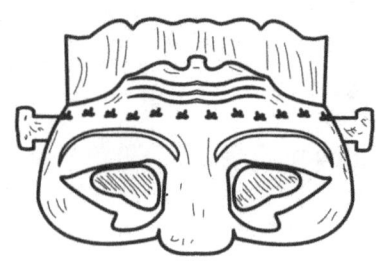

The helm, upturned, is the cup or cauldron of the western gate of water. It is the helkapp that Tubal Cain as the Lord of death wears to grant invisibility. The helm is also symbolic of the mask, which we use in transformational magics, and ecstatic ritual. The helm protects the head, which the Celts perceived as the seat of the soul. Thus, just as the shield protects the physical body from harm, so does the helm, or mask, represent protection of the soul. It is appropriate, then, that the helm be the weapon of the western gate, that place of rest, that realm of the dead, that healer of the soul.

A replica or costume piece (not made of plastic) would work. There are leather helmets of both historical and fantasy origins, as well. It is possible to even construct a leather helm for yourself, if you desire.

Alternatively, you could display a Mask (or multiple masks) in the West. Look to the Dorset Ooser and the Head of ATHO for both inspiration and connection of these symbols.

Copyright Asteria Books 2022

Wands and Woods

Wands have been used since ancient times to command and compel entities, direct power, house spirits, and symbolize the forces of nature. Wooden wands are linked to the symbolism of the World Tree and also draw upon the energies of the species of tree from which they were sourced. Stone and metal wands are a tool of the modern magical practitioner and can be useful for specific workings. Stone wands are great for healing and spirit work, while metal wands are excellent conductors of energy. The best length for a wand is from the crook of the elbow to the tip of the middle finger.

BLACKTHORN ~ a winter tree; sloes ripen and sweeten only after the first frost; has vicious thorns that can cause painful infections; forms dense thickets when left to spread on its own.; used in cudgel-making; associated with cursing and blasting magic.

WILLOW ~ strongly lunar ; found at the edges of streams and lakes, giving them the elemental powers of both earth and water; use it for love, healing, eloquence, and rhythms

BIRCH ~ first to bud; first to grow in bare soil; a symbol of new beginnings; protection, healing, fertility, and rebirth

ASH ~ Celtic and Norse World Tree; symbolizes connections - past & present, spiritual & earthly, lowest & highest, self & cosmos; good for work involving divination, healing, inner journeys, and initiation.

OAK ~ endurance, strength, power, and nobility; the name "druid" derives from *duir*, the Celtic term for the oak; use in magic for strength, wisdom, illumination

APPLE ~ related to the rose family, it is associated with love and beauty; the Celts also linked the Apple to the isle of Avalon, a place of healing and rebirth

HAZEL ~ fertility, wisdom, marriage, divination, healing, protection, intuition, dowsing wands, individuality, finding the hidden, luck and wishes. The Hazel is considered to be the Tree of knowledge for the Celts.

CEDAR ~ Abor Vitae, this is the classical Tree of Life; used for establishing sacred spaces, clearing negative energies, and summoning helpful spirits

Copyright Asteria Books 2019

Mazey Stone

The Mazey Stone (or Troy Stone) is a tool that is virtually unknown in Wicca and Neo-Paganism, despite having very ancient roots and a wide realm of use in both British and Scandinavian folk magick. This "stone" (although it is sometimes inscribed into wood) is a small, personal representation of a labyrinth or maze design that has been extent since Ancient Greece. The same maze (sometimes called a Cretan Maze/Labyrinth) has been built as both a turf maze and a stone maze in large enough scale for a person to walk. Mazey Stones, however, are small enough to be handheld and traced with a finger. Their purpose is multi-part: induce a light trance state, act as a gateway ward, and symbolically connect us to the Red Thread.

Troy Towns

The maze most commonly featured in Mazey Stones has been associated with both Crete (and the labyrinth that held the Minotaur) and also Troy (whose walls were said to be laid out in a seven-layer circuit as part of their elaborate defense). Within both British and Scandinavian place names where turf and stone labyrinths are attested, a great many incorporate some reference to Troy (Caerdroia, Walls of Troy, Troy-town, Trojaborg, etc.)

Symbolism

In Trojan lore, the city's labyrinthine walls were a defensive design aimed at thwarting would-be attackers. Should they make their way into the city (which was difficult for one who didn't know the path), they would be trapped inside. The Cretan lore, however, says that their maze was designed to keep the Minotaur within, thereby protecting the people. When we reframe the idea of "what lies at the heart of the labyrinth" in terms of the Mysteries (or spiritual gnosis and transformation), treading the labyrinth becomes a spiritual and magical act. Furthermore, we can see in the lore additional symbolism attached to the labyrinth-keepers (like Ariadne) and its tools (like the red thread she lays as a guide). The Mazey Stone is one of the practical, physical tools that brings us into the presence of the Divine (both within us and around us). It helps us gain access to the Mysteries.

Gateway Stone

When you are not actively using the Mazey Stone to induce trance or journey work (which is done simply by tracing one's finger along the grooved route of the path — and chanting or humming), the stone can be placed at the entrance to the Compass.

Copyright Asteria Books 2022

Skull and Crossed Bones

The Ancestral skulls of the Coveners are placed a the base of the Stang, along with the cauldron and anvil. A pair of crossed leg bones is also placed there with a Coven skull, as well. Sometimes the Coven Skull is hung from the Stang, in which case the two crossed arrows function in a similar capacity as the crossed leg bones.

The bones are crossed when we are not doing necromantic rituals. But if we want to talk to the Dead, we open the leg bones so they make a vertical channel facing out from the skull. This opens the path of communication.

The skull and bones used for this use are from a once-living being, since these are much more effective than stone, paper mache, ceramic, or glass for purposes of communication. But, if you must make a substitution for real bone, use an alternative that feels good to you.

Avoid plastic for any tool that will carry Spirit. A Witch would do better to carve an apple into a crude skull shape and "skin" a couple of sticks to act as the bones, than use plastic ones.

Of the animal bones you might choose, medium to large mammals are best, for practical reasons. The bones are sturdier and less like to break from being held and moved. Horned/antlered animals are the most preferred, due to their association with the Witch Father.

Personal animal Allies are also great candidates for skulls and bones, as long as they're sturdy enough for this use and legal to own.

Copyright Asteria Books 2022

Coven Dolly

The Dolly is one of the less common bits of folkloric Craft that occasionally shows up in the writings of published Witches. As with many other folkloric pieces, the traditions that have been handed down around the Dolly can vary widely, as do the origin stories or rationales given for her existence.

The Dolly is representative of the Coven Guardian or Familiar. Witches who practice independently might still have one as a House Guardian/Familiar for the home where they live.

The "Hearth Doll" of Old Craft became the "Kitchen Witch Doll" for many Appalachian and Ozark families. These days, they are seen simply as "good luck" – with little awareness of their traditions.

In different parts of the UK, we still see the Hearth Doll (or Chimney Doll) in her place upon the hearth. Gemma Gary's Ros an Bucca Coven used to maintain a website and photo archive of tools that featured just such a doll as this. She is fully decked out with talismans, a beaded and knotted rowan berry necklace, and a hare and is provisioned with a chair, cauldron, and wee blackthorn staff. In essence, she has all the tools she needs to do the work she's been engaged to do.

The Dolly can be simple or elaborate. You can make it according to any number of traditional doll-making methods – or you can purchase a doll (not plastic please) to act as the vessel for the Spirit of your home or Coven. Wooden, corn husk, porcelain, and cloth dolls are all good choices.

The Coven's Dolly is kept at the home where the Coven meets (the Covenstead) and is present for most, if not all rituals. Fashioned as an adult figure (not a child), the Dolly is the vessel of the Coven Familiar and should convey something of that Spirit's nature, if possible.

Copyright Asteria Books 2022

Divination

Augury

From the shadowed pages of this tome, I impart the arcane art of Augury, a practice as old as the feathered kin themselves. Know that the avian creatures, those messengers of the celestial spheres, bear upon their wings the very whispers of destiny.

The Augur, a seeker of hidden truths, must possess a keen eye and a tranquil spirit. He shall observe the birds, not with the gaze of a hunter, but with the reverence of a scholar deciphering ancient glyphs. The manner of their flight, be it swift and direct, or erratic and circling, reveals the currents of fate. The cries they utter, from the sharp, piercing shriek to the soft, melodious trill, are the very voices of the Godds, speaking in a tongue only the initiated can understand.

Let the Augur note the direction from whence they come, for the East brings tidings of beginnings, the West of endings, the North of trials, and the South of blessings. Observe also the lands upon which they alight, for barren ground portends misfortune, while fertile fields promise abundance.

Consider the number of birds, for a solitary bird may signify isolation, while a flock heralds a gathering. The species themselves hold meaning: the raven, a harbinger of omen, for good or ill; the dove, a symbol of peace; the eagle, a sign of power.

Through these observations, the Augur may perceive the threads of destiny, woven by unseen hands. But beware, for misinterpretation breeds falsehood, and the whispers of the birds are fickle, their meanings veiled in shadow. Only through diligent study and unwavering devotion can the true Augur unlock the secrets they hold.

Copyright Asteria Books 2025

Bibliomancy

Bibliomancy is a method by which the very words of written wisdom may illuminate the pathways of fate. Know that within the bound pages of sacred texts, or even the mundane tomes of man, reside the echoes of cosmic truths, waiting to be unveiled.

The Bibliomancer, a seeker of hidden knowledge, must approach this practice with reverence and a tranquil mind. He shall not seek to force the words, but rather allow them to flow as a river, guided by the unseen currents of chance.

Begin by composing a question, a query that weighs upon the soul. Pray for guidance from the Powers you trust and heed. Then, with eyes closed and spirit attuned, allow the hand to fall upon a chosen book. Open it, with eyes closed, trace a path across the page with the finger until a word or passage calls to the inner ear. This is the oracle's response, a message whispered from the realm of the written word.

Consider the context of the passage, for its meaning may be layered and cryptic. A single word can hold a universe of significance, its interpretation shifting with the ebb and flow of circumstance. Let the Bibliomancer meditate upon the chosen words, allowing their essence to permeate the soul.

Be wary, for the unwary mind may misinterpret the subtle nuances of the text. The words are not always literal, but rather symbolic, reflecting the hidden patterns of destiny. Thus, the Bibliomancer must possess a discerning heart, capable of perceiving the subtle whispers hidden within the ink. By this method, the written word becomes a conduit for divine insight, and the pages of a book, a gateway to the unknown.

Prayer Before Bibliomancy

"Ancient Spirit of the written word, I invoke your presence. As I seek guidance within these pages, grant me clarity and discernment. Let my hand find the words meant for my path, and illuminate their true meaning. Shield me from illusion, and open my mind to your wisdom. I offer this moment of reverence, trusting in your guidance to reveal the answers I seek."

Copyright Asteria Books 2025

Candle Readings

The Ceromancer, a seeker of truth in the realm of light and form, approaches this practice with a calm heart and a focused mind. A suitable candle, preferably of a single color, is essential. The flame's quality and the wax's patterns are the keys to interpretation.

Begin by focusing your intention, visualizing the question or situation you seek to understand. Light the candle, allowing the flame to stabilize. Observe the flame's color, size, and movement, as well as the patterns formed by the melting wax.

The flame's characteristics hold symbolic meaning. A bright, steady flame signifies clarity, positive energy, and straightforwardness. A flickering or unstable flame indicates uncertainty, obstacles, or emotional turmoil. A blue flame suggests spiritual influence or communication, while a red flame portends passion, anger, or urgency. A small flame warns of limitations or scarcity, while a large flame signifies abundance or expansion.

The wax's patterns also hold significance. Dripping wax that forms distinct shapes reveals messages. Shapes formed near the candle's base represent the past or present, while those formed further away indicate the future.

Shapes

Animals: represent instincts, primal urges, or specific individuals.

Flowers: signify growth, beauty, or emotional expression. If specific flowers are discernible, the symbolism of those blossoms might also be added to the interpretation.

Numbers: represent time, quantity, or symbolic meaning.

Letters: signify communication or specific words.

Swords or sharp shapes: represent conflict, cutting ties, or decisive action.

Rounded shapes: represent harmony, cycles, or completion.

Wax Movement

Wax dripping straight down: a clear path or straightforward answer.

Wax dripping in spirals: cyclical patterns or repeating events.

Wax dripping unevenly: instability or unpredictable circumstances.

Flame and Wax Combined

A strong blue flame with wax forming a dove shape: spiritual peace and communication.

A flickering red flame with wax forming sharp angles: emotional conflict and decisive action.

Copyright Asteria Books 2025

Cartomancy

Cartomancy, the ancient art of divination using cards, has captivated mystics, scholars, and seekers throughout history. From tarot decks to playing cards to oracle cards, cartomancy techniques offer a window into the past, present, and future, revealing insights and guidance through symbolic interpretation.

Cartomancy encompasses various types of cards, each with its own symbolism and interpretation methods:

1. TAROT CARDS: Tarot decks consist of 78 cards divided into major arcana (22 cards representing major life themes) and minor arcana (56 cards divided into four suits – usually cups, pentacles, swords, and wands – each representing different aspects of life and experiences).
2. PLAYING CARDS: Traditional playing cards, with their suits of hearts, diamonds, clubs, and spades, also lend themselves to divinatory practices. Each suit and number can be interpreted symbolically, reflecting aspects of daily life and relationships.
3. ORACLE CARDS: Specially designed cards that are usually curated around a theme or central concept, these cards are highly symbolic, artistic, and unique.

Techniques of Cartomancy

Shuffling and Drawing: The process begins with shuffling the cards to infuse them with the seeker's energy and intention. Cards are then drawn, either randomly or with a specific spread in mind.

Spreads: Spreads are layouts that determine how cards are placed during a reading. Popular spreads include the Celtic Cross (for detailed insights into a situation), Three-Card Spread (past, present, future), and the Yes/No Spread (simple answers to direct questions).

Intuitive Interpretation: Cartomancy relies heavily on intuition. Readers interpret the cards' symbolism, colors, numbers, and relationships within the spread, weaving together a narrative that speaks to the seeker's concerns or questions.

Symbolism: Each card carries layers of symbolism. For instance, the Fool in tarot can represent new beginnings or taking risks, while the Ace of Cups might symbolize emotional fulfillment or spiritual awakening.

Journaling: Keeping a journal of readings helps track patterns, refine interpretations, and deepen understanding of personal associations with specific cards.

Copyright Asteria Books 2024

Casting Lots

Casting lots is an ancient method of divination, rooted in diverse cultures and traditions. This practice involves using objects like stones, bones, or dice to interpret outcomes.

Types of Lots

Stones and Pebbles -- Gather a collection of stones, each marked with symbols or numbers. Alternatively, stones can be unmarked but embody a variety of shapes, colors, or other distinguishable qualities. Each stone's marking or color may represent specific meanings related to health, prosperity, or relationships.

Dice -- Use standard six-sided dice or specialized dice with symbols. Roll them to generate numbers or patterns, interpreting each roll's significance. Numerical outcomes may correspond to specific outcomes or themes relevant to the question or situation.

Sticks or Bones -- Arrange sticks or bones in patterns or sequences. Their arrangement or order after casting can provide insights into sequences or paths.

Rituals and Preparation

Clarify Purpose: Before casting, define the question or intention clearly. Focus on what guidance or insight is sought from the lots.

Mental Preparation: Clear the mind of distractions and cultivate openness to receive messages or insights from the lots.

Ritual Cleansing: Some traditions involve purifying the objects used for casting lots, such as through smudging with sage or using consecrated water.

Spiritual Alignment: Align with spiritual or cosmic energies through prayers, meditation, or invoking divine guidance before beginning.

Method of Casting

Lots are usually cast by allowing a random number and collection of objects from the set to be pulled from their container and tossed onto a reading surface like a tray or mat. Readers pay attention to how the objects land or arrange themselves. Note any patterns, groupings, or outliers that may influence interpretation.

Casting lots is often very unique to the individual, so be prepared to collect your own set of lots and then assign general meanings to each piece in your set.

Copyright Asteria Books 2024

Dice Reading

From the realm of chance and the geometry of fate, I reveal the art of Dice Divination, a method by which the rolling bones reveal the hidden patterns of destiny. Within the tumbling cubes, marked with modern numerical faces, reside the whispers of fortune, waiting to be deciphered.

The Dice Diviner, a seeker of truth in the realm of chance, approaches the casting with a steady hand and focused mind. The dice are allowed to fall freely, their patterns revealing the currents of destiny.

Begin by formulating a clear question, a query that resonates within your being. Then, with a breath of intention, cast the dice upon a flat surface. For a simple reading, use two six-sided dice (2d6). The sum of the two dice provides a general overview: a low sum (2-6) suggests challenges or delays, a middle sum (7) indicates balance or a turning point, and a high sum (8-12) portends positive outcomes or opportunities.

Each die's individual result offers specific insights. Die one often represents the querent or the situation itself, while die two reflects external influences or the outcome. For example, a 1 on die one might suggest isolation or a need for caution, while a 6 on die two could indicate success or completion.

Consider the relationship between the dice. A double (two identical numbers) amplifies the meaning of that number. A large difference between the two dice signifies a strong contrast or conflict. For a more complex reading, use multiple dice, such as 3d6 or 4d6, assigning each die a specific meaning (e.g., past, present, future; self, others, environment). The sum and individual values of each die are then interpreted in relation to their assigned meanings.

The numbers themselves are not merely numerical values, but symbolic representations. One represents beginnings or individuality, two duality or partnerships, three creativity or communication, four stability or structure, five change or challenges, and six harmony or completion. Through this art, the rolling bones become a conduit for divination, and the patterns they form, a gateway to the hidden truths that lie beyond. Let the dice fall, and let their wisdom guide your path.

Copyright Asteria Books 2024

Domino Readings

The patterns and relationships formed by the tiles of fallen dominoes reveal the interplay of opposing forces, the balance and imbalance that shape our lives. Through this art, the falling stones become a conduit for divination, and the arrangements, a map of the unseen connections that guide our path. Let the tiles fall, and let their wisdom illuminate your understanding.

Begin by formulating a question that explores the balance or imbalance within a situation. Then, either cast the dominoes onto a flat surface or draw a set number from a facedown pile. The patterns formed, and the values revealed, are not random, but reflections of the forces at play.

Consider the layout of the drawn or fallen dominoes. A line of tiles reveals a sequential progression, while a cluster indicates a convergence of influences. The double tiles (tiles with matching numbers on both sides) amplify the meaning of that number, representing a point of emphasis or stability.

Each tile's value, represented by the pips on each side, holds symbolic meaning. Zero represents potential or absence, one represents individuality or beginnings, two represents duality or partnerships, three represents creativity or communication, four represents stability or structure, five represents change or challenges, and six represents harmony or completion.

The relationship between the two sides of a tile is crucial. A tile with a large difference between its two sides indicates a conflict or tension, while a tile with similar values suggests harmony or balance. The total sum of the pips in a reading also provides a general overview, revealing the overall energy of the situation.

Copyright Asteria Books 2025

Dream Interpretation

Dreams have fascinated humanity since ancient times, offering glimpses into the mysterious realms of the subconscious and beyond. In both traditional cultures and modern magical practices, dream interpretation serves as a profound tool for understanding ourselves, navigating life's challenges, and seeking spiritual guidance. Across civilizations, from Mesopotamia to Egypt and beyond, dreams were revered as messages from gods or spirits. Ancient Egyptians believed dreams provided insights into the divine will, influencing decisions both personal and political. Similarly, Greek philosophers and Roman leaders consulted dream oracles for prophecies and guidance in matters of state.

In the 19th century, Sigmund Freud revolutionized dream interpretation with his psychoanalytic theory, proposing that dreams reflect unconscious desires and conflicts. Freud's work laid the foundation for understanding dreams as symbolic narratives that encode deeper psychological truths. Today, dream interpretation in magic blends ancient wisdom with modern insights from psychology and neuroscience. While magical traditions emphasize spiritual guidance and symbolism, contemporary interpretations also consider psychological theories of dreams as reflections of the subconscious mind.

In magical traditions, practitioners employ various techniques to decipher dream messages:

- Symbolism and Divination: Objects, creatures, and actions in dreams are interpreted symbolically, often using divination tools like tarot cards or runes to discern their meanings within a magical context.
- Ritualistic Practices: Before sleep, rituals such as meditation or casting protective spells are performed to influence dream content and enhance spiritual connection.
- Dream Journals: Keeping a detailed record of dreams aids in identifying recurring themes and symbols, facilitating interpretation and personal growth over time.

Engaging with dreams through a magical lens offers numerous benefits:

- Self-Discovery: Exploring dreams unveils hidden aspects of the self and unconscious desires, promoting introspection and self-awareness.
- Manifestation: Dreams serve as a blueprint for manifesting intentions or desires in waking life, aligning magical practice with personal goals and aspirations.
- Healing and Transformation: Confronting fears, resolving emotional conflicts, or receiving spiritual insights through dreams can lead to profound healing and inner transformation.

Whether seeking guidance from divine sources, exploring inner realms, or unlocking the mysteries of existence, dreams provide a profound avenue for both mystical exploration and personal revelation.

Copyright Asteria Books 2024

Egg Readings

From the depths of the primal egg, and the clarity of water, I reveal the art of Oomancy. Through this art, the yolk and water become a mirror reflecting the hidden currents of fate, revealing the answers that lie within.

The Oomancer, a seeker of truth in the fluid realm, approaches this practice with a pure heart and a steady hand. Preparation is key: a fresh, unbroken egg is required, symbolizing the potential held within. Clear, still water, in a transparent glass, provides the canvas upon which fate's image will be painted.

Begin by focusing your intent, visualizing the question or situation you seek to understand. Gently crack the egg, separating the yolk from the white. Carefully deposit the yolk into the glass of water, ensuring it remains whole. Observe the yolk as it settles, and the forms it creates as it interacts with the water.

The shapes and patterns that emerge hold symbolic meaning. A clear, unbroken yolk suggests clarity and straightforwardness. Cloudiness or fragmentation indicates confusion or obstacles. A yolk that sinks directly to the bottom portends stability or grounding, while one that floats near the surface signifies fleetingness or superficiality.

Shapes formed by the yolk hold specific interpretations: a circle represents wholeness or cycles, a line indicates a journey or path, a heart signifies love or emotion, and a cloud suggests uncertainty or vagueness. Bubbles within the water can represent communication or messages, their size and location adding nuance to the reading.

Sample Interpretations:

- A yolk forming a clear, unbroken circle at the bottom with a few small bubbles: a stable and positive situation with minor communications.

- A fragmented yolk with cloudy water: confusion and obstacles are present, requiring careful navigation.

- A yolk forming a line that rises to the surface: a journey or change is imminent, but may be fleeting.

- A yolk forming a heart shape with many small bubbles: a situation involving love or strong emotion with many communications.

Copyright Asteria Books 2025

Geomancy

The Geomancer, a seeker of truth within the terrestrial realm, approaches this practice with a calm spirit.

Here are the figures and their meanings:

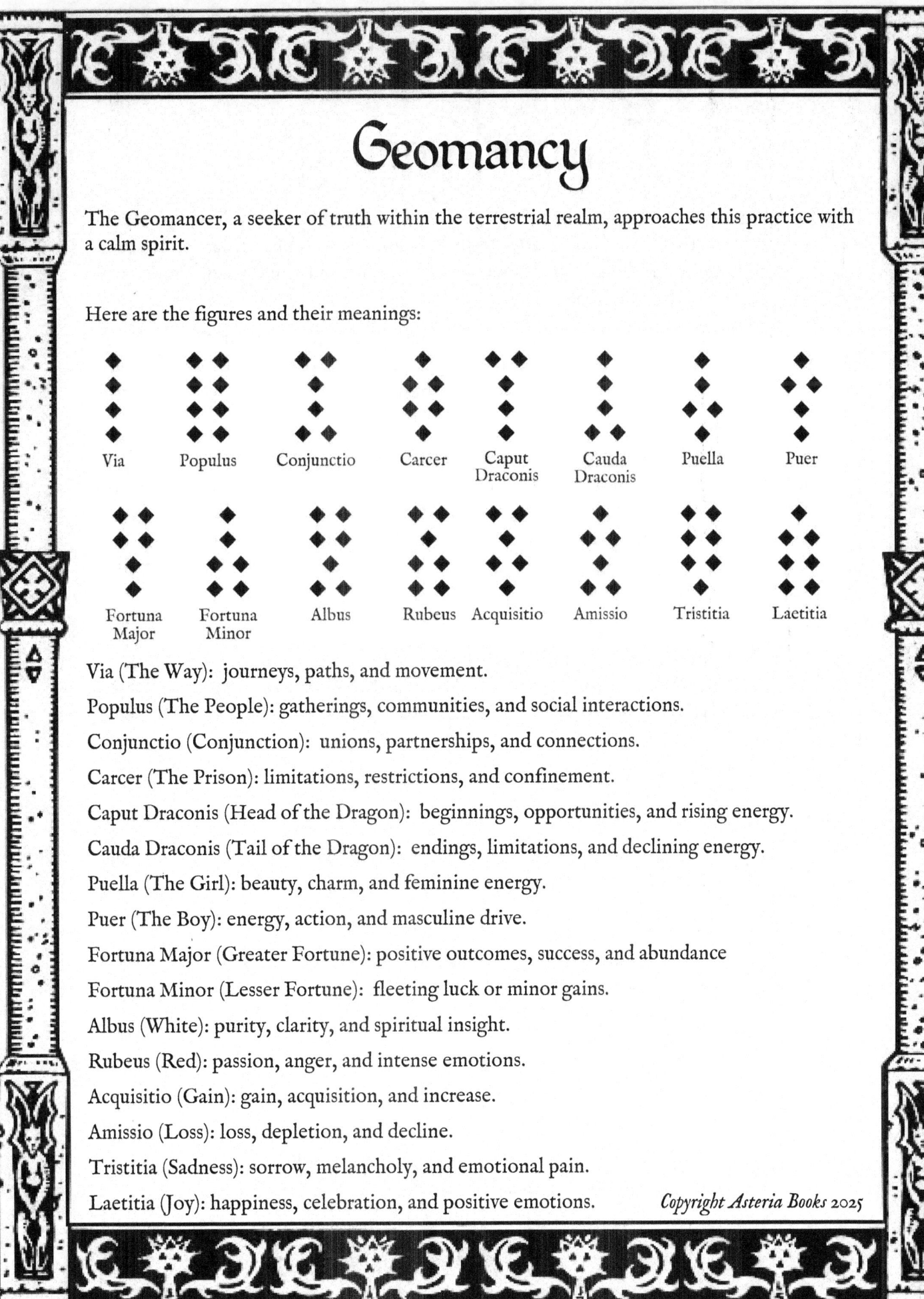

Via (The Way): journeys, paths, and movement.

Populus (The People): gatherings, communities, and social interactions.

Conjunctio (Conjunction): unions, partnerships, and connections.

Carcer (The Prison): limitations, restrictions, and confinement.

Caput Draconis (Head of the Dragon): beginnings, opportunities, and rising energy.

Cauda Draconis (Tail of the Dragon): endings, limitations, and declining energy.

Puella (The Girl): beauty, charm, and feminine energy.

Puer (The Boy): energy, action, and masculine drive.

Fortuna Major (Greater Fortune): positive outcomes, success, and abundance

Fortuna Minor (Lesser Fortune): fleeting luck or minor gains.

Albus (White): purity, clarity, and spiritual insight.

Rubeus (Red): passion, anger, and intense emotions.

Acquisitio (Gain): gain, acquisition, and increase.

Amissio (Loss): loss, depletion, and decline.

Tristitia (Sadness): sorrow, melancholy, and emotional pain.

Laetitia (Joy): happiness, celebration, and positive emotions.

Copyright Asteria Books 2025

Lampadomancy

The Lampadomancer, a seeker of truth in the realm of light and shadow, approaches this practice with a calm heart and a focused mind. A suitable oil lamp, containing pure oil, is essential. The flame's quality and the oil's movement within the vessel are the keys to interpretation.

Begin by focusing your intention, visualizing the question or situation you seek to understand. Light the lamp, allowing the flame to stabilize. Observe the flame's color, size, and movement, as well as the patterns formed by the oil within the lamp.

The flame's characteristics hold symbolic meaning. A bright, steady flame signifies clarity, positive energy, and straightforwardness. A flickering or unstable flame indicates uncertainty, obstacles, or emotional turmoil. A blue flame suggests spiritual influence or communication, while a red flame portends passion, anger, or urgency. A small flame warns of limitations or scarcity, while a large flame signifies abundance or expansion.

The oil's patterns also hold significance. A clear, undisturbed oil surface suggests harmony and balance. Bubbles within the oil can represent communication, messages, or emotional releases. Streaks or lines in the oil indicate journeys, paths, or movement. Dark spots or cloudiness within the oil warn of negativity, obstacles, or hidden influences.

Sample Interpretations:

> A bright, steady blue flame with a clear, undisturbed oil surface: spiritual clarity and harmony are present.

> A flickering red flame with dark spots in the oil: intense emotions and hidden negativity are present, requiring careful attention.

> A small, yellow flame with streaks in the oil: limited resources and a journey or path are indicated.

> A large, steady flame with numerous small bubbles: positive energy and abundant communication are present.

Copyright Asteria Books 2025

Numerology

Embedded within the study of numerology is the belief that certain basic numbers reflect universal Truths which are observable in the natural world and have been reflected in art, poetry, and myth in cultures all over the globe. Studying the way the numbers that are important in our own lives can give us greater clarity into the primal patterns at play in shaping our reality — and our perceptions of that reality.

A person's "Life Path" number is determined by adding together all the digits of their birthday (and adding the resulting digits, until a single digit number (or the number 11) is reached. The Life Path number indicates a soul's purpose in this life. It can also shed insight on the challenges you've experienced in this life. The "Expression" number is determined by assigning a numerical value to each letter in the full name given to you at birth and then adding those numbers together until you have a single digit (or 11), as above. Suffixes like Jr, II, etc. should be omitted. The Expression number is a reflection of the soul's purpose and reflects gifts, talents, abilities, and motivations.

1	2	3	4	5	6	7	8	9
A	B	C	D	E	F	G	H	I
J	K	L	M	N	O	P	Q	R
S	T	U	V	W	X	Y	Z	

Sept. 25, 1975 —> 9/25/1975 —> 9+2+5+1+9+7+5=38 —> 3+8= 11

Laurelei Black —> 3+1+3+9+5+3+5+9+2+3+1+3+2 = 47 —> 4+7 = 11

1 ~ Sun, unity, ambition, courage, the male principle, Divine spark
2 ~ Moon, duality, emotions, harmony, differentiation, the female principle, balance
3 ~ Jupiter, creativity, joy, the triangle, the divine child
4 ~ Earth, will, discipline, equality, the cross, the square, order
5 ~ Mercury, communication, freedom, magic, humanity, the star
6 ~ Venus, love, beauty, wisdom, union, perfect pairing
7 ~ Cosmos, mysticism, spirituality, contemplation
8 ~ Saturn, law, authority, eternity, infinity, As Above/So Below
9 ~ Mars, action, proficiency, completion, the mystic rose
11 ~ Manifestation, Master Number, Justice

Copyright Asteria Books 2019

Molten Metal Readings

The Molybdomancer, a seeker of truth within the realm of metal and water, approaches this practice with a calm spirit and a focused mind. A suitable quantity of molten metal, traditionally lead or tin, and a vessel of cold water are essential.

Begin by melting the metal, ensuring it reaches a liquid state. Carefully pour the molten metal into the cold water, observing the hissing and steaming as it solidifies. The resulting shapes and patterns are then interpreted.

The forms created by the cooled metal hold symbolic meaning. Shapes resembling objects, animals, or letters are interpreted accordingly.

Rounded shapes: signify wholeness, completion, or cycles.

Angular shapes: represent conflict, obstacles, or sharp edges.

Elongated shapes: signify journeys, paths, or connections.

Hollow shapes: represent emptiness, loss, or hidden meanings.

Human or animal shapes: represent people or primal instincts.

Letters or numbers: represent communication or symbolic values.

The texture and surface of the solidified metal also hold significance. Smooth surfaces suggest harmony and clarity, while rough or jagged surfaces indicate discord or obstacles. Bubbles or holes within the metal can represent hidden influences or emotional releases.

Sample Interpretations:

A smooth, rounded shape: a positive outcome or completion of a cycle.

A jagged, angular shape: conflict or obstacles requiring careful navigation.

A long, thin shape: a journey or path with a specific destination.

A hollow, bubble-filled shape: hidden emotions or unresolved issues.

A shape that resembles a letter: a message or communication that is relevant to the question.

Copyright Asteria Books 2025

Palmistry

Palmistry is the divinatory art of telling a person's fortune by examining the lines, shape, and coloring of the hand. It is also known as *chiromancy* after a palm reader who made the art famous. Below is a reproduction of a 17th century palmistry chart.

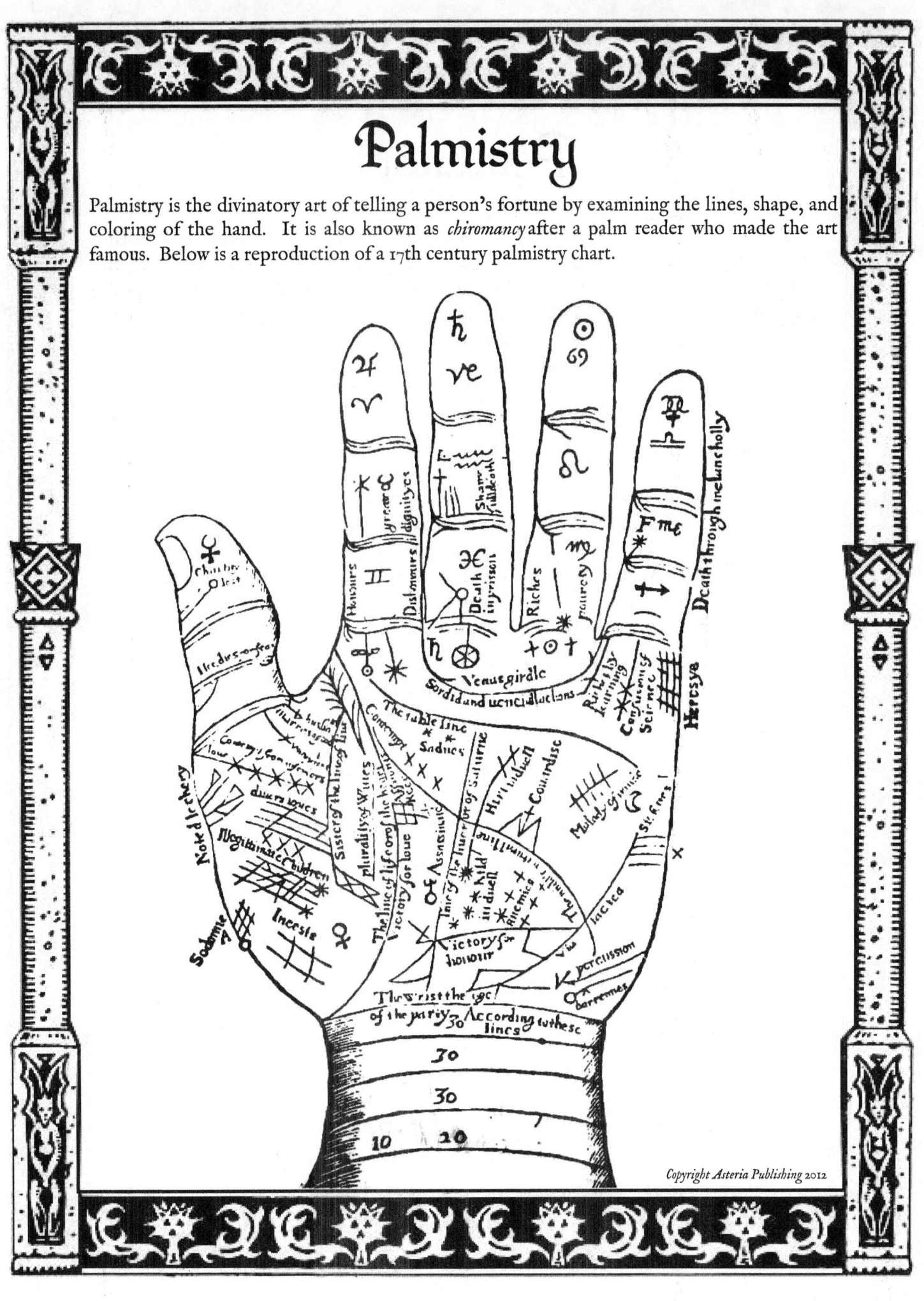

Pendulum

The pendulum is perhaps one of the simplest divination tools to create, carry, and use. It is also, arguably, the least offensive or frightening tool to those unfamiliar with occult studies. In fact, one simple method of pendulum divination common among Christians for determining the sex of an unborn child involves dangling one's crucifix over the belly of a pregnant woman. Straight-line swings indicate a male baby, while circles indicate a female baby.

A pendulum can be created by suspending any type of weight (or "plumb") from a string. Many pendulums are made from semi-precious stones, shells, woods, and metals that were chosen due to their alignments with particular energies. However, you can use any combination of materials that resonates with you. Indeed, a necklace with a pendant or heavy charm that you wear daily may serve as your truest pendulum, as it is already attuned to your energy.

When you wish to use your pendulum for divination, start by holding it in your dominant hand. It helps to put your elbow on a table or hold it close to your side to minimize your movement. Still your mind with a few breaths and then ask the pendulum to show you YES, then show you NO. Make note of the types of swings. For some people, these will always be the same, every time you ask. It is important to begin with this simple exercise, however, because the energy of other individuals (including Spirits) can occasionally change the direction of your pendulum's movements – which would change everything about the reading you conduct. From here, you can conduct a "reading" by asking Yes/No questions.

A pendulum reading can also be conducted using a semi-circular "board" drawn on paper, wood, leather, or cloth onto which you have inscribed letters, numbers, names, or other information you wish the pendulum to indicate. This can be very elaborate and can extend the usefulness of your pendulum into many different areas beyond Yes/No questions.

Pendulums are also very helpful in "dowsing," which is an energetic or intuitive method for finding things. To do this, you can either draw a map and allow the pendulum swings to guide you to the area where the thing you seek is located, or you can write the place names in a semi-circle, as in the "board" method above.

Copyright Asteria Books 2019

Sieve and Shears Readings

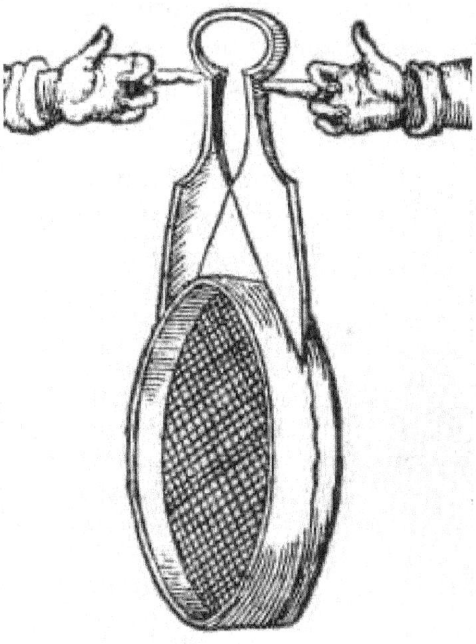

Begin by focusing your intention, visualizing the question or accusation you seek to answer. In ancient practice, this was often used to determine guilt. The shears are inserted into the rim of the sieve, forming a cross shape, and the sieve is suspended. The following "barbarous words" are then spoken:

Dies, mies, jeschet, benedoefet, dowima, enitemaus

The apparatus's movements hold symbolic meaning. If the sieve and shears move or turn when a particular name or word is spoken, it indicates guilt or a connection to the matter at hand. A still apparatus suggests innocence or lack of involvement. The intensity of the movement corresponds to the strength of the connection.

Modern interpretations adapt this ancient practice. Rather than guilt, one can ask questions requiring a yes/no answer. A slight movement towards a designated direction, such as clockwise, indicates "yes," while stillness or movement in the opposite direction, counter-clockwise, signifies "no."

The shears, acting as a fulcrum, amplify the sieve's movements, making subtle shifts more pronounced. Their presence adds a sense of sharpness and precision to the judgment, suggesting a definitive answer.

Sample Interpretations:

A sharp, rapid turn of the sieve and shears when a name is spoken: strong indication of involvement.

A still apparatus during the speaking of a name: indication of innocence.

A slight, deliberate movement of the sieve and shears clockwise: a "yes" answer to a question.

A slight, deliberate movement of the sieve and shears counter-clockwise: a "no" answer to a question.

Copyright Asteria Books 2025

Smoke and Steam Readings

The Capnomancer, a seeker of truth within the realm of vapor and smoke, approaches this practice with a calm spirit and a focused mind. A suitable source of smoke or steam is essential, such as a burning herb, incense, or heated water. The forms and movements of the vapors are the keys to interpretation.

Begin by focusing your intention, visualizing the question or situation you seek to understand. Ignite the herb or incense, or heat the water, allowing the smoke or steam to rise. Observe the patterns formed by the ascending vapors, noting their shape, direction, and density.

The smoke or steam's characteristics hold symbolic meaning. Rising straight upwards signifies clarity, directness, and positive energy. Swirling or erratic patterns indicate uncertainty, confusion, or emotional turmoil. Thin, wispy smoke suggests fleeting influences or subtle messages, while thick, dense smoke portends strong forces or significant events.

Shapes formed by the vapors hold specific interpretations:

Ascending Shapes

Straight lines: represent a clear path or straightforward answer.

Spirals: signify cyclical patterns or repeating events.

Clouds or amorphous shapes: represent uncertainty or hidden influences.

Descending Shapes

Falling or dissipating patterns: represent endings, loss, or decline.

Directional Movement

Smoke moving towards the querent: indicates a direct influence or personal message.

Smoke moving away from the querent: suggests external influences or detachment.

Sample Interpretations:

Thick, dense smoke rising straight upwards: strong positive energy and clear direction.

Thin, wispy smoke swirling erratically: uncertainty and fleeting influences are present.

Smoke forming cloud-like shapes that dissipate quickly: hidden influences are present, but their effects are temporary.

Smoke rising, and forming a distinct line, moving toward the querent: a direct message, with a straight forward answer.

Copyright Asteria Books 2025

Tasseomancy

The Tasseomancer approaches this practice with a calm spirit and a focused mind. A suitable cup, preferably white or light-colored to enhance visibility, and finely ground tea leaves or coffee grounds are essential. The patterns and formations within the cup are the keys to interpretation.

Begin by preparing a cup of tea or coffee, allowing the leaves or grounds to settle. The querent should then drink the beverage, leaving a small amount of liquid and sediment at the bottom. The cup is then swirled three times counter-clockwise, and inverted onto a saucer to drain.

Observe the patterns formed by the remaining leaves or grounds within the cup. Shapes, symbols, and their placement hold symbolic meaning.

Shapes

Animals: represent instincts, primal urges, or specific individuals.

Flowers: signify growth, beauty, or emotional expression.

Numbers: represent time, quantity, or symbolic meaning.

Letters: signify communication or specific words.

Lines: represent journeys, paths, or connections.

Circles: represent cycles, wholeness, or completion.

Placement

Near the rim: events occurring in the near future.

Near the bottom: events occurring in the distant future or past.

On the sides: influences from the querent's surroundings.

Scattered patterns: uncertainty or chaotic influences.

Clumped patterns: focused energy or significant events.

Copyright Asteria Books 2025

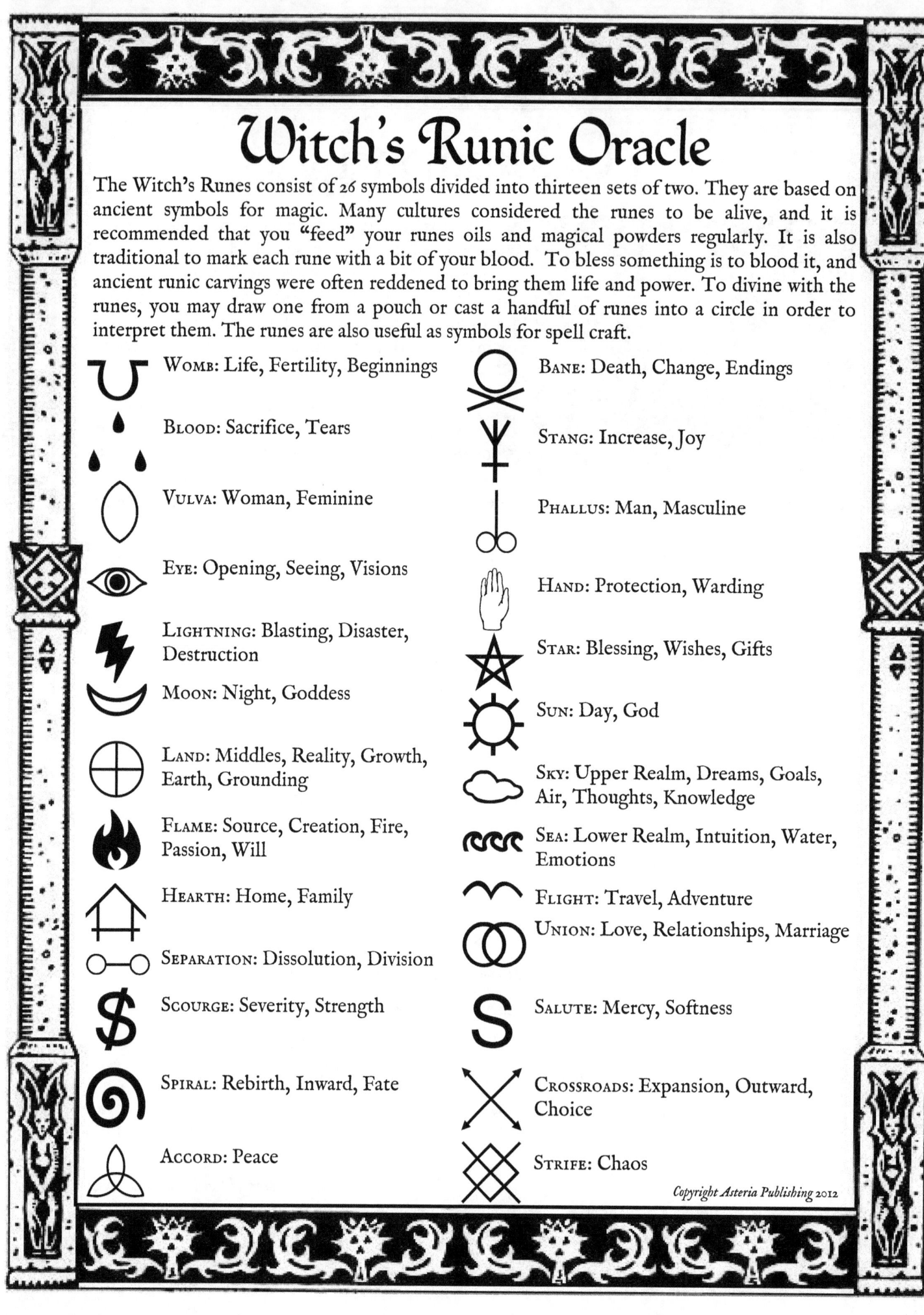

Scrying

Scrying is the divinatory practice of seeking visual messages through the use of a tool or medium. Though you can scry with any of the elements, water scrying might be the oldest version of divination known to humans. It reveals much in connection with our emotions, psyches, past-lives, ancestors - all of the things we associate with the western gate of elemental water and the Underworld. Learning to navigate these waters will help you understand the patterns and issues involved in your life.

Tools Used for Scrying
Water in a black bowl, cup, or cauldron
Crystal bowl, polished stones, scrying jewelry
Black Mirror
Incense smoke
Flames

The technique for scrying in any element is going to be more or less the same. In short, you will enter a meditative state, relax your gaze while looking in the direction of your scrying tool or element, and then simply allow the messages or images to come to you.

Tips and techniques for scrying success

Some people like to add oils or herbs to the water (or choose visionary herbs for the smoke blend, if you are scrying in incense smoke or flames). Some add a silver coin or gemstone to bowl, cauldron, or cup. It is helpful to do this work in a darkened room to limit other visual stimuli. If you are gazing into water, glass, or crystal, light a single candle whose light is shining on the surface of the water or glass, but isn't directly in your line of vision.

Copyright Asteria Books 2019

Making a Dark Mirror

The dark mirror (or "black mirror") is the magical descendant of an obsidian mirror — a disc of polished black volcanic stone used as a scrying glass. While a highly polished piece of naturally occurring stone (such as a black variety of obsidian, tourmaline, onyx, agate, or hematite) can be an amazing scrying surface, it can also be cost prohibitive and might not afford a Witch the opportunity to take part in *crafting* an important personal tool. What follows are basic guidelines crafting one's dark mirror.

Materials Needed:
Glass surface (concave or flat)
Black enamel paint
Paint brush
Black fabric (felt, silk, velvet, wool)
Frame, stand, box (optional)
Adornments (optional)

Essentially, this tool is made by painting the backside of a piece of glass with black enamel (probably 2-3 coats to account for streaks). Enamel works best because it is both durable and glossy.

If you are using a concave piece of glass like a clock glass or an old-fashioned "bubbled" picture frame, you want to paint the outer bowl of the glass so that you will be looking into a clear, glossy black well or pool with the paint on the other side.

While the paint is still tacky, apply your black fabric to the entire backing. This will adhere to the enamel, adding an impenetrable layer of obscurity. No light will come through while you gaze into your mirror, and it will be protected from scratches.

You can encase the mirror in a frame or a wooden box (with a hinged lid, if you like), place it on a stand, or hang it on a wall.

Try to make the whole assembly of a size in which you'll be able to see your whole face at no further than arm's length away.

Embellish your dark mirror with runes, sigils, shells, stones, talismans, or other fetiches to enhance its power and lend you protection while you seek wisdom and guidance.

Copyright Asteria Books 2019

Astrology: An Overview

The ancient art of Astrology is a system of divination and understanding that maps the cosmos' influence upon the earthly realm. This practice, a bridge between the heavens and humanity, seeks to decipher the language of the stars, revealing the hidden patterns that shape our destinies.

Astrology, at its core, is a study of correspondences. The positions and movements of celestial bodies - planets, stars, and luminaries - are seen as symbolic representations of archetypal energies and influences. These influences, perceived as emanating from the cosmos, are believed to interact with and shape the human experience.

The natal chart, a snapshot of the heavens at the moment of birth, serves as the foundation of astrological interpretation. It maps the positions of the planets within the twelve signs and houses, revealing the individual's unique energetic blueprint. This chart, a microcosm of the cosmos, reflects the individual's personality, potential, and life path.

Transits, the ongoing movements of the planets, reveal the dynamic interplay between the natal chart and the current celestial energies. These transits, like cosmic weather patterns, influence daily life, bringing periods of challenge, opportunity, and transformation.

Synastry, the comparison of two natal charts, explores the dynamics of relationships, revealing the compatibility and potential challenges between individuals. Mundane astrology examines the influence of celestial events on world affairs, predicting trends and patterns in politics, economics, and social movements. Horary astrology provides answers to specific questions by examining the astrological chart erected for the moment the question is asked. Electional astrology seeks to find auspicious times for important events, aligning actions with favorable celestial energies.

Astrology is not about rigid determinism, but rather about understanding the cyclical nature of life and the interplay of cosmic forces. It offers a framework for self-awareness, personal growth, and navigating the complexities of existence.

It illuminates the hidden patterns within our lives, empowering us to make informed choices and align ourselves with the rhythms of the universe. It is a tool for understanding, not control, a map of the soul's journey through the cosmos.

Copyright Asteria Books 2025

Astrological Terminology

TRANSITS: The ongoing movements of the planets across the natal chart, revealing the dynamic interplay between current celestial energies and the individual's birth chart. Transits highlight temporary influences, periods of challenge, opportunity, and transformation.

PROGRESSIONS: A symbolic method of advancing the natal chart through time, revealing the unfolding of long-term trends and personal development. Secondary progressions, for example, advance the chart by one day for each year of life.

RETURNS: Charts erected for the moment a planet returns to its natal position, marking significant cyclical events. Solar returns, for example, mark the annual return of the Sun to its birth position, revealing the themes of the upcoming year.

ASCENDANT (ASC): The sign rising on the eastern horizon at the moment of birth, representing the individual's outward persona and initial approach to life.

DESCENDANT (DSC): The point opposite the ascendant, representing partnerships, marriage, and contracts.

MIDHEAVEN (MC): The highest point in the chart, representing career, public image, and ambition.

ORBS: The allowable deviation from the exact degree of an aspect, acknowledging that planetary influences operate within a range.

EPHEMERIS: A table of calculated planetary positions for specific dates and times, essential for accurate chart calculations.

RETROGRADE: The apparent backward movement of a planet from Earth's perspective, symbolizing a period of introspection and reevaluation.

NODES OF THE MOON: The points where the Moon's orbit intersects the ecliptic, representing karmic patterns and life lessons.

VERTEX: A sensitive point in the chart, often associated with fated encounters and karmic connections.

Copyright Asteria Books 2025

Foundational Astronomy Concepts

The ecliptic, the Sun's apparent path across the sky, is the fundamental plane of the solar system. It is the circle traced by the Sun's center as it appears to revolve around Earth once a year. This path, a great circle on the celestial sphere, serves as the central reference point for astrological calculations. The zodiac signs, those twelve divisions of the ecliptic, are therefore tied to the Sun's annual journey.

The celestial sphere, an imaginary sphere of infinite radius surrounding Earth, provides a framework for mapping the positions of celestial objects. It allows us to visualize the apparent movements of the Sun, Moon, planets, and stars. Imagine it as a giant dome above us. The ecliptic, the Sun's path, is a great circle drawn upon this sphere. The planets, as they orbit the Sun, appear to move along or near the ecliptic, their positions constantly shifting against the backdrop of the fixed stars.

The movement of the planets, those wandering stars, is the core of astrological observation. These celestial bodies, each moving at its own pace, weave a complex tapestry of influence as they traverse the zodiac. Their positions, speeds, and aspects to one another reveal the ever-changing dynamics of the cosmos. Understanding their orbital periods and speeds is crucial for calculating transits and progressions.

The ephemeris, a table of calculated planetary positions for specific dates and times, is an indispensable tool for astrologers. It provides the precise coordinates of the planets, allowing for accurate chart calculations and interpretations. This table, a celestial almanac, allows one to understand where each planet was at any given time. The ephemeris is essential for calculating natal charts, transit charts, and other astrological calculations.

Copyright Asteria Books 2025

The Zodiac

Aries: The Ram, born of fire and ruled by Mars, embodies fiery initiation, impulsive action, and the pioneering spirit.

Taurus: The Bull, born of earth and ruled by Venus, embodies grounded sensuality, steadfast persistence, and the appreciation of beauty.

Gemini: The Twins, born of air and ruled by Mercury, embodies intellectual curiosity, communicative agility, and the duality of perception.

Cancer: The Crab, born of water and ruled by the Moon, embodies emotional sensitivity, nurturing instincts, and the deep connection to home and family.

Leo: The Lion, born of fire and ruled by the Sun, embodies radiant creativity, regal charisma, and the desire for self-expression.

Virgo: The Virgin, born of earth and ruled by Mercury, embodies analytical precision, practical efficiency, and the pursuit of perfection.

Libra: The Scales, born of air and ruled by Venus, embodies harmonious balance, diplomatic grace, and the pursuit of justice.

Scorpio: The Scorpion, born of water and ruled by Pluto (traditionally Mars), embodies intense passion, transformative power, and the exploration of hidden depths.

Sagittarius: The Archer, born of fire and ruled by Jupiter, embodies expansive optimism, philosophical exploration, and the pursuit of higher knowledge.

Capricorn: The Goat, born of earth and ruled by Saturn, embodies disciplined ambition, pragmatic achievement, and the respect for tradition.

Aquarius: The Water-Bearer, born of air and ruled by Uranus (traditionally Saturn), embodies innovative idealism, rebellious independence, and the pursuit of collective progress.

Pisces: The Fish, born of water and ruled by Neptune (traditionally Jupiter), embodies compassionate empathy, dreamlike intuition, and the surrender to universal consciousness.

Copyright Asteria Books 2025

Tropical v. Sidereal Astrology

The Tropical and Sidereal Zodiacs are two different systems that both seek to map the heavens. However, they diverge in their foundational principles, leading to distinct interpretations of astrological influences.

The Tropical Zodiac, the more commonly used system in Western astrology, is anchored to the Earth's relationship with the Sun. It begins at the vernal equinox, the moment the Sun crosses the celestial equator from south to north, marking the beginning of Aries. This system divides the ecliptic into twelve equal segments, each 30 degrees in length, corresponding to the traditional zodiac signs. The Tropical Zodiac is therefore tied to the seasons, with Aries always beginning at the spring equinox in the Northern Hemisphere.

The Sidereal Zodiac, prevalent in Vedic astrology, is anchored to the fixed stars. It acknowledges the Earth's precession, the slow wobble of its axis that causes the equinoxes to shift against the backdrop of the stars. This system uses a fixed point in the celestial sphere, often the star Spica, to define the beginning of Aries. As a result, the Sidereal Zodiac shifts over time, currently lagging behind the Tropical Zodiac by approximately 24 degrees.

The key difference lies in their reference points. The Tropical Zodiac is seasonal, emphasizing the Earth's relationship to the Sun, while the Sidereal Zodiac is stellar, emphasizing the Earth's relationship to the fixed stars. This difference leads to variations in planetary placements between the two systems. A planet in Aries in the Tropical Zodiac might fall into Pisces in the Sidereal Zodiac, for example.

The choice between the two systems is a matter of philosophical and practical consideration. Tropical astrologers emphasize the seasonal archetypes and their influence on human experience, while Sidereal astrologers emphasize the cosmic backdrop and the influence of the fixed stars. Both systems offer valuable insights, but their interpretations diverge due to their distinct foundational principles. Understanding this difference is crucial for navigating the diverse landscape of astrological practice.

Copyright Asteria Books 2025

Astrology & the Human Body

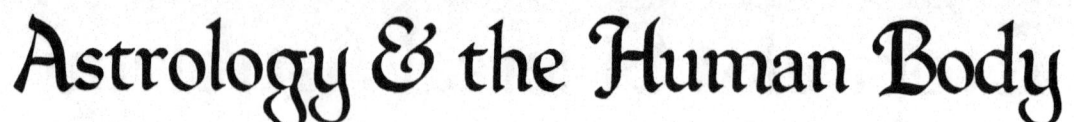

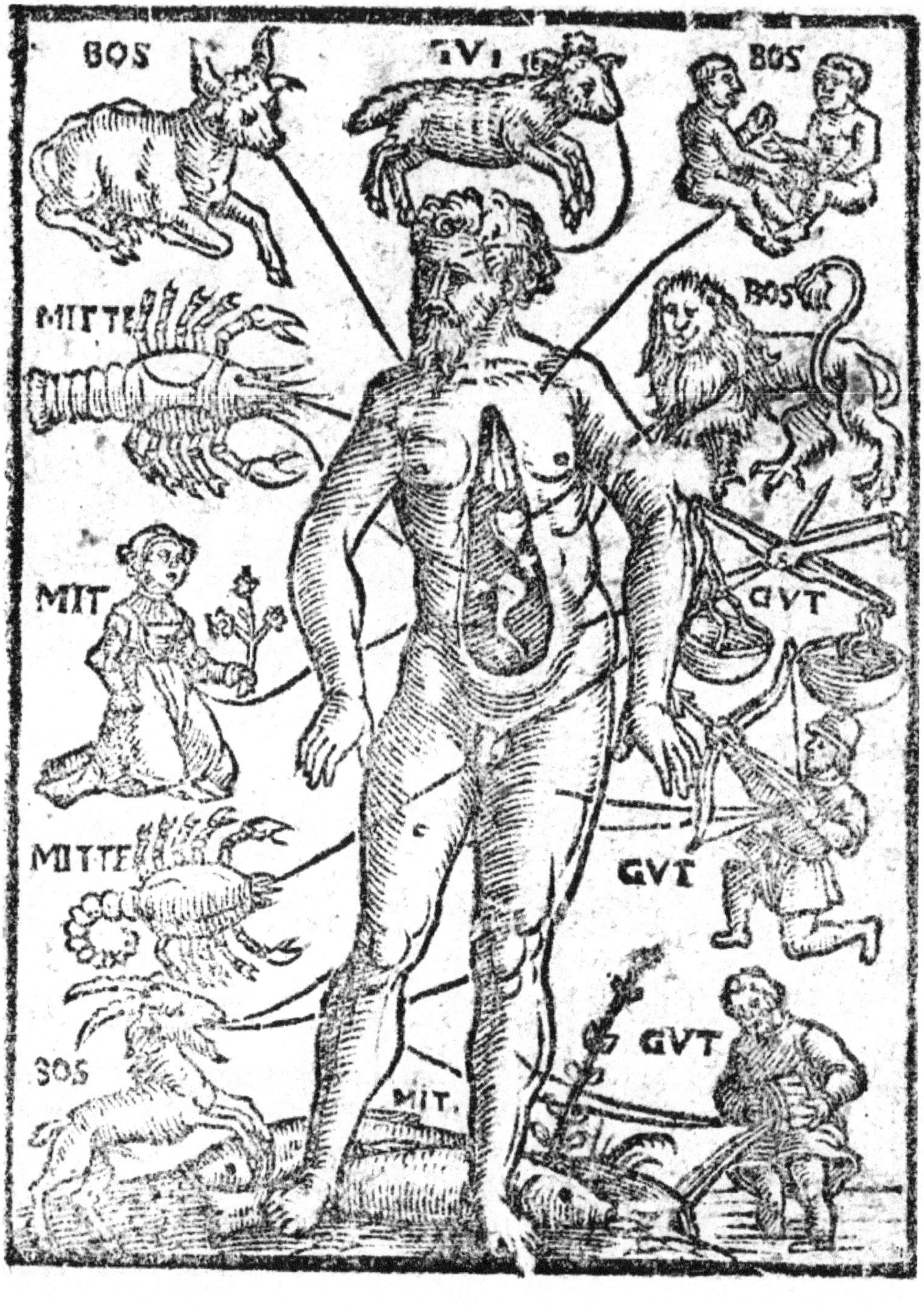

Copyright Asteria Books 2025

The Planets

The Planets of our solar system are the cosmic actors that shape the theater of human experience. These celestial bodies, both classical and modern, weave a tapestry of influence, their movements and aspects revealing the hidden currents of fate.

The classical planets, those visible to the naked eye, represent the fundamental energies of human existence:

- Sun: The radiant heart, embodying vitality, ego, and the core self.
- Moon: The reflective soul, embodying emotions, instincts, and the subconscious.
- Mercury: The swift messenger, embodying intellect, communication, and adaptability.
- Venus: The alluring beauty, embodying love, harmony, and the appreciation of aesthetics.
- Mars: The fiery warrior, embodying drive, passion, and the urge to assert oneself.
- Jupiter: The expansive benefactor, embodying growth, abundance, and the pursuit of higher knowledge.
- Saturn: The stern teacher, embodying discipline, structure, and the lessons of time.

The outer planets, discovered with the aid of telescopes, represent generational influences, shaping the collective consciousness:

- Uranus: The rebellious innovator, embodying change, revolution, and the breaking of boundaries. Its influence is generational, shaping societal shifts and technological advancements.
- Neptune: The dreamy idealist, embodying illusion, spirituality, and the dissolution of boundaries. Its influence is generational, shaping artistic movements and collective dreams.
- Pluto: The transformative destroyer, embodying power, transformation, and the exploration of hidden depths. Its influence is generational, shaping societal power structures and collective shadow work.

Copyright Asteria Books 2025

Retrogrades

Retrograde motion, from our Earth-bound vantage point, occurs when a planet's orbital speed appears slower than Earth's, creating the illusion of backward movement. This shift in perspective alters the planet's expression, turning its energies inward, towards the realm of the subconscious and the revisiting of past experiences.

Mercury Retrograde prompts a review of communication, thought processes, and travel. Expect delays, misunderstandings, and a need to revisit past conversations or projects. It is a time for careful consideration and meticulous attention to detail.

> Venus Retrograde invites reflection on relationships, values, and aesthetics. Past connections may resurface, and a reevaluation of personal values and artistic expression is encouraged. It is a time for introspection in matters of the heart and beauty.

Mars Retrograde prompts a reevaluation of drive, passion, and assertiveness. Past conflicts may resurface, and a reassessment of personal boundaries and anger management is advised. It is a time for channeling energy inward, towards self-reflection and controlled action.

> Jupiter Retrograde invites reflection on beliefs, philosophies, and personal growth. Past opportunities may resurface, and a reassessment of one's worldview and expansion is encouraged. It is a time for internalizing wisdom and reflecting on personal philosophies.

Saturn Retrograde prompts a reevaluation of discipline, structure, and responsibility. Past obligations may resurface, and a reassessment of personal boundaries and long-term goals is advised. It is a time for internalizing lessons learned and restructuring one's foundations.

> Uranus Retrograde and innovations may resurface, and a reassessment of personal liberation and societal change is encouraged. It is a time for internalizing change and embracing unconventional perspectives.

Neptune Retrograde invites reflection on illusions, spirituality, and artistic expression. Past dreams and ideals may resurface, and a reassessment of personal beliefs and spiritual connections is encouraged. It is a time for internalizing spiritual insights and confronting illusions.

> Pluto Retrograde prompts a reevaluation of power, transformation, and hidden depths. Past transformations and power struggles may resurface, and a reassessment of personal shadow work and societal power structures is advised. It is a time for internalizing transformative processes and confronting the depths of the psyche.

Copyright Asteria Books 2025

The Houses

The planetary houses, numbered in a clockwise sequence, divide the zodiac into twelve segments, each representing a specific arena of human experience.

1st House (Ascendant): The house of self, personality, and physical appearance. It reveals the individual's outward expression, their initial approach to life, and their first impressions.

2nd House: The house of possessions, values, and finances. It reveals the individual's relationship with material resources, their sense of self-worth, and their financial stability.

3rd House: The house of communication, siblings, and short journeys. It reveals the individual's communication style, their intellectual curiosity, and their interactions with their immediate environment.

4th House (Imum Coeli): The house of home, family, and roots. It reveals the individual's relationship with their family, their sense of belonging, and their emotional foundations.

5th House: The house of creativity, romance, and children. It reveals the individual's creative expression, their romantic inclinations, and their relationship with children.

6th House: The house of work, health, and service. It reveals the individual's daily routines, their approach to work, and their physical well-being.

7th House (Descendant): The house of partnerships, marriage, and contracts. It reveals the individual's approach to relationships, their ideal partner, and their legal agreements.

8th House: The house of transformation, shared resources, and the occult. It reveals the individual's capacity for transformation, their relationship with shared resources, and their interest in hidden matters.

9th House: The house of philosophy, higher education, and long journeys. It reveals the individual's philosophical beliefs, their pursuit of higher knowledge, and their experiences with foreign cultures.

10th House (Midheaven): The house of career, public image, and ambition. It reveals the individual's professional aspirations, their public standing, and their sense of purpose.

11th House: The house of friendships, groups, and ideals. It reveals the individual's social connections, their involvement in groups, and their humanitarian ideals.

12th House: The house of hidden enemies, subconscious, and spirituality. It reveals the individual's hidden vulnerabilities, their subconscious patterns, and their connection to the spiritual realm.

Copyright Asteria Books 2025

The Elements and Astrology

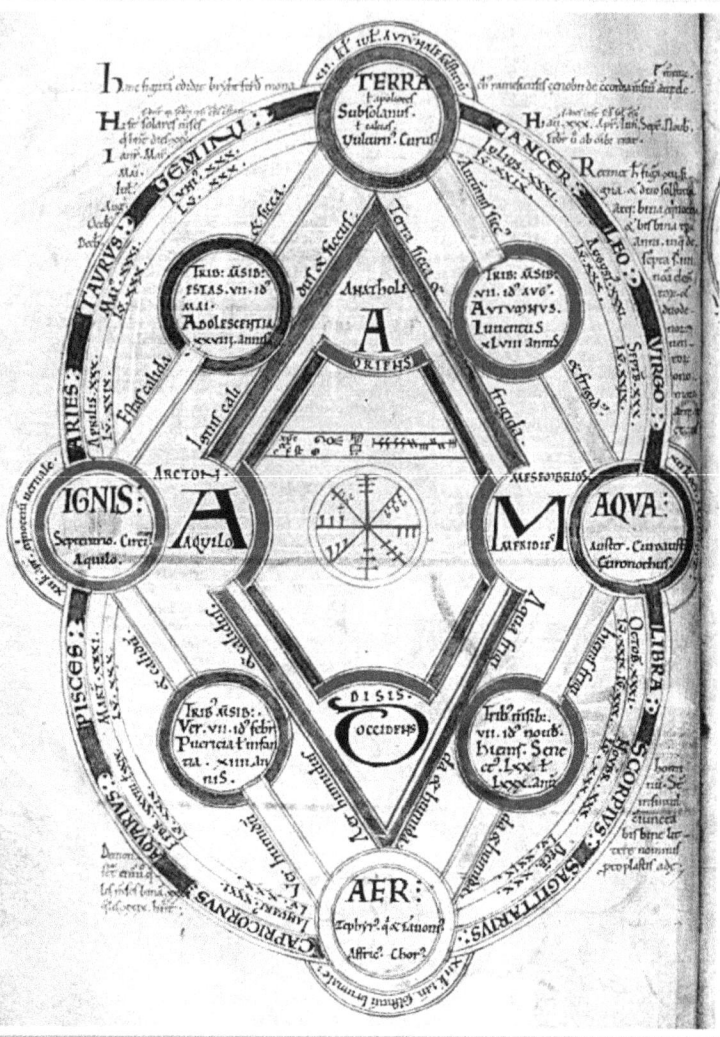

The four elements, the building blocks of the material world, represent distinct energetic qualities which are manifested in the study of astrology.

Fire (Aries, Leo, Sagittarius): Represents passion, action, and inspiration. It embodies the spark of creation, the drive to assert oneself, and the pursuit of ideals. Fire signs are energetic, enthusiastic, and driven.

Earth (Taurus, Virgo, Capricorn): Represents stability, practicality, and material reality. It embodies groundedness, perseverance, and the appreciation of tangible things. Earth signs are reliable, patient, and focused on security.

Air (Gemini, Libra, Aquarius): Represents intellect, communication, and social interaction. It embodies mental agility, objectivity, and the pursuit of knowledge. Air signs are communicative, adaptable, and thrive on intellectual stimulation.

Water (Cancer, Scorpio, Pisces): Represents emotions, intuition, and the subconscious. It embodies sensitivity, empathy, and the connection to the inner world. Water signs are emotional, intuitive, and guided by feeling.

Copyright Asteria Books 2025

Modalities

IN ASTROLOGOS.

Cardinal (Aries, Cancer, Libra, Capricorn): Represents initiation, action, and the drive to begin new projects. Cardinal signs are assertive, proactive, and focused on initiating change. They are the starters, the catalysts.

Fixed (Taurus, Leo, Scorpio, Aquarius): Represents stability, persistence, and the ability to maintain focus. Fixed signs are determined, loyal, and focused on maintaining stability. They are the sustainers, the keepers.

Mutable (Gemini, Virgo, Sagittarius, Pisces): Represents adaptability, flexibility, and the ability to adjust to change. Mutable signs are versatile, communicative, and focused on adapting to circumstances. They are the adapters, the transitioners.

Copyright Asteria Books 2025

Astrological Aspects

Celestial aspects are the geometric relationships that define the energetic connections between celestial bodies. These aspects, like cosmic conversations, shape the flow of energy within the natal chart and during transits, revealing the harmonious and challenging dynamics that influence our lives.

Conjunction (0°): The union of two planets, amplifying their energies and blending their influences. This aspect represents a potent fusion, a merging of forces that can manifest as intense focus or internal conflict.

Opposition (180°): The tension of polarities, the push and pull between opposing forces. This aspect represents a dynamic interplay between contrasting energies, often leading to awareness of duality and the need for balance.

Square (90°): The friction of obstacles, the clash of conflicting energies. This aspect represents challenges, tension, and the need for action to overcome obstacles. It is a catalyst for growth and transformation.

Trine (120°): The harmony of flow, the ease of compatible energies. This aspect represents natural talent, effortless expression, and harmonious integration. It facilitates creativity and positive expression.

Sextile (60°): The opportunity for collaboration, the gentle flow of supportive energies. This aspect represents potential, opportunity, and the ability to work harmoniously with others. It fosters communication and cooperation.

The concept of orbs acknowledges that these aspects are not exact, but rather operate within a range of degrees. An orb is the allowable deviation from the exact degree of an aspect. The size of the orb varies depending on the planets involved and the type of aspect.

    Larger orbs are generally allowed for the Sun and Moon, as their influence is considered more powerful.

    Smaller orbs are used for personal planets like Mercury, Venus, and Mars, as their influence is more immediate and personal. Outer planets like Jupiter, Saturn, Uranus, Neptune, and Pluto may have larger orbs, reflecting their broader, more generational influence.

    The size of the orb also influences the strength of the aspect. A tighter orb, closer to the exact degree, indicates a stronger and more pronounced influence. A wider orb, further from the exact degree, indicates a weaker and more subtle influence.

Copyright Asteria Books 2025

Types of Charts

Star charts can be crafted for various purposes, unveiling the intricate dance of planetary energies and illuminating different facets of our existence.

- Natal Chart: The cornerstone of astrological interpretation, a snapshot of the heavens at the moment of birth. It reveals the individual's unique energetic blueprint, their personality, potential, and life path. This chart is the foundation for understanding one's inherent strengths, weaknesses, and tendencies.

- Transit Chart: A dynamic map that overlays the current positions of the planets onto the natal chart, revealing the ongoing interplay of celestial energies. It illuminates the temporary influences shaping daily life, highlighting periods of challenge, opportunity, and transformation.

- Synastry Chart: A relational map that compares two natal charts, revealing the dynamics of interpersonal connections. It explores the compatibility, potential challenges, and karmic patterns between individuals, illuminating the nature of their relationship.

- Composite Chart: A relational map that combines two natal charts into a single chart, representing the relationship itself as an entity. It reveals the shared energy and purpose of the relationship, highlighting its strengths, weaknesses, and potential for growth.

- Horary Chart: A query-based map erected for the moment a specific question is asked. It provides answers to specific inquiries by analyzing the planetary positions and aspects at the time of the query, revealing the likely outcome of the situation.

- Electional Chart: A timing-based map used to determine auspicious times for important events, such as weddings, business ventures, or medical procedures. It seeks to align actions with favorable celestial energies, maximizing the potential for success.

- Mundane Chart: A world-event map that examines the influence of celestial events on global affairs, such as political trends, economic cycles, and natural disasters. It provides insight into the collective energies shaping societal patterns.

- Solar Return Chart: A yearly-cycle map erected for the moment the Sun returns to its natal position, marking the individual's solar birthday. It reveals the themes and energies that will dominate the upcoming year.

- Lunar Return Chart: A monthly-cycle map erected for the moment the Moon returns to its natal position, marking the individual's lunar return. It reveals the emotional themes and patterns that will dominate the upcoming month.

- Progressed Chart: A symbolic map that progresses the natal chart forward in time, revealing the unfolding of long-term trends and personal development. It illuminates the inner changes and psychological shifts that occur throughout life.

Copyright Asteria Books 2025

Understanding the Natal Chart

The natal chart, a map of the heavens at the moment of one's first breath, holds the keys to understanding personality, potential, and destiny.

The first step in reading a natal chart is to identify the placement of planets within the twelve signs and houses. Each planet represents a distinct archetypal energy, while each sign colors that energy with its unique qualities. The houses, representing different areas of life, reveal where these energies manifest.

For example, Mars in Aries in the 10th house indicates a forceful and assertive approach to career (10th house), expressed with the directness and impulsivity of Aries, and amplified by the raw energy of Mars. Conversely, Venus in Cancer in the 4th house suggests a loving and nurturing approach to home and family (4th house), expressed with the sensitivity and emotional depth of Cancer, and guided by the harmonious influence of Venus.

The ascendant (ASC), also known as the rising sign, is the sign rising on the eastern horizon at the moment of birth. It represents the individual's outward persona, their initial approach to life, and their first impressions. It is the mask they wear in social situations, the filter through which they interact with the world.

The descendant (DSC), opposite the ascendant, represents partnerships, marriage, and contracts. It reveals the individual's ideal partner and their approach to relationships. It reflects the qualities they seek in others, and the dynamics they create in close partnerships.

The midheaven (MC), the highest point in the chart, represents career, public image, and ambition. It reveals the individual's professional aspirations, their public standing, and their sense of purpose. It reflects their drive for achievement and their contribution to the world.

The imum coeli (IC), opposite the midheaven, represents home, family, and roots. It reveals the individual's relationship with their family, their sense of belonging, and their emotional foundations. It reflects their need for security and their connection to their past.

These four angles - ASC, DSC, MC, and IC - form the framework of the natal chart, defining the individual's relationship with self, others, career, and home. They are the cardinal points of the chart, the axes around which the planetary energies revolve.

Reading a natal chart is a process of synthesis, of weaving together the various planetary placements, sign qualities, house positions, and angular relationships. It requires both knowledge and intuition, a blending of analytical skill and empathetic understanding. The natal chart is not a static blueprint, but a dynamic map of potential, a guide for navigating the intricate landscape of life.

Copyright Asteria Books 2025

Fool's Journey

From the shadowed depths of the Major Arcana are revealed the twenty-two keys to the soul's journey, each a gateway to profound understanding. These cards, unlike their lesser brethren, speak of archetypal forces, the grand narratives that shape our destinies. We, the Fool, follow a hero's journey from folly to wisdom.

The Fool, numbered zero, begins the journey, a symbol of boundless potential and untamed spirit. The Magician, with his tools of manifestation, teaches the power of will. The High Priestess, veiled in mystery, whispers of intuition and hidden knowledge. The Empress, abundant and fertile, embodies creation and nurturing. The Emperor, structured and authoritative, represents control and order.

Through trials and tribulations, the seeker encounters the Hierophant, the Lovers, the Chariot, and Justice, each imparting vital lessons. The Hermit, solitary and wise, illuminates the path of introspection. The Wheel of Fortune turns, revealing the cyclical nature of fate. Strength tempers the spirit, while the Hanged Man reveals the power of surrender.

Death transforms, Temperance balances, and the Devil tempts. The Tower shatters illusions, and the Star offers hope. The Moon reveals hidden shadows, and the Sun illuminates clarity. Judgment calls for reckoning, and the World completes the cycle. These are the archetypes, the grand narratives, the keys to unlocking the soul's deepest mysteries.

Copyright Asteria Books 2025

3 Card/Stone Readings

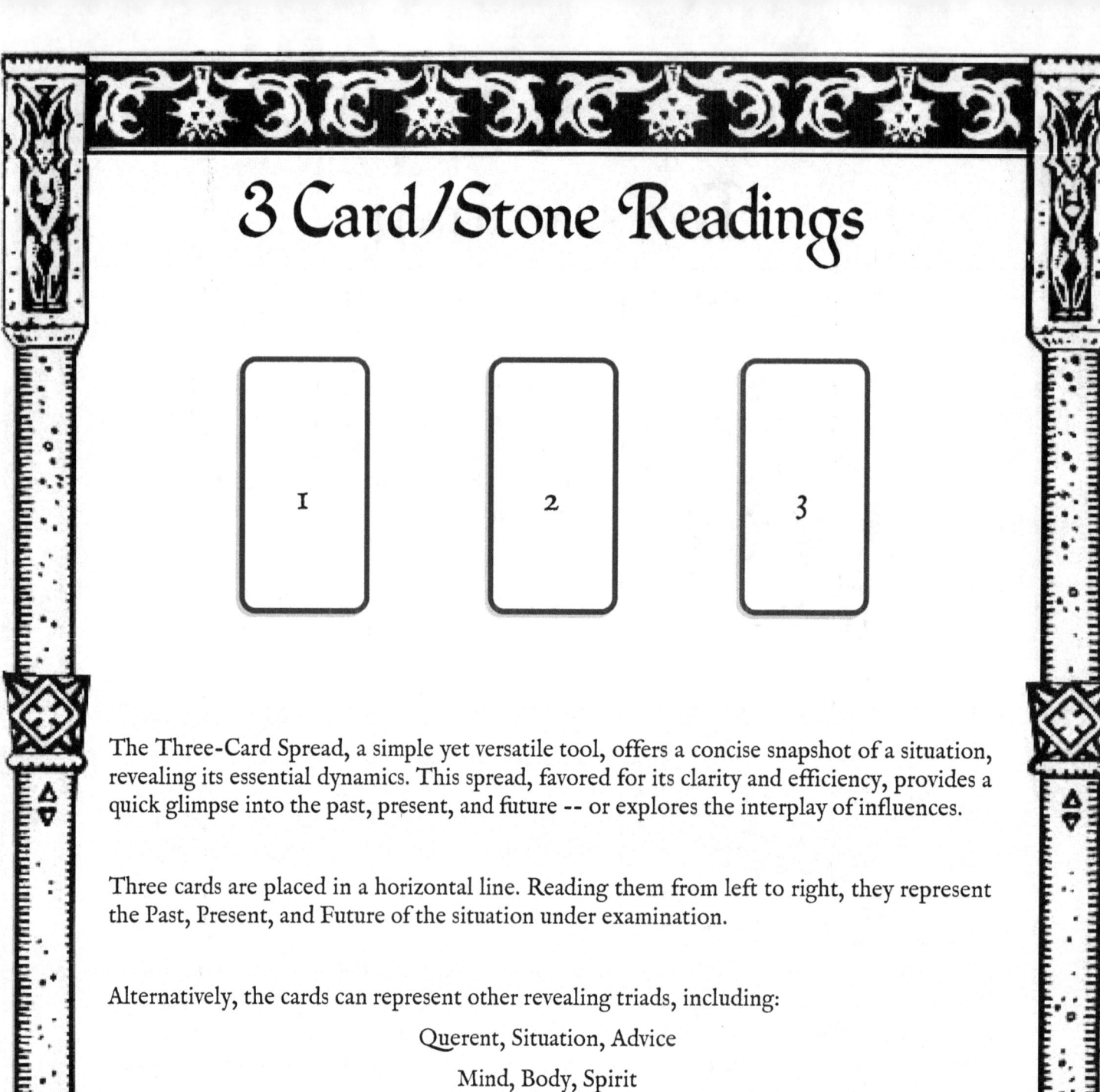

The Three-Card Spread, a simple yet versatile tool, offers a concise snapshot of a situation, revealing its essential dynamics. This spread, favored for its clarity and efficiency, provides a quick glimpse into the past, present, and future -- or explores the interplay of influences.

Three cards are placed in a horizontal line. Reading them from left to right, they represent the Past, Present, and Future of the situation under examination.

Alternatively, the cards can represent other revealing triads, including:

> Querent, Situation, Advice
>
> Mind, Body, Spirit

This flexibility allows the spread to be adapted to a wide range of questions and circumstances. The simplicity of the three-card layout allows for quick and direct interpretations, focusing on the core elements of the situation.

The relationships between the cards are crucial. A harmonious flow between the cards suggests a smooth progression, while conflicting cards indicate challenges or obstacles. The overall tone of the spread, whether positive or negative, provides a quick overview of the situation's trajectory.

Copyright Asteria Books 2025

Chalice and Blade Spread

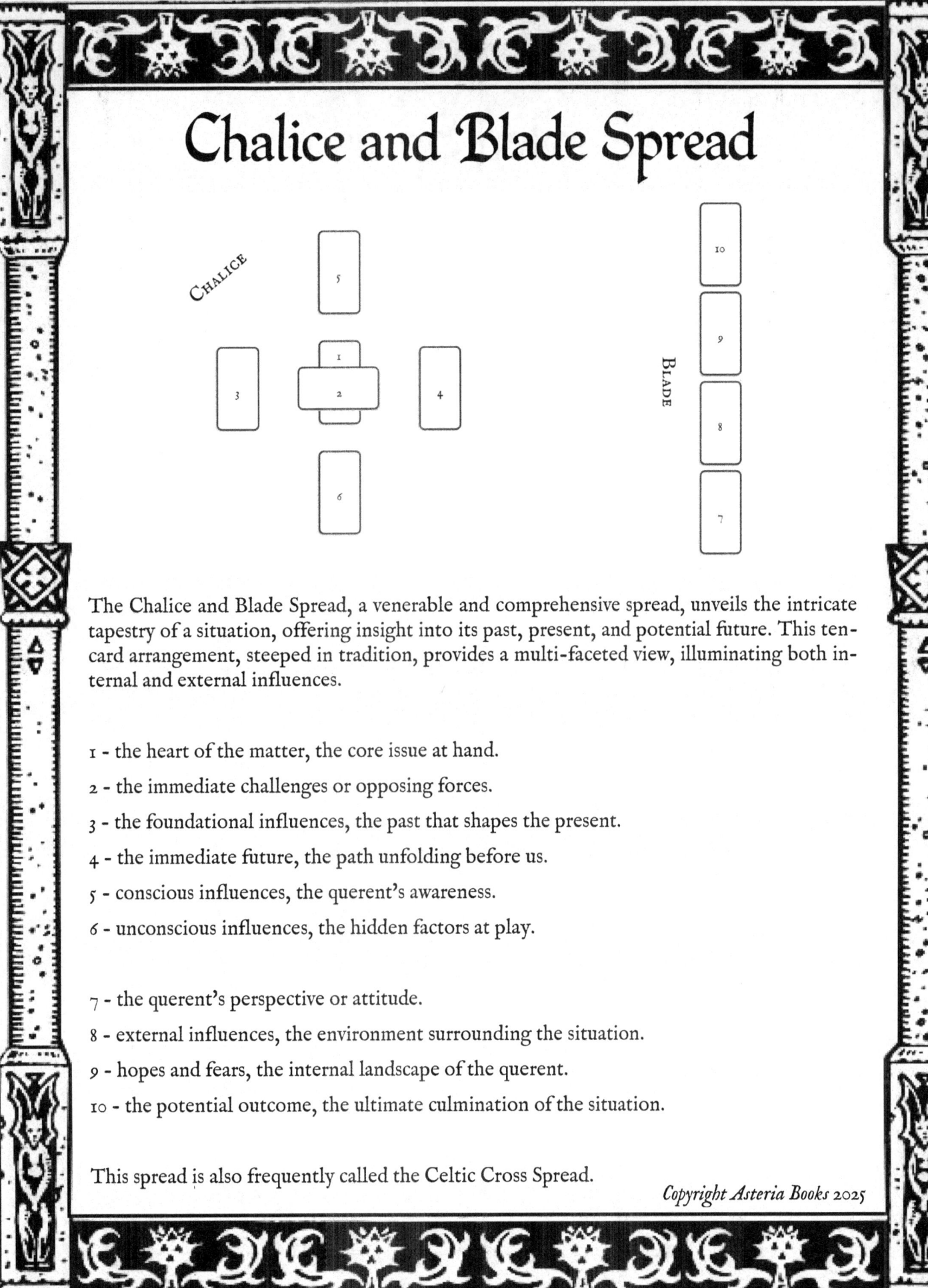

The Chalice and Blade Spread, a venerable and comprehensive spread, unveils the intricate tapestry of a situation, offering insight into its past, present, and potential future. This ten-card arrangement, steeped in tradition, provides a multi-faceted view, illuminating both internal and external influences.

1 - the heart of the matter, the core issue at hand.

2 - the immediate challenges or opposing forces.

3 - the foundational influences, the past that shapes the present.

4 - the immediate future, the path unfolding before us.

5 - conscious influences, the querent's awareness.

6 - unconscious influences, the hidden factors at play.

7 - the querent's perspective or attitude.

8 - external influences, the environment surrounding the situation.

9 - hopes and fears, the internal landscape of the querent.

10 - the potential outcome, the ultimate culmination of the situation.

This spread is also frequently called the Celtic Cross Spread.

Copyright Asteria Books 2025

Crowley Spread

The Crowley 15-Card Spread (often called the Thoth Spread or sometimes the English Spread), is rooted in a Tree of Life framework, offering an even deeper dive into the intricate dynamics of a situation. Designed by Aleister Crowley, this spread aims to map the complex interplay of energies, revealing hidden motivations, karmic patterns, and the potential for profound transformation. This spread is especially well-suited for use with the Thoth Tarot, whose associations vary in some ways from the more common Rider-Waite-Smith tarot systems.

This arrangement allows for a detailed exploration of the spiritual and psychological dimensions at play.

This spread introduces layers of complexity, illuminating the subtle interactions between different aspects of the situation. They reveal the hidden pathways of influence, the unconscious drives, and the potential for spiritual growth and self-discovery. It delves into the karmic implications, the potential for transformation, and the ultimate outcome, which is often presented as a profound revelation.

This spread requires a willingness to confront the deeper, often hidden, aspects of the psyche. It is a powerful tool for those seeking profound self-knowledge and spiritual exploration, offering a comprehensive map of the inner and outer landscapes that shape our destinies.

Copyright Asteria Books 2025

Major Arcana

0. The Fool: Untamed spirit, boundless potential, a leap of faith into the unknown.

1. The Magician: Manifestation, will, the power to shape reality with tools at hand.

2. The High Priestess: Intuition, hidden knowledge, the veiled mysteries of the subconscious.

3. The Empress: Abundance, fertility, creation, the nurturing embrace of nature.

4. The Emperor: Structure, authority, control, the imposition of order upon chaos.

5. The Hierophant: Tradition, dogma, spiritual guidance, the bridge between the divine and mortal.

6. The Lovers: Choice, union, harmony, the delicate balance of duality.

7. The Chariot: Willpower, victory, control, the triumphant surge towards a goal.

8. Strength: Inner fortitude, courage, taming the wild beast within.

9. The Hermit: Solitude, introspection, wisdom gleaned from inner reflection.

10. Wheel of Fortune: Cycles, fate, the turning tides of destiny.

11. Justice: Balance, fairness, karmic retribution, the scales of truth.

12. The Hanged Man: Sacrifice, surrender, altered perspective, seeing the world upside down.

13. Death: Transformation, endings, rebirth, the inevitable cycle of change.

14. Temperance: Balance, harmony, moderation, the alchemical fusion of opposites.

15. The Devil: Temptation, bondage, shadow self, the allure of the material.

16. The Tower: Sudden upheaval, destruction, shattering illusions, the lightning strike of truth.

17. The Star: Hope, inspiration, healing, the guiding light in darkness.

18. The Moon: Intuition, illusions, hidden fears, the veiled realm of the subconscious.

19. The Sun: Vitality, joy, clarity, the radiant light of truth.

20. Judgment: Awakening, rebirth, karmic reckoning, the call to higher purpose.

21. The World: Completion, integration, fulfillment, the culmination of the soul's journey.

Copyright Asteria Books 2025

Minor Arcana: Court Cards

These cards, the people of the suits, speak of roles, behaviors, and the nuanced interactions that shape our lives.

Pages: The messengers, the learners, the youthful expressions of the suit's energy. They embody potential, curiosity, and the initial stages of development within their respective elements. They often represent messages, opportunities, or new beginnings.

Knights: The movers, the seekers, the dynamic forces of the suit's energy. They embody action, movement, and the pursuit of goals. They often represent journeys, challenges, or the expression of passionate energy.

Queens: The nurturers, the keepers, the receptive and intuitive expressions of the suit's energy. They embody emotional maturity, inner wisdom, and the ability to cultivate and maintain. They often represent feminine energy, emotional support, or the embodiment of the suit's qualities.

Kings: The rulers, the masters, the authoritative and decisive expressions of the suit's energy. They embody leadership, control, and the ability to manifest and direct. They often represent masculine energy, authority, or the mastery of the suit's domain.

Wands (Fire)
- Page: Energetic, enthusiastic, a spark of inspiration.
- Knight: Impulsive, passionate, driven by ambition.
- Queen: Charismatic, creative, confident and inspiring.
- King: Authoritative, visionary, a leader of action.

Cups (Water)
- Page: Emotional, sensitive, a messenger of feelings.
- Knight: Romantic, idealistic, driven by emotions.
- Queen: Empathetic, nurturing, deeply connected to emotions.
- King: Compassionate, wise, emotionally mature.

Swords (Air)
- Page: Curious, communicative, a messenger of intellect.
- Knight: Driven, argumentative, quick-witted and sharp.
- Queen: Intelligent, perceptive, clear and discerning.
- King: Authoritative, logical, a master of intellect.

Pentacles (Earth)
- Page: Practical, grounded, a student of the material world.
- Knight: Diligent, patient, focused on material goals.
- Queen: Nurturing, practical, grounded and abundant.
- King: Stable, prosperous, a master of the material realm.

Copyright Asteria Books 2025

Minor Arcana: Pips

The forty seeds of experience, the "pips" of the Minor Arcana, are each a stage in the unfolding of earthly and emotional realms. These cards, the numbered vessels of the suits, speak of the daily currents of life, the ebb and flow of our immediate realities.

Wands (Fire): Speak of action, creativity, will, and spiritual drive. They chronicle the spark of inspiration, the flame of ambition, and the journey towards manifestation.

Cups (Water): Speak of emotions, relationships, intuition, and love. They chart the flow of feelings, the depths of connection, and the tides of the heart.

Swords (Air): Speak of intellect, communication, conflict, and truth. They delineate the sharpness of thought, the clarity of words, and the battles of the mind.

Pentacles (Earth): Speak of material possessions, security, work, and the physical world. They map the growth of resources, the stability of foundations, and the tangible aspects of life.

Aces: The genesis, the raw potential, the spark of an element's influence, a pure expression of its suit's essence.

Twos: Duality, balance, choices, the initial interactions and partnerships within the suit's domain.

Threes: Growth, expression, creativity, the first fruits of labor within the suit's sphere.

Fours: Stability, structure, foundations, the establishment of boundaries and patterns within the suit's realm.

Fives: Conflict, challenge, change, the disruption of established patterns within the suit's influence.

Sixes: Harmony, cooperation, success, the resolution of conflict and the achievement of balance within the suit.

Sevens: Reflection, evaluation, challenges to progress, the questioning and assessment within the suit's journey.

Eights: Movement, action, change, the swift and decisive progression within the suit's narrative.

Nines: Culmination, near-completion, introspection, the nearing of fruition within the suit's experience.

Tens: Completion, burdens, endings, the full expression of the suit's energy, often leading to a shift or change.

Copyright Asteria Books 2025

Nordic Runes: An Overview

The Norse runes held a profound significance within the ancient Nordic cosmology, transcending their function as a mere alphabet. They were perceived as potent symbols, acting as conduits to the deeper, mystical layers of the universe.

Runes were deeply intertwined with the fabric of Norse cosmology, believed to embody the fundamental forces of nature and the cosmos, serving as keys to understanding the hidden workings of the world. The Norns, the weavers of fate, were said to utilize runes to shape destiny, highlighting their connection to the very essence of existence.

Beyond their linguistic value, runes were employed in divination, magic, and ritual practices, thought to possess inherent power, capable of influencing events and connecting with spiritual realms. The act of inscribing runes was not simply writing; it was an invocation, a channeling of the energies they represented. Each rune held a complex web of symbolic meaning, representing concepts, forces, and aspects of the human experience. Thus the runes were far more than letters, they were gateways to whole realms of meaning, used to help people understand their place in the cosmos, and to manipulate its forces.

The myth of Odin's acquisition of the runes, through his self-sacrifice, underscores their sacred nature, solidifying their status as divine knowledge, imbued with profound wisdom.

They are not mere symbols, but living energies, waiting to be awakened by the seeker who approaches them with reverence and understanding. Their wisdom, gleaned from the depths of time, offers a profound connection to the primal forces that shape our existence, a testament to the enduring power of the Runes. They are the whispers of the past, the echoes of the gods, and the tools for shaping the future.

Copyright Asteria Books 2025

Runic Divination

The Norse alphabet varied a bit from place to place and changed somewhat over time, but one of the more commonly used versions today consists of 24 letters that are divided into three sets called *aettr*, which were ruled by specific Gods. Runes were often considered *alive* and therefore needed to be fed, usually with ritual oils, powders, and (at least in their initial blessing) a bit of the Runester's own blood. To divine with the Runes, you can draw a single Rune from a pouch (or three, for a more well-rounded view), or you can cast the entire set onto a circular field, reading only those runes that are face up within the circle. The Runes are also very helpful as symbols for magic and can be combined to create powerful bindrune sigils.

Freya's Aett

Fehu (F) Increase of wealth and possessions, protection of valuables. Used to send energy on its way, fire in its uncontrolled, primal state.

Uruz (U,V) Used to create change, healing, vitality, strength, to boost energy of magickal work.

Thurisaz (Th) Beginning new projects, luck- the hand of fate helping you, protection, the hammer of Thor, opening gateways.

Ansuz (A) Communications, wisdom and clarity, to attract others to your cause, increase magickal energy.

Raido (R) Safe travel, movement, obtaining justice in an issue, used to keep a situation from stagnating.

Kenaz (K) The hearth fire, artistic pursuits, healing, love and passion, creativity, strength.

Gebo (G) Gifts, partnerships on all realms, sex magick, brilliance, integration of energies.

Wunjo (W, V) Joy, happiness, love, fulfillment in career and home life, the icing on the cake.

Heimdall's Eight

Hagalaz (H) Slow, steady pace, no disruptions, asking for a hand from fate within a situation you do not control.

Nauthiz (N) Need, desire, fulfilling those needs, love and sex magick, motivation created by distress.

Isa (I) Cessation of energy, freezing an issue where it stands, cooling relationships, separation, division.

Jera (Y) Harvesting tangible results from efforts already sown, fertility, culmination of events, abundance.

Eihwaz (EI) Banishing magick, removal of obstacles and delays, invoking foresight, clearing up hidden issues and situations.

Perdhro (P) Unexpected gains, hidden secrets coming to light, discovering that which has been lost, spiritual evolution.

Algiz (Z) Protection, fortunate influences, fate on your side, victory and success, good luck and personal strength.

Sowulo (S, Z) Victory, power, strength, health, the rune of the sun, vitality, drive to work and produce.

Tir's Eight

Teiwaz (T) Victory, leadership, success over other competitors, increase in finances, virility and passion (especially for men).

Berkana (B) Growth, abundance, fertility, Mother Earth, protection, the zenith of an idea or situation.

Ehwaz (E) Abrupt changes, moving into new home and environment, travel, swift change in situation.

Mannaz (M) Cooperation, teamwork, collaboration, help and aid from others, beginning new projects, especially with others.

Laguz (L) Intuition, imagination, success in studies, creativity, vitality and passion (especially for women).

Inguz (NG) Fertility, successful conclusion to issue or situation, ending one cycle and beginning another.

Dagaz (D) Increase and expansion, prosperity, growth, major turning points in life, turning in new directions.

Othila (O) Material possessions and protection of those possessions, inheritance (can be genetic traits inherited from elders).

Copyright Asteria Books 2018

Rune Lore and Myth

From the frost-rimed halls of Asgard, and the shadowed depths of Yggdrasil, I chronicle the tales that bind the Runes to the very fabric of Norse cosmology. These glyphs, more than mere symbols, are woven into the legends of gods and giants, their power resonating through the ages.

Odin, the Allfather, hung upon the windswept branches of Yggdrasil, pierced by his own spear, for nine long nights. This harrowing ordeal, a sacrifice of self to self, granted him the knowledge of the Runes. He heard their whispers, felt their power coursing through him, and etched them into the very bark of the World Tree. This act of self-sacrifice imbued the Runes with divine power, making them conduits for the very essence of creation.

The Runes are not merely tools of divination; they are woven into the tales of creation, destruction, and rebirth. They appear in the sagas, inscribed upon weapons, woven into spells, and carved into standing stones. They were used in daily life, for protection, healing, and communication. They were also used in more ritualistic settings, to invoke the gods, to bind spells, and to divine the future.

The Norse world was one of constant struggle, a battle against the forces of chaos. The Runes, born from this harsh reality, reflect this duality. They can be used for both creation and destruction, for healing and harm. Understanding the cultural context of the Runes is crucial to their proper use. They are not to be trifled with, but approached with respect and reverence, for they hold within them the echoes of a world where gods and giants walked the earth, and where fate was a force to be reckoned with.

Copyright Asteria Books 2025

Galdr

Using the art of Galdr, the runic chant, the voice becomes a conduit for the very energies of the Runes. Through carefully crafted words and resonant tones, the Galdrmadr, the rune-singer, awakens the slumbering power within these sacred glyphs.

Galdr is not mere recitation; it is a weaving of sound, a vibration that resonates with the primal forces of the cosmos. Each rune, with its unique name and phonetic value, possesses a distinct frequency, a resonance that echoes through the nine worlds. By chanting these names, by shaping the sounds into specific patterns, the Galdrmadr aligns their own energy with the rune's essence.

The voice becomes a living instrument, a channel for the flow of runic power. The tones are not arbitrary; they are carefully chosen to resonate with the specific energy of each rune. The vowels, long and drawn out, amplify the rune's inherent qualities, while the consonants, sharp and percussive, direct the energy towards a specific purpose.

The words themselves are imbued with power, often drawn from ancient kennings and poetic forms. They are not merely descriptive; they are invocations, commands, and affirmations, shaping the reality around the Galdrmadr. The rhythm and cadence of the chant are crucial, creating a hypnotic state that allows the rune's energy to permeate the mind and spirit.

Galdr is used for a variety of purposes: to invoke the protection of Algiz, to enhance the clarity of Ansuz, to channel the raw power of Uruz, and so on. Galdr can be used for healing, for divination, for binding spells, and for shaping the very fabric of fate. The Galdrmadr, through the power of their voice, becomes a weaver of destiny, shaping the world with the ancient sounds of the Runes.

Copyright Asteria Books 2025

Stadhagaldr

Practicing Stadhagaldr, the runic postures, is a method by which the body becomes a living vessel for the energies of the Runes. Through carefully crafted stances and focused intent, the rune-master, embodies the very essence of these sacred glyphs.

Stadhagaldr is not mere physical exercise; it is a ritualistic dance, a channeling of primal forces through the body's form. Each rune, with its unique shape and symbolic meaning, corresponds to a specific posture, a stance that aligns the body with the rune's inherent energy.

The body becomes a living rune, a conduit for the flow of cosmic power. The limbs are positioned to mirror the rune's shape, creating a physical representation of its energy. The spine aligns with the rune's vertical axis, grounding the practitioner and connecting them to the earth. The breath flows rhythmically, drawing in and releasing the rune's energy.

The mind focuses on the rune's meaning, visualizing its form and chanting its name. This mental focus, combined with the physical posture, creates a powerful resonance, a vibration that aligns the practitioner's energy with the rune's essence. The rune-master becomes a living embodiment of the rune, channeling its power through their physical form.

Stadhagaldr is used for a variety of purposes: to invoke the protection of Algiz, the practitioner raises their arms, mirroring the rune's shape, becoming a living shield. To channel the strength of Uruz, the practitioner adopts a powerful stance, grounding themselves and drawing in the earth's raw energy. To enhance the clarity of Ansuz, the practitioner stands tall, opening their throat and allowing the rune's energy to flow through their voice.

Stadhagaldr is also called Runic Yoga by some, and was first developed as a practice in the 1920's. The rune-master can also adapt this practice to something akin to "mudras" – or yoga of the hands – by forming the hands and fingers into runic shapes.

Copyright Asteria Books 2025

Rune Carving and Blessing

The rune-carver approaches this task with reverence and focused intent, for these are not mere symbols, but vessels of primal power.

The choice of wood is paramount, each type imbued with its own inherent energies. Yew, for its connection to the cycles of life and death; ash, for its association with Yggdrasil, the World Tree; birch, for its nurturing and protective qualities. The wood is carefully selected, cleansed, and prepared, a blank canvas awaiting the rune's mark.

With a sharpened blade, the runes are meticulously carved, each stroke deliberate and precise. The shapes are not merely drawn, but etched into the very essence of the wood, awakening the slumbering energies within. As each rune is formed, its name is whispered, its meaning visualized, imbuing the carving with intent.

Once the runes are carved, they must be blessed, consecrated to their sacred purpose. This ritual is a communion between the rune-carver and the runes, a binding of their energies. The runes are bathed in moonlight, cleansed with smoke from sacred herbs, and anointed with oils infused with runic power.

The rune-carver then invokes the gods, calling upon Odin, the Allfather, and the other deities associated with the runes. They chant galdr, the runic songs of power, awakening the energies within the carved staves. The runes are held aloft, bathed in the light of the sun or moon, and imbued with the rune-carver's own life force (blood).

Finally, the runes are wrapped in cloth, a sacred shroud, and stored in a place of honor. They are now ready for use, potent vessels of runic power, waiting to be cast, chanted, and wielded by the skilled hand of the rune-carver. They are no longer mere wood, but living runes, conduits for the forces that shape our destinies.

Copyright Asteria Books 2025

Rune Casting

The Rune Master approaches this practice with reverence and focused intent, seeking to decipher the whispers of destiny.

The simplest method involves drawing runes from a bag, each rune pulled with focused intent, representing a specific aspect of the query. This method allows for a direct and personal connection with the runes, each draw guided by intuition.

Another method involves casting the runes onto a cloth, a sacred space marked with symbols and sigils. The runes are thrown, their landing positions and orientations revealing the interplay of forces at work. The patterns formed by the fallen runes are then interpreted, revealing the threads of fate.

Basic spreads, like the Three-Rune Spread, offer concise insights. The first rune, drawn or cast to the left, represents the past, the foundational influences shaping the present. The second rune, in the center, reveals the present situation, the immediate challenges or opportunities. The third rune, to the right, illuminates the potential future, the likely outcome or path ahead.

The Nine-Rune Spread, a more complex arrangement, delves deeper into the situation's intricacies. The runes are cast or drawn in a pattern resembling the nine worlds of Norse cosmology, revealing the interplay of forces across multiple realms. This spread illuminates the spiritual, emotional, and material aspects of the query, offering a comprehensive overview of the situation's dynamics.

The interpretation of runic spreads requires both knowledge and intuition. The Rune Master must understand the individual meanings of the runes, as well as their relationships to one another within the spread. The patterns formed by the fallen runes are not random, but rather a reflection of the forces at play, revealing the hidden currents that shape our destinies. The Rune Master becomes a conduit for these forces, deciphering the whispers of fate and guiding the seeker towards understanding.

Copyright Asteria Books 2025

Runic Crafting and Talismans

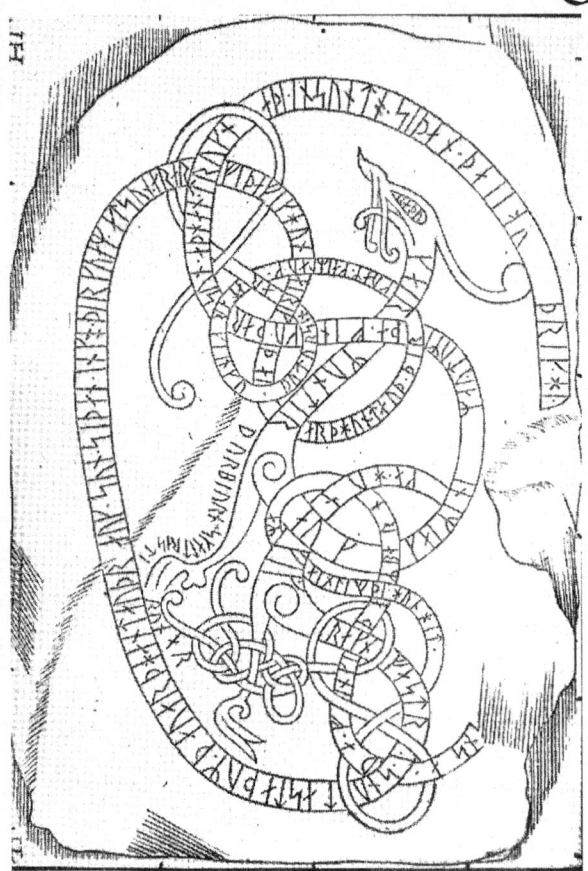

The rune-smith selects materials with care, each imbued with its own inherent energies. Metal, for its durability and conductivity; stone, for its grounding and protective qualities; wood, for its connection to the natural world. The chosen material is then shaped and prepared, a blank canvas awaiting the runic inscription.

Runic binding, the art of combining runes into sigils, is a crucial aspect of talisman creation. Runes are chosen for their specific meanings and energies, then interwoven into a single, cohesive symbol. This binding amplifies the runes' power, creating a focused and potent force. The rune-smith visualizes the desired outcome, imbuing the sigil with intent.

The runes are then inscribed upon the chosen material, each stroke deliberate and precise. The shapes are not merely drawn, but etched into the very essence of the material, awakening the slumbering energies within. As each rune is formed, its name is whispered, its meaning visualized, imbuing the carving with intent.

The talisman or amulet is then blessed, consecrated to its sacred purpose. This ritual is a communion between the rune-smith and the crafted object, a binding of their energies. The object is bathed in moonlight, cleansed with smoke from sacred herbs, and anointed with oils infused with runic power.

Ethical considerations are paramount in runic magic. The rune-smith must approach this practice with respect and responsibility, understanding the potent forces they are working with. Runes are not to be used for frivolous purposes or to inflict harm. They are tools for balance and harmony, for protection and guidance.

Safety is also crucial. Runic energies are powerful and can be unpredictable. The rune-smith must be grounded and centered, maintaining a clear intention and a strong connection to the earth. They must understand the potential consequences of their actions and proceed with caution. The runes are not playthings, but tools of profound power, to be wielded with wisdom and reverence.

Copyright Asteria Books 2025

Bindrunes

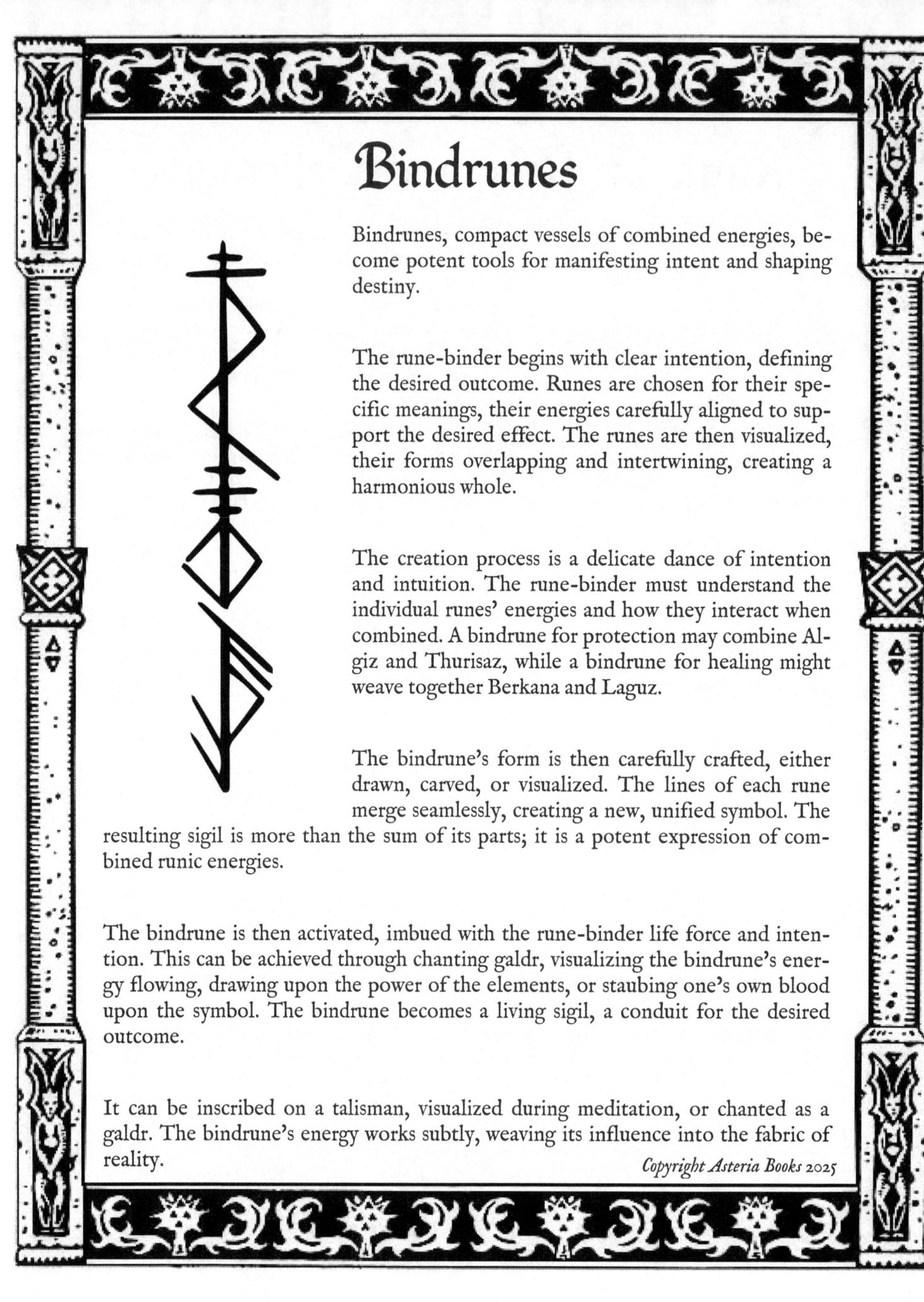

Bindrunes, compact vessels of combined energies, become potent tools for manifesting intent and shaping destiny.

The rune-binder begins with clear intention, defining the desired outcome. Runes are chosen for their specific meanings, their energies carefully aligned to support the desired effect. The runes are then visualized, their forms overlapping and intertwining, creating a harmonious whole.

The creation process is a delicate dance of intention and intuition. The rune-binder must understand the individual runes' energies and how they interact when combined. A bindrune for protection may combine Algiz and Thurisaz, while a bindrune for healing might weave together Berkana and Laguz.

The bindrune's form is then carefully crafted, either drawn, carved, or visualized. The lines of each rune merge seamlessly, creating a new, unified symbol. The resulting sigil is more than the sum of its parts; it is a potent expression of combined runic energies.

The bindrune is then activated, imbued with the rune-binder life force and intention. This can be achieved through chanting galdr, visualizing the bindrune's energy flowing, drawing upon the power of the elements, or staubing one's own blood upon the symbol. The bindrune becomes a living sigil, a conduit for the desired outcome.

It can be inscribed on a talisman, visualized during meditation, or chanted as a galdr. The bindrune's energy works subtly, weaving its influence into the fabric of reality.

Copyright Asteria Books 2025

Rune Staves

Runestaves, crafted from wood or stone, become focused conduits for a specific rune's power and tools for amplifying its influence.

The Runesmith begins with selecting a suitable material, often wood corresponding to the rune's nature - birch for Berkana, yew for Eihwaz. The material is then carefully shaped and prepared, becoming a blank canvas for the rune's inscription.

The chosen rune is then meticulously carved or inscribed upon the stave, each stroke imbued with intent. The Runesmith visualizes the rune's energy flowing into the material, awakening its inherent power. The carving is not merely a symbol, but a conduit, a channel for the rune's essence.

The runestave is then activated, consecrated to its specific purpose. This can be achieved through chanting galdr, visualizing the rune's energy resonating within the stave, or anointing it with oils infused with corresponding herbs and also with the Runesmith's own blood. The stave becomes a living embodiment of the rune's power.

The use of a runestave is focused and direct. It can be held during meditation, placed upon an altar, or used as a focal point for ritual work. A runestave carved with Algiz, for example, can be used for protection, its energy radiating outwards, warding off negative influences. A runestave carved with Sowilo can be used to amplify personal power, its energy bringing clarity and focus.

The runestave acts as an amplifier, concentrating and directing the rune's energy towards a specific goal. It is a tool for focused intent, a way to channel the potent power of a single rune into a tangible form, allowing the Runesmith to wield its influence with precision and purpose.

Copyright Asteria Books 2025

Freyja's Aett

FREYA IN HER CHARIOT.

Freyja's aett, the first family of Norse runes, held a foundational significance in ancient Nordic cosmology. This grouping represented the primal forces and fundamental aspects of existence, forming the bedrock upon which the later aettir built. As a cohesive unit, they embodied the raw potential of creation, the initial spark that ignited the cosmos.

This aett was deeply connected to the themes of beginnings, primal energies, and the establishment of order. It symbolized the shaping of the world from chaos, the emergence of life, and the inherent power that drives all things. The runes within this aett were seen as gateways to understanding these fundamental principles, offering insights into the very nature of being and the forces that shaped the world. They represented the raw, unbridled potential that underpins all subsequent manifestations, laying the groundwork for the unfolding of fate and destiny.

Copyright Asteria Books 2025

Fehu

Fehu (fay-hoo) represents cattle, wealth, and mobile property.

Divinationally, it signifies prosperity, abundance, and the attainment of material or spiritual rewards. It can also indicate a loss of possessions if reversed or ill-aspected.

Fehu is a rune of beginnings, representing the initial spark of creation and the potential for growth. Its energy promotes the flow of resources and the manifestation of desires.

Magically, Fehu can be used to attract wealth, enhance financial stability, and foster generosity. It can also be employed in rituals to increase personal power and strengthen one's connection to the material world. To use it in magic, visualize the rune glowing with golden light, representing the flow of abundance, or inscribe it on a green candle for prosperity spells.

Meditating on Fehu can help align one's energy with the frequency of wealth and attract opportunities for financial growth. Its energy is dynamic and forward-moving, encouraging action and decisive steps towards achieving one's goals.

Copyright Asteria Books 2025

Uruz

Uruz (oo-rooz) represents the wild ox, symbolizing primal strength, untamed potential, and raw, vital energy.

In divination, it signifies raw power, physical health, unexpected change, determination, and endurance. It speaks of the untamed forces of nature and the inherent strength within oneself. Uruz can indicate a need to tap into one's inner reserves of power to overcome obstacles and navigate challenging situations. It signifies a period of significant change or transformation, often requiring courage and resilience.

Magically, Uruz can be used to strengthen willpower, enhance physical healing, ground oneself in the present moment, and harness primal energy. It can aid in overcoming obstacles, building stamina, and connecting with the earth's vital forces. To use it in magic, visualize the rune glowing with a deep red or brown light, symbolizing the earth's energy, or inscribe it on a piece of leather for grounding rituals.

Meditating on Uruz can help one connect with their inner strength and tap into their reserves of resilience. Its energy is powerful and direct, encouraging decisive action and the harnessing of one's inner power to achieve desired outcomes.

Copyright Asteria Books 2025

Thurisaz

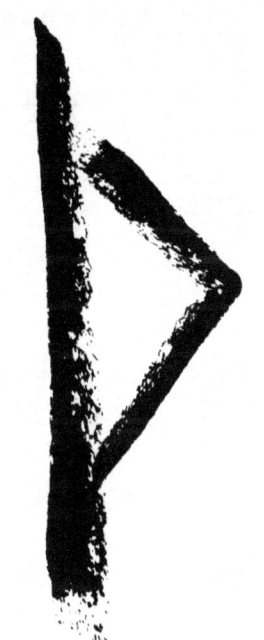

Thurisaz (thoo-ree-sahz) represents the thorn, symbolizing primal chaos, defensive force, and the destructive power of giants.

In divination, it signifies challenges, tests, and the need for careful consideration. It can represent a powerful force, either destructive or protective, depending on context. Thurisaz speaks of potential conflict, both internal and external, and the need to confront obstacles with wisdom and strength. It can also indicate a gateway to new beginnings, but only after overcoming significant challenges.

Magically, Thurisaz can be used for protection, banishing negative energies, and invoking the power of Thor. It can aid in breaking down barriers, confronting fears, and asserting one's boundaries. To use it in magic, visualize the rune glowing with a sharp, red light, symbolizing defensive energy, or inscribe it on a piece of iron for protection spells.

Meditating on Thurisaz can help one confront and overcome inner demons and external threats. Its energy is forceful and direct, demanding respect and careful consideration of its power.

Copyright Asteria Books 2025

Ansuz

Ansuz (ahn-sooz) represents the mouth, or Odin, symbolizing divine breath, communication, and wisdom.

In divination, it signifies messages, inspiration, and the flow of knowledge. It can indicate unexpected insights, divine guidance, and the power of spoken words. Ansuz speaks of the importance of communication, both with others and with the divine. It suggests a time for listening, learning, and seeking wisdom. It can also represent creative inspiration and the ability to articulate one's thoughts and ideas effectively.

Magically, Ansuz can be used to enhance communication skills, invoke divine inspiration, and access hidden knowledge. It can aid in public speaking, writing, and any form of communication. To use it in magic, visualize the rune glowing with a bright, blue light, symbolizing clarity and inspiration, or inscribe it on a piece of parchment for communication spells.

Meditating on Ansuz can help one connect with their inner wisdom and receive divine guidance. Its energy is insightful and communicative, encouraging open dialogue and the pursuit of knowledge.

Copyright Asteria Books 2025

Raido

Raido (rye-thoh) represents the wagon or journey, symbolizing movement, rhythm, and the cyclical nature of life.

In divination, it signifies travel, both physical and spiritual, and the alignment of one's path. It can indicate a journey, a change of direction, or a need to find balance and harmony. Raido speaks of the natural rhythms of life and the importance of staying on one's true path. It suggests a time for reflection, planning, and adapting to change. It can also represent communication through travel or the bringing together of disparate elements.

Magically, Raido can be used for safe travels, aligning with one's destiny, and finding rhythm and balance. It can aid in planning journeys, both literal and metaphorical. To use it in magic, visualize the rune glowing with a vibrant, orange light, symbolizing movement and direction, or inscribe it on a compass for safe travel spells.

Meditating on Raido can help one find their true path and align with the natural flow of life. Its energy is dynamic and directional, encouraging movement and the pursuit of one's goals.

Copyright Asteria Books 2025

Kenaz

Kenaz (kay-nahz) represents the torch or beacon, symbolizing controlled fire, creative energy, and illumination.

In divination, it signifies knowledge, skill, and the ability to shed light on hidden things. It can indicate inspiration, creativity, and the application of knowledge. Kenaz speaks of the controlled use of fire, both literally and metaphorically, representing the power to transform and create. It suggests a time for applying skills, pursuing creative endeavors, and gaining clarity. It can also represent healing, passion, and the ability to bring light into darkness.

Magically, Kenaz can be used to enhance creativity, ignite passion, and illuminate hidden truths. It can aid in healing, craftsmanship, and the pursuit of knowledge. To use it in magic, visualize the rune glowing with a warm, red-orange light, symbolizing creative fire, or inscribe it on a candle for illumination spells.

Meditating on Kenaz can help one access their creative potential and gain clarity in their endeavors. Its energy is focused and illuminating, encouraging the application of knowledge and the expression of creativity.

Copyright Asteria Books 2025

Gebo

Gebo (geh-boh) represents a gift or offering, symbolizing partnership, balance, and the exchange of energy.

In divination, it signifies gifts, both given and received, and the importance of reciprocity. It can indicate partnerships, alliances, and the harmonious exchange of energy between individuals or forces. Gebo speaks of the sacredness of giving and receiving, highlighting the importance of balance and mutual respect. It suggests a time for collaboration, cooperation, and the sharing of resources. It can also represent contracts, agreements, and the strengthening of bonds through shared experiences.

Magically, Gebo can be used to enhance partnerships, attract gifts, and promote harmonious relationships. It can aid in strengthening bonds, creating alliances, and fostering mutual understanding. To use it in magic, visualize the rune glowing with a warm, golden light, symbolizing generosity and balance, or inscribe it on a piece of amber for partnership spells.

Meditating on Gebo can help one cultivate gratitude and foster harmonious relationships. Its energy is balanced and reciprocal, encouraging mutual respect and the sharing of gifts.

Copyright Asteria Books 2025

Wunjo

Wunjo (woon-yoh) represents joy, harmony, and the fulfillment of desires.

In divination, it signifies happiness, success, and the attainment of goals. It can indicate a period of prosperity, contentment, and the enjoyment of positive outcomes. Wunjo speaks of the importance of harmony, both within oneself and in relationships with others. It suggests a time for celebration, gratitude, and the appreciation of life's blessings. It can also represent the coming together of disparate elements into a harmonious whole.

Magically, Wunjo can be used to attract joy, enhance happiness, and foster positive relationships. It can aid in achieving goals, celebrating success, and creating a harmonious environment. To use it in magic, visualize the rune glowing with a bright, golden-yellow light, symbolizing joy and harmony, or inscribe it on a piece of birch wood for happiness spells.

Meditating on Wunjo can help one cultivate a positive mindset and attract positive experiences. Its energy is uplifting and harmonious, encouraging joy and the celebration of life.

Copyright Asteria Books 2025

Hagal's Aett

Hagal's aett, the second family of Norse runes, carried the weight of growth, transformation, and the challenges of the journey through life. This group represented the development and evolution of the primal forces established by Freyja's aett, focusing on the interactions between those forces and the complexities of existence.

As a group, they symbolized the processes of change, the trials of growth, and the necessary sacrifices that accompany progress. This aett underscored the dynamic nature of the cosmos, highlighting the constant flux and interplay between opposing forces. It explored themes of resistance, perseverance, and the honing of inner strength. These runes were perceived as guides through the difficult passages of life, offering insights into navigating adversity and embracing transformation. They represent the cultivation of potential, the forging of character, and the acceptance of the ever-shifting tides of fate.

Copyright Asteria Books 2025

Hagalaz

Hagalaz (hah-gah-lahz) represents hail, symbolizing destructive natural forces, sudden disruption, and tests of fate.

In divination, it signifies challenges, unavoidable events, and the need for resilience. It can indicate a period of hardship, unexpected setbacks, and the breaking down of old structures. Hagalaz speaks of forces beyond one's control, demanding adaptation and inner strength. It suggests a time for facing adversity, accepting the inevitable, and learning from difficult experiences. It can also represent a cleansing process, where destruction precedes renewal.

Magically, Hagalaz can be used for protection against negative forces, breaking unwanted patterns, and accepting fate. It can aid in weathering storms, both literal and metaphorical. To use it in magic, visualize the rune glowing with a cold, white-blue light, symbolizing icy power, or inscribe it on a piece of crystal for protection spells.

Meditating on Hagalaz can help one find inner strength and resilience in the face of adversity. Its energy is disruptive and transformative, encouraging acceptance and adaptation.

Nauthiz

Nauthiz (now-thiz) represents need or necessity, symbolizing hardship, resistance, and the inner strength required to overcome adversity.

In divination, it signifies restriction, delay, and the need for patience. It can indicate a period of scarcity, challenges, and the necessity to endure difficult times. Nauthiz speaks of the importance of resilience, perseverance, and the development of inner strength through hardship. It suggests a time for confronting limitations, accepting responsibility, and finding creative solutions to problems. It can also represent the fire of friction, the spark that ignites innovation in times of need.

Magically, Nauthiz can be used to strengthen willpower, overcome obstacles, and find solutions in challenging situations. It can aid in endurance, patience, and the development of inner resources. To use it in magic, visualize the rune glowing with a dark, smoky gray light, symbolizing hardship and resilience, or inscribe it on a piece of dark wood for endurance spells.

Meditating on Nauthiz can help one find inner strength and navigate difficult times. Its energy is restrictive yet transformative, encouraging perseverance and the development of inner resources.

Copyright Asteria Books 2025

Isa

Isa (ee-sah) represents ice, symbolizing stillness, stagnation, and the freezing of energy.

In divination, it signifies a period of pause, blockage, and the need for patience. It can indicate a standstill, a lack of progress, and the need to conserve energy. Isa speaks of the power of stillness, the potential for frozen energy, and the necessity to accept periods of inactivity. It suggests a time for reflection, introspection, and the acceptance of limitations. It can also represent the need to solidify plans and conserve resources.

Magically, Isa can be used to freeze unwanted situations, halt negative influences, and create a sense of stillness. It can aid in meditation, introspection, and the conservation of energy. To use it in magic, visualize the rune glowing with a cold, white light, symbolizing frozen energy, or inscribe it on a piece of clear quartz for stillness spells.

Meditating on Isa can help one find inner peace and accept periods of inactivity. Its energy is still and restrictive, encouraging patience and introspection.

Copyright Asteria Books 2025

Jera

Jera (yay-rah) represents the harvest or year, symbolizing cycles, rewards, and the natural flow of time.

In divination, it signifies the reaping of what has been sown, the culmination of efforts, and the cyclical nature of life. It can indicate a period of prosperity, abundance, and the fulfillment of long-term plans. Jera speaks of the importance of patience, perseverance, and the understanding that all things come in their own time. It suggests a time for celebrating achievements, appreciating the fruits of one's labor, and recognizing the cyclical nature of existence. It can also represent legal matters, contracts, and the establishment of just rewards.

Magically, Jera can be used to ensure a successful harvest, promote long-term success, and align with the natural rhythms of life. It can aid in legal matters, contracts, and the manifestation of desired outcomes. To use it in magic, visualize the rune glowing with a golden-brown light, symbolizing harvest and abundance, or inscribe it on a piece of wheat or oak for prosperity spells.

Meditating on Jera can help one align with the natural cycles of life and manifest long-term success. Its energy is cyclical and rewarding, encouraging patience and the appreciation of the fruits of one's labor.

Eihwaz

Eihwaz (eye-wahz) represents the yew tree, symbolizing endurance, protection, and the connection between life and death.

In divination, it signifies strength in adversity, foresight, and the ability to navigate transitions. It can indicate a period of transformation, spiritual growth, and the need for perseverance. Eihwaz speaks of the yew's enduring nature, its deep roots, and its connection to both the physical and spiritual realms. It suggests a time for facing fears, accepting change, and understanding the cyclical nature of existence. It can also represent protection, defense, and the ability to bridge different worlds.

Magically, Eihwaz can be used for protection, spiritual guidance, and navigating transitions. It can aid in connecting with ancestors, strengthening inner resilience, and facing mortality with courage. To use it in magic, visualize the rune glowing with a deep, dark green light, symbolizing the yew's strength, or inscribe it on a piece of yew wood for protection spells.

Meditating on Eihwaz can help one gain spiritual insight and navigate life's transitions with grace. Its energy is protective and transformative, encouraging endurance and spiritual growth.

Copyright Asteria Books 2025

Perthro

Perthro (per-thro) represents the lot cup or womb, symbolizing fate, mystery, and the hidden aspects of life.

In divination, it signifies hidden influences, chance, and the unfolding of destiny. It can indicate secrets, mysteries, and the exploration of the unknown. Perthro speaks of the unpredictable nature of fate, the hidden forces that shape our lives, and the potential for unexpected outcomes. It suggests a time for introspection, delving into the subconscious, and exploring the mysteries of existence. It can also represent birth, rebirth, and the cyclical nature of life.

Magically, Perthro can be used for divination, exploring hidden truths, and influencing fate. It can aid in unlocking mysteries, accessing intuition, and understanding the deeper patterns of life. To use it in magic, visualize the rune glowing with a deep, dark blue or black light, symbolizing mystery and hidden knowledge, or inscribe it on a piece of bone or dark stone for divination spells.

Meditating on Perthro can help one access their intuition and explore the hidden aspects of themselves and the world around them. Its energy is mysterious and transformative, encouraging introspection and the exploration of the unknown.

Copyright Asteria Books 2025

Algiz

Algiz (al-ghiz) represents the elk or protection, symbolizing divine protection, defense, and spiritual connection.

In divination, it signifies protection from harm, divine guidance, and heightened awareness. It can indicate a need for vigilance, the presence of protective forces, and the strengthening of spiritual defenses. Algiz speaks of the divine shield, the connection to higher powers, and the ability to ward off negative influences. It suggests a time for seeking protection, strengthening spiritual boundaries, and trusting in divine guidance. It can also represent heightened intuition, psychic awareness, and the ability to perceive danger.

Magically, Algiz can be used for protection, warding off negative energies, and strengthening spiritual connections. It can aid in creating protective shields, invoking divine assistance, and enhancing psychic abilities. To use it in magic, visualize the rune glowing with a bright, silver or white light, symbolizing divine protection, or inscribe it on a piece of silver or crystal for protection spells.

Meditating on Algiz can help one connect with their spiritual guides and strengthen their psychic defenses. Its energy is protective and uplifting, encouraging trust in divine guidance and the strengthening of spiritual boundaries.

Copyright Asteria Books 2025

Sowilo

Sowilo (so-wee-loh) represents the sun, symbolizing power, victory, and the life-giving force.

In divination, it signifies success, clarity, and the attainment of goals. It can indicate a period of vitality, positive energy, and the manifestation of desired outcomes. Sowilo speaks of the sun's radiant energy, the power to overcome obstacles, and the achievement of victory. It suggests a time for harnessing inner strength, pursuing goals with confidence, and basking in the light of success. It can also represent healing, enlightenment, and the realization of one's full potential.

Magically, Sowilo can be used to enhance vitality, attract success, and invoke the power of the sun. It can aid in healing, manifesting goals, and strengthening one's personal power. To use it in magic, visualize the rune glowing with a bright, golden-yellow light, symbolizing solar energy, or inscribe it on a piece of gold or sunstone for success spells.

Meditating on Sowilo can help one tap into their inner power and manifest their desires. Its energy is radiant and powerful, encouraging confidence and the pursuit of one's full potential.

Tyr's Aett

Tyr's aett, the third family of Norse runes, embodies the culmination of cycles, the reaping of rewards, and the wisdom gained through experience. This final family represents the integration of the primal energies and transformative journeys of the previous aettir, focusing on the outcomes and lasting legacies of those processes.

As a cohesive group, this aett symbolizes the attainment of knowledge, the manifestation of destiny, and the cyclical nature of existence. It highlights the importance of reflection, the understanding of interconnectedness, and the acceptance of the inevitable flow of time. These runes were seen as guides to comprehending the deeper patterns of fate, offering insights into the rewards of perseverance and the significance of lasting impact. They represent the harvest of accumulated wisdom, the fulfillment of potential, and the recognition of the cyclical nature of life, death, and rebirth.

Copyright Asteria Books 2025

Tiwaz

Tiwaz (tee-wahz) represents the god Tyr, symbolizing justice, sacrifice, and unwavering courage.

In divination, it signifies victory through self-sacrifice, honor, and the pursuit of truth. It can indicate a period of conflict, the need for decisive action, and the importance of upholding justice. Tiwaz speaks of the god Tyr's commitment to fairness and the willingness to make sacrifices for the greater good. It suggests a time for standing up for one's beliefs, facing challenges with courage, and upholding principles. It can also represent legal matters, contracts, and the pursuit of justice.

Magically, Tiwaz can be used to enhance courage, ensure victory in legal matters, and invoke the power of justice. It can aid in strengthening willpower, upholding principles, and facing challenges with integrity. To use it in magic, visualize the rune glowing with a bright, blue-silver light, symbolizing justice and courage, or inscribe it on a piece of steel or lapis lazuli for legal spells.

Meditating on Tiwaz can help one cultivate courage and stand up for what is right. Its energy is just and courageous, encouraging integrity and the pursuit of truth.

Copyright Asteria Books 2025

Berkana

Berkana (ber-kah-nah) represents the birch tree, symbolizing growth, fertility, and nurturing.

In divination, it signifies new beginnings, family, and the feminine principle. It can indicate a period of growth, healing, and the nurturing of relationships. Berkana speaks of the birch's gentle strength, its connection to nature, and its role as a symbol of fertility and renewal. It suggests a time for nurturing projects, fostering growth, and embracing the feminine aspects of life. It can also represent family, home, and the creation of a safe and supportive environment.

Magically, Berkana can be used to enhance fertility, promote healing, and nurture relationships. It can aid in creating a peaceful home, fostering growth, and strengthening family bonds. To use it in magic, visualize the rune glowing with a soft, green light, symbolizing growth and nurturing, or inscribe it on a piece of birch wood or a green candle for fertility spells.

Meditating on Berkana can help one cultivate a nurturing spirit and create a harmonious environment. Its energy is gentle and nurturing, encouraging growth and the strengthening of relationships.

Copyright Asteria Books 2025

Ehwaz

Ehwaz (eh-wahz) represents the horse, symbolizing partnership, trust, and harmonious cooperation.

In divination, it signifies teamwork, loyalty, and the smooth progression of journeys. It can indicate a period of collaboration, mutual understanding, and the strengthening of bonds. Ehwaz speaks of the strong connection between horse and rider, representing the importance of trust and cooperation in achieving shared goals. It suggests a time for building partnerships, fostering harmony, and working together towards common objectives. It can also represent transportation, movement, and the smooth flow of energy.

Magically, Ehwaz can be used to strengthen partnerships, enhance communication, and promote harmonious cooperation. It can aid in teamwork, negotiation, and the smooth progression of projects. To use it in magic, visualize the rune glowing with a light, gray-blue light, symbolizing partnership and trust, or inscribe it on a piece of leather or horsehair for collaboration spells.

Meditating on Ehwaz can help one cultivate trust and build strong, harmonious relationships. Its energy is balanced and cooperative, encouraging teamwork and mutual understanding.

Copyright Asteria Books 2025

Mannaz

Mannaz (man-naz) represents humanity, symbolizing the self, social order, and the interconnectedness of people.

In divination, it signifies human potential, intelligence, and the importance of community. It can indicate self-awareness, social interaction, and the need for cooperation. Mannaz speaks of the collective human experience, the strengths and weaknesses of humanity, and the importance of social harmony. It suggests a time for self-reflection, understanding one's role in society, and fostering positive relationships. It can also represent intellectual pursuits, communication, and the development of personal potential.

Magically, Mannaz can be used to enhance social connections, improve communication, and promote self-understanding. It can aid in group work, community building, and personal growth. To use it in magic, visualize the rune glowing with a clear, light blue light, symbolizing human intellect, or inscribe it on a piece of paper or parchment for communication spells.

Meditating on Mannaz can help one gain self-awareness and foster positive social interactions. Its energy is social and intellectual, encouraging cooperation and personal growth.

Laguz

Laguz (lah-gooze) represents water, symbolizing flow, intuition, and the subconscious mind.

In divination, it signifies emotions, dreams, and the hidden depths of the psyche. It can indicate intuition, psychic abilities, and the need to trust one's inner voice. Laguz speaks of the fluid nature of water, the ebb and flow of emotions, and the connection to the subconscious. It suggests a time for exploring inner depths, trusting intuition, and embracing the fluidity of life. It can also represent healing, cleansing, and the flow of energy.

Magically, Laguz can be used to enhance intuition, promote healing, and connect with the subconscious. It can aid in dream work, psychic development, and emotional balance. To use it in magic, visualize the rune glowing with a deep, blue-green light, symbolizing water's depth, or inscribe it on a piece of seashell or blue stone for intuition spells.

Meditating on Laguz can help one connect with their inner wisdom and embrace the flow of life. Its energy is fluid and intuitive, encouraging emotional balance and psychic awareness.

Copyright Asteria Books 2025

Ingwaz

Ingwaz (ing-wahz) represents the god Ing, symbolizing fertility, potential, and the inner self.

In divination, it signifies potential energy, inner strength, and the completion of cycles. It can indicate a period of rest, incubation, and the gathering of resources for future endeavors. Ingwaz speaks of the fertile earth, the potential for growth, and the importance of inner strength and self-reliance. It suggests a time for reflection, consolidation, and the preparation for new beginnings. It can also represent home, family, and the safe containment of energy.

Magically, Ingwaz can be used to enhance fertility, promote inner peace, and gather strength for future endeavors. It can aid in creating a safe space, fostering growth, and consolidating energy. To use it in magic, visualize the rune glowing with a deep, earthy green light, symbolizing fertile potential, or inscribe it on a piece of fertile earth or a green candle for growth spells.

Meditating on Ingwaz can help one connect with their inner strength and prepare for new beginnings. Its energy is contained and fertile, encouraging reflection and the gathering of resources.

Copyright Asteria Books 2025

Othala

Othala (oh-thah-lah) represents ancestral property or homeland, symbolizing heritage, inheritance, and the connection to one's roots.

In divination, it signifies family, tradition, and the importance of ancestral connections. It can indicate inheritance, property, and the need to honor one's lineage. Othala speaks of the importance of heritage, the strength derived from one's ancestors, and the connection to one's homeland. It suggests a time for honoring traditions, respecting family ties, and understanding one's place within a larger lineage. It can also represent property, possessions, and the transmission of knowledge through generations.

Magically, Othala can be used to strengthen family bonds, honor ancestors, and secure property. It can aid in connecting with one's heritage, protecting possessions, and preserving traditions. To use it in magic, visualize the rune glowing with a warm, brown-gold light, symbolizing ancestral connection, or inscribe it on a piece of family heirloom or a stone from one's homeland for inheritance spells.

Meditating on Othala can help one connect with their ancestors and honor their heritage. Its energy is grounding and traditional, encouraging respect for lineage and the preservation of heritage.

Copyright Asteria Books 2025

Dagaz

Dagaz (dah-gahz) represents day or dawn, symbolizing awakening, clarity, and the breakthrough of light.

In divination, it signifies a major shift, a period of enlightenment, and the dawn of a new era. It can indicate positive change, clarity of vision, and the overcoming of obstacles. Dagaz speaks of the transition from darkness to light, the moment of clarity, and the potential for significant transformation. It suggests a time for embracing change, shedding old patterns, and welcoming new beginnings. It can also represent balance, harmony, and the merging of opposites.

Magically, Dagaz can be used to bring about positive change, illuminate hidden truths, and usher in a new era. It can aid in achieving breakthroughs, overcoming obstacles, and manifesting positive outcomes. To use it in magic, visualize the rune glowing with a bright, white-yellow light, symbolizing dawn and clarity, or inscribe it on a white candle or a piece of clear quartz for enlightenment spells.

Meditating on Dagaz can help one embrace change and welcome new beginnings with clarity and optimism. Its energy is transformative and illuminating, encouraging positive change and the dawn of a new era.

Copyright Asteria Books 2025

The Blank Rune

Thw controversial Blank Rune, or Wyrd, is a relatively modern addition to runelore, and many practitioners do not include it in their practice. For those who do, it is a symbol of the ultimate mystery, the fate that lies beyond our comprehension. This rune, unlike its brethren, bears no mark, no glyph; yet its presence speaks volumes, a silent testament to the forces that shape our destinies.

Its appearance in a casting is a potent omen, a stark reminder that some things are beyond our grasp. It signifies the presence of forces beyond our understanding, the unseen currents that shape our lives. It speaks of the limitations of divination, the boundaries of human knowledge.

The Blank Rune's meaning is not negative, nor is it positive. It is simply neutral, a reflection of the unknown. It can represent a period of uncertainty, a time when the future is veiled in shadow. It can also signify a profound shift, a turning point where fate takes an unexpected turn.

Its presence demands humility and acceptance. It reminds us that we are not masters of our destinies, but rather participants in a grander cosmic dance. It urges us to relinquish control, to surrender to the flow of Wyrd, and to trust in the unfolding of events.

The Blank Rune is a powerful reminder that not all questions have answers, and not all paths are clear. It is a symbol of the ultimate mystery, the void from which all things arise, and to which all things return. It is the silent whisper of fate, the echo of the unknowable, a reminder that even within the runes, there are secrets that remain forever hidden.

Copyright Asteria Books 2025

Energy and Using Power

The Power

The Divine Power inherent within the natural world (including human bodies) is the energy source upon which Witches draw for magical workings. This Power has been known to both ancient and contemporary societies around the world by a variety of names, including numen (Roman), maegen (Anglo-Saxon), mana (Polynesian), teotl (Aztec), and shekinah (Semitic). Very often, cultures encountering these societies have misunderstood this in-dwelling power as a Deity in its own right, when in truth, it is the expression of the deific force of Creation, Life, Death, and the great Mysteries.

Within traditional witchcraft, the Power is called the Cunning Fire or Witchfire, visualized as a blue-green flame. It is reflected in an alcohol fire burning in the cauldron or a candle burning between the horns of the stang. In these symbols, we see the green-fire of the Witchfather, an emerald jewel ablaze on his brow as he brings Illumination to Humanity.

A skilled witch draws Power not just from her own body but from the environment around her, the earth below her, and the cosmos beyond her. Power flows freely through and around the body unless blockages or dis-ease are present. Before consciously drawing Power for a ritual or spell, the cunning person should always take a moment to align the Three Souls and tap into the Power outside herself so as to avoid depleting her own energy.

Meditation and visualization exercises enable the witch to see the Power more clearly with the mind's eye, which makes it easier to control and direct. They also help the witch to feel the flow of Power as something different than a surge of emotion, which can ebb and flow with the tide of circumstance.

The witch's tools help contain, direct, and shape the Power while methods such as the "Eight Ways of Making Magic" help raise Power. A skilled witch will be able to access and use Power without exterior tools and utilizing very simple methods, even having developed a full repertoire of techniques.

Copyright Asteria Books 2019

Grounding & Centering

Your energy can be "off" in lots of ways that would benefit from grounding and centering techniques. You may need to realign your energy if you are feeling spacy, disoriented, clumsy, confused, overwhelmed, anxious, agitated, hyper, drained, etc. You might have too much energy coursing through your system, not enough energy, someone else's energy, or just too many conflicting energetic desires of your own.

"To ground one's energy" means to root oneself, to draw energy from the earth, and to allow one's excess energy to flow into the earth. If you are familiar at all with the electrical trade, it is much like grounding an electrical current. This allows for better flow and steadier, more focused control of the energy current running through your system (your physical, spiritual, emotional, and energetic bodies).

There are many ways to accomplish energetic grounding. The simplest is to make yourself aware of your energetic connection to the earth and allow your energy to balance out with it. You're standing right on it, all the time. Even if you're inside a building, only thin layers of concrete (rock) separate you from (and yet connect you to) the Earth. Visualize that connection and tap in. Or, if you need to get hands on, go outside and get your hands and feet in some dirt, on some stones. Stomp, dance, walk. Move your energy in rhythm with the ground, and this alone will ground you.

"To center one's energy" refers to the practice of bringing one's energetic awareness into a core energy center in the body. Centering is about focus and clearing the mind of distractions. It helps us to be present in the moment. Bring your focus to the energy center in your belly or your heart, for best results.

One can center using a number of techniques and tools. If you have just grounded, you now have an open channel to the ground below you. Do the same for the sky above. It is exactly the same, except you are reaching up and drawing on celestial energy (starfire), which you gently draw into your energetic body. Your head, heart, and belly are the cauldrons, wheels, *receptacles* of those energies, which swirl and mingle within you. Let them expand and fill you with the energy you need, and then let them recede back to a comfortable space where you can move about your day. Know that you can always reach up or reach down and touch into those primal and eternal energies to draw on them. And you can always rebalance, if needed.

Copyright Asteria Books 2019

Eight Ways of Making Magick

You can combine many of these ways to produce more Power.

1. MEDITATION OR CONCENTRATION ~Focused concentration on a subject is the most basic form of raising and sending energy. Meditation is a deeper form of concentration, and can be enhanced through specific postures and gestures.
2. CHANTS, SPELLS, INVOCATIONS ~ We speak the Universe into being. Chanting brings "enchantment." Spells were once written or "spelled" documents detailing the results desired. Invocations and evocations are vocal magic calling on Spirits and Gods for aid in our desires.
3. PROJECTION OF THE ASTRAL BODY, OR TRANCE ~In truth, all of the ways of making magic seek to bring the magician into a form of trance, even if it is very light. Through trance we perceive other realms and can manipulate the energy links that connect all things as one.
4. INCENSE, DRUGS, WINE, ETC. ~ Entheogens (substances which enable us to embody the Gods) have a long and storied history in the Craft. They have been used in flying ointments, transformation elixirs, herbal incenses, smokes, anointing oils, washes, and any herbal mixture you can think of. Wine, of course, is central to the Red Meal, and also serves as a gentle way to let slip our egos and find ourselves outside of consensus reality when used in moderation. All can be dangerous, some are illegal. A few are lethal, even in small amounts. This Path of Power should not be attempted by the untrained Witch.
5. DANCING ~Dancing may be the oldest form of celebration and communication. It is central to the raising of power through the treading of the mill.
6. *USE OF THE CORDS* ~ Warricking cords are often used to restrict blood flow to produce the desired trance state, frequently in combination with body postures also intended to restrict circulation. Ladders are used in knot magic.
7. THE SCOURGE ~ Light, rhythmic application of the scourge at the base of the spine can produce trance just as would a steady drumbeat, or the use of the lamed step. Some covens use a scourge as part of initiatory or other gateway rituals, where the strike of the flails can either be mild, moderate, or even more severe. In these cases, the symbolism of the scourge varies widely from coven to coven, but the effect is almost always to alter consciousness in some way.
8. *THE GREAT RITE* ~ The Great Rite "in truth" is the act of sexual congress between two individuals who have each invoked a God or Goddess. The Great Rite "in symbol" is routinely performed in the Wiccan version of the eucharistic sacrament, in which a cup and a blade represent the creative forces of the universe that bless the cakes and wine. Sex magick is a great source of power, but it should be approached cautiously and consentingly by all parties.

Copyright Asteria Books 2019

Energy Centers of the Body

There are many ways to view the energy centers, or "wheels," within the body. The current, most codified and widespread view arising from Eastern tantric practice proposes seven wheels, but others suggest radically different numbers and positions. The energy wheels illustrated here align with a traditional northern European shamanic (and Craft) view of the energetic body. The wheel in the belly is linked to the Black Soul, the lunar tides, and the digestive and reproductive systems. The heart wheel is connected to the Red Soul, the heart fire, Witchblood, respiration, circulation, and self-expression. The head wheel is connected to the White Soul, star-fire, the HGA, universal consciousness, intuition, and intellect.

Copyright Asteria Books 2019

The Lame Step

The lame step is one of the old and identifying markers of Witches and of their God. And their Goddess. Nursery rhymes show us the evidence of the lame step in magic, the Forge God -- the first and mightiest God of Witchcraft -- is more often lamed than not, and the Witches' Goddess hobbled on a goose's foot.

The Forge God and the Lame Step

The lame step could be said to originate, as it relates to magic, with the God of the Forge. Nearly all Forge Gods were depicted with a lame step or a misshapen leg in antiquity. The mundane reason for this was very likely due to the residual heavy metal poisoning suffered by actual smiths -- or the fact that otherwise strong men who had suffered some crippling childhood disease or injury could still be trained to blacksmith work. Whatever the case, the image of the smith is intimately linked with that of a hobbled or ham-strung, yet powerful, man. A man who understands something related to the alchemical process, and therefore magic. In the case of T'Qayin and Azazel, this image is that of a goat-footed God. The goat-foot is one variation of the lame step, and it is very intimately linked to the forge. Heavy metal poisoning bunched the muscles of the leg in a way that it pulled the smith's legs and foot up into a position like he was walking on a stiletto heel.

The Goose-Footed Goddess

The lame step appears again in the Witches' Goddess in at least one instance. In France, there is a notable story of La Reine Pedauque, the goose-footed queen. She is the original Mother Goose. Mother Goose, is so closely related to the Teutonic Hulda that they are reflections of one another. Frau Hulda, Holda, Holle, Hel rides a goose through the night sky and is a spinner. She is the Dark Grandmother and the White Lady. With her goose-foot, she shows us another aspect of the lame step.

Use of the Lame Step

The lame step is a marker for those who walk between the worlds. Symbolically, it represents having one foot in consensus reality and one foot in the realms beyond the veil. The lame step is a way of showing that you are between the worlds. It is the most basic step in Witch dances and is used when Treading the Mill.

Copyright Asteria Publishing 2012

Energy Links & Link Cutting

Intense encounters, repetitive interactions, and magical workings create energetic links between us and the other people, places, and sometimes even the objects involved in those situations. Magical links are created between us and the target(s) of our spellcraft, whether we bless or blast. Through these links, the sacrifice or cost of our magic is extracted and we remain connected to the work. Similarly, when we make or take oaths from covenmates or life partners, we forge magical links that bind our lives and fates together. Our bonds to parents, children, friends, mentors, and sex partners all create links. While these links can be positive sources of power and support, they are also capable of draining our energy reserves and distracting our focus. This is especially true when we are maintaining links to people or situations that are manipulative, controlling, traumatic, or otherwise troubling. It is helpful, then, to take time to periodically tend to these links and cleanse our energetic bodies. While some links (especially those created by specific oaths) my not be entirely removable, most can be uprooted, and all can be minimized.

Rite of Link Cutting

Materials:
Black-Handled Knife
Bowl of Salt Water
Blanket or Towel
Florida Water
Besom

This ritual is best done with partner, as there are areas of your energetic body you can't fully reach, and you will likely need someone to support you through the emotionally-challenging links as you uproot them.

You may wish to take a cleansing ritual bath before beginning. Cast your compass as you normally do. Working skyclyd upon your blanket or towel, lightly "scrape" the edge of your athame over your entire body to cut the links, flinging the cut strands to the floor around you.

Work slowly. Links are most common at the joints and orifices, but they can occur anywhere. They may be as thin as spiderwebs or as thick as cables. You may need to work longer on certain links. You may need help, and you may need to process the emotional sludge that pulls free with the link. Do not forget to cut the links on your scalp, face, behind your ears, and around your genitals.

When your blade drags, sticks, or feels sluggish (or if you *see* or otherwise sense that it is time), rinse it in the saltwater, and then continue cutting links. (Care for your blade when done.)

Sweep the sludgy links out of your space and out the backdoor when you're done, dumping the saltwater on top. Bless your body and besom with sprinkles of Florida Water.

Copyright Asteria Books 2019

Seething

Seething is a linguistic derivative of Seiðr (Seithr), which is a type of sorcery that was practiced in Norse society during the Late Scandinavian Iron Age. Modern witches use seething as a way to shamanically get outside of themselves, into an altered state, and to raise the Power for charging a spell, tool, or talisman or to come into contact with Spirits. Whether the seething practice that has come down to us is a well-distilled form of the sorcery practiced by Norse women (for it was primarily a women's magic) or a corruption of it, that is hard to say. Based on the resources we have (the Eddas, etc), it seems that what we practice now is very much linked to what they did then.

"To seethe" has also come to mean "to be turbulent, to boil." The word had this definition by the Middle Ages, which tells us that the trance state achieved by this technique is not one of calm and peace. Much like the name suggests, you will be "working yourself up" when you seethe.

There are two basic modern interpretations of the practice of seething. The first method is very much like the practice of Treading the Mill. The witch bears a gandreigh (riding pole), such as a staff, broom, or stang. He treads a wide circle while focusing power on a central point, such as a central stang, altar, or lead witch. Alternately, the witch may choose to use their own gandreigh as the focal point and circle around it while holding it as the axis point.

The second method of seething is a seated variation in which the witch raises a great deal of great emotion and force of Will through the act of rocking back and forth (or side to side, or in a circle). Breath control, muscle flutters, and chanting are adjunct techniques used to deepen this practice. While it sounds complex, even simple rhythmic control of the physical body frees the mind to wander as it will. Here, the gandriegh can still be employed to tap out rhythms for the witch to "ride" into trance.

Copyright Asteria Books 2019

Widdershins & Deosil

The terms deosil and widdershins come to common Craft usage from older German and Gaelic terms that refer generally to clockwise and counter-clockwise movements, respectively.

Deosil is a more modern spelling of the Irish and Scots Gaelic terms meaning "right" or "sunwise" -- as in "turning in the direction of the sun." It was considered propitious to turn to the right and to favor right-handed movements, a propensity that carried over into ritual practice and was handed down into superstition to the point that some people even believed that drinking or performing other actions with the left hand could prove to be fatal.

Widdershins, on the other hand, comes from an old Germ word *widersinnig ("against"* + *"sense")*. This form of "sense" is actually most closely related to words like "practicality" and "aptness." So, to move widdershins is to move against the norm. This bears out when we look at the way the word was cited in the Oxford English Dictionary's entry in an early attestation from 1513, where it was found in the phrase "widdersyns start my hair", i.e. my hair stood on end.

Some traditions have strict rules about only moving deosil or only moving widdershins within the caim. Many Traditional Witches use both types of movement during ritual, though we use them very deliberately. We acknowledge that every step within the compass is an act of treading the mill. Be cognizant with each step you take of whether or not you are building on the magick of the work you are aiming to do, or if you are unwinding it by moving contrary-wise.

You can use the mill to lead you either up and out or down and within. When treading sunwise, the energy rises upward, spiraling us into the first realm. Treading widdershins brings the energy down into the land where we can access the third realm. Neither of these movements is more desirable than the other, they are both as necessary and as benign as the positive and negative poles of a magnet.

Copyright Asteria Books 2018

Witch Flight

At its most basic level, Witch Flight is the same as astral projection or soul journeying. (We sometimes call it "hedge-crossing" since we are crossing the boundaries between the worlds.) But Witch Flight differs a bit in execution from what is usually called astral travel, etc. We have seen and discussed some aspects of those differences already. Namely, folkloric Witches often make use of a Fetch and a Gandreid (or Gandreigh) when flying.

The Fetch is an etheric "body" that the Black Soul inhabits while traveling in the Unseen Realms. It is anchored to the physical realm through the use of a "fetish" or "fetich" that houses the Fetch when not in use.

The Gandreid is a riding pole that is (in its most essential form) a representation of the World Tree and acts as your "steed" while you travel. It can be a stang, a staff, or a broom. And it is the Witch's hobby horse. Our own Sleipnir with his 8 legs in each of the worlds that are hung within Yggdrasil. It is the Spiral Castle, with its 8 arms reaching to the Castles and Gates.

There are many, many reasons to cross the hedge. At first, our motivations are usually experiential. We want to see and discover what is there. Meet the inhabitants of the Unseen. Encounter the places and objects that are there. Eventually, though, we go "out and about" in search of information, as a way to performing healings (or blastings), or to engage with the Powers or other Witches. All of the reasons that are common to shamanic practitioners for soul journeying apply to us, as well.

There is no single way to fly. We use the term "flight" to encompass any soul journey, even when we don't necessarily picture ourselves flying across the skies. We can follow a guided meditation with the aid of flying ointment or sabbat tea – perhaps with our Gandreid under or between our knees or held lengthwise across our bodies. We can dance with staff or stang in hand, falling to the ground in a trance, and let our Spirits wander free. We can tap out a rhythm with our Stang on the ground and/or tap an arrow against the shaft of the Stang while chanting or intoning the runes (performing galdr). We can seethe while sitting, , swaying and rocking to loosen our Spirits.

Copyright Asteria Books 2022

Geise

A geis (or geas – plural, geise/geasa) is a type of personal taboo (either prohibition or obligation) that often has a magical component to it. It can be laid upon a person by another person/Being, or it can be taken on by that person directly.

No matter how the geis comes to be, it can be viewed as either a blessing or a curse. In my experience, when a person takes on a prohibitive geis of their own volition, they tend to see it less as a curse and more as a sacrifice. For example, I have a good friend who can't consume caffeine due to a magical agreement. Additionally, I am completely unable to eat rabbit meat (the flesh of one of my most present and potent Animal Allies) without getting ill.

In folklore and mythology, it is not uncommon to see this type of obligation appearing in groups of three, though some mythic figures are recounted as observing several.

Often the geis takes the form of a prohibition against a certain action or circumstance, such as never turning back once a journey is begun, never telling your true name, never eating a certain food, etc. However, it can also be an obligation one must perform when given the opportunity – such as always eating the food offered by a woman, always place one's feet in the lap of a maiden while sitting, etc.

There is often great power in observing a geis. Just be warned that once begun, it can't be ended (unless a time limit was built into the original geis). Failing to meet the obligation or observe the prohibition is often linked to the gravest of misfortunes.

You may never encounter this sort of sacred obligation. Then again, you may find that a certain act of spellwork or a votary obligation for a particular Spirit/Godd looks very much like a geis, in your practice.

Copyright Asteria Books 2022

On Oaths & Vows

Oaths

In their strictest sense, oaths are promises that draw upon the authority and power of a larger institution, governing body/individual, or spiritual presence. There is an implication of divine (or institutional) retribution or penalty if the oath is broken or otherwise unfulfilled. The greater Power is called upon to stand witness to the promise, offering support in the execution of the promise, and accountability in the case of its breaking. Oaths are very frequently made in public (or semi-public) settings, invoking a sense of accountability to, by, and for the community.

Think: oath of office, oath of allegiance, Hippocratic oath, promissory oath

Vow

Technically speaking, a vow is made to someone or something for the purpose of dedicating oneself in service and loyalty. This is also a sacred promise, but it is generally of a more personal nature than an oath. Likewise, the accountability for vows is often a more private matter, often kept with the parties between whom the vow was made. In the ancient world, a vow would be accompanied by a votary offering – a symbolic gift or sacrifice that demonstrates the regard the person holds for the obligation being undertaken. One notable place where this custom remains intact is in the giving of a ring as an accompaniment to wedding vows.

Think: wedding vows, vow of silence, vow of celibacy, vow of poverty

Breaking/Keeping Troth

The breaking or keeping of oaths and vows can often mean the difference between breaking and keeping bonds. "Oath-breaking" is considered a grievous betrayal within traditional communities – covens, included. And breaking a vow often signals the dissolution of the relationship.

Your own Will and Word are invoked in the making of both oaths and vows. Consider well the damage that you do to the integrity and power of both your Will and your Word when these sacred promises are cast aside. You diminish your ability to call these forward in the future.

Breaking troth can also be seen as cursing yourself. You, of your freewill, spoke the words of your promise in a sacred setting, calling upon Mighty Ones to be the keepers of these oaths/vows. They (the Powers) will hold true, even if you do not, which might mean bringing misery and suffering upon yourself.

Copyright Asteria Books 2022

Hair Binding and Covering

Hair retains profound spiritual and magical significance in both ancient and modern pagan traditions, acting as a conduit for personal power and connection to the divine. Hair binding and covering aren't simply aesthetic choices, but ritualistic acts imbued with symbolic meaning.

Unbound hair continues to be associated with wildness, untamed energy, and a direct link to the natural world. Modern practitioners, like their ancient counterparts, might wear their hair loose during rituals to channel raw power and connect with primal forces. Conversely, bound or covered hair symbolizes control, protection, and respect for the sacred. It signifies marital status, spiritual devotion, or a period of mourning in many contemporary practices.

Hair covering, particularly, serves as a protective barrier against negative energies or unwanted spiritual influences. Veils or head coverings are often worn during rituals or in sacred spaces to maintain focus and prevent the dissipation of personal power. This practice remains a form of reverence, acknowledging the presence of deities or spirits.

Hair binding, through braids, knots, or cords, is still a way to weave intention and energy into the hair itself. Specific patterns or materials amplify desired qualities or invoke particular deities. Cords of certain colors bind specific energies, while braids represent the weaving of fate or the binding of spells.

Ultimately, the practices of hair binding and covering remain deeply personal and vary across pagan traditions, both ancient and modern. They serve as tangible expressions of spiritual beliefs and magical practices, transforming hair from a simple physical feature into a potent symbol of power and connection.

Copyright Asteria Books 2025

Sex Magick in Trad Craft

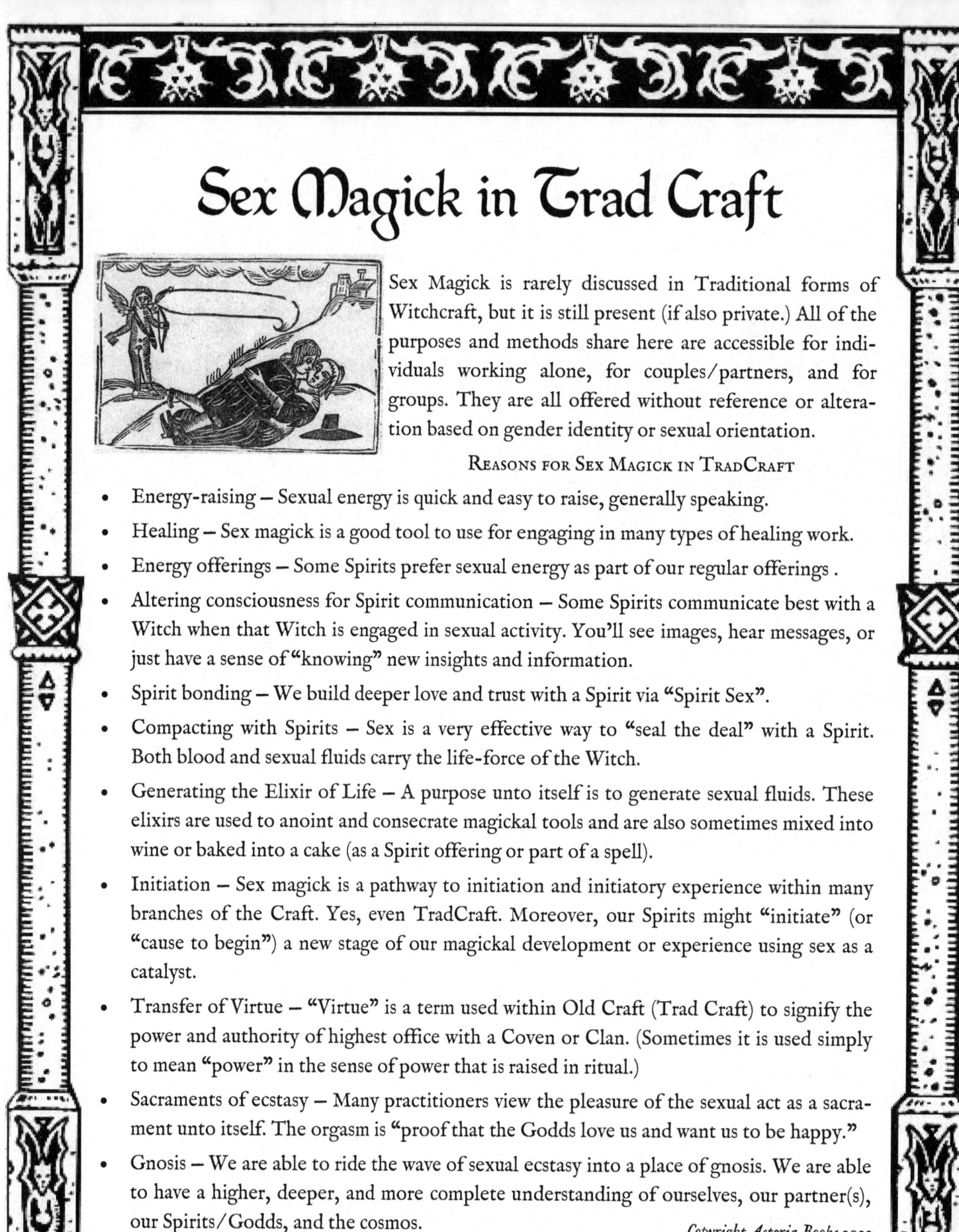

Sex Magick is rarely discussed in Traditional forms of Witchcraft, but it is still present (if also private.) All of the purposes and methods share here are accessible for individuals working alone, for couples/partners, and for groups. They are all offered without reference or alteration based on gender identity or sexual orientation.

Reasons for Sex Magick in TradCraft

- Energy-raising — Sexual energy is quick and easy to raise, generally speaking.
- Healing — Sex magick is a good tool to use for engaging in many types of healing work.
- Energy offerings — Some Spirits prefer sexual energy as part of our regular offerings.
- Altering consciousness for Spirit communication — Some Spirits communicate best with a Witch when that Witch is engaged in sexual activity. You'll see images, hear messages, or just have a sense of "knowing" new insights and information.
- Spirit bonding — We build deeper love and trust with a Spirit via "Spirit Sex".
- Compacting with Spirits — Sex is a very effective way to "seal the deal" with a Spirit. Both blood and sexual fluids carry the life-force of the Witch.
- Generating the Elixir of Life — A purpose unto itself is to generate sexual fluids. These elixirs are used to anoint and consecrate magickal tools and are also sometimes mixed into wine or baked into a cake (as a Spirit offering or part of a spell).
- Initiation — Sex magick is a pathway to initiation and initiatory experience within many branches of the Craft. Yes, even TradCraft. Moreover, our Spirits might "initiate" (or "cause to begin") a new stage of our magickal development or experience using sex as a catalyst.
- Transfer of Virtue — "Virtue" is a term used within Old Craft (Trad Craft) to signify the power and authority of highest office with a Coven or Clan. (Sometimes it is used simply to mean "power" in the sense of power that is raised in ritual.)
- Sacraments of ecstasy — Many practitioners view the pleasure of the sexual act as a sacrament unto itself. The orgasm is "proof that the Godds love us and want us to be happy."
- Gnosis — We are able to ride the wave of sexual ecstasy into a place of gnosis. We are able to have a higher, deeper, and more complete understanding of ourselves, our partner(s), our Spirits/Godds, and the cosmos.

Copyright Asteria Books 2022

Sacred Touch

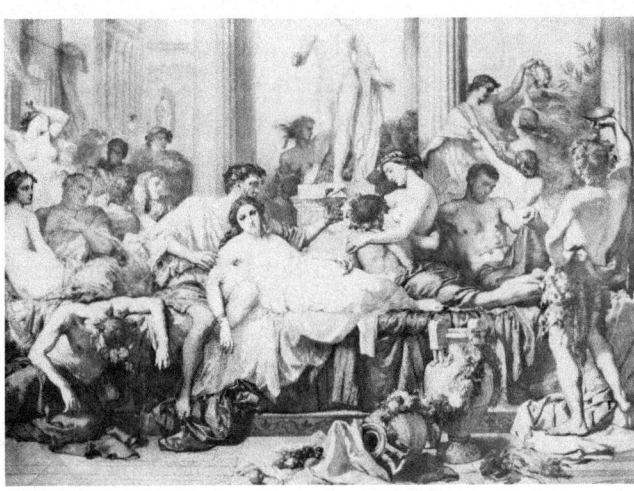

The Sacred Touch Ceremony was first developed and taught within the Qadishti Movement of sacred sexuality by Michael A. Manor. It is a simple and expandable ritual that offers an egalitarian and accessible approach to sacred sexuality for all participants.

Sacred Space is prepared (laying the compass, etc), and the participants are seated in a circle. Participants are dressed or disrobed to their level of comfort, and they may add or remove clothing at any time. Members of the ceremony take turns occupying a place in the middle of the circle, where they may assume any posture they prefer (sitting, lying prone or supine, etc).

Before any touching begins, the participant in the central space states both their preferences and their boundaries in terms of touch. Sometimes, group boundaries are in place, as well — ie, no touching genitals or breasts, no penetrative sexual acts, etc. Precautions are always taken to prevent fluid exchange and to encourage safer sex (condoms, dental dams, nitrile gloves, etc.), and a safe word is always in place to halt all touch immediately. Those occupying the ring of the circle offer touch up to their own level of comfort and boundaries, after the preferences and boundaries have been stated by the individual whose turn it is to receive. Everyone is offered time in the center to be a receive of touch.

Participants are given ample time in the center in order to experience loving touch. The group often comes to a natural stopping point together without words being exchanged. Even without penetration or orgasm (or, in some cases, without any nudity at all), participants often experience a climactic and euphoric state of well-being, connection, and intimacy. (These benefits are linked to the neural affects of bilateral, asynchronous touch, which is being studied within psychology for its healing features.)

Copyright Asteria Books 2022

Hieros Gamos

The Hieros Gamos (Sacred Marriage, in Greek) is a ritual of sacred sexuality and sex magick that is found in many traditional cultures and ancient religions. Our earliest records and recollections around this ritual are from Enheduanna. In the poem called the "Courtship of Inanna and Dumuzi," we see the ritual marriage of the Queen/Priestesses/Goddess with the Shepherd/Priest (who becomes King as a result of their union).

How to Perform a Heiros Gamos

The execution of this ritual is fairly straightforward, although that doesn't necessarily mean that it is "simple." It can take place between two (or more?) partners of any gender, as long as all of the partners involved are able to successfully invoke a possessory state with a preferred Spirit/Deity. Often, preparatory actions (such as bathing, dressing, adorning with jewelry, applying make-up, inviting the partner to the bedchamber, and disrobing) are ritualized and sometimes involve secondary parties who fulfill roles as a traditional maid or squire — someone who helps their lord or lady get dressed.

The partners each invoke their respective Spirits/Deities, and they proceed to have sex in this fully-invoked state. They might recite invocation chants for each other, or they might each do this for themselves. This can be done simultaneously (if silent invocation processes are used) or one at a time. There are two poems that are used widely among Witches of all sorts for the purpose of calling forth the WitchMother and WitchFather — "The Charge of the Goddess" and "The Invocation of the Horned God." Both were written by Doreen Valiente, who worked closely with both Gardner and Cochrane. Alternatively, you might use a temple hymn associated with the Spirit/Deity, or even write your own.

The purpose for Traditional Witches within the Hieros Gamos isn't fecundity in land and people. It is gnosis. It is enlightenment. It is seeing the Truth of ourselves, or our partners, and of the Spirits we have invoked together.

Copyright Asteria Books 2022

Cosmology and Magical Theory

The Airts

The Airts of Traditional Craft correspond to different elemental quarters than those found in Wiccan and Ceremonial traditions. The Airts are based on old "Celtic" lore.

The North - Air
Values: Intellect, Thoughts, Inspiration, Communication, Flight, Divination
Colors: White, sky blue, black, silver
Symbols: Circle, bird, bell, flute, chimes, clouds, Sylphs, the Angel
Tools: Keek stone, flail, knives
Weapons: Staff/Spear
Musical Instruments: Reed instruments
Times: Imbolc, Midnight, Winter, Old Age
Places: Sky, mountaintop, treetop, bluffs, summit of a mound
Zodiac: Aquarius, Gemini, Libra
Sense: Scent
Power: To Know
Process: Chanting, Visualization, Reading, Speaking, Praying, Singing, Fragrance, Charms

The East - Fire
Values: Passion, Power, Will, Energy, Courage, Strength, Light
Colors: Red, orange, amber
Symbols: Triangle, lightning, flame, candle, Salamanders, the Lion
Tools: The lamp, wand, staff
Weapons: Sword
Musical Instruments: String Instruments
Times: Beltane, Dawn, Spring, Youth
Places: Volcanoes, ovens, hearths, bonfires, deserts
Zodiac: Aries, Leo, Sagittarius
Sense: Sight
Power: To Will
Process: Dancing, Burning, Candle-magic, Solar magic, Mirrors

The South - Earth
Values: Growth, Experience, Authority, Money, Physicality, Security, Nourishment
Colors: Black, brown, russet, green
Symbols: Square, cornucopia, scythe, salt, stone, Gnomes, the Bull
Tools: The casting bowl, pentacles, horns
Weapons: Shield
Musical Instruments: Drums
Times: Lammas, Noon, Summer, Coming of Age
Places: Caves, forests, fields, gardens, canyons
Zodiac: Capricorn, Taurus, Virgo
Sense: Touch
Power: To Keep Silent
Process: Burying, Grounding, Binding, Eating, Totemic magic, Wortcunning, Clay figures, Dirts

The West - Water
Values: Emotions, Intuition, Cleansing, Mystery, Sacrifice
Colors: Grey, turquoise, blue, indigo
Symbols: Crescent, shell, boat, anchor, cup, Undines, the Eagle
Tools: The chalice or quaiche, cauldron
Weapons: Helm
Musical Instruments: Chimes
Times: Samhain, Twilight, Autumn, Adulthood
Places: Oceans, rivers, lakes, waterfalls, wells, beaches, baths
Zodiac: Cancer, Scorpio, Pisces
Sense: Taste
Power: To Dare
Process: Bathing, Healing, Drinking, Baptism, Charged Waters, Blood magic

Copyright Asteria Publishing 2012

Elemental Air

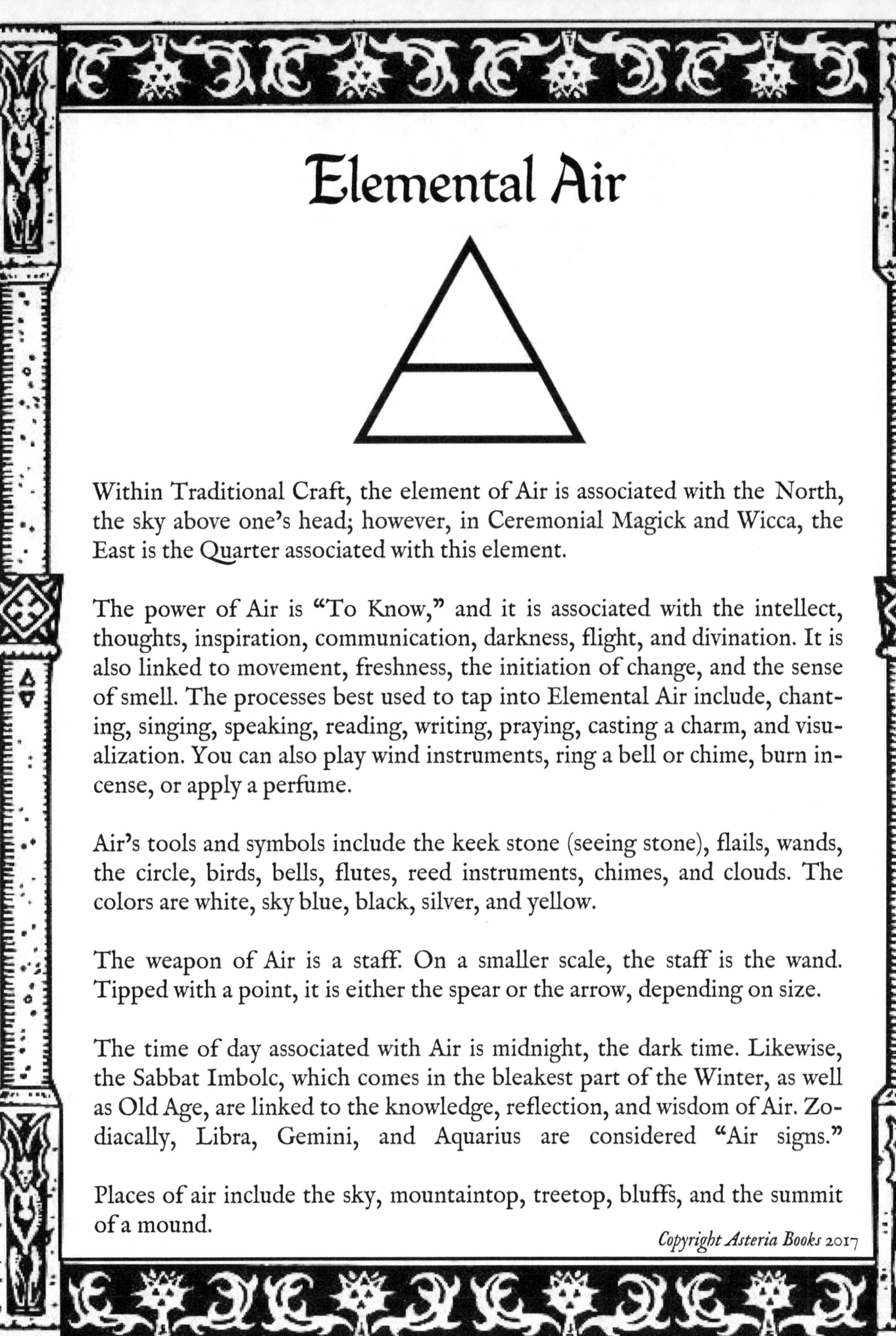

Within Traditional Craft, the element of Air is associated with the North, the sky above one's head; however, in Ceremonial Magick and Wicca, the East is the Quarter associated with this element.

The power of Air is "To Know," and it is associated with the intellect, thoughts, inspiration, communication, darkness, flight, and divination. It is also linked to movement, freshness, the initiation of change, and the sense of smell. The processes best used to tap into Elemental Air include, chanting, singing, speaking, reading, writing, praying, casting a charm, and visualization. You can also play wind instruments, ring a bell or chime, burn incense, or apply a perfume.

Air's tools and symbols include the keek stone (seeing stone), flails, wands, the circle, birds, bells, flutes, reed instruments, chimes, and clouds. The colors are white, sky blue, black, silver, and yellow.

The weapon of Air is a staff. On a smaller scale, the staff is the wand. Tipped with a point, it is either the spear or the arrow, depending on size.

The time of day associated with Air is midnight, the dark time. Likewise, the Sabbat Imbolc, which comes in the bleakest part of the Winter, as well as Old Age, are linked to the knowledge, reflection, and wisdom of Air. Zodiacally, Libra, Gemini, and Aquarius are considered "Air signs."

Places of air include the sky, mountaintop, treetop, bluffs, and the summit of a mound.

Copyright Asteria Books 2017

Elemental Earth

Within Traditional Craft, the element of Earth is associated with the South, the ground below one's feet; however, in Ceremonial Magick and Wicca, the North is the Quarter associated with this element.

The power of Earth is "To Keep Silent," and it is associated with growth, experience, authority, money, physicality, security, and nourishment. It is also linked to fertility, abundance, and the sense of touch. The processes best used to tap into Elemental Earth include burying, grounding, binding, eating, totemic magic, and wortcunning or herbalism. You can also play drums or touch coarse, firm, or dense textures.

Earth's tools and symbols include the casting bowl, pentacles, horns, the square, cornucopias, scythes, salt, stone, clay figures, and dirts. Gnomes the Bull are considered the creatures of Earth. The colors are black, brown, russet, green.

The weapon of Earth is a shield. On a smaller scale, the shield is a plate or paten, and it can be viewed as the altar itself.

The time of day associated with Earth is noon, the productive time. Likewise, the Sabbat Lammas, which comes at the height of Summer, as well as Coming of Age, are linked to the virility, productivity, and abundance of Earth. Zodiacally, Capricorn, Virgo, and Taurus are considered "Earth signs."

Places of Earth include the caves, forests, fields, gardens, canyons.

Copyright Asteria Books 2017

Elemental Fire

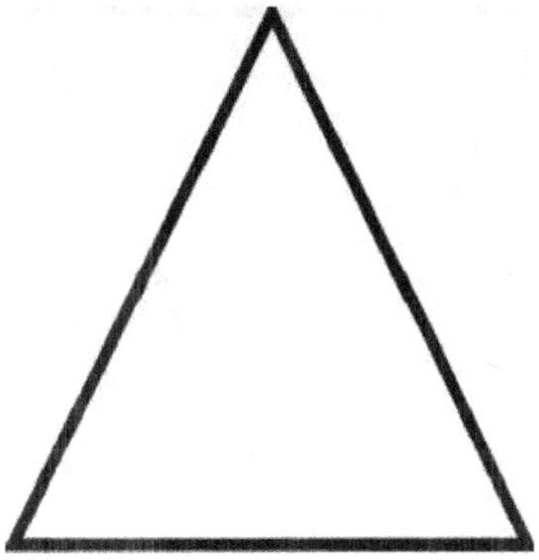

Within Traditional Craft, the element of Fire is associated with the East and the rising sun; however, in Ceremonial Magick and Wicca, the South is the Quarter associated with this element.

The power of Fire is "To Will," and it is associated with passion, power, will, energy, courage, strength, and light. It is also linked to sexuality, transformation, and the sense of sight. The processes best used to tap into Elemental Fire include dancing, burning, candle magic, solar magic, and mirror magic. You can also play string instruments or engage in an activity that makes you sweat.

Fire's tools and symbols include the lamp, wand, sword, triangle, lightning, flame, and candle. Salamanders and the Lion are considered the creatures of Fire. The colors are red, orange, amber .

The weapon of Fire is a sword, having been formed and strengthened within the flames. On a smaller scale, the knife is a versatile blade possessing the same qualities and honed for a more specific purpose.

The time of day associated with Fire is dawn, the fiery beginning of each day. Likewise, the Sabbat Beltaine, which comes at the height of Spring, as well as Youth, are linked to the passion, activity, and inception of Fire. Zodiacally, Leo, Sagittarius, and Aries are considered "Fire signs."

Places of Fire include Volcanoes, ovens, hearths, bonfires, deserts .

Copyright Asteria Books 2017

Elemental Water

▽

Within both Traditional Craft and the Ceremonial and Wiccan systems, the element of Water is associated with the West, the place of the setting sun.

The power of Water is "To Dare," and it is associated with emotions, intuition, cleansing, Mystery, and sacrifice. It is also linked to death, the ancestors, healing, and the sense of taste. The processes best used to tap into Elemental Water include bathing, drinking, baptism, and blood magic. You can also play chimes or charge waters for use in magic.

Water's tools and symbols include the chalice or quaiche, cauldron, crescent, shell, boat, and anchor. Undines and the Dolphin are considered the creatures of Water. The colors are grey, turquoise, blue, and indigo.

The weapon of Water is the helmet, being an armored bowl.

The time of day associated with Water is twilight, the end of each day. Likewise, the Sabbat Samhain, which comes at the end of the Autumn harvest, as well as Adulthood, are linked to the transition, submersion, and healing of Water. Zodiacally, Pisces, Cancer, and Scorpio are considered "Water signs."

Places of Water include oceans, rivers, lakes, waterfalls, wells, beaches, and baths.

Copyright Asteria Books 2017

Laws of Magic

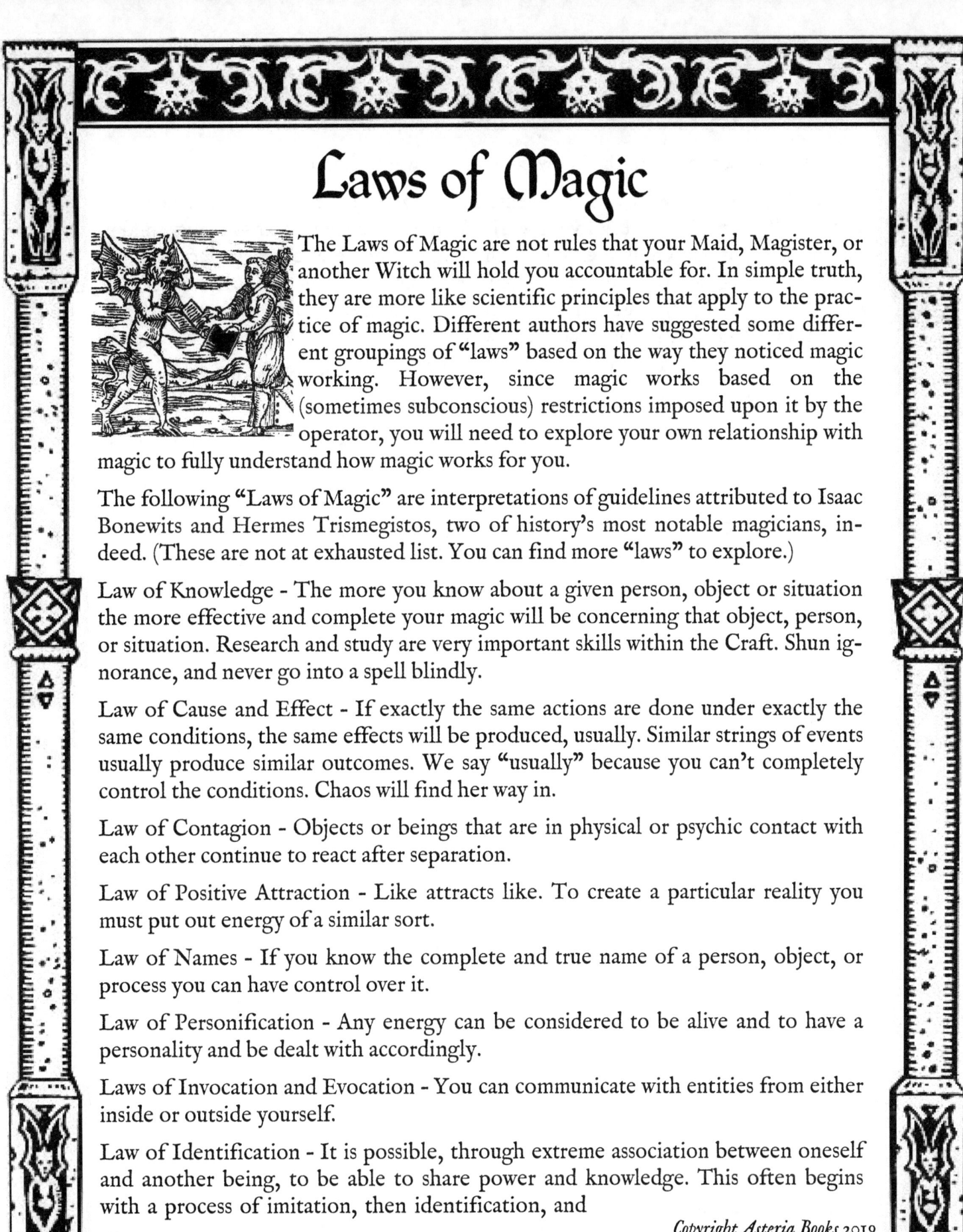

The Laws of Magic are not rules that your Maid, Magister, or another Witch will hold you accountable for. In simple truth, they are more like scientific principles that apply to the practice of magic. Different authors have suggested some different groupings of "laws" based on the way they noticed magic working. However, since magic works based on the (sometimes subconscious) restrictions imposed upon it by the operator, you will need to explore your own relationship with magic to fully understand how magic works for you.

The following "Laws of Magic" are interpretations of guidelines attributed to Isaac Bonewits and Hermes Trismegistos, two of history's most notable magicians, indeed. (These are not at exhausted list. You can find more "laws" to explore.)

Law of Knowledge - The more you know about a given person, object or situation the more effective and complete your magic will be concerning that object, person, or situation. Research and study are very important skills within the Craft. Shun ignorance, and never go into a spell blindly.

Law of Cause and Effect - If exactly the same actions are done under exactly the same conditions, the same effects will be produced, usually. Similar strings of events usually produce similar outcomes. We say "usually" because you can't completely control the conditions. Chaos will find her way in.

Law of Contagion - Objects or beings that are in physical or psychic contact with each other continue to react after separation.

Law of Positive Attraction - Like attracts like. To create a particular reality you must put out energy of a similar sort.

Law of Names - If you know the complete and true name of a person, object, or process you can have control over it.

Law of Personification - Any energy can be considered to be alive and to have a personality and be dealt with accordingly.

Laws of Invocation and Evocation - You can communicate with entities from either inside or outside yourself.

Law of Identification - It is possible, through extreme association between oneself and another being, to be able to share power and knowledge. This often begins with a process of imitation, then identification, and

Copyright Asteria Books 2019

ultimately possession until the knowledge and power is shared.

Law of Personal Universes - Every sentient being is the center of his or her own universe. You are the center of your world. You experience your own reality, and it may or may not be exactly the same as the reality anyone else has. In fact, it can't be. We've all agreed to certain terms and arrangements, which we call "consensus reality." On some level, though, your universe is different than all others, and you are the one ultimately in control of your world.

Law of Pragmatism - If you believe it, if it works for you, no matter on what level of reality it works, then it is true and real.

Law of True Falsehoods (Law of Paradox) - It is possible to be wrong and still be correct.

Law of Unity - Everything is connected. Ultimately, each object that you think of as solid is nothing more than a collection of atoms - energy. Trees, buildings, gasses, people, tectonic plates, and paper plates - we're all energy, and we're all connected to each other. Given all the other laws, this means that we have an effect, both magical and mundane, on absolutely everything.

Law of Mentalism - The Classical Greeks referred to the Supreme Being as the All. Sometimes the All was also called the "logos," which means "word," but it also means everything having to do with a person's words or speech, including their thoughts and reasoning. The Law of Mentalism reminds us that the All is mind itself, and the All encompasses everything in the universe. Magic is an act of thinking.

Law of Correspondence - All things are related. The physical, spiritual, and mental realms are connected, with one flowing out the other. The separations that we perceive between them are illusions.

Law of Vibration - Everything vibrates. Nothing rests. Modern science has confirmed that everything vibrates, just at different frequencies. Our eyes perceive light frequencies at different wavelengths as various colors in the spectrum. The same principal applies to auditory perception. New breakthroughs and understandings are happening all the time in the realm of quantum physics to confirm what magicians and Witches have practiced for millennia.

Law of Polarity - Everything has its opposite. According to Hermetics, opposites are actually the same in their core nature, but they differ in their degree or rank. As examples, you can think about heat and cold, peace and war, love and hate.

Law of Rhythm - There is a constant flow of energy. The tide always turns. The cycle always continues. When the pendulum swings to the right, it will eventually swing equally to the left. This is the reason why there is always some price to be paid for magic.

Ethical Witchcraft

The Ardanes (Witch Laws) and the Wiccan Rede are relative newcomers to the practice of the Craft of the Wise. They were both devised in the middle of the last century to make Witchcraft more palatable and acceptable to our largely Abrahamic society. The Craft (in its truest sense) does not offer a moral guidepost. It is a system of magic, a way of reaching out to the Unseen World and being more closely a part of it. The Black Goddess, White Goddess, Tubal Qayin – do not look to them for your moral compass, for they are Nature's Compass, Magic's Compass. They are Powers, neither "male-" nor "bene-" (bad, good).

You are responsible and accountable to yourself, your Clan, your Cuveen, your community, your country, and your world. How you keep yourself on your path is up to you.

That being said, as a piece of Craft Lore (and even as a starting place in thinking about your own ethics), it is interesting to look at the Ardanes and the Rede. Bear in mind that these pieces are modern constructs with occasional bits of arcana thrown into the mix. Some of the advice contained within them is worth a look. Other pieces seem very out of keeping with the Craft as we know it.

The Ardanes or Ordains first appeared in Craft documentation in 1957, when Gerald Gardner presented them to his coven after a disagreement about his own interactions with the media while insisting on secrecy within the coven. No known record of them in any older documentation exists prior to that date. These Laws have had several iterations, and they vary amongst covens/Traditions who hold to them. Some are anachronistic, misogynistic, or oddly Christo-centric.

Many, if not most, Witchcraft traditions use the Wiccan Rede as the foundation of their code of ethics. The first published form of the Wiccan Rede is a couplet that appeared in 1964 by Doreen Valiente: "Eight words the Wiccan Rede fulfill, An it harm none, Do what ye will." Rede is a Middle English word meaning "advice or council," while, in this case, an is an archaic conjunction meaning "if." Other versions, have been written since then, but this is the basic tenant of Wiccan ethics.

Ultimately, each Witch must pursue a line of *independent* thought regarding ethics and a Code. In other words: know what YOU believe to be ethical behavior and hold to it. Remember that ethics and morals are not really about being held accountable to a power higher than yourself. If you believe an action is wrong, and you proceed in doing it, you will pay a price for doing it.

Copyright Asteria Books 2015

The World Tree

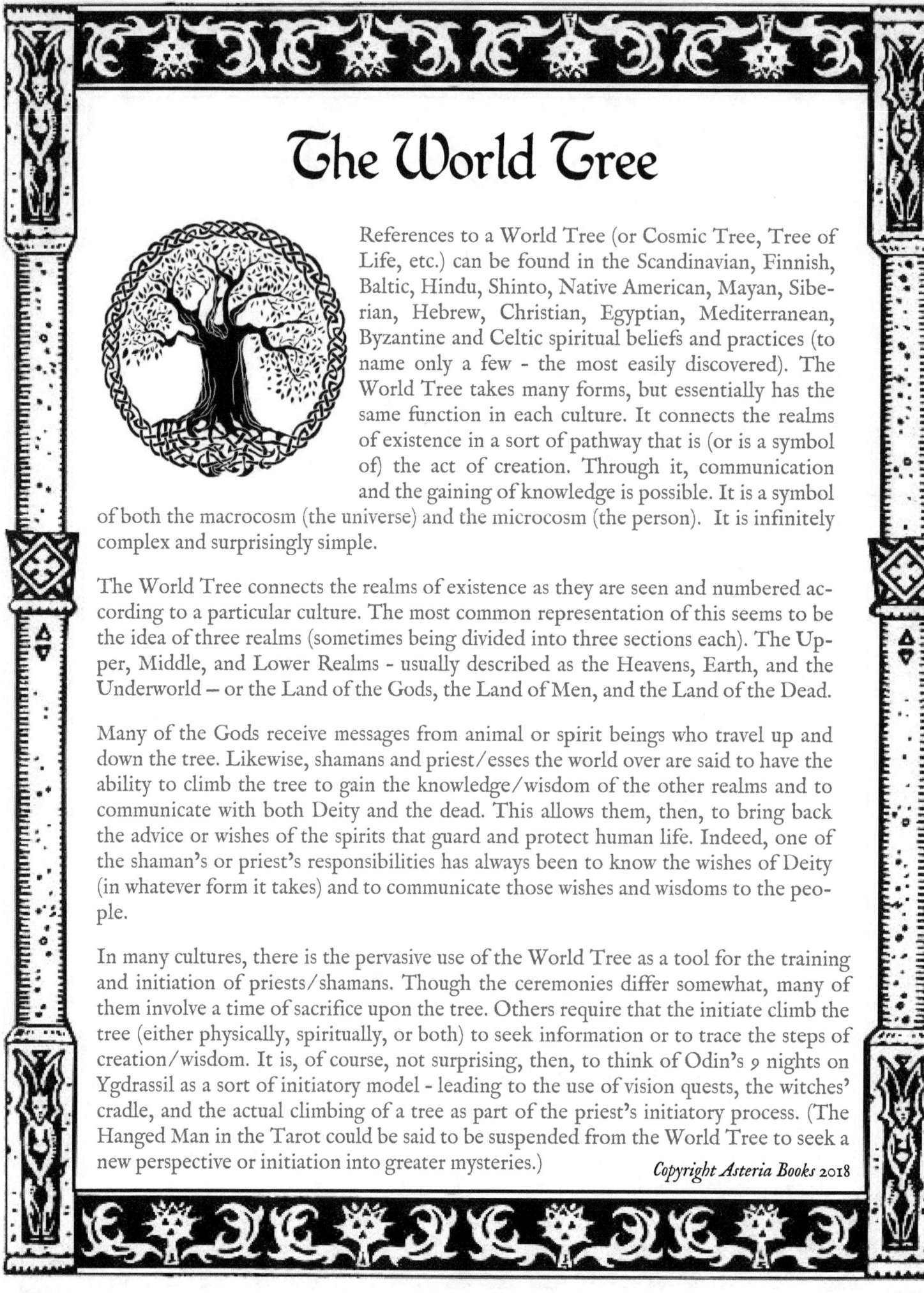

References to a World Tree (or Cosmic Tree, Tree of Life, etc.) can be found in the Scandinavian, Finnish, Baltic, Hindu, Shinto, Native American, Mayan, Siberian, Hebrew, Christian, Egyptian, Mediterranean, Byzantine and Celtic spiritual beliefs and practices (to name only a few - the most easily discovered). The World Tree takes many forms, but essentially has the same function in each culture. It connects the realms of existence in a sort of pathway that is (or is a symbol of) the act of creation. Through it, communication and the gaining of knowledge is possible. It is a symbol of both the macrocosm (the universe) and the microcosm (the person). It is infinitely complex and surprisingly simple.

The World Tree connects the realms of existence as they are seen and numbered according to a particular culture. The most common representation of this seems to be the idea of three realms (sometimes being divided into three sections each). The Upper, Middle, and Lower Realms - usually described as the Heavens, Earth, and the Underworld — or the Land of the Gods, the Land of Men, and the Land of the Dead.

Many of the Gods receive messages from animal or spirit beings who travel up and down the tree. Likewise, shamans and priest/esses the world over are said to have the ability to climb the tree to gain the knowledge/wisdom of the other realms and to communicate with both Deity and the dead. This allows them, then, to bring back the advice or wishes of the spirits that guard and protect human life. Indeed, one of the shaman's or priest's responsibilities has always been to know the wishes of Deity (in whatever form it takes) and to communicate those wishes and wisdoms to the people.

In many cultures, there is the pervasive use of the World Tree as a tool for the training and initiation of priests/shamans. Though the ceremonies differ somewhat, many of them involve a time of sacrifice upon the tree. Others require that the initiate climb the tree (either physically, spiritually, or both) to seek information or to trace the steps of creation/wisdom. It is, of course, not surprising, then, to think of Odin's 9 nights on Ygdrassil as a sort of initiatory model - leading to the use of vision quests, the witches' cradle, and the actual climbing of a tree as part of the priest's initiatory process. (The Hanged Man in the Tarot could be said to be suspended from the World Tree to seek a new perspective or initiation into greater mysteries.)

Copyright Asteria Books 2018

The Evil Eye

Many cultures all over the world share a common belief in a type of curse or hex that is transmitted (usually) unwittingly through a glare or glance in which the caster is filled with envy, praise, or covetousness. It can also be transmitted, intentionally or unintentionally, by people with green or blue eyes — which is why protective charms to ward against this curse are so often blue, green, or turquoise.

The evil eye is also called the *invidious eye*, the *envious eye*, *ayin ha'ra* (Hebrew), *malocchio* (Italian), *mal ojo* (Spanish), *jettatore* (Sicilian), the *stink eye* (Hawaiian), *nazar* (Turkish), and *bla band* (Farsi).

While the eye itself is a receptive sensory organ, the power of the evil eye is insidious in its ability to send curses outward in a projective manner often unbeknownst to the own doing the cursing. In a traditional context, the person who sends the curse does not necessarily intend the afflicted target any harm. They simply admire and covet what they don't already have. For this reason, mothers in cultures where a belief in the evil eye is prevalent might respond, "Oh, but he's got dirt on him," when told their baby is beautiful. Without saying something seemingly "mean," the child might attract the evil eye and become sick — or even die!

Perils related to the evil eye include wasting, illness, blight, injury, plain bad luck, and possibly death.

Hamsa   Mano Fica   Mano Cornuto   Cornicello

Charms against the evil eye are sometimes also simply called "the evil eye" and take the shape of a blue, green, or turquoise circle banded in white to represent the eye. Various hand gestures and horns (with their phallic connotations) are also reputed to ward against the evil eye. Eyes, hands, and horns have all been fashioned into jewelry, charms, and art that can be displayed on bodies, in homes, and in vehicles to offer the most possible protection against the threat of this malevolent glare.

Copyright Asteria Books 2019

The Humours

Around 450 BCE, Aristotle advocated for the theory of a Four Element system as the basis for which all things in the Universe (including the human body and psychological temperament) are comprised. Elemental philosophy took shape in Hippocratic medicine in the form of "humors" — a system of fluids related to the elements of Earth, Air, Fire, and Water. Imbalances in the humors, which are most often attributed to the positions of the stars at the time of an individual's birth, can cause constitutional and psychological weaknesses or overbalances. The job of the physician (or, in some later cases, the alchemist) was to create medicines or apply procedures to rebalance the humors. These philosophies dominated medical practice through the mid 1500's — and still held influence until the 1800's.

PHLEGMATIC ~ Water; the Moon; Cancer, Scorpio, Pisces; Mucus; White; calm, quiet, easygoing, meditative, organized, dependable, conservative, caring, following, contemplative, diplomatic, peaceful, feminine, unmotivated, lazy, selfish, stingy, stubborn

SANGUINE ~ Air; Venus; Gemini, Libra, Aquarius; Blood; Red; outgoing, charismatic, warm, friendly, responsive, lively, amorous, optimist, lively, carefree, compassionate, entertaining, generous, restless, loud, obnoxious, egocentric, insecure, exaggerative,

MELANCHOLIC ~ Earth; Saturn; Taurus, Virgo, Capricorn; Black Bile; Black; gifted, perfectionist, conscientious, loyal, aesthetic, idealistic, sensitive, analytical, creative, spiritual, moody, poetic, artistic, pessimistic, critical, touchy, vengeful, martyrish, judgmental, pompous, manic, flippant, unsociable

CHOLERIC ~ Fire; Mars; Aries, Leo, Sagittarius; Yellow Bile; Brown; determined, independent, productive, decisive, practical, athletic, optimistic, confident, quick, leading, energetic, passionate, masculine, insensitive, hostile, sarcastic, domineering, proud, impatient, obstinate, hot-tempered, sadistic

Copyright Asteria Books 2019

Meeting at the Crossroads

Liminal places are those locales that can be described as neither here nor there, and since time immemorial, they have been considered the very best places to meet the Witchfather (or Witchmother) and perform spells. Liminal spaces might be include the mouth of a cave (neither in the belly of the earth, nor upon the land's breast), at the seashore (neither in the ocean, nor upon dry land), at a doorway (neither inside the house, nor yet outside its bounds). But the liminal place that has fired the imagination and bred some of the most enduring folklore is that of the crossroads – the place where two or more roads come together and the traveler can stand for a moment in true limbo, on their way to anywhere.

It is in this place of balance, of limitless possibility, of undiscovered potential that magic and initiation are possible. The Seeker of the Mysteries has access to all that Is, Was, and Will Be.

Cultures from all over the globe have expressed this concept in a myriad of ways. Some embrace it, and some fear it. The Keeper of these Mysteries is most often viewed as a devil, demon, whore, or hag, but sometimes they are known as the Master, Light Bearer, Psychopomp, Key Holder. (Sometimes they are both loved and feared, for the Mysteries that illuminate and set the soul aflame can also consume one with madness if not grounded and tempered.) Hekate and Hermes both held this role in ancient Greece. In Africa (and African-diaspora) religions we see Legba/Elegua (and several others) as well as Pomba Gira. Odin was honored at crossroads in parts of Denmark and elsewhere in the Norse world.

Folklore holds that rulers, dancers, musicians, artists, and merchants – just to name a few – have all made deals with the Devil at the crossroads to increase their talents, fame, power, and fortune. Perhaps the truer tale is that these intrepid (or desperate) seekers quested for mastery of their natural gifts. They may have come away changed by their initiation, startled by the Keeper they encountered there, but their work was fueled by Cunning Fire after they had gone down to those crossroads.

Copyright Asteria Books 2019

The Pentagram

First attested in ancient Sumer, the pentagram is one of the oldest and most recognizable symbols contemporarily associated with witchcraft and the occult. It is a five-pointed star formed by five straight lines enclosed in a circle.

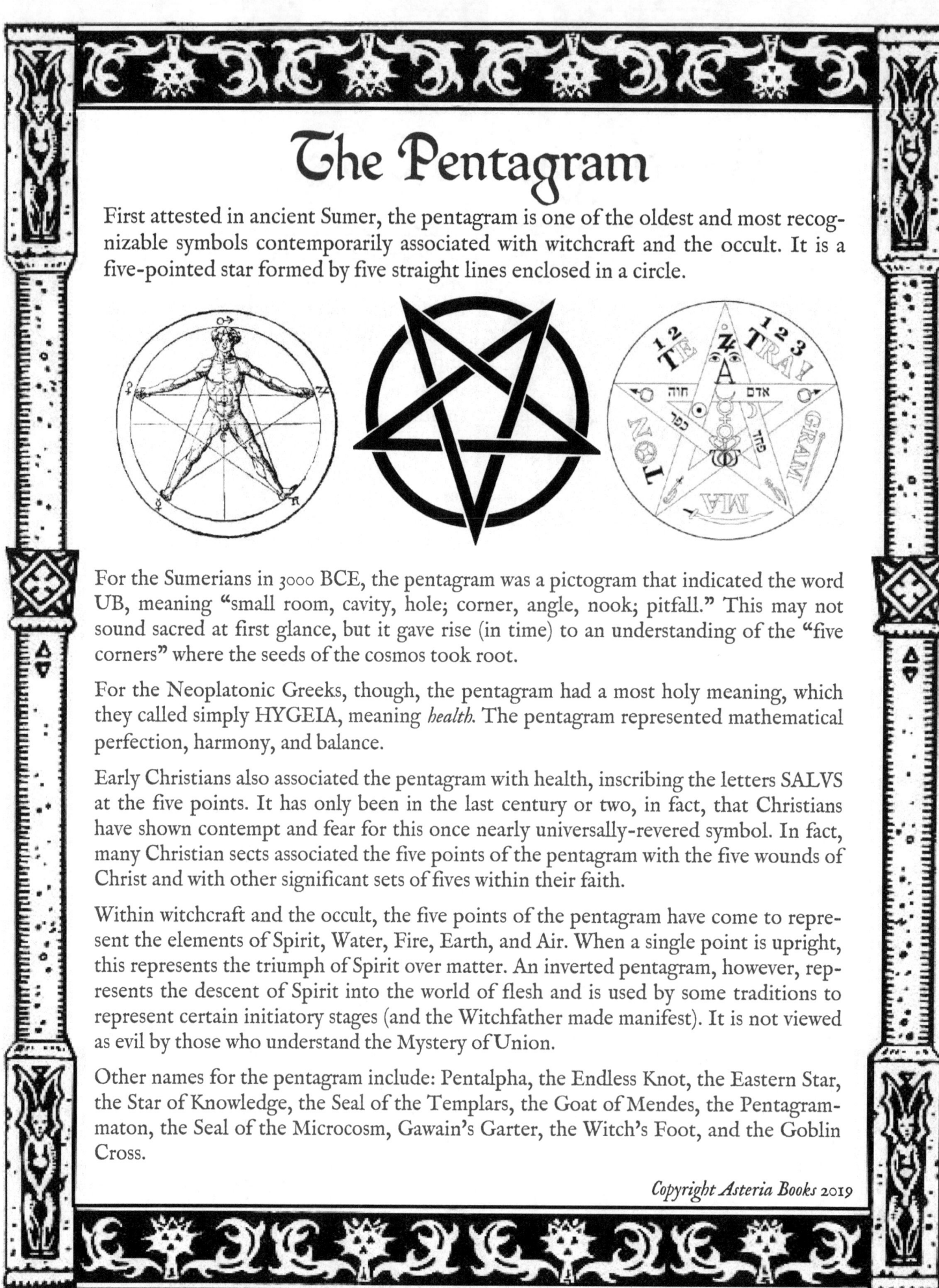

For the Sumerians in 3000 BCE, the pentagram was a pictogram that indicated the word UB, meaning "small room, cavity, hole; corner, angle, nook; pitfall." This may not sound sacred at first glance, but it gave rise (in time) to an understanding of the "five corners" where the seeds of the cosmos took root.

For the Neoplatonic Greeks, though, the pentagram had a most holy meaning, which they called simply HYGEIA, meaning *health*. The pentagram represented mathematical perfection, harmony, and balance.

Early Christians also associated the pentagram with health, inscribing the letters SALVS at the five points. It has only been in the last century or two, in fact, that Christians have shown contempt and fear for this once nearly universally-revered symbol. In fact, many Christian sects associated the five points of the pentagram with the five wounds of Christ and with other significant sets of fives within their faith.

Within witchcraft and the occult, the five points of the pentagram have come to represent the elements of Spirit, Water, Fire, Earth, and Air. When a single point is upright, this represents the triumph of Spirit over matter. An inverted pentagram, however, represents the descent of Spirit into the world of flesh and is used by some traditions to represent certain initiatory stages (and the Witchfather made manifest). It is not viewed as evil by those who understand the Mystery of Union.

Other names for the pentagram include: Pentalpha, the Endless Knot, the Eastern Star, the Star of Knowledge, the Seal of the Templars, the Goat of Mendes, the Pentagrammaton, the Seal of the Microcosm, Gawain's Garter, the Witch's Foot, and the Goblin Cross.

Copyright Asteria Books 2019

Powers of the Sphinx

There are said to be four primary things essential to magic. These four principles are the Powers of the Sphinx: To Know, To Will, To Dare, and To Keep Silent.

Eliphas Lévi indicates where to start in our endeavor to use the Powers of the Sphinx: "When one does not know, one should will to learn. To the extent that one does not know, it is foolhardy to dare, but it is always well to keep silent."

Thus the Four Powers are employed much like steps in a process; we must know before we can will, and so on. This idea is reinforced in Lévi's *Transcendental Magick*: "To learn how to will is to learn how to exercise dominion. But to be able to exert will power you must first know; for will power applied to folly is madness, death, and hell." Also: "In order to Dare we must Know; in order to Will, we must Dare; we must Will to possess empire and to reign we must Be Silent."

These four principle powers relate to the four fixed signs of the Zodiac, and the four magical elements. Together these faces of the fixed signs of the Zodiac create the four creatures composing the Sphinx.

Latin	Power	Sphinx	Zodiac	Element
Scire	To know	Human	♒ Aquarius	△ Air
Velle	To will	Lion	♌ Leo	△ Fire
Audere	To dare	Eagle	♏ Scorpio	▽ Water
Tacere	To keep silent	Bull	♉ Taurus	▽ Earth

For our purposes, there is no substitute for any of these powers. Firstly, it is imperative to Know one's Craft ins far as one can at the level that they currently are. Secondly, one must have proper force of Will in order to raise and direct power for a purpose. Thirdly, a magician or Witch must have great Daring to walk the Crooked Path, to travel to other realms and stand in sacred space. Finally -- and this is the most sacred and most challenging Power, as it is the Power of Earth, which is lowest of matter and closest to beginning over at Spirit -- is the Power to Keep Silent. In Silence is Wisdom, and there are many Mysteries that cannot be spoken of but must only be felt with the soul.

Copyright Asteria Publishing 2012

Under the Rose

To work "Under the Rose" means to work in secrecy, taken from the Latin *subrosa*. Most modern covens assume a level of secrecy for some or all of their meetings and rituals and hold both their membership and meeting place confidential as a matter of precaution. This clandestine air has a two-fold purpose. One is a simple safety measure. The other is an act of guardianship relative to the Mysteries.

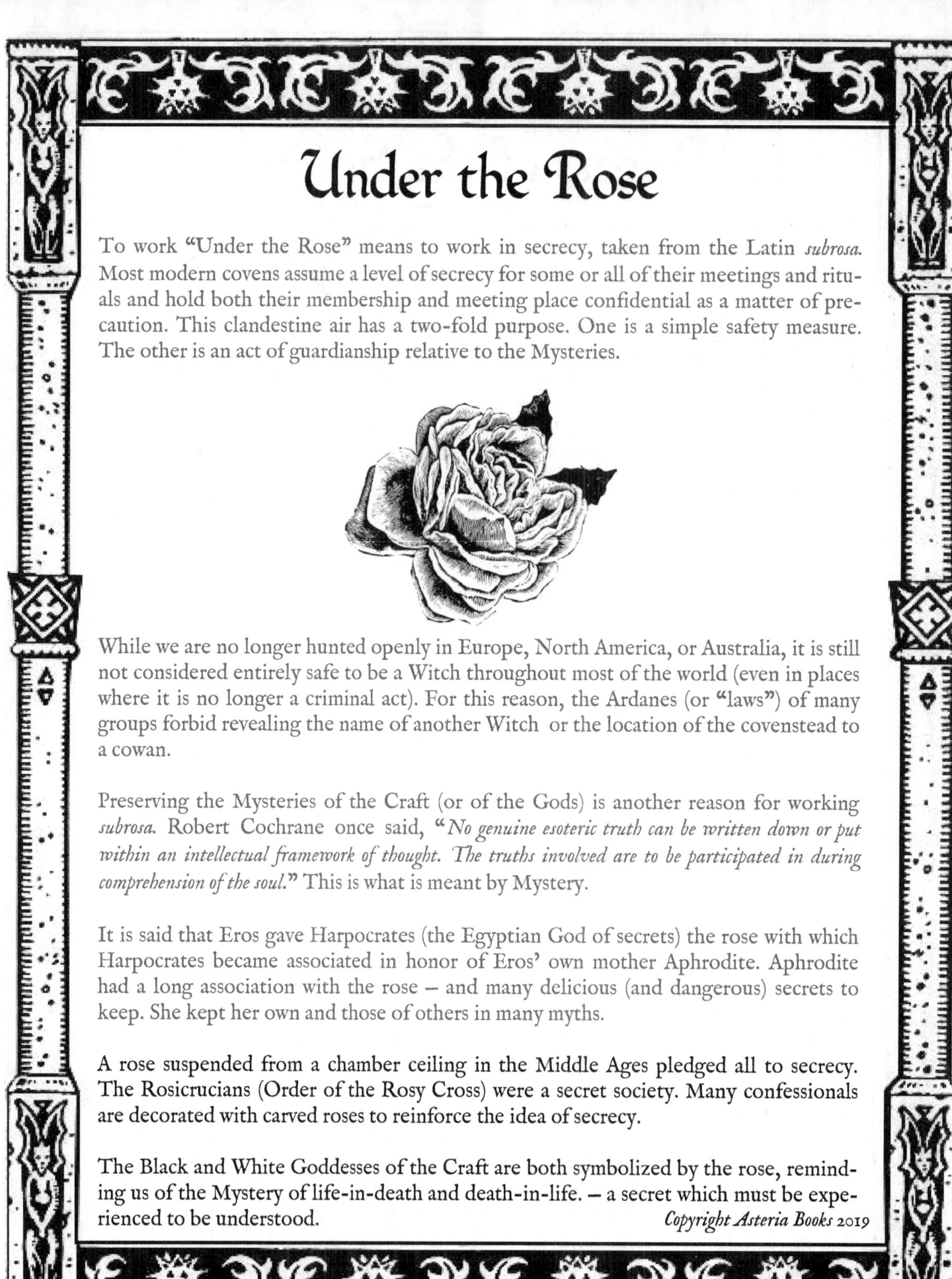

While we are no longer hunted openly in Europe, North America, or Australia, it is still not considered entirely safe to be a Witch throughout most of the world (even in places where it is no longer a criminal act). For this reason, the Ardanes (or "laws") of many groups forbid revealing the name of another Witch or the location of the covenstead to a cowan.

Preserving the Mysteries of the Craft (or of the Gods) is another reason for working *subrosa*. Robert Cochrane once said, "*No genuine esoteric truth can be written down or put within an intellectual framework of thought. The truths involved are to be participated in during comprehension of the soul.*" This is what is meant by Mystery.

It is said that Eros gave Harpocrates (the Egyptian God of secrets) the rose with which Harpocrates became associated in honor of Eros' own mother Aphrodite. Aphrodite had a long association with the rose — and many delicious (and dangerous) secrets to keep. She kept her own and those of others in many myths.

A rose suspended from a chamber ceiling in the Middle Ages pledged all to secrecy. The Rosicrucians (Order of the Rosy Cross) were a secret society. Many confessionals are decorated with carved roses to reinforce the idea of secrecy.

The Black and White Goddesses of the Craft are both symbolized by the rose, reminding us of the Mystery of life-in-death and death-in-life. — a secret which must be experienced to be understood.

Copyright Asteria Books 2019

The Three Realms

In many cultures where shamanism is practiced spiritual movement takes place in three planes, worlds, or realms. The three realms are the world above (the sky, heaven, land of the gods), the world around (the land, middle-earth, place of the elemental gates, land of the nature spirits), and the world below (the sea, the underworld, land of the dead). In Celtic lore these realms are named *Ceugent* (ky-jent), *Gwyned*, and *Abred*.

Sky, land, and sea,
Three-in-one, one-in-three.
-Celtic prayer

Shamans use certain techniques of trance to access these realms. In many cultures a tree or pole is visualized as standing at the center of all things, reaching up into the sky and down into the underworld. Shamans use this pole to climb or descend to other realms. In our tradition we use the image of the Spiral Castle, Caer Sidhe, spinning around to open its gate to the different points of the wheel of the year. Its spire reaches up to the stars, and its caverns are home to the great forge and the cauldron. The pole is symbolized literally in our circles by the raising of the stang. By its virtue we can "ride" the stang to any place in the realms, though we may also use our own personal riding-pole, or gandreigh, to do so.

First Realm	Second Realm	Third Realm
Ceugent	Gwyned	Abred
Upperworld, Upper Realm, Realm of Sky, Wind	Earth world, Center world, Realm of Land, Middle Earth	Underworld, Realm of the Sea
Otherworld	Consensus reality	Underworld
Birth, beginnings	Middles	Death, endings
The mind	Living bones and flesh	Emotion
Breath	Physicality	Inner self
Metacognition	Consciousness	Subliminal, Unconscious, Subconcious
Perspective	Limits and limitations	Deep mystery
Movement, setting in motion (beginning)	Progress, action, doing	Rest
Struggle and enlightenment	Going through something	Truth beyond substance or thought
Preservation: the undying realm, absence of decay	Day-to-day struggles and concerns	Healing the soul
Expansion/expansiveness	Manipulation of perception/glamory	Empathy
First arm of the Triskle	Second arm of the Triskle	Third arm of the Triskle
Spire of the Spiral Castle	Place of the Doorway of the Spiral Castle	Initiation chamber beneath the the Castle
Entry through flight or climbing	No entry needed (already in this realm)	Entry through caves, wells, barrows, etc.
Black Knife/Athame	White Knife/Kerfane	Red Knife/Shelg

Copyright Asteria Publishing 2012

The Triple Soul

Many world shamanic traditions, recognize either a tripartite soul or three souls in one body. These three souls, for us, correspond to the triple colors of witchcraft - red, black, and white.

The first soul is the Black Soul, or "spirit." This is our astral body, and it is capable of traveling beyond this world into other realms while we live. The spirit is what we identify as our Self, our ego. It is our identity in this lifetime, and it is an exact copy of "us" in the astral realms, although it can take any form you wish for it as the Fetch. Upon death, the spirit (Black Soul) may wander as a ghost or revenant, it may stay to act as a guide or guardian to others, or it may travel back to the cosmic cauldron where its energy will dissolve to create new spirits.

The second soul is the Red Soul, or "eternal soul." We often call this the Bone Soul, as it lives in the bones of each of us and cannot be destroyed. It is the divine spark of the Witchfather's blood within every true Witch's heart. The Bone Soul, after death, is awarded a period of rest in Ynys Avalon (Elphame, the Summerlands, as you prefer), after which it is reborn. The eternal soul holds our past life memories and our connection to our ancestors.

The third soul is the White Soul, or "higher self." It is also known as the Holy Guardian Angel. The higher self exists just above our bodies, like a crown or halo. Inspiration, enlightenment, and divine wisdom all come to us through the higher self. It is one of the main goals of a witch to gain knowledge of this higher self and to commune with it regularly. The eternal soul (Red/Bone Soul) is alchemically married to the higher self (White Soul), and so true lasting communion is reveled to us upon death - and possibly even within our lifetimes.

Copyright Asteria Books 2018

The Black Soul

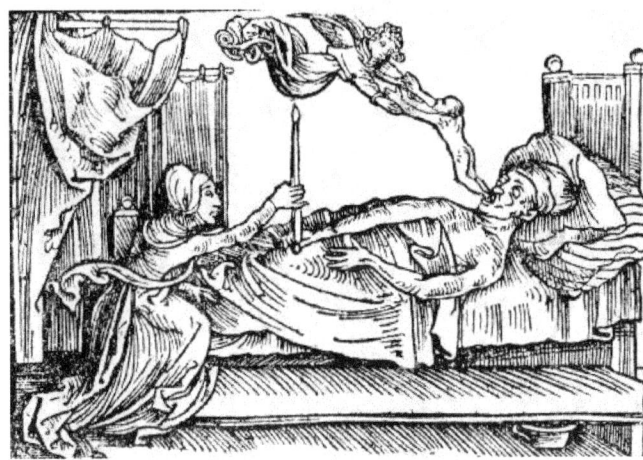

The Black Soul is that part of the spirit that retains memories and the personality connected to a particular life. It is very individual, and it is separate from the Higher Self (White Soul) and the Eternal Soul (Red Soul). It is the part of the energy structure that may become a ghost, haunting a particular location; but more often, it is the Black Soul who acts as a guiding Ancestor for future generations.

If you've talked to the Mighty Dead via a medium, talking board, your own clairvoyance, or other tool, this is the Black Soul of that Ancestor. The White and Red Souls have remained together and gone on to do other work, probably as another incarnate being. The Black Soul has remained here to act as a guide.

While still living and working with the White and Red Souls as part of the YOU that you are right now, your Black Soul is able to leave your body through witch flight and Fetch work. Some spiritual traditions call this astral travel. What they are calling the astral body, we are calling the Black Soul.

When Isobel Gowdie famously said, "I shall go into a hare," she was talking about sending her Black Soul out to roam in flight. The hare was a favorite choice of Fetch among Witches for its associations with the moon, shapeshifting, graveyards, and fertility.

Copyright Asteria Books 2018

White Soul

The White Soul is generally called the "Higher Self." In some traditions, it is called the "Holy Guardian Angel" (or HGA). Other names for this Soul from other religious systems include Augoeides (Neo-Platonism), Daemon (Platonism), Atman (Hinduism), God Self, etc.

Those who are able to see and interpret the aura often describe the White Soul as a crown or halo. In individuals with a very well-developed White Soul, this corona is often more visible and sometimes manifests as a visible star or bird above the head (especially when viewed in shamanic or highly receptive trance states).

Those on a path of enlightenment are said to be seeking "knowledge" of and "conversation" with the White Soul, and practices related to meditation, reflection, and invocation will all help the true seeker clarify their Soul's purpose and gain a better understanding of itself. Natural by-products of this "knowledge and conversation" are inspiration and wisdom.

The White Soul is the truest and purest Self, the Soul that is God-like in the sense that it is a Deity unto itself. It knows its Divinity and calls you to know it of yourself, as well. In rare glimpses throughout your mortal life, you will have true alignment of all Three Souls (as well as all Three Realms) and see yourself fully for the immortal and Divine Being you are.

Copyright Asteria Books 2018

Red Soul

The Red Soul (or Bone Soul) is eternal and linked in a sort of alchemical marriage to the White Soul. Whereas the Black Soul is only with you for a single lifetime, your Red and White Souls are bound together throughout all your lives, deaths, and periods of rest and reflection that come in between.

We call the Red Soul the "Bone Soul" as a nod to both the blood-producing marrow that reminds us of our connection to Tubal Qayin and also because of this Soul's ability to connect us with those in our bloodline, both physically and spiritually. Here, we see the old maxim, "Blood calls to blood," play out again and again as we reincarnate into the same family lines in multiple lives or are connected to the same soul-mates in several incarnations. In this sense, the marrow is the Red Thread that connects the line of Witches back to Qayin. The Red Soul also acts as the thread that links the Black and White Souls, thereby connecting us to our Selves.

Where the Black Soul is responsible for our sense of self and identity in this life, and the White Soul is responsible for our sense of purpose and learning throughout all our lives, the Red Soul is the agent of our deepest connection to our world, our work, and our loved ones.

Copyright Asteria Books 2018

Witch Blood & Witch Marks

Witch Marks

During the Medieval European witch trials, there was a belief that during a witch's initiation the Witchfather (whom the world called "Devil") would place his mark somewhere upon the body of the witch. Many of these same marks have been associated with *spiritual gifts* in cultures who were not so consumed with "witch frenzy." European witch hunters and Inquisitors would search the bodies of women and men accused of cunning craft looking for extra teeth, supernumerary nipples, red hair, unusual birthmarks, double-crowned skulls, etc. Historically (and contemporarily) many witches have taken a special tattoo at the time of initiation to mark themselves as a member of the People. These tattoos vary in shape and location by Clan.

Witch Blood

It is said that the blood of the Witchfather is passed via the bloodline – which is rooted in lore from the book of Enoch. This is part of the reason why the Craft at large is referred to as "the Family" and groupings of covens who operate under similar practices are called Clans. This heritage is often marked in terms of "lineage" and phrases like "daughter coven" are used to denote ancestry. While many who are newly drawn to the Craft many be unable to verify their Craft lineage (not having been taught by a blood relative), there is a common understanding that "blood calls to blood" and that those called to the crooked path are heeding the call of T'Qayin himself, whose blood sings in their veins. By forging the blood bond with him directly, you are igniting the Red Thread of the Craft – a link that no other can deny or break asunder.

The Kuthun

A kuthun is a magical inheritance that allows a witch to pass her power in this life to her spiritual descendant. It is a physical object that is tied to her work as a cunning person and acts as an incentive to teach her Arte to another.

Copyright Asteria Books 2019

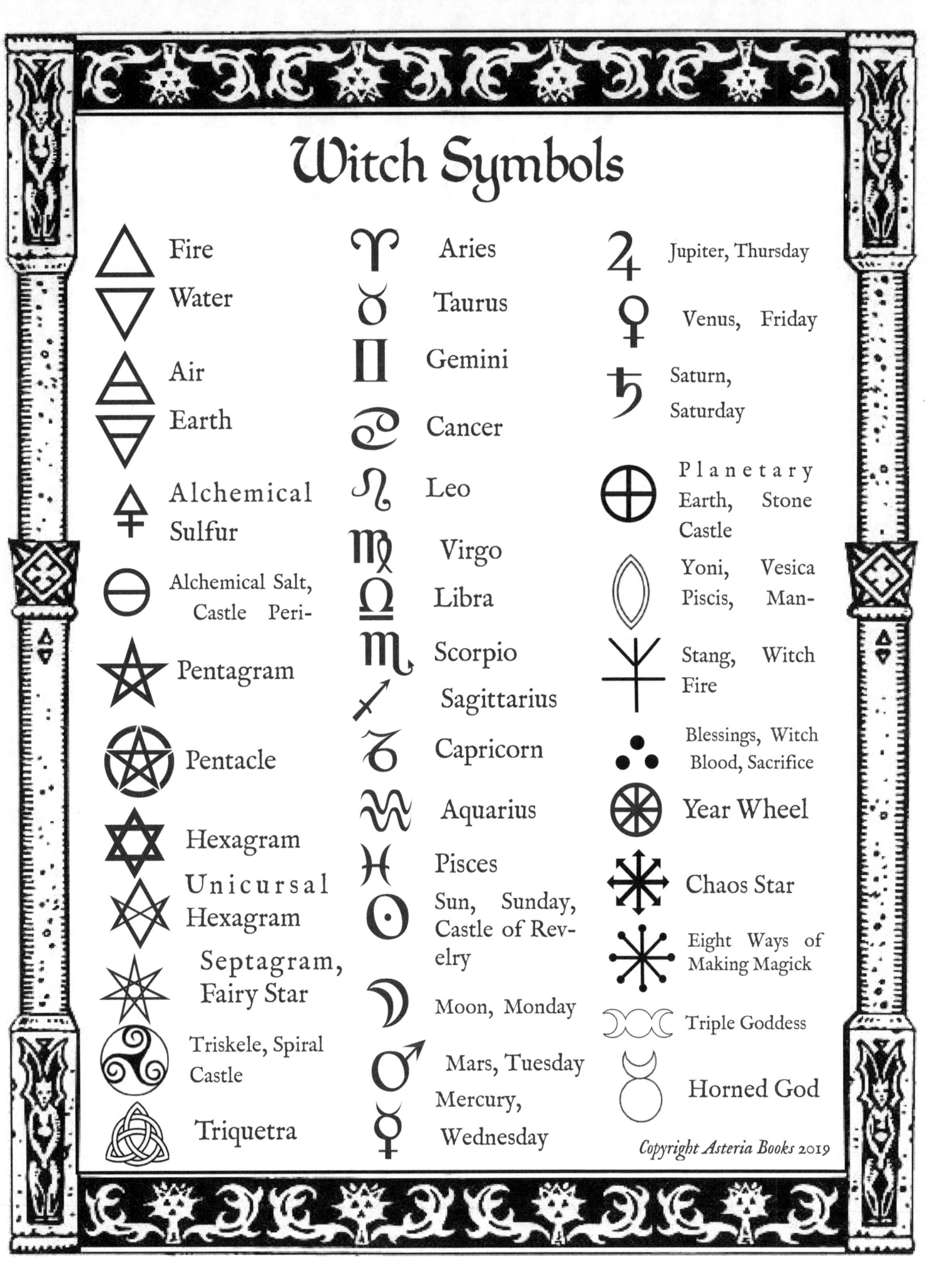

Models of Magic

One of the most difficult aspects of working or talking with other Witches or Magicians is often finding the common *ground* in the common *language* we share. We are all doing magic, but we aren't all approaching it the same way. A German Magician called Frater U:.D:. broke down the distinctions in the ways different magic-users approach and talk about magic into this system of models.

Spirit Model -- This is the most traditional model of magic, and it is one that most Traditional Witches operate from, at least in part. In this model, the Witch/Magician/Shaman, recognizes Spirits as entities separate from themselves and enlists their aid in magical endeavors via bargaining, prayer, contract, partnership, etc. The Spirits can range from nature Spirits to Ancestors to daemons to Godds, etc. Many practitioners of this model operate within a set of strictly prescribed parameters and must meet obligations as instructed by their Spirits and their religious tradition.

Energy Model -- Those who operate within this model view the world and everything in it as a set of interconnecting vibrational energies. By tapping into the correct vibrational pattern or energy level, change can be affected. Light, color, sound, emotion, and intention are all part of the energy spectrum, as are thoughts, diseases, etc. By aligning with the desired energy, the outcome can be reached. This model was in evidence as early as the start of Hermetic practice and has its roots in Gnostic and early Platonic thought.

Psychological Model -- This relatively modern model is heavily influenced by the work of Jungian psychology and is the basis for a great deal of modern ceremonial magick. It posits that one's entire reality is a projection of their thought and that by changing their thoughts, they can change the world. Spirits of every sort, then, are archetypal expressions of the magician, and magic is the process of conforming the reality to the Will by virtue of shifting the thought processes of the magician.

Information Model -- This model is very modern and says that energy on its own is "dumb" and required information for direction. Conversely, information on its own lacks intent and energy. Within this model, however, it is possible to transmit vast quantities of information across time and space to "program" objects and energies to accomplish a magical objective.

Meta Model -- Sometimes called "Chaos Model," Meta Model practitioners are aware of the models and see their strengths. They are able to choose between and blend models to best suit the working at hand. The "whatever works" philosophy is the hallmark of Meta Model.

Copyright Asteria Books 2021

The Witches' Dance Floor

One of the "known secrets" of folkloric Witchcraft is that Witches travel to meet each other using Soul journey techniques, and these meetings happen in what some might call "astral temples." That is a very New Age sounding term for what some of our European Craft ancestors would have called the Brocken (or Blocksburg — the highest mountain peak in Northern Germany) or the Hexentanzenplatz (hexen = witches', tanzen = dancing, platz = place).

The Brocken was a specific place that was associated with Witchcraft rituals in the pre-modern era in Europe. Other mountains had similar honors and associations. There are peaks and groves, caves and heaths on every inhabited continent that have come to be known as gathering places for Witches.

Here is what I know of the place: I cross water and fields and stars during my flight. It is in a high place, with a grove of sacred trees encircling it. We know these Tree Allies. It is a broad, open place. Hard-packed earth on a table of rock. Flat. A bonfire is usually set in the center, and stars swim in the dark sky overhead. Witches and Familiars of every ilk revel together here. A huge banquet is laid on a table. The WitchFather and WitchMother preside over the scene — though I can only ever approach one of them at a time. (If I see Him, She is unavailable to me on that flight — and vice versa.)

What do we do there? All manner of magic can be undertaken from here. All manner of journeys can lead out from here. At its most basic level, we can allow our Souls to play, revel, heal, and be inspired here.

The act of meeting in this place is often called "Meeting at the Sabbat." Walpurgis/Beltaine is the Sabbat most strongly associated with this gathering, but since this "astral temple" exists outside of time, we are in the "eternal now" when we arrive there. That means we can access that otherworldly Witches' Sabbat from whatever date and time we find ourselves within the physical world. In other words, you don't have to wait until the first of May to go.

Copyright Asteria Books 2022

Triskele and Triquetra

The triskele and triquetra, both tri-spiral symbols, resonate deeply within cosmological understanding across various pagan traditions. Though distinct in form, they share a fundamental representation of triplicity, a concept central to many ancient worldviews.

The triskele, with its dynamic, spiraling arms, embodies cycles of motion: birth, death, and rebirth; past, present, and future; or the three realms of earth, sea, and sky. It signifies progress, competition, and the constant flux of existence, mirroring the celestial movements and seasonal shifts. Its spiraling nature suggests continuous evolution and the interconnectedness of these cycles.

The triquetra, a more static, interlaced knot, represents the unity of three distinct elements. It symbolizes the interconnectedness of mind, body, and spirit; the triple goddess (maiden, mother, crone); or the three realms in a more balanced, harmonious form. Its interwoven design emphasizes the indivisible nature of these triplicities, highlighting their inherent connection and interdependence.

Both symbols, therefore, act as visual representations of cosmological principles, reflecting the cyclical nature of time and the interconnectedness of all things.

Copyright Asteria Books 2025

www.ingramcontent.com/pod-product-compliance
Lightning Source LLC
Chambersburg PA
CBHW060257240426
43661CB00060B/2815